Welcome to McGraw-Hill's GREe

Congratulations! You've chosen the GRE guide from America's leading educational publisher. You probably know us from many of the textbooks you used in college. Now we're ready to help you take the next step — and get into the graduate program of your choice.

This book gives you everything you need to succeed on the test. You'll get in-depth instruction and review of every topic tested, tips and strategies for every question type, and plenty of practice exams to boost your test-taking confidence.

In addition, in the following pages you'll find:

- **How to Use This Book**: Step-by-step instructions to help you get the most out of your test-prep program.

- **How to Use the Practice Tests**: Tips and strategies to guide your test-taking practice and to help you understand GRE scoring.

- **Your GRE Training Schedule and GRE Emergency Plan**: How to make the best use of your time, even if the test is just days away.

- **50 Top Strategies for Test Day**: Use this list to check your knowledge, or as a last-minute refresher before the exam.

- **Information for International Test-takers**: Find out what you need to know if you plan to take the test outside of the United States.

- **Getting the Most from the Free Online Practice Tests**: Log on to the companion website for more test-taking practice.

ABOUT McGRAW-HILL EDUCATION

This book has been created by a unit of McGraw-Hill Education, a division of The McGraw-Hill Companies. McGraw-Hill Education is a leading global provider of instructional, assessment, and reference materials in both print and digital form. McGraw-Hill Education has offices in 33 countries and publishes in more than 65 languages. With a broad range of products and services — from traditional textbooks to the latest in online and multimedia learning — we engage, stimulate, and empower students and professionals of all ages, helping them meet the increasing challenges of the 21st century knowledge economy.

How to Use This Book

This book provides all the material you need to score well on the GRE. It will teach you the knowledge that is required for this difficult exam, and it also provides ample opportunities for you to test yourself with full-length practice tests. At the end of the book you'll find a GRE vocabulary list, a glossary of GRE math terms, and additional test-taking resources.

Count backward from your GRE test day to determine how much preparation time you have. If you have at least three weeks but preferably twelve to eighteen weeks before test day, you should work through this entire book. You can follow the five-step program shown below. If you have less than three weeks, go to the GRE Emergency Plan on page 6A.

1 Start with the Diagnostic Test
The Diagnostic Test in Chapter 3 of this book is a simulated full-length GRE. Take it as the first step in your test-preparation program. It will help you to pinpoint areas of strength and weakness in your knowledge base and your skill set. After you have scored the Diagnostic Test, you should review the parts of the chapters that cover any content areas you found difficult.

2 Learn Test-taking Strategies
Chapter 4 describes important test-taking strategies that can help you earn extra points. You'll learn about strategic thinking, relaxation techniques, and when to guess if you don't know the answer to a question.

3 Get Ready for GRE Analytical Writing
Chapter 6 offers tips and strategies for writing the two essays required in the Analytical Writing section. Also provided is information about how your essays will be scored. You'll find typical writing prompts as well as sample student responses to show you what makes a high-scoring GRE essay.

4 Prepare for the Verbal and Quantitative Reasoning Sections
Chapters 7 and 8 provide complete review and practice for the Verbal and Quantitative Reasoning sections of the GRE. Each chapter offers concept reviews and specific strategies for answering the given question types, along with plenty of practice exercises with answers. As you work through these chapters, pay close attention to topics and question types that were particularly difficult for you on the Diagnostic Test.

5 Take the Practice Tests
Part IV of this book contains full-length practice GRE tests with complete explanations. Additional practice tests are available online at **www.mhpracticeplus.com**. Use these tests to check your progress, to gain experience with the GRE format, and to learn to pace yourself to get your highest score.

How to Use the Practice Tests

▶ **Take the Diagnostic Test Under Realistic Testing Conditions**
Time yourself strictly. You need to have an accurate picture of what your performance would be like if test day were today. A good place to take the test is a library; it will be relatively quiet, just like a testing center.

▶ **After Your Review, Tackle the Practice Tests**
When you have finished your review of the instructional material in Chapters 4–8, start tackling the practice tests in Part IV of this book and on the companion website. Each one is a full-length simulated GRE. These tests contain some variations in style and mix of question types. This approach is intentional so that you can get a taste of all the various formats and styles that can appear on a GRE exam.

▶ **Review the Explanations as Necessary**
There is an explanation for each of the practice questions in this book. You will probably not need to read all of them. Sometimes you can tell right away why you answered a particular question wrong. We have seen countless students smack themselves on the forehead and say, "stupid mistake." We try to refer to these errors as "concentration errors." Everyone makes them from time to time, and you should not worry when they occur. Try to distinguish between concentration errors and any actual holes in your knowledge base. If you have time, read the explanations for any questions that were challenging for you.

▶ **Keep Your Score Results in Perspective**
GRE scores are sensitive to factors such as fatigue and stress. So don't get worried if you see some variations due to an off day or because the practice test exposed a weakness in your knowledge base or skill set. Just use the information that you gather as a tool to help you improve.

▶ **A Note on Scoring the Practice Tests**
The scoring scale of the GRE is changing along with the test. This presents a challenge for the authors of this book as we go to print with extremely limited information from the test-makers at ETS. We are including here an explanation that is as thorough as it can be at this time without engaging in speculation that might mislead the reader.

ETS has announced a new scoring scale. The old 200–800 scale will no longer be used. In short, the Verbal Reasoning and Quantitative Reasoning scoring range is now 130–170, in 1-point increments. This means that there are 41 gradients instead of the 61 gradients on the old scale. Analytical Writing will still be rated on the 0–6 scale. In November 2011, ETS is scheduled to release a conversion table to allow comparison to the old scale, after they review the performance of test takers on the new exam. For test takers who take the "old" GRE General Test prior to August 2011, and submit scores after November 2011, ETS will report the 200–800 scaled scores along with estimated scores on the 130–170 scale and associated percentiles. For all test takers who take the GRE revised General Test, the scores will only be reported on the 130–170 scale with associated percentiles.

What follows is simply our best guess based on currently available information. Please keep in mind that all values are approximate and the actual scale may differ significantly. On the old scale, the verbal scores associated with each percentile were consistently lower than quantitative scores. ETS may take this opportunity to "re-center" those scores. We will have to wait and see. In any case, the percentile ranking will be reported to the graduate programs that you send your scores to and that is still a competitive measure comparing you to all other applicants who took a comparable GRE exam.

Percentile	OLD SCALE		NEW SCALE	
	Quant.	Verbal	Quant.	Verbal
90th	780	620	168	167
75th	720	560	155	151

Because the percentile ranking is determined by comparing each test taker to the entire group of test takers who take the same exam, it is nearly impossible to give a good estimate of how a specific raw score will translate into a scaled score. As we have stated in past editions, do not get too hung up on practice test scores. The goal is to do your best on test day and this material will help you to do that; the idea is to learn something from each practice experience. Keep in mind that you do not need to be perfect in order to get a great score and be admitted to your chosen program.

GRE Training Schedule

At least four weeks before your GRE

- Find a quiet place, such as a library, and take the Diagnostic Test (Chapter 3) under actual test conditions. Time yourself strictly. Evaluate your results and pinpoint your areas of strength and weakness. Read chapters 1 and 2. Download the *POWERPREP* II® software from ETS if you haven't done so already. Register for the GRE exam following the procedures described at **www.gre.org**.

The first three to four weeks of training

- Don't worry about timing. At your leisure, work through the first two GRE practice tests in this book or on the companion website. Think about how the questions and passages are put together and study whatever other sources you need to so that you can fill any holes in your knowledge base. Read chapters 4–10 in this book.

Two weeks before your GRE

- Take your first "dress rehearsal" exam — we recommend the *POWERPREP* II® software. Time yourself strictly. Use the results to fine-tune the last part of your training. Review relevant chapters in this book.

One week before your GRE

- Take your second "dress rehearsal" exam. If it doesn't go well, don't get too worried. Try to figure out what went wrong and review the explanations provided and the other relevant portions of this book. There is still time to consolidate your gains and continue to improve. Start planning a fun event for after your GRE!

Two to three days before your GRE

- Make a practice run to the testing center. Figure out what you are going to wear on test day. Gather your materials together (ticket, ID, pencils, calculator). Adjust your sleep schedule, if necessary, so that you are able to wake up by 7:00 A.M. and be thinking clearly by 8:00 A.M. Confirm your plans for fun after the exam!

The day before your GRE

- Rest and relaxation are the order of the day. Do little or no practice or studying. Get some physical activity so that you are better able to sleep and because the endorphins that you release in your brain will help with stress management. Make sure that you take care of your transportation issues and wake-up plan.

Test Day!

- Get up early. Eat breakfast. Read something to get you "warmed up." Bring your materials. Be on time. Avoid any fellow test-takers who are "stress monsters." Remember your game plan for each section. Don't forget to breathe evenly and deeply, and don't tire yourself out with needless physical exertion like tensing up your muscles while taking your GRE. When the test is finished, try not to think about it until you get your score report.

GRE Emergency Plan

If you have only a day or two before your GRE, you should take the following steps. They are listed in order of priority so you should do as many of them as you can before your test.

1. Seriously consider rescheduling

Rather than taking your exam with little or no preparation, you should look at your calendar and the GRE website and wait to take your GRE if you can do so and still get the information to your schools of choice before their deadlines.

2. Relax

Even if you don't have enough time to reschedule, you can get some useful information out of this book that will help you to pick up a few points that you might not have gotten otherwise.

3. Take the Diagnostic Test

There is a psychological theory called "Test Re-Test" that says that you should do a little bit better on a second GRE than a first GRE, even if you don't do any preparation in between. So make the Diagnostic Test in this book your first practice GRE. Time yourself strictly and do it all in one sitting.

4. Review the strategies in Chapter 4

Those are the high-yield test-taking strategies that will get you the most extra points on test day.

5. Read through the content chapters

Focus on the content areas you know you will struggle with on the GRE.

6. Do as many practice questions as you can in your weakest area

Look at the explanations to gain a better understanding of how to approach the questions.

7. Get some sleep

Being well rested will have a bigger impact on your score than staying up all night "cramming." There is a significant skill component on this test. It is not all about knowledge. So you can't learn enough information to guarantee a higher score.

50 Top Strategies for Test Day

When it's almost test day, and you've read this book and taken the Practice Tests, make sure you review this page and the pages that follow. Here you'll find 50 essential strategies that can definitely help you earn more points on the GRE. You'll see longer explanations of each strategy, along with examples, in the review portions of this book. The purpose of these pages is to provide a handy, all-in-one, last-minute reminder of these valuable concepts. Use this review to check your test readiness and make sure you're prepared to get your best score.

General Test-Taking Strategies

Relax
1. Don't panic if you are having a hard time answering the questions! You do not have to answer all of the questions correctly to get a good score.
2. Take a few moments to relax if you get stressed during the test. You will feel better.

Be Aware of Time
3. Pace yourself. Budget enough time for each question so that you won't have to rush at the end of the section.
4. Stay focused. Ignore the things going on around you that you cannot control.

Guess Carefully
5. You can skip around within a section, so answer the questions that are easiest for you, saving the more difficult questions for the end. Keep moving so that you can answer as many of the "easy" questions as possible and only guess on those that are more difficult or time-consuming.
6. There is no direct scoring penalty for wrong answers, so it pays to answer every question, even if you have to guess.
7. When you don't know the answer and need to guess, try to make an educated guess by eliminating answer choices that you know are wrong. The more you can eliminate, the better your chance of getting the question right.

Strategies for the Computer-based Test

The Computer System
8. In your Analytical Writing essays, take a few moments to check your spelling and grammar. The word processing software that you will use does not include a spell checker or a grammar checker.
9. Be aware of scroll bars. Some images and text are too big to fit on your screen and require you to scroll down to view them.
10. The online calculator should be used sparingly. Take the time to learn how to use it before you begin testing.

Answering Questions
11. Within a test section, if you have time, you can return to a question that you answered earlier and change your answer if you think a change is warranted. But be very careful about changing your mind. When answering questions, your first instinct is often the right one.
12. Be aware that the Verbal and Quantitative portions of the test are partially computer-adaptive. That is, if you do well on the first Verbal or Quantitative section, the computer will give you a more difficult second section.

GRE Verbal

Reading Comprehension

13 Read the questions first and make a mental note when the questions refer to specific lines, words, or boldfaced text. Do not try to memorize — just get an idea of what you should be looking for.

14 Read each passage for Topic, Scope, and Purpose. Then skim for structure. Try to isolate one topic word or sentence for each paragraph. Don't spend precious time trying to "learn" details.

15 Try to distinguish between details that are factual and details that are the opinions of the author.

16 Try to predict an answer before looking at the answer choices. If an answer choice matches your predicted answer, it is most likely correct.

17 Paraphrase when you need to. Putting the question and answer choices into your own words often makes them easier to understand.

18 Remember that some Reading Comprehension questions ask you to select more than one answer choice. Carefully consider ALL of the answer choices before making your selections.

Sentence Equivalence

19 Remember that for Sentence Equivalence questions, you must select two answer choices. Always consider ALL of the answer choices before you make your selections.

20 Use the Latin roots, prefixes, and suffixes to figure out what hard words mean.

21 Let the context of the sentence guide you. Try to look for "clue" words and phrases in the sentence that might suggest a contrast or comparison.

22 Try filling in the blank with your own words before you look at the answer choices. If you find answer choices that are similar to yours, they are most likely correct.

23 When you think that you have the correct answers, read the entire sentence to yourself, using your choices in the blank. If it makes sense, then mark your answers on the computer screen.

24 Consider slight variations in the meaning of each word.

Text Completions

25 Read through the text once to get an idea of context.

26 Pay attention to "clue" words in the text, such as transition words, that will help you to identify the structure of the text.

27 Start with the blank that seems the most simple to fill, and then work on the others.

28 Once you've made your selections, check the text for logic and grammar.

GRE Analytical Writing

Issue Task

29 Discuss the issue from any perspective. Remember, there is no correct position. Choose the position that you can most strongly support.

30 No matter which position you take, make sure you have compelling reasons and examples to support it. Make sure you consider how someone might challenge or question your position.

31 Do not worry about the number of examples included in your essay or the length of your essay; focus on the quality of your ideas.

Argument Task

32 Carefully read the given argument. Pay attention to the structure of the argument and the statements or claims, assumptions, implications, and supporting evidence given or left out.

33 Remember, your task is to find flaws in the logic of the argument, NOT agree with, disagree with, prove, or disprove the argument.

34 Do not worry about the number of examples or the length of your essay; focus on the quality of your critique.

GRE Quantitative

General Math Strategies

The following strategies can be applied to all of the GRE math sections

35 Draw pictures on your scratch paper as necessary to help you figure out problems.
36 Look for a way to reason through the problem. Use your on-screen calculator only if you really need it.
37 When reading word problems, translate them into mathematical equations. ("Carrie has 3 more CDs than Amy" is equivalent to C = A + 3)
38 Remember to estimate or "ball-park" answers when you can. It is often possible to eliminate all but the correct answer choice without doing any actual math.

Multiple-choice Questions

39 Make sure that you understand what information is given and what question is being asked. Paraphrase if necessary.
40 Many questions will allow you to "reason" your way an answer by performing only a few or even no calculations. Avoid lengthy and complicated calculations when possible.
41 Remember that some questions call for more than one correct answer. For these questions, be sure to carefully analyze ALL of the answer choices. Don't just select the first correct answer you see and move on.

Data Analysis Questions

42 Before answering each question, scan the given data.
43 Many of the questions will allow you to approximate an answer by making a visual comparison only. Avoid performing calculations when possible.
44 Do not base your answer to any question on an assumption or any outside information. Use only the data given.
45 You might be asked to select more than one correct answer, so pay close attention to the format of the question.

Quantitative Comparison Questions

46 Many comparisons require estimation only. Avoid lengthy and complicated calculations.
47 Be sure to take into account any information given that applies to both quantities.
48 If one quantity is sometimes greater or sometimes less than the other quantity, then the relationship cannot be determined from the information (Answer choice D means that no one can determine the answer, not just that you can't determine the answer.)

Numeric Entry Questions

49 Read the question carefully and be sure to provide the type of answer indicated.
50 You will not have any answer choices to guide you, so check your answer and make sure it is logical based on the information provided in the question.

25 Math Concepts You Absolutely Need to Know

1. The area of a circle is $A = \pi r^2$, where r is the radius of the circle.
2. The circumference of a circle is $C = 2\pi r$, where r is the radius of the circle. The circumference can also be expressed as πd, because the diameter is always twice the radius.
3. The area of a rectangle is $A = lw$, where l is the length of the rectangle and w is the width of the rectangle.
4. The area of a triangle is $A = \frac{1}{2}bh$, where b is the base of the triangle and h is the height of the triangle.
5. The volume of a rectangular prism is $V = lwh$, where l is the length of the rectangular prism, w is the width of the rectangular prism, and h is height of the rectangular prism.
6. The volume of a cylinder is $V = \pi r^2 h$, where r is the radius of one of the bases of the cylinder and h is the height of the cylinder.
7. The perimeter is the distance around any object.
8. The Pythagorean Theorem states that $c^2 = a^2 + b^2$, where c is the hypotenuse of the triangle and a and b are two sides of the triangle.
9. The following are angle measures and side lengths for Special Right Triangles:

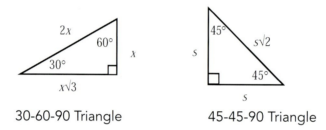

30-60-90 Triangle 45-45-90 Triangle

10. In an equilateral triangle, all three sides have the same length, and each of the angles equals 60°.
11. In an isosceles triangle, two sides have the same length, and the angles opposite those sides are congruent.
12. The complete arc of a circle has 360°.
13. A straight line has 180°.
14. A prime number is any number that can only be divided by itself and 1.
15. Squaring a negative number yields a positive result.
16. To change any fraction to a decimal, divide the numerator by the denominator.
17. If two numbers have one or more divisors in common, those are the common factors of the numbers.
18. To calculate the mean, or average, of a list of values, divide the sum of the values by the number of values in the list.
19. The median is the middle value of a list of numbers that is in either ascending or descending order.
20. The mode is the value that appears the greatest number of times in a list.
21. A ratio expresses a mathematical comparison between two quantities. (1/4 or 1:4)
22. A proportion is an equation involving two ratios. (1/4 = x/8 or 1:4 = x:8)
23. When multiplying exponential expressions with the same base, add the exponents.
24. When dividing exponential expressions with the same base, subtract the exponents.
25. When raising one power to another power, multiply the exponents.

Information for International Test-takers

Every year, more and more international students take the GRE General Test. Of the more than 670,000 tests administered in 2009, approximately 172,000, or more than 25%, were taken by non-U.S. citizens. If you are an international student who is planning to take the GRE in order to pursue graduate or business school studies in the United States, these pages will provide some information that can help make the process easier for you. We also suggest that you visit the official GRE website, www.ets.org/gre, for further details and updates. The site is maintained by Educational Testing Service (ETS), the organization that creates and administers the test.

The GRE General Test is currently offered as a computer-based test in the United States, Canada, and many other countries. The test is offered in a paper-based format in areas of the world where computer-based testing is not available.

Arranging to Take the GRE

Finding a Testing Center

With permanent testing centers located in countries all around the world, most applicants should not have trouble finding a place to take the test. If there are no centers near your home, you will need to travel to one. When you register for the GRE, you will need to schedule a test appointment at specific testing center. Go to www.ets.org/gre for a complete listing of testing centers worldwide.

Registering for the Test

Register early to get your preferred test date and to receive your test preparation material in time to prepare for the test. Remember that testing appointments are scheduled on a first-come, first-served basis. There are four ways you can register for the computer-based General Test: on the Internet, by phone, by fax, and by mail. Major credit cards are accepted to pay for registration.

- **To register via the Internet**, visit www.ets.org/gre.
- **To register by phone**, call your local test center directly, or call the Prometric® Candidate Services Call Center. You can call Monday through Friday, 8:00 A.M.–8:00 P.M. Eastern Time (excluding holidays) at 1-443-751-4820 or 1-800-GRE-CALL (1-800-473-2255). You will receive a confirmation number, reporting time, and test center address when you call.
- **To register by fax**, you must download and complete the International Test Scheduling form, then fax it to the appropriate Regional Registration Center (RRC). The form must be received at least seven days before your first-choice test date. A confirmation number, reporting time, and the test center address will be faxed or mailed to you. If you provide an e-mail address, you may receive a confirmation by e-mail. The list of RRCs is updated frequently, so be sure to visit www.ets.org/gre for the most current information.
- **To register by mail**, download and complete the Authorization Voucher Request Form and mail the appropriate payment and voucher request form to the address printed on the voucher. Allow up to four weeks for processing and mail delivery. When you receive your voucher, call to schedule an appointment; be sure to make your appointment prior to the expiration date on the voucher.

Standby testing is available at permanent test centers on a first-come, first served, space available basis in the United States, American Samoa, Guam, U.S. Virgin Islands, Puerto Rico, and Canada only.

If you must cancel or reschedule a testing appointment, contact the appropriate registration center no later than 10 full days before your appointment (not including the day of your test or the day of your request). Keep in mind that you cannot reschedule between sites served by different Regional Registration Centers.

NOTE: You can register for the paper-based General Test either online or by mail. Use a credit card, a money order, or a certified check when registering by mail. Download and complete the registration form and mail the completed form with payment to the address printed on the form. ETS must receive your registration form by the registration deadline, which can be found at **www.ets.org/gre**. Allow at least four weeks for processing.

The Day of the Test

If you are testing outside of your country of origin, then you must present your signed passport as your primary identification document. If you do not, ETS may automatically cancel your test scores. In addition, if your passport is not written using English language letters, you must also present another form of identification that includes a recent, recognizable photo and is written in English.

If you are taking the test within a European Union country, you may use your valid national European identity card. Your card must be signed.

Be sure to follow all the testing center instructions and procedures set by the testing center. Some of these procedures are outlined in Chapter 2 of this book, "Taking the GRE."

Test Preparation for International Students

ETS is very careful to make sure that the GRE is not biased against international test-takers. All questions are pre-tested by being included in unscored "experimental" test sections given to both U.S. and international test-takers. If statistics prove that any of the new questions put the international test-takers at a disadvantage, those items never appear on the test. Still, international test-takers face certain challenges.

The Language Barrier

The biggest and most obvious difficulty for international test-takers is the language barrier. Many people residing outside of the United States who sign up to take the GRE are non-native English speakers. The entire test, including instructions and questions, is in English. One part of the test is focused on verbal skills and another part is a writing test, which requires not only an understanding of the language but a command of it. Your English writing, reading comprehension, and grammar skills are directly tested on the GRE. Most experts advise non-native English speakers to read as much in English as they can in the months leading up to the test. Other activities that might help you are creating and using flash cards with difficult English words on them and practicing your English by communicating with others who speak the language.

To improve your understanding of spoken English, you can watch American TV shows (often now available online). Keep a journal and express your thoughts about what you've read and seen in writing. Your goal should be to practice presenting evidence in a cohesive and interesting way to support your arguments in the writing section of the exam. When you read items from American publications, pay particular attention to how the writers gather evidence and present it because there are often subtle cultural differences at play. Remember that the quantitative part of the GRE is also in English so it's a good idea to review math formulas and glossaries in English.

Becoming Familiar with Standardized Tests

Getting acquainted with standardized tests is another must-do for international test takers. This type of exam is a part of the average American's educational experience but is not necessarily a cultural norm in other parts of the world. Some people outside the United States may be unfamiliar with multiple-choice questions. These are questions in which you are given from several choices for the correct answer. There are strategies for choosing the best one when you're not sure. For example, you can eliminate answers that you know are incorrect and then choose among the remaining choices. This is called "taking an educated guess," and it can improve your chances of picking the correct answer. Timing is a very important part of standardized tests. Keeping calm is the first step to overcoming the pressure. Taking practice tests is key to learning how to pace yourself to maximize your performance in a limited time period. Taking practice tests will also help you become familiar with the test format. Understanding the instructions for each part of the test in advance can save you time during the exam because you won't have to spend time on the instructions in addition to the other reading you have to do.

Testing Your English Language Skills

If you received your undergraduate degree from an institution in a country whose official language is not English, the graduate program to which you are applying will likely require you to submit proof of your English proficiency along with your GRE scores. Most institutions accept scores on either the TOEFL (Test of English as a Foreign Language) or the IELTS (International English Language Testing System); many now also accept scores on the newer PTE (Pearson Test of English). Check with the programs to which you are applying for information about their test requirements. There is no specific passing score on these tests; graduate institutions set their own requirements.

- **TOEFL:** The TOEFL iBT is an Internet-based test administered on 30 to 40 dates a year at more than 4500 sites around the world. A paper-based version (TOEFL PBT) is still used but only in a few locations where Internet access is not reliable. For more information including the format of the test, scoring, and registration, visit **www.ets.org/toefl**. The TOEFL iBT captures the test taker's speech and uses this to measure English speaking ability in a standardized manner. Multiple-choice questions are used to measure reading and listening abilities. Two essay questions are used to measure writing abilities.
- **IELTS:** The IELTS is a paper-based test created at Cambridge University in the UK. It consists of four modules — Listening, Reading, Writing, and Speaking. Question types include multiple choice, sentence completion, short answer, classification, matching, labeling, and diagram/chart interpretation. The Speaking test is a face-to-face interview with a certified examiner. IELTS has two versions: Academic and General Training. The Academic test is for those who want to study at a tertiary level in an English-speaking country. The General Training test is for those who want to do work experience or training programs, enroll in secondary school, or migrate to an English-speaking country. For more information, visit **www.ielts.org**.
- **PTE:** The PTE was developed by Pearson, an international educational testing and publishing company. Like the TOEFL iBT, it is administered at testing centers on a computer (there is no paper version). Visit www.pearsonpte.com for more information about the PTE and updated lists

of the schools that accept it and the locations where it is given. Like the TOEFL, the PTE uses multiple-choice questions plus essay questions to measure reading, listening, and writing skills. A 30-second audio clip of the test taker's speech is sent to schools along with the test scores.

One Last Hurdle: The Student Visa

Nonresidents of the United States need to obtain a visa to live in the United States. Once you have chosen a graduate program and have been accepted, you will need to begin the process of obtaining your student visa.

Getting a student visa to study in the United States is not as difficult as getting an H1-B visa to work in the country after graduation. Experts, including the U.S. government, suggest that students begin the student visa process as early as possible. Besides needing the time to complete the required forms, you will also need to schedule an appointment for the required embassy consular interview, and the waiting times for this vary and can be lengthy.

Visa Requirements

During the student visa process, you are expected to prove that you have adequate financing to study in the United States, ties to your home country, and a likelihood that you will return home after finishing your studies. In addition, you will have to participate in an ink-free, digital fingerprint scan and provide a passport valid for travel to the United States and with a validity date at least six months beyond your intended period of stay.

Your school will provide you with an I-20 form to complete. The school will use this to register you with the Student and Exchange Visitor Information System (SEVIS), an Internet-based system that maintains accurate and current information on nonimmigrant students and exchange visitors and their families. If you have a spouse and/or children who will be joining you, you must register them with SEVIS as well. You'll also need to submit a completed and signed nonimmigrant visa application with forms DS-156 and DS-158. A 2" × 2" photo that meets certain requirements, which you can find at the U.S. Department of State website, **www.travel.state.gov**, is necessary as well.

Transcripts, diplomas from previous institutions, scores from standardized tests such as the TOEFL or IELTS, and proof you can afford the school (think income tax records, original bank books and statements) are things you should have on hand when applying for your visa. If you have dependents, you will also need documents that prove your relationship to your spouse and children, such as a marriage license and birth certificates.

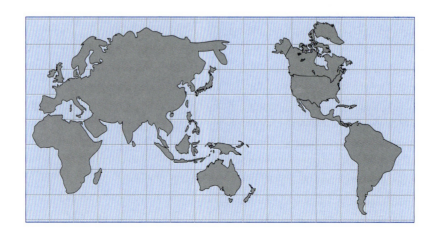

Getting the Most from the Free Online Practice Tests

Visit **MHPracticePlus.com/GRE** for your free access to additional complete GRE practice tests. Each one is a complete interactive exam with automatic timing and scoring, as well as detailed explanations for every question. You'll also see a list of other GRE study resources available from McGraw-Hill.

Accessing the Tests

At the website, click on the words "GRE Center." You'll be taken to a web page that offers full-length practice GREs. Click on a test section to begin.

Taking the Tests

Main Menu

On the Main Menu, when you move the cursor over "Practice Test 1" or "Practice Test 2," you will see a list of the test sections. Choose a section by moving the cursor over it, then click on the Start Section button (or, under Analytical Writing, on the name of the writing task). You have the option of taking each section as a timed test or as an untimed test. If you choose the timed test mode, a countdown clock will appear at the upper right corner of the screen.

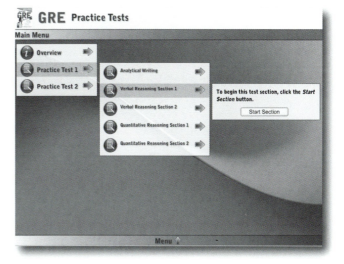

You will then be shown the View Instructions screen for that test section. It presents the directions for each question type. When you close the View Instructions screen, the first question will appear.

Answering Questions

To answer questions, click on the answer circle beside the letter of your choice. At the bottom right corner of the screen you will see a note such as "2 of 20," telling you how many questions are in the section and which question you are answering. After answering each question, click on one of the two arrows at either side of that note to go to the next or previous question.

At any time you may roll your cursor over the **Question Status** at the bottom left corner for the

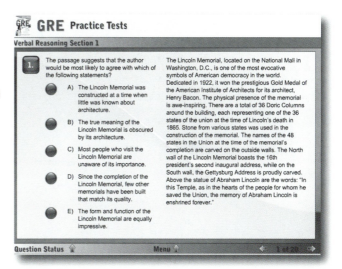

screen to see the total number of questions in the section and which ones you have answered or not answered.

Menu Options

At the bottom center of the screen you will see a **Menu** button. Roll your cursor over that button to see these choices:

- **Exit Program:** Choose this option if you wish to exit the program. Then, if you wish to resume work on to the same test section, relaunch the program. From the Main Menu, you will have the opportunity to complete the section that you exited or to restart it from the beginning.

- **Score and Exit Section:** You may choose this option at any time while working on a test section. You will get a new dialogue box that will tell how many questions in the section you answered correctly and allow you to review the questions, your answers, the correct responses, and the explanations. See "Scoring the Practice Tests" below for more information.

- **Save and Exit Section:** This option takes you back to the Main Menu. Your work will be saved, and whenever you go back to the Main Menu, you will have the opportunity to complete or restart the section that you exited.

- **View Instructions:** Choose this option if you wish to see the instructions for the question type or types in the test section where you are currently working.

Scoring the Practice Tests

After you answer the last question in a section, if you have not answered all of the preceding questions, you will be prompted to roll your cursor over the Question Status button to see which ones you have not answered. You can then return to them and answer them if you wish. Then return to the final question in the section.

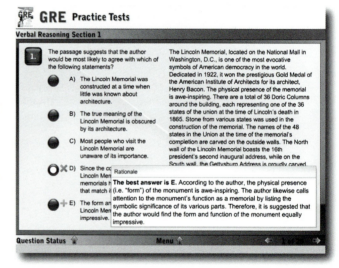

You will then be asked if you wish to score and exit the section. If you click "Score and Exit," you will see a new dialogue box that will tell you how many of the questions in the section you answered correctly. You will then be asked, "Would you like to review the section now?" If you click "yes," the questions will appear one by one on the screen as shown at right.

There will be an "X" next to every one of your answers and a "+" next to every correct answer. For each question, you will also see an inset panel with the explanation ("rationale") for the correct answer. You may then navigate away or close the program.

Later, if you return to the Main Menu and roll your cursor over the section that you completed, you will see a dialogue box that will tell you when you completed the section and how you scored. You can then either review your work on the section, or restart it and take it again.

2011–2012
EDITION

McGraw-Hill's
New GRE

Graduate Record Examination General Test

2011–2012 EDITION

McGraw-Hill's
New GRE

Graduate Record Examination General Test

Steven W. Dulan
and the Faculty of Advantage Education

New York | Chicago | San Francisco | Lisbon | London
Madrid | Mexico City | Milan | New Delhi | San Juan | Seoul
Singapore | Sydney | Toronto

The McGraw·Hill Companies

Copyright © 2011, 2009 by The McGraw-Hill Companies, Inc. All rights reserved. Printed in the United States of America. Except as permitted under the United States Copyright Act of 1976, no part of this publication may be reproduced or distributed in any form or by any means, or stored in a database or retrieval system, without the prior written permission of the publisher.

1 2 3 4 5 6 7 8 9 10 11 12 13 14 15   QDB/QDB   1 9 8 7 6 5 4 3 2 1

Book alone:
ISBN 978-0-07-174259-7
MHID 0-07-174259-x
ISSN 1946-1275

Book/CD set:
ISBN: P/N 978-0-07-174264-1 of set
         978-0-07-174266-5

MHID: P/N 0-07-174264-6 of set
         0-07-174266-2
ISSN 1946-1275

Printed and bound by Quad/Graphics-Dubuque

McGraw-Hill books are available at special quantity discounts to use as premiums and sales promotions, or for use in corporate training programs. To contact a representative, please e-mail us at bulksales@mcgraw-hill.com.

GRE® is a registered trademark of Educational Testing Service (ETS), which was not involved in the production of, and does not endorse, this product.

Product or brand names used in this book may be trade names or trademarks. Where we believe that there may be proprietary claims to such trade names or trademarks, the name has been used with an initial capital or it has been capitalized in the style used by the name claimant. Regardless of the capitalization used, all such names have been used in an editorial manner without any intent to convey endorsement of or other affiliation with the name claimant. Neither the author nor the publisher intends to express any judgment as to the validity or legal status of any such proprietary claims.

About the Author

Steven W. Dulan, J.D., has been involved with GRE preparation since 1989. A former U.S. Army Infantry Sergeant, Steve scored in the 99th percentile on every standardized test he has ever taken. After graduating from Michigan State, Steve attended The Thomas M. Cooley Law School on a full Honors Scholarship. While attending law school, Steve continued to teach standardized test prep classes (including ACT, SAT, PSAT, GRE, GMAT, and LSAT) an average of 30 hours each week, and tutored some of his fellow law students in a variety of subjects and in essay exam writing techniques. Professor Dulan has also served as an instructor at Baker University, Cleary University, Lansing Community College, The Ohio State University-Real Estate Institute, and The Thomas M. Cooley Law School. Guest lecturer credits include Michigan State University, University of Michigan, Detroit College of Law, Marquette University, Texas Technical University, University of Miami, and Wright State University.

Thousands of students have benefited from Steve's instruction, coaching, and admissions consulting, and have entered the graduate programs of their choice. Steve's students have gained admission to some of the most prestigious institutions of higher learning in the world, and have received numerous scholarships and fellowships of their own. Since 1997, Steve has served as the president of Advantage Education® (**www.AdvantageEd.com**), a company dedicated to providing effective and affordable test prep education in a variety of settings, including one-on-one tutoring via the Internet worldwide using its Personal Distance Learning® system. The information and techniques included in this book are the result of Steve's experiences with test preparation students at all levels over many years.

Acknowledgments

I would like to acknowledge the outstanding contribution of the faculty and staff of Advantage Education. Your hard work and dedication have made this endeavor a success. You are not only the smartest but also the best.

The following Advantage Education staff members deserve special thanks for their extra efforts:

Senior Editor and Project Manager: Amy Dulan

Contributing Authors/Editors: Pamela Chamberlain, Lisa DiLiberti, Megan Hettwer, Matt Mathison, Blair Morley, Ryan Particka, Jordan Pearce, Andrew Sanford, and Amanda Thompson

Contents at a Glance

PART I: Introduction to the GRE General Test

| CHAPTER 1 | Overview of the GRE | 3 |
| CHAPTER 2 | Taking the GRE | 11 |

PART II: Preparing for the GRE General Test

CHAPTER 3	GRE Diagnostic Test	19
CHAPTER 4	GRE General Testing Strategies	73
CHAPTER 5	Introduction to GRE Logic	83
CHAPTER 6	GRE Analytical Writing	97
CHAPTER 7	GRE Quantitative	127
CHAPTER 8	GRE Verbal	153

PART III: Content Area Review

| CHAPTER 9 | Basic GRE Math Review | 181 |
| CHAPTER 10 | Basic GRE Verbal Review | 237 |

PART IV: Practicing for the GRE General Test

CHAPTER 11	GRE Practice Test 1	261
CHAPTER 12	GRE Practice Test 2	315
CHAPTER 13	GRE Practice Test 3	369

Appendixes

APPENDIX A	GRE Vocabulary List	425
APPENDIX B	Glossary of GRE Math Terms	457
APPENDIX C	Additional Resources	469

Contents

Part I: Introduction to the GRE General Test

CHAPTER 1 Overview of the GRE — 3
- GRE Format — 4
- GRE Question Types — 5
  - Analytical Writing — 5
  - Verbal — 6
  - Quantitative — 8
  - More on the Computer-based Test — 10
- What's Next? — 10

CHAPTER 2 Taking the GRE — 11
- Registering for the GRE General Test — 11
- Taking the GRE General Test — 12
- Scoring the GRE General Test — 13
  - Scoring the General Test Analytical Writing Section — 13
  - Scoring the General Test Verbal and Quantitative Sections — 13
  - A Note on Scoring the Practice Exams in This Book — 14
  - What Your Scores Mean to Schools — 14
- Test-Takers with Disabilities — 14
- What's Next? — 15

Part II: Preparing for the GRE General Test

CHAPTER 3 GRE Diagnostic Test — 19
- GRE Diagnostic Test Answer Key — 61
- GRE Diagnostic Test Answer Explanations — 63

CHAPTER 4 GRE General Testing Strategies — 73
- Knowledge, Skills, and Abilities (KSA) — 73
- Focus on the Easy Stuff — 75
- Stay "On Point" — 75
- Simplify — 76
- Guess Wisely — 76
- Manage Stress — 77
- Relax to Succeed — 77

Specific Relaxation Techniques	78
Be Prepared	78
Know Yourself	78
Rest	79
Eat Right	79
Breathe	79
Take Mental Breaks	79
Have a Plan of Attack	79
Be Aware of Time	80
Listen to Music	80
Some Strategies for the Computer-based Test	80
What to Expect on Test Day	81
Take a Dry Run	81
Wake Up Early	81
Dress for Success	81
Fuel Up	81
Bring Supplies	81
Warm Up Your Brain	82
Plan a Mini-Vacation	82
What's Next?	82
CHAPTER 5 Introduction to GRE Logic	**83**
Arguments	84
Context	85
Chain of Reasoning	85
Assumptions	86
Validity, Truth, and Soundness	86
Conditionals	87
Sufficiency	88
Necessity	88
Negation	89
Fallacies	90
Slippery Slope	90
Percent versus Number	91
Sampling Error	91
Correlation versus Causation	92
Equivocation	92
Ad Hominem Arguments	93
Appeal to Authority	93
Appeal to Majority: The Quantity/Quality Fallacy	94
Circular Argument	94
Begging the Question	95
Reductio ad Absurdum	95
What's Next?	96

CHAPTER 6 GRE Analytical Writing	97
Breaking Down Analytical Writing	98
Scoring the Analytical Writing Sections	98
What the GRE Readers Are Looking For	99
Writing Techniques	100
Writing Strategies	100
Clearly State Your Position	101
Present Your Ideas Logically	101
Review and Correct Your Essay	101
Issue Task	102
The Time Limit	102
The Issue	102
Your Response	102
Sample Essay Prompt 1: Analyze an Issue	105
Sample Essay Prompt 2: Analyze an Issue	109
Argument Task	113
The Time Limit	113
The Argument	113
Your Response	113
Sample Essay Prompt 1: Analyze an Argument	116
Sample Essay Prompt 2: Analyze an Argument	120
Practice Writing Prompts	124
Issue Task Practice	124
Argument Task Practice	124
What's Next?	125

CHAPTER 7 GRE Quantitative	127
Multiple-choice Questions	128
Anatomy of a GRE Multiple-choice—Select One Answer Question	128
Anatomy of a GRE Multiple-choice—Select One or More Answers Question	129
General Strategies for Multiple-choice Questions	130
Multiple-choice Practice Questions	138
Answers and Explanations	141
Quantitative Comparison Questions	143
Anatomy of a GRE Quantitative Comparison Question	143
General Strategies for Quantitative Comparison Questions	144
Quantitative Comparison Practice Questions	146
Answers and Explanations	148
Numeric Entry Questions	149
Anatomy of a GRE Numeric Entry Question	149
General Strategies for Numeric Entry Questions	149

Numeric Entry Practice Questions	150
Answers and Explanations	150
What's Next?	151

CHAPTER 8 GRE Verbal — 153

Sentence Equivalence Questions	153
Anatomy of a GRE Sentence Equivalence Question	154
General Strategies for Sentence Equivalence Questions	155
Practice Sentence Equivalence Questions	158
Answers and Explanations	161
Reading Comprehension Questions	162
Anatomy of a GRE Reading Comprehension Question	162
General Strategies for Reading Comprehension Questions	164
Reading Comprehension Question Content Types	168
Practice Reading Comprehension Questions	171
Answers and Explanations	173
Text Completion Questions	174
Anatomy of a GRE Text Completion Question	174
General Strategies for Text Completion Questions	174
Practice Text Completion Questions	175
Answers and Explanations	176
What's Next?	177

Part III: Content Area Review

CHAPTER 9 Basic GRE Math Review — 181

Numbers and Operations	182
The Properties of Integers	182
Real Numbers	182
Order of Operations (PEMDAS)	183
Decimals	184
Fractions and Rational Numbers	185
Squares and Square Roots	186
Exponents	186
Scientific Notation	187
Mean, Median, and Mode	187
Ratio, Proportion, and Percent	188
Absolute Value	189
Simple Probability and Outcomes	189
Factors and Multiples	189
Exercises: Numbers and Operations	190
Basic Operations	190
Squares and Square Roots	191
Exponents	192

Scientific Notation	192
Mean, Median, and Mode	192
Ratio, Proportion, and Percent	193
Absolute Value	193
Simple Probability and Outcomes	194
Factors and Multiples	194
Answers and Explanations	195
Basic Operations	195
Squares and Square Roots	196
Exponents	196
Scientific Notation	197
Mean, Median, and Mode	197
Ratio, Proportion, and Percent	198
Absolute Value	199
Simple Probability and Outcomes	200
Factors and Multiples	201
Algebra and Functions	203
Linear Equations with One Variable	203
Polynomial Operations and Factoring Simple Quadratic Expressions	203
Systems of Equations	204
Inequalities	205
Functions	205
Exercises: Algebra and Functions	206
Linear Equations with One Variable	206
Polynomial Operations and Factoring Simple Quadratic Equations	206
Systems of Equations	207
Linear Inequalities with One Variable	207
Functions	207
Answers and Explanations	208
Linear Equations with One Variable	208
Polynomial Operations and Factoring Simple Quadratic Equations	209
Systems of Equations	210
Linear Inequalities with One Variable	212
Functions	213
Geometry	214
Coordinate Geometry	214
Triangles	216
Quadrilaterals, Lines, Angles	217
Some Other Polygons	219
Circles	220
Three-Dimensional Figures	221
Exercises: Geometry	221
Coordinate Geometry	221
Properties and Relations of Plane Figures	222

Angles, Parallel Lines, and Perpendicular Lines	222
Perimeter, Area, and Volume	224
Answers and Explanations	224
Coordinate Geometry	224
Properties and Relations of Plane Figures	226
Angles, Parallel Lines, and Perpendicular Lines	228
Perimeter, Area, and Volume	228
Word Problems and Data Analysis	231
Word Problems	231
Data Analysis	231
Exercises: Word Problems and Data Analysis	232
Translating Word Problems	233
Data Analysis	234
Answers and Explanations	235
Translating Word Problems	235
Data Analysis	235
What's Next?	236

CHAPTER 10   Basic GRE Verbal Review   237

Grammar Rules	237
Subject/Verb Agreement	238
Nouns and Pronouns	239
Verbs and Verb Forms	242
Sentence Construction	242
Punctuation Rules	245
Commas	245
Apostrophes	247
Colons and Semicolons	248
Parentheses and Dashes	250
End Punctuation	250
Rhetoric	251
Commonly Misused Words	251
What's Next?	257

Part IV: Practicing for the GRE General Test

CHAPTER 11   GRE Practice Test 1   261

GRE Practice Test 1 Answer Key	304
GRE Practice Test 1 Answer Explanations	306

CHAPTER 12   GRE Practice Test 2   315

GRE Practice Test 2 Answer Key	357
GRE Practice Test 2 Answer Explanations	359

CHAPTER 13 GRE Practice Test 3	**369**
GRE Practice Test 3 Answer Key	411
GRE Practice Test 3 Answer Explanations	413

Appendixes

APPENDIX A GRE Vocabulary List	**425**
APPENDIX B Glossary of GRE Math Terms	**457**
APPENDIX C Additional Resources	**469**

2011–2012 EDITION

McGraw-Hill's
New GRE

Graduate Record Examination General Test

PART I

Introduction to the GRE General Test

CHAPTER **1** **OVERVIEW OF THE GRE**

CHAPTER **2** **TAKING THE GRE**

1
Overview of the GRE

CHAPTER GOALS
- Learn how the GRE is structured.
- Find out what kinds of questions are on the test.
- Study examples of each question type.
- Learn about the computer adaptive test format.

The Graduate Record Examination (GRE) General Test is required by most institutions and programs granting Master or Doctorate degrees, although it is not required by all programs. Not surprisingly, the most competitive programs generally have higher score requirements. Some programs also require Subject Tests, which are beyond the scope of this volume. You should speak to the admissions department at the school to which you are applying to confirm whether you will need to take one or more of the subject tests. For more information on the GRE Subject Tests, visit **www.gre.org/gre**.

The GRE does not measure your knowledge of business procedures or law, or any specific content area. In addition, it does not measure your value as a person, nor does it predict your success in life. However, the GRE does a fairly good job of predicting how hard you will have to work to understand the material in your chosen program. If you prepare for this test seriously now, you'll sharpen your comprehension, math, and reasoning skills, and be able to focus on the relevant information in your course work much more easily once you start graduate school.

GRE Format

GRE Tip

The GRE is offered as a paper-based test in certain areas of the world where computer testing is not available. International test-takers can find more information in the Welcome section at the start of this book.

The GRE General Test is a computer-based (or, in some locations, paper-based) test that includes five scored sections: one Analytical Writing section (with two scored writing tasks), two Quantitative sections, and two Verbal sections. Your test will also include an experimental section, called the "pretest" section, which is mixed in with the other sections of the test and appears as either a Verbal or a Quantitative section. There might also be a "research" section, which will always be the final section presented if you have one included in your test. The answers on the pretest and research sections will not count toward your GRE score. The questions are meant to help the test writers at Educational Testing Service (ETS) refine their methods and try out new material that may be included in future GRE tests. The pretest is not identified and will seem like just another test section as you work through it. The research section, if you have one on your test, will be identified as such.

The GRE always begins with the two Analytical Writing tasks: the Issue Task and the Argument Task. For both tasks, if you are taking the computer-based GRE, you will write your response using the word processor that is built into the GRE software. The Verbal and Quantitative Sections may appear in any order on your test. When working on these sections, you may skip around, first answering questions that you find less challenging, then coming back to the more difficult questions. Once you have completed a section, you may not go back to it. You are allowed a total of 3 hours and 45 minutes for the computer-based GRE, including the unscored section, and a total of 4 hours and 5 minutes for the paper-based GRE, including the unscored section. Chapter 6 of this book discusses Analytical Writing in detail, while Chapters 7 and 8 cover the Quantitative and Verbal sections, respectively.

The basic time breakdown is shown in the following chart. (Note that all sections after Analytical Writing can appear in any order on your actual test, except for the research section, which will come last.)

GRE Test Format (Computer Based)

Section	Number of Questions	Time Limit
Analytical Writing	Issue Task Argument Task	30 minutes 30 minutes
Verbal (2 sections)	20 questions per section	35 minutes per section
Quantitative (2 sections)	20 questions per section	30 minutes per section
Unscored (experimental Verbal or Quantitative Section)	Varies	Varies
Research (your GRE might not include this section—if it does, this section will be at the end)	Varies	Varies

GRE Test Format (Paper Based)

Section	Number of Questions	Time Limit
Analytical Writing	Issue Task	30 minutes
	Argument Task	30 minutes
Verbal (2 sections)	25 questions per section	35 minutes per section
Quantitative (2 sections)	25 questions per section	40 minutes per section
Unscored (experimental Verbal or Quantitative Section)	Varies	Varies

Your GRE may contain questions that are similar to released GRE questions that appear on the POWERPREP® software or in official GRE publications, such as *The Official Guide to the GRE Revised General Test*. Be very careful when responding to these questions because they might be slightly different from the questions that you remember. There might be different facts in the question stem and there might be different answer choices.

GRE Question Types

In order to simplify the sometimes complicated information on the GRE, you must first understand what you're looking at. The following section provides a simple overview of the kinds of GRE questions that you will encounter.

Analytical Writing

The Analytical Writing section consists of an Issue Task and an Argument Task. You are expected to write essays that address each task. Here are typical examples of what you might see:

Issue Task

You will have 30 minutes to organize your thoughts and compose a response that represents your point of view on the issue. Do not respond to any issue other than the one presented; a response to any other issue will receive a score of 0.

Issue Topic

"Leaders should focus more on the needs of the majority than on the needs of the minority."

Discuss whether you agree or disagree with the statement. Use relevant reasons and examples to support your point of view. In developing and supporting your position, consider ways in which the statement might or might not hold true. Explain how those considerations affect your point of view.

Argument Task

You will have 30 minutes to organize your thoughts and compose a response that critiques the given argument. Do not respond to any argument other than the one given; a response to any other argument will receive a score of 0.

Argument Topic

The following appeared as part of an article in a health and fitness magazine:

"Several volunteers participated in a study of consumer responses to the new Exer-Core exercise machine. Every day for a month, they worked out on the machine for 30 minutes in addition to maintaining their normal fitness regimen. At the end of that month, most of the volunteers reported a significant improvement in both their stamina and muscle condition. Therefore, it appears that the Exer-Core exercise machine is truly effective in improving a person's overall general health and fitness."

Critique the reasoning used in the argument above. You are not being asked to discuss your point of view on the argument. You should identify and analyze the central elements of the argument, the underlying assumptions that are being made, and any supporting information that is given. Your critique can also discuss other information that would strengthen or weaken the argument or make it more logical.

Strategies to help you write high-scoring essays are included in Chapter 6, "GRE Analytical Writing."

Verbal

The Verbal sections of the GRE General Test include Sentence Equivalence, Reading Comprehension, and Text Completion questions. The questions do not appear in any predetermined order, nor is there any set number of each question type on any given GRE General Test. You should take as many practice tests as you can in order to become familiar with the format of the GRE verbal section.

Strategies specific to each of the question types outlined below can be found in Chapter 8, "GRE Verbal."

Sentence Equivalence

Select the words that, when inserted in the blank(s), best fit the context of the sentence and complete the sentence in the same manner.

Because of his _____, Brian's guests felt very welcome and comfortable staying at his house for the weekend.

- [A] animosity
- [B] hospitality
- [C] determination
- [D] wittiness
- [E] severity
- [F] generosity

Reading Comprehension

The GRE has three types of Reading Comprehension questions: Multiple-choice, Select One Answer; Multiple-choice, Select One or More Answers; and In-passage. The reading passages are usually just one or two paragraphs in length, and the number of questions per passage varies from one to six. The different types of questions do not appear in any predetermined order, nor is there a set number of each question type on every GRE General Test. A sample of each of the three question types is shown below.

Questions 1 to 3 are based on the following passage.

Scientists know very little about the eating habits of our ancestors who lived over two and a half million years ago. To solve this problem, scientists have started examining chimpanzees' hunting behavior and diet to find clues about our own prehistoric past. It is not difficult to determine why studying chimpanzees might be beneficial. Modern humans and chimpanzees are actually very closely related. Experts believe that chimpanzees share about 98.5 percent of our DNA sequence. If this is true, humans are more closely related to chimpanzees than they are to any other animal species.

1. The main purpose of the passage is to
   - (A) explore biological and physiological similarities between humans and chimpanzees
   - (B) examine the hunting behavior and diet of chimpanzees and compare it to human activity
   - (C) discuss the health benefits of eating and hunting meat while simultaneously predicting the effect of this behavior on chimpanzee offspring
   - (D) bring attention to the pioneering research of Dr. Jane Goodall in Tanzania
   - (E) educate the public on the impact that tool use had on early human societies

GO ON TO NEXT PAGE

Consider each of the three choices separately and select all that apply.

2. With which of the following statements is the author most likely to agree?
   - [A] Organisms that share a large percentage of DNA share similar characteristics.
   - [B] It has been difficult to study the eating habits of ancient man.
   - [C] Human behavior cannot be determined by comparing it to the behavior of animals.

3. Select the sentence that indicates a solution to the problem identified in the passage.

Text Completion

Choose one entry for each blank from the corresponding column of choices. Fill in the blanks in the way that best completes the text.

Experts believe that humans have 10 trillion cells in their bodies, which (i) _____ any number of essential genetic elements; scientists often marvel at what incredible (ii) _____ would ensue should the cells become jumbled or misunderstand their purpose.

Blank (i)	Blank (ii)
(A) govern	(D) order
(B) organize	(E) method
(C) dislocate	(F) chaos

Quantitative

The Quantitative sections of the GRE General Test include the following question types.

- Quantitative Comparison
- Multiple-choice—Select One Answer
- Multiple-choice—Select One or More Answers
- Numeric Entry

In each Quantitative section, the Quantitative Comparison questions always come first. The other question types do not appear in any predetermined order, nor is there any set number of each question type on every GRE General Test. The Multiple-choice and Numeric Entry questions may appear as discrete (stand-alone) items, or they may be part of a set of questions based on the data in a table, chart, or other graphic. You should take as many practice tests as you can in order to become familiar with the format of the GRE Quantitative section.

Strategies specific to each of the question types outlined here can be found in Chapter 7, "GRE Quantitative."

Quantitative Comparison

Compare Quantity A and Quantity B and select:

- Ⓐ if Quantity A is greater
- Ⓑ if Quantity B is greater
- Ⓒ if the two quantities are equal
- Ⓓ if the relationship cannot be determined from the information given

Quantity A	Quantity B
$-(3)^4$	$(-3)^4$

> **NOTE**
> Some Quantitative Comparison questions provide additional information centered between two columns. This information will help you to compare the two quantities. Refer to Chapter 7, "GRE Quantitative," for more details.

Multiple-choice—Select One Answer

For multiple-choice questions, unless you are directed otherwise, you should select a single answer choice.

1. When jogging, a runner takes 24 complete steps in 10 seconds. At this rate, approximately how many complete steps does the runner take in 144 seconds?
   - Ⓐ 34
   - Ⓑ 104
   - Ⓒ 154
   - Ⓓ 240
   - Ⓔ 346

Multiple-choice—Select One or More Answers

For this kind of multiple-choice question, the directions will tell you to choose all answers that apply. If the question specifies how many answer choices to select, select exactly that number of choices.

GO ON TO NEXT PAGE

2. Which two of the following integers have a product less than −80?
   - A −11
   - B −10
   - C −3
   - D 8

Numeric Entry

For the following question, write your answer in the box.

Solve the equation for x: $2(x-3)+9=4x-7$

More on the Computer-based Test

The computer-based GRE is partially computer-adaptive, which means that when you complete the first Verbal or first Quantitative section, the computer may give you a more difficult second Verbal or Quantitative section, depending on how well you performed on the first section. This process allows for a more accurate assessment of your individual ability level in a given subject area.

Within each section, you do not have to answer the questions in the order in which they are presented, and you do not have to confirm an answer in order to move to the next question. You are free to skip questions, and you do not have to answer every question in the section. If you have time, you can return to questions you skipped or weren't sure about, and you can change an answer you decide is incorrect. However, once time runs out for a section, you cannot return to that section later.

Only minimal computer skills are required to take the GRE. We suggest that you familiarize yourself with the computer adaptive system by downloading the free POWERPREP® software available at **www.gre.org**. Review the tutorials and testing tools prior to test day so that you know how the process works.

What's Next?

Chapter 2, "Taking the GRE," includes information on how to register for the GRE, what to expect at the testing center, and how the GRE is scored. We also provide a review of the policies governing test-takers with disabilities.

Taking the GRE

CHAPTER GOALS

- Get information about registering for the GRE.
- Find out what rules you must follow at the testing center.
- Learn how each part of the test is scored.

As mentioned in Chapter 1, the GRE General Test is designed to help graduate school admissions departments assess applicants. GRE scores are used to augment undergraduate records and transcripts and to provide a standard of measure for comparing all applicants.

The first step in taking the GRE is to register for an appropriate test date and location. If you are an international student, please also read the Welcome Section at the start of this book.

Registering for the GRE General Test

You can register for the GRE on the Internet, by telephone, or by U.S. mail. You will schedule your GRE test on a first-come, first-served basis at a testing location near you. The test is offered throughout the year at many locations around the United States. The GRE is also given in many countries worldwide. The full list of locations, and other registration details, can be found online at **www.ets.org**.

You can register via telephone by calling 1-800-GRE-CALL (1-800-473-2255). Registrations sent by mail can take up to four weeks to process. You must send the appropriate forms, either those printed directly from the GRE website or those found in the GRE Bulletin. The latter is available at many college counseling offices, as well as online. After you register, you will receive both detailed information about your testing center and free test prep materials, including the POWERPREP® software mentioned previously.

As of the printing of this book, you can take one GRE per calendar month. In addition, you can take a maximum of five GRE tests within any 12-month period. When you send your GRE scores to graduate schools, they see all scores from all GRE tests that you have taken within the past five years. You cannot choose to reveal scores only from a certain test date. How schools treat multiple-test scores varies. Some use only your most recent score, while others average the scores of each of your tests. Contact the admissions department of the programs to which you are applying for more information.

Taking the GRE General Test

One of the reasons the GRE is a useful tool for admissions departments is that it is a standardized test administered in the same way to all test-takers. In order to maintain this level of standardization, administration of the GRE is governed by some very specific rules, including, but not limited to, the following:

- You must have acceptable and valid ID; if you do not, you will not be admitted into the test center.
- You must use exactly the name that appears on your primary ID to register for the GRE and gain admittance to the test center.
- You must adhere to test center personnel requirements; failure to do so could result in expulsion from the test center.
- You cannot bring personal items such as cell phones, pagers, cameras, calculators, and the like.
- You must sign the confidentiality statement at the test center.

NOTE

The rules governing the computer-based GRE are different from those governing the paper-based test. Visit www.ets.org for more information on the test administration process.

Scoring the GRE General Test

On the GRE General Test, you will receive separate scores for Analytical Writing, Verbal Reasoning, and Quantitative Reasoning. The scores are calculated as follows.

Scoring the General Test Analytical Writing Section

Each essay receives a score from two highly trained readers using a 6-point holistic scale. This means that the readers are trained to assign a score based on the overall quality of an essay in response to a specific task. If the two scores differ by more than one point on the scale, a third reader steps in to resolve the discrepancy. In this case, the first two scores are dropped and the score given by the third reader is used. Otherwise, the scores from the two readers are averaged so that a single score from 0 to 6 (in half-point increments) is reported. If no essay response is given, a No Score (NS) is reported for this section. If an essay response is provided for one of the two writing tasks, the task for which no response is written receives a score of zero. Scoring guidelines are provided in Chapter 6, "GRE Analytical Writing." Your actual essays will also be reviewed by the Essay-Similarity-Detection software at Educational Testing Service (ETS) to ensure that your work is original.

Scoring the General Test Verbal and Quantitative Sections

Your scores on these two portions of the test will depend on your specific performance on the questions given as well as the number of questions answered correctly in the allotted time. First, for each measure, a raw score is computed based on the number of questions answered correctly. Then, using statistical methods, each raw score is converted to a scaled score that takes account of small differences between test forms. For the computer-based test, the conversion process also takes account of the fact that the test is partially adaptive; that is, depending how well you perform on the first Verbal and first Quantitative question, the computer may give you a second Verbal or Quantitative question that is more difficult. The purpose of statistically generating a scaled score is to make sure that scores achieved by test-takers on one GE test form are comparable to the same scores achieved on other GRE test forms. The Verbal and Quantitative scores are each reported on a 130–170 score scale, in 1 point increments. If you answer no questions at all in either section, a No Score (NS) is reported.

A Note on Scoring the Practice Exams in This Book

Because actual GRE tests are scored using scales that are unique to each test form, this book only includes a guideline for interpreting scores on the simulated practice tests. As you work through this book, you should take additional practice exams with the official POWERPREP® software. It contains the same scoring "engine" as the real GRE exam and can give you a very good idea of how you should expect to do on test day. At this stage, and throughout most of your practice, you should not worry excessively about your test scores; your goal should be to learn something from every practice experience and to become familiar with the format and types of questions on the GRE.

What Your Scores Mean to Schools

You can select up to four institutions to receive your score report. Generally, score reports will be sent to you and the institutions selected 10 to 15 days after you complete the test. Most graduate programs elect to use GRE scores as an admissions tool because GRE scores are a reliable measure of an individual's capacity to perform at the graduate level, and because GRE scores provide a consistent means by which to evaluate applicants. Admissions professionals also take into account an applicant's grade point average, personal interviews, and letters of recommendation. However, because each of these methods of evaluation is variable and subjective, admissions departments need a standardized tool to provide a more objective measure of academic success.

Test-Takers with Disabilities

ETS provides additional information for test-takers with disabilities that includes guidelines for documenting disabilities, suggestions for test-takers, and the necessary forms required to obtain special accommodations. For test-takers with documented disabilities, these accommodations might include the following:

- Additional or extended testing time and breaks
- Allowance of medical devices in the testing center and special computer equipment
- A reader, a sign language interpreter, and recording devices

Accommodation requests must be made in advance and by following the guidelines set forth in *The Bulletin Supplement for Test Takers with Disabilities*, available as a download on **www.ets.org**. Documentation review could take several weeks, so be sure to submit all of the required forms and information at least two months prior to your desired test date.

What's Next?

The Diagnostic Test in Chapter 3 should be your next step. It will help you to focus on areas of strength and weakness in your knowledge base and skill set. After you've assessed your current readiness for the GRE, focus on the remaining chapters in this book to maximize your GRE score.

PART II

Preparing for the GRE General Test

CHAPTER 3 **GRE DIAGNOSTIC TEST**

CHAPTER 4 **GRE GENERAL TESTING STRATEGIES**

CHAPTER 5 **INTRODUCTION TO GRE LOGIC**

CHAPTER 6 **GRE ANALYTICAL WRITING**

CHAPTER 7 **GRE QUANTITATIVE**

CHAPTER 8 **GRE VERBAL**

3
GRE Diagnostic Test

CHAPTER GOALS

- Take a simulated full-length GRE under actual test conditions.
- Check your results using the Answer Key.
- Review the explanations for each question, particularly those for questions you answered incorrectly or did not answer at all.
- Use the results to plan your GRE preparation program, focusing on areas you need to improve.

This diagnostic test can assist you in evaluating your current readiness for the Graduate Record Examination (GRE). Sample questions representing each section of the GRE are included to help you pinpoint areas of strength and weakness in your knowledge base and your skill set. Don't worry if you are unable to answer many or most of the questions at this point. The rest of this book contains information and resources to help you to maximize your GRE score.

We suggest that you make this diagnostic test as much like the real test as possible. Find a quiet location, free from distractions, and make sure that you have pencils and a timepiece. The simulated GRE in this chapter consists of five sections: one Analytical Writing task (in two parts), two Verbal Reasoning sections, and two Quantitative Reasoning sections, each with 20 questions. You should allow approximately 3 hours and 30 minutes to complete the entire test. The test sections should be completed in the time indicated at the beginning of each section and in the order in which the sections appear. You may skip around within a section, but complete each section before you move on to the next one.

Within each section there are several different types of questions. Make sure that you read and understand all directions before you begin.

- Circle your answers on the test so that you can compare your answers to the correct answers listed in the Answer Key on page 61.
- When asked to select a sentence in a passage that meets a certain description, circle or underline the sentence you choose.
- Carefully review the explanations, paying close attention to the questions you missed. Reviewing explanations for questions you answered correctly is helpful because it reinforces "GRE thinking."

Remember, your score on the actual GRE will depend on many factors, including your level of preparedness and your fatigue level on test day.

As you work through this and the other simulated tests in this book, you should be aware that they are not actual tests. They are reasonably accurate simulations written by GRE experts. They contain basically the same mix of question types as a real GRE. If you work through all of the material provided, you can rest assured that there won't be any surprises on test day. The biggest difference between these tests and your real GRE is the fact that these are paper tests and you will take your GRE using a computer. We've tried to mimic the computer test as much as possible, but you should definitely plan to do some practicing with the free software available at **www.gre.org** from the authors of the GRE. For more information regarding the differences between the simulated test in this book and your actual GRE, refer back to Chapter 1, "Overview of the GRE," and Chapter 2, "Taking the GRE."

The Diagnostic Test begins on the next page.

GRE Diagnostic Test

SECTION 1   **ANALYTICAL WRITING**

SECTION 2   **VERBAL REASONING**

SECTION 3   **VERBAL REASONING**

SECTION 4   **QUANTITATIVE REASONING**

SECTION 5   **QUANTITATIVE REASONING**

                     ANSWERS AND EXPLANATIONS

SECTION 1

Analytical Writing

PART 1. ANALYZE AN ISSUE

30 minutes

You will have 30 minutes to organize your thoughts and compose a response that represents your point of view on the issue. Do not respond to any issue other than the one presented; a response to any other issue will receive a score of 0.

Issue Topic

"The government should provide funding for school music programs so that music can flourish and be available to all members of the community."

Discuss whether you agree or disagree with the statement. Use relevant reasons and examples to support your point of view. In developing and supporting your position, consider ways in which the statement might or might not hold true. Explain how those considerations affect your point of view.

Analytical Writing

PART 2. ANALYZE AN ARGUMENT

30 minutes

You will have 30 minutes to organize your thoughts and compose a response that critiques the given argument. Do not respond to any argument other than the one given; a response to any other argument will receive a score of 0.

Argument Topic

"When Marion Park first opened, it was the largest, most popular park in town. While it is still the largest park, it is no longer as popular as it once was. Recently collected statistics reveal the park's drop in popularity: About 45 cars per day enter the park. On the other hand, tiny Midtown Park in the center of downtown is visited by more than 125 people on a typical weekday. One obvious difference is that Midtown Park, unlike Marion Park, can utilize parking spaces along Main Street and along various side streets. Therefore, if Marion Park is to regain its popularity, the town council will obviously need to approve funding for additional parking."

Critique the reasoning used in the argument above. You are not being asked to discuss your point of view on the argument. You should identify and analyze the central elements of the argument, the underlying assumptions that are being made, and any supporting information that is given. Your critique can also discuss other information that would strengthen or weaken the argument or make it more logical.

SECTION 2

Verbal Reasoning

30 Minutes
20 Questions

This section consists of three different types of questions: Reading Comprehension, Text Completion, and Sentence Equivalence. To answer the questions, select the best answer from the answer choices given. Reading Comprehension questions appear in sets; Text Completion and Sentence Equivalence questions are independent. The questions will be presented in random order. Read the following directions before you begin the test.

Reading Comprehension Questions

Directions:
Multiple-choice Questions—Select One Answer Choice: These are the traditional multiple-choice questions with five answer choices from which you must select one.

Multiple-choice Questions—Select One or More Answer Choices: These questions provide three answer choices; select all that are correct.

Select-in-Passage: Choose the sentence in the passage that meets a certain description.

Text Completion Questions

Directions: Select one entry from the corresponding column of choices for each blank. Fill all blanks in the way that best completes the text.

Sentence Equivalence Questions

Directions: Select the two answer choices that, when used to complete the sentence, fit the meaning of the sentence as a whole and produce completed sentences that are alike in meaning.

Questions 1 to 3 are based on the following passage.

Sending a robot into space to gather information is a viable option, but should only be regarded as that—an option. Even the most technologically advanced robots cannot and should not replace manned missions to outer space. Certainly it is cheaper and less dangerous to launch a computer probe that can gather reams of

GO ON TO NEXT PAGE

data, but often the information obtained by a machine only serves to produce more questions than it answers. Therefore, the space program should allow manned missions to follow up on those initial information-gathering robotic ventures.

While manned missions are more costly than are unmanned missions, they are also more successful. Robots and astronauts use much of the same equipment in space, but a human is more capable of calibrating those instruments correctly and placing them in appropriate and useful positions. A computer is often neither as sensitive nor as accurate as a human in managing the same terrain or environmental circumstances. Robots are also not as equipped as humans to solve problems as they arise, and robots often collect data that is not helpful or even desired. A human, on the other hand, can make instant decisions about what to explore further and what to ignore.

For Question 1, select one answer choice.

1. The passage supplies information to answer which of the following questions?
    - (A) What is the cost of launching a computer probe into space?
    - (B) What type of information can safely be ignored when exploring outer space?
    - (C) How much information can a computer probe gather in outer space?
    - (D) What is the next level in space exploration?
    - (E) Are unmanned space missions more economical than manned space missions?

2. Select the sentence that offers potential advantages to using robots as information gatherers in space.

    Certainly it is cheaper and less dangerous...

For Question 3, select one answer choice.

3. According to the passage, all of the following are advantages of humans over robots EXCEPT
    - (A) humans can more accurately manage the data collected
    - (B) humans can apply critical thinking skills to new situations
    - (C) humans can only calibrate instruments designed by robots
    - (D) humans are more sensitive to environmental changes
    - (E) humans are better at preparing instrumentation for use in space

Question 4 is based on the following passage.

Coffee seems to be one of the world's biggest and most enduring passions, as coffee houses continue to pop up on every corner, each one sporting beans from multiple exotic and sometimes completely unfamiliar locations. Although usually referred to as coffee beans, they are actually closer to berries, which grow on bushes found on slopes several thousand feet above sea level in places like Brazil. The berries are soaked, dried, sorted, and finally roasted for various amounts of time, depending on how strong and dark the consumer prefers his coffee.

For Question 4, select one answer choice.

4. Which of the following can be inferred from the overall process involved in preparing coffee beans?
   - Ⓐ Coffee beans must be roasted longer than coffee berries.
   - Ⓑ Soaking is the lengthiest step in the preparation process.
   - Ⓒ Consumer preference regarding the final strength and color of coffee varies.
   - Ⓓ A consumer's passion for coffee determines exactly how the beans are processed.
   - Ⓔ The more exotic and unfamiliar the coffee bean, the longer it takes to prepare.

For Questions 5 to 7, select one entry from the corresponding column of choices for each blank. Fill all blanks in the way that best completes the text.

5. Body language involves a combination of multiple facial (i) _____ and various physical positions to convey its unique (ii) _____ message.

Blank (i)	Blank (ii)
Ⓐ movements	Ⓓ oral
Ⓑ expressions	Ⓔ strident
Ⓒ appearances	Ⓕ nonverbal

6. Although the scientist's recommendations may have been (i) _____, the students had trouble following his (ii) _____ presentation and were, therefore, against his proposal.

Blank (i)	Blank (ii)
Ⓐ absurd	Ⓓ organized
Ⓑ realistic	Ⓔ empirical
Ⓒ ubiquitous	Ⓕ convoluted

7. The New Zealand Storm Petrel was a bird long thought (i) _____, but in 2003 several birds were spotted for the first time in 150 years, apparently having (ii) _____ themselves on the predator-free Hauraki Islands during the (iii) _____.

Blank (i)	Blank (ii)	Blank (iii)
Ⓐ extinct	Ⓓ buried	Ⓖ interim
Ⓑ endangered	Ⓔ initiated	Ⓗ search
Ⓒ dormant	Ⓕ secreted	Ⓘ extension

Part II: Preparing for the GRE General Test

Questions 8 to 11 are based on the following passage.

By any measure, computers are among the most influential and powerful tools of the modern age. They represent the high-tech revolution that has transformed the ways in which human beings interact with each other and with the world at large. Seemingly, computers are the very definition of the modern era. Although modern computers have only been a part of our everyday world for a few decades, a discovery made just over a century ago found that the concept behind them is far older than anyone could have imagined. In fact, according to the experts who have studied an ancient Greek shipwreck, one particular "computer" dates back more than 2,000 years.

Made of metal, this mechanism is approximately the size of a shoebox. It was found in 1901 by divers working off the isle of Antikythera. Uncertain of the mechanism's function, the divers named it after the island near which it was found. At the time, the Antikythera was in terrible shape from being underwater for so long. Its pieces had merged into a broken mass and all experts could deduce was that it had something to do with astronomy. Recently, thanks to a combination of advanced imaging methods and x-ray computer tomography, scientists have been able to re-create the possible design of the apparatus.

The Antikythera mechanism once had at least 30 bronze gears with as many as 225 hand-cut teeth. Scientists believe it was designed to compute eclipses of the sun and moon a number of years into the future, as well as show the motions of the planets. While experts are still uncertain as to why the device was made, there is no doubt that its technology was at least 1,000 years ahead of its time.

For Question 8, select one answer choice.

8. The primary purpose of the passage is to
   - (A) explain how computers were originally designed
   - (B) provide details on how to compute solar and lunar eclipses
   - (C) introduce the concept of an ancient device with a modern application
   - (D) describe the discovery of a computer-like machine designed more than 2,000 years ago
   - (E) show how x-ray computer tomography has helped scientists explore ancient discoveries

For Question 9, consider each of the choices separately and select all that apply.

9. The author of the passage most likely mentions that the divers were uncertain as to the Antikythera's function because
   - [A] it demonstrates that computers are not very important to people in today's society
   - [B] it reinforces the notion that computers are a tool of the modern age
   - [C] it contradicts earlier theories regarding ancient technology

10. Select the sentence in the passage that presents an argument for the surprising and unusual nature of this discovery.

[handwritten: Although modern computers have only...]
[handwritten: → While experts are still uncertain...]

For Question 11, consider each of the choices separately and select all that apply.

11. The passage suggests that, compared to modern computers, the Antikythera
    - [A] did not influence subsequent technological advances
    - [B] did not become obsolete within a short time of its creation
    - [C] did not confuse researchers

Question 12 is based on the following passage.

Over the years there have been countless fans of the classic Hanna-Barbera cartoon character Yogi Bear. The cartoon series enjoyed by young and old alike revolved mostly around the misadventures of this loveable bear and his sidekick Boo-Boo as they attempted to snag "pic-a-nic" baskets in the made-up land of Jellystone Park. It's not often that people think about where the ideas for these cartoons characters came from, which brings up an interesting point: do bears actually search for food left in picnic baskets and unattended campsites? Anyone who has watched an episode of the classic cartoon can see that the bears' behavior goes far beyond the limits of what is natural. The thing that must be explored, then, is which of those humorous antics were license on the part of Hanna-Barbera, and which were actually based on a bear's normal behaviors.

For Question 12, select one answer choice.

12. The passage implies which of the following about the cartoon character Yogi Bear?
    - (A) Yogi's behavior is based exclusively on that of wild bears.
    - (B) Yogi's penchant for picnic baskets is purely fictional.
    - (C) Yogi's humorous antics are not necessarily grounded in reality.
    - (D) Yogi's behavioral patterns have been described extensively by naturalists.
    - (E) Yogi's actions consistently mimic those of bears in the wild.

GO ON TO NEXT PAGE

For Question 13, select one entry from the corresponding column of choices for each blank. Fill all blanks in the way that best completes the text.

13. Many people suspect that (i) _____ humans are only a few inventions away since it is already possible to (ii) _____ many body parts with improvements made out of plastic and metal, and many key organs can be (iii) _____ from one body to another.

Blank (i)	Blank (ii)	Blank (iii)
Ⓐ artificial	Ⓓ articulate	Ⓖ stabilized
Ⓑ geriatric	Ⓔ discard	Ⓗ transferred
Ⓒ mortal	Ⓕ replace	Ⓘ filched

Questions 14 and 15 are based on the following passage.

There are few portraits in the world as famous as Leonardo da Vinci's *Mona Lisa*, but the identity of the model for the legendary painting has been an enduring mystery for countless people. Now some experts believe that the young woman might have been an Italian named Lisa Gherardini, the wife of an affluent silk merchant and government figure. Other researchers suspect it might have been Isabella of Aragon, the Duchess of Milan. Whoever she was, the mystery woman certainly gave the world one of its most mysterious smiles.

For Question 14, select one answer choice.

14. Which of the following sentences can be inferred about the *Mona Lisa* painting from this passage?
    Ⓐ The model for the *Mona Lisa* was a very happy and kind woman.
    Ⓑ The *Mona Lisa* is one of the most well known portraits in the world.
    Ⓒ Leonardo da Vinci's paintings all contained some kind of mystery in them.
    Ⓓ The painting was apparently supposed to be a present to the Duchess of Milan.
    Ⓔ Lisa Gherardini must have been a very patient person to sit for such a detailed portrait.

For Question 15, consider each of the choices separately and select all that apply.

15. Which of the following statements about the portrait is supported by the passage?
    Ⓐ The portrait is the subject of ongoing controversy.
    Ⓑ The portrait was of a single unidentified woman.
    Ⓒ The portrait's model was smiling as the picture was painted.

For Questions 16 through 20, select the two answer choices that, when used to complete the sentence, fit the meaning of the sentence as a whole and produce completed sentences that are alike in meaning.

16. The problem with activists is that far too often they merely _____ the protection of various ecosystems, instead of taking a lead role in their management.
    - [A] circumvent
    - [B] abridge
    - [C] diversify
    - [D] advocate
    - [E] abhor
    - [F] support

17. When practicing with a bow and arrow, it is _____ to be aware of both the velocity and the trajectory of one's arrows if one wishes to hit the target.
    - [A] irrelevant
    - [B] necessary
    - [C] conventional
    - [D] prudent
    - [E] detrimental
    - [F] insightful

18. As we traveled to college for the first time, the family car was _____ with books, clothing, appliances, and other necessities.
    - [A] keen
    - [B] indigent
    - [C] barren
    - [D] pallid
    - [E] laden
    - [F] overflowing

19. The _____ of sediment in the river caused concern among environmentalists and industrialists alike; the water levels in the river were being reduced almost daily.
    - [A] accretion
    - [B] disposal
    - [C] depletion
    - [D] alienation
    - [E] ethnology
    - [F] accumulation

GO ON TO NEXT PAGE

20. Running a marathon is an _____ task, taking months of both physical and mental preparation and training before actually running a grueling 26.2 miles.
   - [A] arduous
   - [B] ambiguous
   - [C] involuntary
   - [D] eloquent
   - [E] overt
   - [F] ambitious

STOP.
This is the end of Section 2. Use any remaining time to check your work.

SECTION 3

Verbal Reasoning

30 Minutes
20 Questions

This section consists of three different types of questions: Reading Comprehension, Text Completion, and Sentence Equivalence. To answer the questions, select the best answer from the answer choices given. Reading Comprehension questions appear in sets; Text Completion and Sentence Equivalence questions are independent. The questions will be presented in random order. Read the following directions before you begin the test.

Reading Comprehension Questions

Directions:
Multiple-choice Questions—Select One Answer Choice: These are the traditional multiple-choice questions with five answer choices from which you must select one.

Multiple-choice Questions—Select One or More Answer Choices: These questions provide three answer choices; select all that are correct.

Select-in-Passage: Choose the sentence in the passage that meets a certain description.

Text Completion Questions

Directions: Select one entry from the corresponding column of choices for each blank. Fill all blanks in the way that best completes the text.

Sentence Equivalence Questions

Directions: Select the two answer choices that, when used to complete the sentence, fit the meaning of the sentence as a whole and produce completed sentences that are alike in meaning.

GO ON TO NEXT PAGE

For Questions 1 through 3, select the two answer choices that, when used to complete the sentence, fit the meaning of the sentence as a whole and produce completed sentences that are alike in meaning.

1. Because of his _____, Brian's guests felt very welcome and comfortable staying at his house for the weekend.
   - A animosity
   - B hospitality
   - C determination
   - D wittiness
   - E severity
   - F receptiveness

2. Some of the earliest bicycles came equipped with solid wooden wheels that were annoyingly _____ to break or crack at the worst moment.
   - A fabricated
   - B constructed
   - C prone
   - D unlikely
   - E debatable
   - F liable

3. Skin contains millions of sensory receptors which inform the brain, through electrical _____, when you have injured yourself.
   - A compulsions
   - B thrusts
   - C impulses
   - D signals
   - E flashes
   - F imitations

Questions 4 and 5 are based on the following passage.

Scientists believe that by raising atmospheric pressure and surface temperature, it is possible to transform the climate of Mars to the point where humans would be able to live there. The process by which a hostile or unsuitable environment is transformed into one that can sustain human life is called *terraforming*. In addition to potentially providing an alternate home for the people of Earth in the future, this undertaking may also allow scientists to test hypotheses about the process of global warming, which is a highly pertinent issue affecting our planet today.

For Question 4, consider each of the choices separately and select all that apply.

4. Which of the following can be inferred from the passage regarding the Martian atmosphere?
   - [A] It has a lower pressure than Earth's atmosphere.
   - [B] It has a higher surface temperature than Earth.
   - [C] It can most certainly be transformed to be more like Earth's atmosphere.

For Question 5, select one answer choice.

5. The passage addresses which of the following consequences of terraforming?
   - (A) The creation of a more hospitable planet.
   - (B) The risk of overpopulation.
   - (C) The elimination of suitable environments.
   - (D) The depletion of the atmosphere.
   - (E) The production of greenhouse gases.

Question 6 is based on the following passage.

A baby polar bear named Knut at the Berlin Zoo is the epicenter of a debate about animal rights and the ethics of keeping animals in captivity. Knut and his brother were abandoned by their mother after being born at the zoo. Knut's sibling died, and Knut himself would have died as well, had the zoo officials not intervened. The zoo workers have been bottle-feeding the bear, and providing it with nourishment and care. Yet certain animal-rights activists say that the bear would have been better off dead than raised by humans, and some go as far as to say that Knut should be killed. They believe that the current treatment of the bear is inhumane, and will lead to future difficulty for Knut in interacting with other polar bears. They argue that since the mother rejected the cub, the zoo workers should have abided by the laws of nature, and the cub should have been allowed to die. Others have argued that in light of the fact that polar bears are an endangered species, it makes sense to keep as many bears as possible alive in captivity so that they can breed.

For Question 6, select one answer choice.

6. The author mentions animal-rights activists in order to
   - (A) explain how Knut became an orphan
   - (B) exonerate the zoo workers
   - (C) depict Knut's caretakers as unprofessional
   - (D) foster the impression that polar bear's cannot exist in the wild
   - (E) point out a counterargument to the zoo's position

GO ON TO NEXT PAGE

Questions 7 to 8 are based on the following passage.

The male/female gender binary dominates Western culture, yet it is far from universal. For example, in India you might encounter a "hijra"—a member of the third sex. They are considered neither man nor woman. Although many of them are physically male, traditionally they refer to themselves as female and dress appropriately. This third gender is referenced in the earliest available records from the Indian Subcontinent, and was an established presence in the Vedic culture. There is no equivalent of hijras in the contemporary Western conceptualization of gender.

For Question 7, consider each of the choices separately and select all that apply.

7. The passage suggests which of the following about gender in Western culture?
   - [A] Most, if not all, members of modern Western civilization consider themselves either male or female.
   - [B] Contemporary Western civilization does not believe in the concept of hijra.
   - [C] The idea of male/female binary gender is not generally considered the norm of contemporary Western civilization.

8. Select the sentence that indicates the historical aspect of hijra.

For Questions 9 and 10, select one entry from the corresponding column of choices for each blank. Fill all blanks in the way that best completes the text.

9. Experts believe that humans have ten trillion cells in their bodies which (i) _____ any number of essential genetic elements, and they often marvel at what incredible (ii) _____ would ensue should the cells become jumbled or misunderstand their purpose.

Blank (i)	Blank (ii)
Ⓐ govern	Ⓓ order
Ⓑ organize	Ⓔ method
Ⓒ dislocate	Ⓕ chaos

10. According to color psychologists, certain hues tend to reflect particular personality _____; violet, for example, indicates a tendency towards mysticism and intuition, while brown suggests an uncomfortable and aimless character.

Ⓐ flaws
Ⓑ aptitudes
Ⓒ traits
Ⓓ endowments
Ⓔ imperfections

Questions 11 to 13 are based on the following passage.

When I was preparing for my two-week vacation in southern Africa, I realized that the continent would be like nothing I had ever seen. I wanted to explore the urban streets as well as the savannah; it's always been my goal to have experiences on vacation that most other tourists fail to find. When my plans were finalized, I left for Africa. The cultural differences were stunning, and made for plenty of laughter and confusion, but always ended up bringing smiles to our faces. What's funny now, though, more than ever, is how ridiculous I must have seemed to the people of one village when I played with their dog. Apparently, the role of dogs in America is nothing like it is in Africa.

I am convinced that African dogs could clobber their American counterparts, if only because African dogs are forced to be self-reliant. The relationship between a typical African dog and his owner is one of tangible mutualism. I say tangible because the African sees himself as the dominant creature not to be bothered by the dog, but nevertheless responsible for providing for it. Hence, no attempts at behavioral training are ever made with African dogs. Instead, the African seizes power with a chunk of scrap meat and a bowl of water. The dog soon learns to quit yapping and biting at the hand that feeds him. Never does the African speak to the animal. I'm not even sure such dogs get names. Their behavior becomes interestingly balanced, however, much to the surprise of the compassionate American dog lover.

For Questions 11 to 13, select one answer choice.

11. According to information provided by the passage, which of the following traits would the author most likely ascribe to African dog owners?
    - (A) affectionate
    - (B) abusive
    - (C) pragmatic
    - (D) deceitful
    - (E) antagonistic

12. The author of the passage is primarily concerned with presenting
    - (A) a description of cultural differences
    - (B) an overview of animal behavior
    - (C) a history of international tourism
    - (D) evidence to refute a global theory
    - (E) an account of animal cruelty

GO ON TO NEXT PAGE

13. The passage addresses which of the following differences between African dogs and American dogs?
    - Ⓐ African dogs do not have owners, whereas American dogs do.
    - Ⓑ African dogs undergo intense behavioral training, while American dogs remain untrained.
    - Ⓒ African dogs learn to respect their owners, but American dogs cannot be disciplined.
    - Ⓓ African dogs retain more independence from their owners than do American dogs.
    - Ⓔ African dogs are more dominant over their owners than are American dogs.

For Questions 14 to 16, select one entry from the corresponding column of choices for each blank. Fill all blanks in the way that best completes the text.

14. Long considered one of the most beautiful of the planets, Saturn has rings that scientists believe (i) _____ the wreckage of scattered moons, but that is partially just (ii) _____ as, so far, no spaceship has been able to bring any ring material specimens back to Earth.

Blank (i)	Blank (ii)
Ⓐ consist of	Ⓓ experimentation
Ⓑ revolve around	Ⓔ speculation
Ⓒ resulted in	Ⓕ vacillation

15. Many American physicians would be quite (i) _____ if the terribly unhealthy, but quite tasty traditional Scottish cult (ii) _____ of chocolate bars dipped in batter and deep fried was served in restaurants throughout the United States.

Blank (i)	Blank (ii)
Ⓐ appalled	Ⓓ remedy
Ⓑ delighted	Ⓔ entrée
Ⓒ mystified	Ⓕ delicacy

16. Conspiracy theories commonly revolve around the concept that an individual or an entire organization has, for a myriad of reasons, _____ events or a series of events in order to fool others, as in the theory that the moon landings were actually events staged in Earth.

Ⓐ devised
Ⓑ manipulated
Ⓒ ignored
Ⓓ plotted
Ⓔ exposed

Question 17 is based on the following passage.

Traditional critical scholarship has considered a literary work the product of one focused mind, along with its social influences, struggling to achieve self-expression. In such a context, the author's intended meaning, especially as it may be inferred by the circumstances surrounding his life and the work, is extremely important: the author's intention should be taken as the gold standard in determining what constitutes an accurate and valid reading of the text. A natural outgrowth of measuring the validity of readings by this standard is the rejection of those readings that do not fit what the author intended, or what the surrounding culture expected the author to intend.

For Question 17, select one answer choice.

17. In the passage, "gold standard" most nearly means
    - (A) monetary normalcy
    - (B) natural outgrowth
    - (C) financial custom
    - (D) cultural expectation
    - (E) best practice

Question 18 is based on the following passage.

A civilization's level of advancement can be judged to an astonishing degree of accuracy by examining what it does with its sewage. Prehistoric people either behaved much like animals by individually burying their excretions, or they placed their waste in foul-smelling communal pit toilets. Later on, rivers were used as receptacles for bodily refuse to wash the offal out to sea. By the Roman times, plumbing had been invented to bring the river to inland settlements—though wastewater still flowed back out into the same rivers that might elsewhere be used for drinking. It is only in the modern age, at the pinnacle of human culture as achieved by western civilization, that we have developed systems for washing soiled water in treatment plants, where it can be chemically treated until it is safe to release back into the hydrosphere.

For Question 18, select one answer choice.

18. Based on the attitudes displayed in the passage, with which of the following statements would the author most likely disagree?
    - (A) An unsanitary habit may nonetheless be preferable to behaving like the other animals in the environment.
    - (B) The world would be a cleaner place if people worldwide had better access to facilities to treat sewage water.
    - (C) Improving sanitation has been a common goal of developing societies, as people seek to live in a cleaner environment.
    - (D) Burying excrement was remarkably environmentally sound, as it enabled human waste to return to the earth without soiling water.
    - (E) Designing an effective plumbing system both signified and mandated a certain level of complexity in the social structure.

Questions 19 and 20 are based on the following passage.

Although a number of inventions not only change society but also bring the inventor enormous pride and even paychecks, some fizzle out because they just do not succeed as hoped. In fact, even the most famous inventors encounter some failed concepts. One of the world's most prestigious inventors, Thomas Alva Edison, creator of the light bulb and the phonograph, tried to introduce the idea of cabinets and other furniture made out of concrete. This furniture was too heavy and too expensive to ever become popular, thus proving that nobody is always right.

For Question 19, consider each of the choices separately and select all that apply.

19. Which of the following statements about Edison can be inferred from the passage?
    - [A] Edison was one of the world's most esteemed and influential inventors.
    - [B] Concrete furniture was the only one of Edison's inventions to ultimately fail.
    - [C] The light bulb and the phonograph were extremely successful inventions by Edison.

20. Select the sentence within the paragraph that describes why sales of Edison's concrete furniture turned out to be unsuccessful.

STOP.
This is the end of Section 3. Use any remaining time to check your work.

SECTION 4

Quantitative Reasoning

35 Minutes
20 Questions

This section includes four types of questions: Multiple-choice Questions (Select One Answer Choice *and* Select One or More Answer Choices), Numeric Entry Questions, and Quantitative Comparison Questions. Read the following directions before you begin the test.

General Information:
Numbers: All of the numbers used in this section are real numbers.

Figures: Assume that the position of all points, angles, etc. are in the order shown and the measures of angles are positive.

Straight lines can be assumed to be straight.

All figures lie in a plane unless otherwise stated.

The figures given for each question provide information to solve the problem. The figures are not drawn to scale unless otherwise stated. To solve the problems, use your knowledge of mathematics; do not estimate lengths and sizes of the figures to answer questions.

Multiple-choice Questions

Select One Answer Choice

Directions: These questions are multiple-choice questions that ask you to select only one answer choice from a list of five choices.

Select One or More Answer Choices

Directions: Select one or more answer choices according to the specific question directions.

If the question does not specify how many answer choices to select, select all that apply.

The correct answer may be just one of the choices or as many as all of the choices, depending on the question.

No credit is given unless you select all of the correct choices and no others.

If the question specifies how many answer choices to select, select exactly that number of choices.

GO ON TO NEXT PAGE

48 Part II: Preparing for the GRE General Test

Numeric Entry Questions

Directions: Enter your answer in the answer box(es) below the question.

Equivalent forms of the correct answer, such as 2.5 and 2.50, are all correct. Fractions do not need to be reduced to lowest terms.

Enter the exact answer unless the question asks you to round your answer.

Quantitative Comparison Questions

Directions: These questions give you two quantities, Quantity A and Quantity B. Compare the two quantities and choose one of the following answer choices:

  A if Quantity A is greater;
  B if Quantity B is greater;
  C if the two quantities are equal;
  D if you cannot determine the relationship based on the given information.

Note: Information and/or figures pertaining to one or both of the quantities may appear above the two columns. Any information that appears in both columns has the same meaning for both Quantity A and Quantity B.

You will also be asked Data Interpretation questions, which are grouped together and refer to the same table, graph, or other data presentation. These questions ask you to interpret or analyze the given data. The types of questions may be Multiple-choice (both types) or Numeric Entry.

> Each of Questions 1 to 7 presents two quantities, Quantity A and Quantity B. Compare the two quantities. You may use additional information centered above the quantities if such information is given. Choose one of the following answer choices:
>
> Ⓐ if Quantity A is greater;
> Ⓑ if Quantity B is greater;
> Ⓒ if the two quantities are equal;
> Ⓓ if you cannot determine the relationship based on the given information.

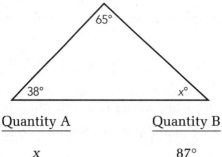

	Quantity A	Quantity B	
1.	x	87°	Ⓐ Ⓑ Ⓒ Ⓓ

	Quantity A	Quantity B	
2.	The average (arithmetic mean) of 16, 23, and 52	The average (arithmetic mean) of 15, 24, and 51	Ⓐ Ⓑ Ⓒ Ⓓ

$x=4$

	Quantity A	Quantity B	
3.	$3x^4$	750	Ⓐ Ⓑ Ⓒ Ⓓ

A rectangular box is 5 feet wide and 6 feet high and has a volume of 120 cubic feet.

	Quantity A	Quantity B	
4.	4 feet	The length of the box	Ⓐ Ⓑ Ⓒ Ⓓ

	Quantity A	Quantity B	
5.	The probability of tossing two "Tails" in a row with a fair coin	The probability of pulling out a red colored piece of candy from a bag containing 3 blue, 4 red, and 5 yellow pieces of candy	Ⓐ Ⓑ Ⓒ Ⓓ

	Quantity A	Quantity B	
6.	The number of hours in a week	The number of months in 14 years	Ⓐ Ⓑ Ⓒ Ⓓ

	Quantity A	Quantity B	
7.	The standard deviation of test scores of five students who score 71, 75, 83, 89, and 77	The standard deviation of test scores of five students who score 81, 85, 93, 99, and 87	Ⓐ Ⓑ Ⓒ Ⓓ

GO ON TO NEXT PAGE

8. For senior class pictures, a photographer charges x dollars to make a negative, $\frac{7x}{10}$ dollars for each of the first 20 prints, and $\frac{x}{10}$ dollars for each print in excess of 20 prints. If $80 is the total charge to make a negative and 30 prints, what is the value of x?

   (A) 3
   (B) 4
   (C) 5
   (D) 6
   (E) 7

9. If Tom traveled 45 miles in 12 hours and Jim traveled four times as far in one-third the time, what was Jim's average speed, in miles per hour?

   (A) 5
   (B) 15
   (C) 30
   (D) 45
   (E) 90

For Question 10, write your answer in the box.

10. Solve the equation for x: $2(x-3)+9=4x-7$

    $x = \boxed{5}$

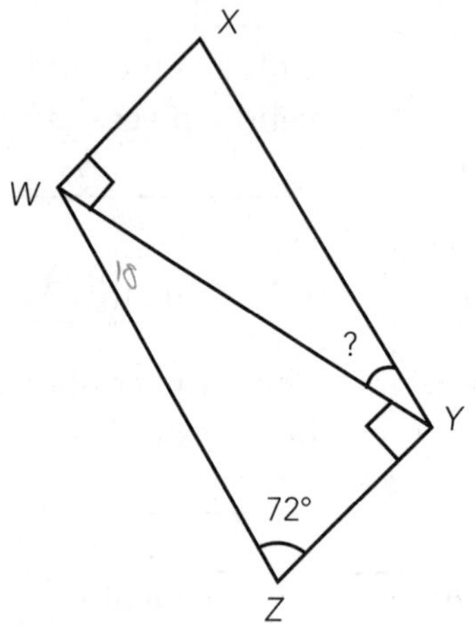

11. In parallelogram WXYZ shown above, WY is perpendicular to YZ and the measure of angle WZY is 72°. What is the measure of angle XYW?

    (A) 12°
    (B) 18°
    (C) 36°
    (D) 58°
    (E) 72°

12. Which of the following is equivalent to the inequality $3x-6>6x+9$?

    Ⓐ $x>-5$
    Ⓑ $x<-5$
    Ⓒ $x>-2$
    Ⓓ $x<3$
    Ⓔ $x>3$

For Question 13, select all the answer choices that apply.

13. You know that x is a positive integer. Which of the following statements individually provide(s) sufficient additional information to determine whether the square root of x is also an integer?
    Select all such statements.

    Ⓐ x is the square of an integer.
    Ⓑ The square root of x is the square of an integer.
    Ⓒ $0<x<10$

Refer to the following graphs for Questions 14 to 17.

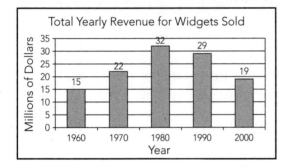

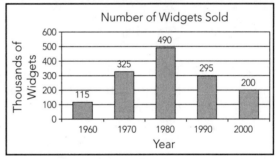

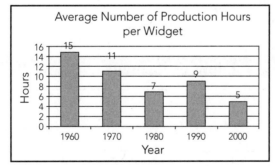

GO ON TO NEXT PAGE

14. In 1990, the total revenue for widgets sold was about how many times as great as the number of widgets sold?
    - A) 3
    - B) 10
    - C) 65
    - D) 98
    - E) 120

For Question 15, write your answer in the box.

15. In 1970, if the cost to produce one widget was $0.07, what would have been the total cost to produce the number of widgets sold during that year?

16. The percent decrease in average number of production hours per widget from 1990 to 2000 was approximately
    - A) 44%
    - B) 36%
    - C) 34%
    - D) 32%
    - E) 27%

17. In how many of the years shown was the number of widgets sold at least three times the number of widgets sold in 1960?
    - A) Four
    - B) Three
    - C) Two
    - D) One
    - E) None

Refer to the following graph for Question 18.

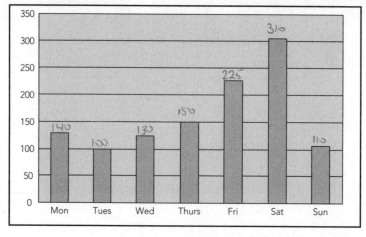

18. The number of hamburgers sold at a stand near the beach for a given week in the summer is shown in the previous chart. Approximately what was the ratio of hamburgers sold on the weekdays (Monday through Friday) to hamburgers sold on the weekend (Saturday and Sunday)?

   (A) 2:5
   (B) 16:29
   (C) 3:4
   (D) 29:16
   (E) 5:2

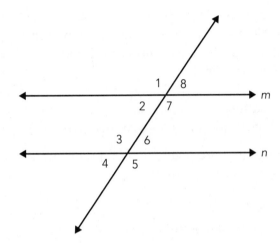

For Question 19, select all the answer choices that apply.

19. In the figure above, m // n. Which of the angles are supplementary to ∠1?   Supplementary?

   (A) ∠2
   (B) ∠3
   (C) ∠5
   (D) ∠6
   (E) ∠7

For Question 20, write your answer in the box.

20. In the number 21,437.89, how many times greater is the place value of the "3" than the place value of the "9"?

STOP.
This is the end of Section 4. Use any remaining time to check your work.

SECTION 5

Quantitative Reasoning

35 Minutes
20 Questions

This section includes four types of questions: Multiple-choice Questions (Select One Answer Choice *and* Select One or More Answer Choices), Numeric Entry Questions, and Quantitative Comparison Questions. Read the following directions before you begin the test.

General Information:
Numbers: All of the numbers used in this section are real numbers.

Figures: Assume that the position of all points, angles, etc. are in the order shown and the measures of angles are positive.

Straight lines can be assumed to be straight.

All figures lie in a plane unless otherwise stated.

The figures given for each question provide information to solve the problem. The figures are not drawn to scale unless otherwise stated. To solve the problems, use your knowledge of mathematics; do not estimate lengths and sizes of the figures to answer questions.

Multiple-choice Questions

Select One Answer Choice

<u>Directions:</u> These questions are multiple-choice questions that ask you to select only one answer choice from a list of five choices.

Select One or More Answer Choices

<u>Directions:</u> Select one or more answer choices according to the specific question directions.

If the question does not specify how many answer choices to select, select all that apply.

The correct answer may be just one of the choices or as many as all of the choices, depending on the question.

No credit is given unless you select all of the correct choices and no others.

If the question specifies how many answer choices to select, select exactly that number of choices.

Numeric Entry Questions

Directions: Enter your answer in the answer box(es) below the question.

Equivalent forms of the correct answer, such as 2.5 and 2.50, are all correct. Fractions do not need to be reduced to lowest terms.

Enter the exact answer unless the question asks you to round your answer.

Quantitative Comparison Questions

Directions: These questions give you two quantities, Quantity A and Quantity B. Compare the two quantities and choose one of the following answer choices:

- **A** if Quantity A is greater;
- **B** if Quantity B is greater;
- **C** if the two quantities are equal;
- **D** if you cannot determine the relationship based on the given information.

Note: Information and/or figures pertaining to one or both of the quantities may appear above the two columns. Any information that appears in both columns has the same meaning for both Quantity A and Quantity B.

You will also be asked Data Interpretation questions, which are grouped together and refer to the same table, graph, or other data presentation. These questions ask you to interpret or analyze the given data. The types of questions may be Multiple-choice (both types) or Numeric Entry.

Each of Questions 1 to 7 presents two quantities, Quantity A and Quantity B. Compare the two quantities. You may use additional information centered above the quantities if such information is given. Choose one of the following answer choices:

- **Ⓐ** if Quantity A is greater;
- **Ⓑ** if Quantity B is greater;
- **Ⓒ** if the two quantities are equal;
- **Ⓓ** if you cannot determine the relationship based on the given information.

	Quantity A	Quantity B	
1.	15 percent of 90	90 percent of 15	Ⓐ Ⓑ Ⓒ Ⓓ

	Quantity A	Quantity B	
2.	$n^2(n^3)^5$	$(n^5)^2$	Ⓐ Ⓑ Ⓒ Ⓓ

GO ON TO NEXT PAGE ➤

56 Part II: Preparing for the GRE General Test

16+12=28

	Quantity A	Quantity B	
3.	The perimeter of a rectangle whose width is 6 cm. and whose diagonal measures 10 cm.	The perimeter of an equilateral triangle in which one side length is 10 cm.	Ⓐ Ⓑ Ⓒ Ⓓ

30

$$9x - 2y = 16$$
$$3x + 7y = 82$$

	Quantity A	Quantity B	
4.	$x + y$	10	Ⓐ Ⓑ Ⓒ Ⓓ

In the rectangular coordinate plane, points A, B, and C have coordinates (8, 9), (5, 9), and (5, 6), respectively.

	Quantity A	Quantity B	
5.	AB	AC	Ⓐ Ⓑ Ⓒ Ⓓ
	3	$3\sqrt{2}$	

x is an integer greater than 2.

	Quantity A	Quantity B	
6.	3^{2x-3}	3^x	Ⓐ Ⓑ Ⓒ Ⓓ
	If 7=3", 2=3'	3^7 3^2	

	Quantity A	Quantity B	
7.	The cost of p apples at a cost of $r+7$ cents each	The cost of 7 peaches at a cost of $(p+r)$ cents each	Ⓐ Ⓑ Ⓒ Ⓓ

$p(r+7) = \$$ $7(p+r) = \$$
$7p+7r = \$$ $7p+7r = \$$

8. A sub sandwich and a soda at a basketball game's concession stand costs $3.40. A family purchases three sub sandwiches and two sodas, and the total cost is $9.10. What is the cost of a soda?
   - Ⓐ $1.00
   - Ⓑ $1.10
   - Ⓒ $1.15
   - Ⓓ $1.20
   - Ⓔ $1.40

For Question 9, select all the answer choices that apply.

9. If $\sqrt{g}$ is an integer, which of the following numbers could *not* equal g? Select all such numbers.
   - Ⓐ 0
   - Ⓑ 4
   - Ⓒ 8

10. A department store ran an advertisement in the paper, stating that 17% of the cost of a provided grocery bag of items would be deducted at the cash register. If an individual placed $180 worth of merchandise in the bag, what would be the discounted price of the items, before taxes (rounded to the nearest dollar)?
    - Ⓐ $144
    - Ⓑ $149
    - Ⓒ $156
    - Ⓓ $163
    - Ⓔ $168

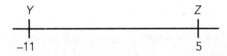

11. On the number line above, what is the coordinate of the point between Y and Z that is three times as far from point Z as from point Y?
    - Ⓐ 1
    - Ⓑ −1
    - Ⓒ −3
    - Ⓓ −7
    - Ⓔ −9

GO ON TO NEXT PAGE

For Question 12, write your answer in the box.

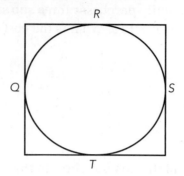

12. In the figure above, a square is circumscribed about a circle with a diameter of 20 cm. Points Q, R, S, and T are the midpoints of the square's sides. What is the total area, in cm², of the square?

400 cm²

13. Of the following values, which is the *greatest*?

    (A) $1 \div \dfrac{1}{3}$ 3

    (B) $1 \times \dfrac{1}{3}$ $\dfrac{1}{3}$

    (C) $1 - \dfrac{1}{3}$ $\dfrac{2}{3}$

    (D) $\dfrac{1}{3} - 1$ $-\dfrac{2}{3}$

    (E) $1 + \dfrac{1}{3}$ $\dfrac{4}{3}$

Refer to the following information and tables for Questions 14 to 17.

Andrew fitted an electric toy car with hard rubber wheels that had deep treads and placed the car on a smooth, flat surface. Andrew started the car and a stopwatch at the same time. Andrew stopped the stopwatch as the car crossed the 75-foot mark. He calculated the results of 3 separate trials as shown in the table below.

Procedure 1	
Trial Number	Time in seconds
1	22.8
2	23.2
3	22.5

Andrew repeated the procedure, except he fitted the car with soft rubber wheels that were smooth and lacked treads. The results are shown in the table below.

Procedure 2	
Trial Number	Time in seconds
1	57.0
2	56.2
3	56.9

14. What was the average time the car with the soft wheels took to cross the 75-foot mark?
    - A) 22.8 seconds
    - B) 33.9 seconds
    - C) 39.8 seconds
    - D) 56.7 seconds
    - E) 170.1 seconds

15. Assuming that the car traveled at a constant speed, approximately how far had the car with hard wheels traveled in Trial 3 after 11.25 seconds?
    - A) 22.5 feet
    - B) 37.5 feet
    - C) 75.0 feet
    - D) 253.125 feet
    - E) Not enough information is given.

16. During which procedure and trial did the car travel at the highest speed?
    - A) Procedure 1, Trial 1
    - B) Procedure 1, Trial 2
    - C) Procedure 1, Trial 3
    - D) Procedure 2, Trial 1
    - E) Procedure 2, Trial 3

17. Assuming the car in Procedure 1 traveled at a constant speed, approximately how long would it take the car to travel 100 feet?
    - A) 100 seconds
    - B) 68.4 seconds
    - C) 30.4 seconds
    - D) 25 seconds
    - E) 22.8 seconds

GO ON TO NEXT PAGE

18. Which of the following is equal to ¼ of 0.1 percent?
    - Ⓐ 0.000025
    - Ⓑ 0.00025
    - Ⓒ 0.0025
    - Ⓓ 0.025
    - Ⓔ 0.25

For Question 19, write your answer in the boxes.

19. There are six members on a committee, four women and two men. They agree to randomly pull two names out of a hat to serve as Chair and Secretary for the group. What is the probability that both of the men are chosen? Give the probability as a fraction in lowest terms.

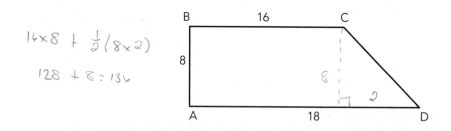

20. What is the area of the trapezoid shown above?
    - Ⓐ 50
    - Ⓑ 86
    - Ⓒ 136
    - Ⓓ 288
    - Ⓔ 2,304

STOP.
This is the end of Section 5. Use any remaining time to check your work.

GRE Diagnostic Test Answers and Explanations

Answer Key

Section 2. Verbal Reasoning

1. E
2. "Certainly it is cheaper…than it answers."
3. C
4. C
5. B, F
6. B, F
7. A, F, G
8. D
9. C
10. "While they are still uncertain… 1,000 years ahead of its time."
11. A, B
12. C
13. A, F, H
14. B
15. A, B
16. D, F
17. B, D
18. E, F
19. A, F
20. A, F

Section 3. Verbal Reasoning

1. B, F
2. C, F
3. C, D
4. A
5. A
6. E
7. A, C
8. "This third gender…presence in the Vedic culture."
9. B, F
10. C
11. C
12. A
13. D
14. A, E
15. A, F
16. B
17. E
18. A
19. A, C
20. "This furniture was too heavy…to ever become popular."

Section 4. Quantitative Reasoning

1. B
2. A
3. A
4. C
5. B
6. C
7. C
8. C
9. D
10. 5
11. B
12. B
13. A, B
14. D
15. 22,750
16. A
17. D
18. E
19. A, D
20. 1,000

Section 5. Quantitative Reasoning

1. C
2. D
3. B
4. A
5. B
6. D
7. D
8. B
9. C
10. B
11. D
12. 400
13. A
14. D
15. B
16. C
17. C
18. B
19. $\frac{1}{15}$
20. C

Chapter 3: GRE Diagnostic Test 63

Answer Explanations

Section 1. Analytical Writing Parts 1 and 2

Because grading the essay is subjective, we've chosen not to include any "graded" essays here. Your best bet is to have someone you trust, such as your personal tutor, read your essays and give you an honest critique. Make the grading criteria mentioned in Chapter 7, "GRE Analytical Writing Assessment," available to whomever grades your essays. If you plan on grading your own essays, review the grading criteria and be as honest as possible regarding the structure, development, organization, technique, and appropriateness of your writing. Focus on your weak areas and continue to practice in order to improve your writing skills.

Section 2. Verbal Reasoning

1. **The best answer is E.** According to the passage, unmanned missions cost less than manned missions, which makes them more economical.
2. **The best answer is:** *Certainly it is cheaper and less dangerous to... than it answers*. This sentence mentions two potential benefits to robotic exploration of space: lower cost and less danger.
3. **The best answer is C.** Humans may be better at calibrating instruments, but the passage makes no mention of who or what might design those instruments.
4. **The best answer is C.** According to the passage, coffee berries are roasted different lengths of time in order to change the strength and color of the coffee. These differences are a response to consumer preference.
5. **The best answer is B and F.** The sentence describes the look of the face and also refers to communication, which best fits "expressions" for Blank (i). Because the passage discusses "body language" and makes no reference to speech, "nonverbal" is the best choice for Blank (ii).
6. **The best answer is B and F.** The use of the conjunction "although" indicates that the two main clauses of the sentence will oppose each other. Since the students rejected the proposal, a negative response, the first choice has to be positive, like "realistic." The second choice explains why they rejected the proposal: it was "convoluted," or difficult to follow.
7. **The best answer is A, F, and G.** The conjunction "but" indicates that Blank (i) should be filled with something opposite to the idea of living birds, like "extinct." The birds were unseen for 150 years, which indicates that they had hidden themselves. Therefore, Blank (ii) is "secreted," which here means "hidden." Finally, Blank (iii) is a synonym for the 150-year gap, i.e. "interim."
8. **The best answer is D.** The passage describes an ancient scientific device that functions like a computer and whose purpose is not currently understood by modern scientists.

9. **The best answer is C only.** According to the passage, scientists believe that the technology of the Antikythera mechanism was 1,000 years ahead of its time. That implies that scientists must reconsider their theories about how technology developed in the ancient world.
10. **The best answer is:** *While they are still uncertain as to why the device was made, there is no doubt that its technology was at least 1,000 years ahead of its time.* This sentence tells the reader that the device is unique and surprising to experts.
11. **The best answer is A and B.** Choice A is implied by the 1,000-year gap in technology development. Choice B is implied because the device computed data several years into the future.
12. **The best answer is C.** According to the passage, the cartoon bears' humorous antics were license on the part of Hanna-Barbera and were far beyond the natural behavior of real bears.
13. **The best answer is A, F, and H.** The choice "artificial" is supported by the description of body parts made out of plastic and metal. These parts can then "replace" natural parts to create "artificial" human beings. "Transferred" is a logical replacement for the third blank, as "filched" is too negative and "stabilized" doesn't make sense in this context.
14. **The best answer is B.** According to the passage, there are few portraits as famous as the *Mona Lisa*. Therefore, it is one of the best known.
15. **The best answer is A and B.** According to the passage, there is disagreement among experts about who sat for the *Mona Lisa*. This supports choice A by describing "controversy," and choice B by implying that the woman is, as yet, unidentified.
16. **The best answer is D and F.** Activists, by definition, act to promote their cause. Therefore, "advocate" is a best choice because it implies action in favor of something. "Support" is a close synonym and completes the sentence in a similar manner.
17. **The best answer is B and D.** "Necessary" and "prudent" both complete the sentence in a logical fashion by indicating the importance of assessing both velocity and trajectory.
18. **The best answer is E and F.** The list of items in the car suggests that it was very full. "Laden" and "overflowing" both convey that idea.
19. **The best answer is A and F.** The reduction in water levels implies that sediment in the river is increasing. "Accretion" and "accumulation" both convey that idea.
20. **The best answer is A and F.** The description of long preparation time and a "grueling" race imply a difficult task. "Arduous" and "ambitious" both convey challenge and difficulty, making them the best choices for this question.

Section 3. Verbal Reasoning

1. **The best answer is B and F.** The two choices are synonyms for welcoming gestures by a host to a guest.
2. **The best answer is C and F.** The passage implies that the wheels were likely to break at inconvenient times. "Prone" and "liable" are synonyms that convey that idea.
3. **The best answer is C and D.** "Impulses" and "signals" match the scientific tone of the sentence, while also conveying the idea that messages of some kind are sent to indicate pain.
4. **The best answer is A.** According to the passage, it would be necessary to raise the atmospheric pressure of Mars to make it possible for humans to live there, or in other words, to make it like Earth's.
5. **The best answer is A.** According to the passage, terraforming turns hostile environments into hospitable ones by creating environments that can sustain human life.
6. **The best answer is E.** According to the passage, certain animal-rights activists disagree with the zoo's policy of raising the bear by hand. Their arguments provide a counterargument to the zoo's position on raising abandoned polar bear cubs.
7. **The best answer is A and C.** According to the passage, Westerners generally consider gender to be binary; that is either male or female. It can be inferred that they, therefore, consider themselves to be either male or female (choice A). Consequently, they do not consider the possibility of a third gender in contemporary society (choice C). The fact that hijra does not exist in Western contemporary culture does not suggest either belief or disbelief in the concept.
8. **The best answer is:** *This third gender is referenced in the earliest available records from the Indian Subcontinent, and was an established presence in the Vedic culture.* The mention of records and Vedic culture indicates the historical aspect of hijra.
9. **The best answer is B and F.** The sentence does not suggest that the cells control the genetic elements, but rather that the cells house the elements in an organized manner. If that organization is disrupted, or jumbled, the opposing state of "chaos" would occur.
10. **The best answer is C.** According to the sentence, color psychologists identify individual colors with particular characteristics or qualities in personalities. This matches the definition of "trait."
11. **The best answer is C.** According to the passage, Africans do not speak to their dogs or give them names, which would eliminate "affectionate." However, the relationship is never described in negative terms. Instead, its "tangible mutualism" implies a pragmatic or practical approach.
12. **The best answer is A.** The passage sets up a description of the relationship between Africans and their dogs by contrasting it with the same relationship in America. This comparison of cultural differences supports answer choice A.

66 Part II: Preparing for the GRE General Test

13. **The best answer is D.** According to the passage, African dogs are more self-reliant than American dogs. This implies that they retain more independence from their owners than American dogs.
14. **The best answer is A and E.** Logically, Saturn's rings are believed to be made up of the wreckage of scattered moons. Therefore, "consist of" is the best fit for the first blank. The contrasting conjunction "but," however, indicates a doubt to that belief. Therefore, "speculation" is the best fit for the second blank.
15. **The best answer is A and F.** The phrase "terribly unhealthy" indicates a negative term like "appalled" for the first blank. The adjective "tasty" indicates a more positive term, like "delicacy," for the second blank. The chocolate bars are clearly a dessert item, so "entrée" is not a good choice.
16. **The best answer is B.** The phrase "to fool others" indicates deliberate trickery. The choice "manipulated" best matches the idea of trickery and deceit.
17. **The best answer is E.** The "gold standard" is often used as a metaphor meaning "the best of its kind." In this case, the passage describes the best practice or approach to determining an accurate and valid reading of the text.
18. **The best answer is A.** This question asks the reader to identify the statement with which the author would likely disagree. Since the author does not indicate that he believes the pit toilets are preferable to buried waste, and in fact, suggests that he finds them equally distasteful, choice A is best.
19. **The best answer is A and C.** Choice A is indicated because the passage calls Edison one of the world's most prestigious inventors. Choice C is indicated because the light bulb and the phonograph are given as examples of why Edison is so esteemed.
20. **The best answer is:** *This furniture was too heavy and expensive to ever become popular.* According to the passage, the concrete furniture was unpopular. Therefore, it is implied that sales were unsuccessful.

Section 4. Quantitative Reasoning

1. **The correct answer is B.** To answer this question correctly you must remember that the sum of the interior angles of a triangle is 180°. Therefore, $x = 180 - 65 - 38$, or 77. Therefore, Quantity B (87) is greater than Quantity A (77).
2. **The correct answer is A.** The sum of the values in Quantity A (91) is greater than the sum of the values in Quantity B (90), so the average of Quantity A is greater than the average of Quantity B.
3. **The correct answer is A.** When $x = 4$, Quantity A is equivalent to $3(4)^4$, or $3(256)$; Quantity B = 750, which is equivalent to $3(250)$. Therefore, Quantity A is greater than Quantity B.

4. **The correct answer is C.** To solve this problem remember that the volume is calculated by multiplying the length by the width by the height ($l \times w \times h$). Set up an equation to find the length of the box:
$$l \times 5 \times 6 = 120$$
$$l \times 30 = 120$$
$$l = 4$$
The quantities are equal.

5. **The correct answer is B.** The probability of tossing two tails in a row is $\frac{1}{2} \times \frac{1}{2} = \frac{1}{4}$. The probability of pulling out the red piece of candy is 4 out of 12, which equals $\frac{1}{3}$.

6. **The correct answer is C.** To answer this question, simply calculate the number of hours in a week (24×7, or 168) and the number of months in 14 years (12×14, or 168). The quantities are equal.

7. **The correct answer is C.** The test scores in Quantity B are each 10 points higher than the scores listed in Quantity A. The mean for Quantity B would be 10 points greater than the mean for Quantity A, but the standard deviations would remain the same.

8. **The correct answer is C.** You are given that the cost of the negative is x dollars and that the cost of the first 20 prints is $\frac{7x}{10}$ dollars per print. You are also given that any number of prints over 20 is $\frac{x}{10}$ dollars per print. The question stem indicates that $80 is the total charge to make a negative and 30 prints. You know that the first 20 prints will cost $\frac{7x}{10}$ dollars per print and the remaining 10 prints will cost $\frac{x}{10}$ dollars per print. Set up an equation and solve for x, as follows:

$$x + 20\left(\frac{7x}{10}\right) + 10\left(\frac{x}{10}\right) = 80$$
$$x + \left(\frac{140x}{10}\right) + \left(\frac{10x}{10}\right) = 80$$
$$x + 14x + x = 80$$
$$16x = 80$$
$$x = 5$$

9. **The correct answer is D.** You are given that Tom traveled 45 miles in 12 hours and that Jim traveled four times as far in one-third the time. That means that Jim traveled 45×4, or 180 miles in $12 \times \left(\frac{1}{3}\right)$, or 4 hours. Therefore, Jim traveled $\frac{180}{4}$, or 45 miles per hour.

10. **The correct answer is 5.** To solve this problem, isolate x on the left side of the equation by performing the necessary calculations:
$$2(x-3)+9=4x-7$$
First, distribute the 2:
$$2x-6+9=4x-7$$
Next, perform the addition on the left side:
$$2x+3=4x-7$$
Now, subtract 3 from both sides:
$$2x=4x-10$$
Next, subtract $4x$ from each side:
$$-2x=-10$$
Finally, divide both sides by -2:
$$x=5$$

11. **The correct answer is B.** According to the figure, angle WZY is 72°. Note that angle WYZ is 90°, which means that angle ZWY must be 18° (180−72−90=18). Therefore, the angle in question must also be 18°.

12. **The correct answer is B.** To answer this question, solve the inequality by isolating x on the left side (remember to switch the sign in the final step!):
$$3x-6>6x+9$$
$$-3x>15$$
$$x<-5$$

13. **The correct answer is A and B.** Statement (A) can be expressed as $x=t^2$, where t is any nonzero integer. In this case, the square root of x equals the square root of t^2, which is t or $-t$, depending on whether t is positive or negative, respectively. In either case, the square root of x is an integer. Therefore, statement (A) alone is sufficient. Statement (B) is also sufficient because the square of an integer must also be an integer. Statement (C) indicates that x is a positive integer less than 10, which is not sufficient to determine whether the square root of x is also an integer.

14. **The correct answer is D.** According to the graphs, in 1990 total revenue was $29 million and the number of widgets sold was 295,000. Because 295,000 is slightly less than 10% of 29,000,000, the total revenue must have been just under 100 times greater than the number of widgets sold.

15. **The correct answer is 22,750.** According to the graphs, in 1970, 325,000 widgets were sold; at $0.07 per widget, the total cost would have been 325,000($0.07), or $22,750.

16. **The correct answer is A.** According to the graphs, from 1990 to 2000, the average number of production hours per widget decreased from 9 to 5. To calculate the percent decrease, divide the difference between the starting value and ending value (9−5) by the starting value: $\frac{4}{9}=0.44$, which is equivalent to 44%.

17. **The correct answer is D.** The first step in solving this problem is to calculate three times the number of widgets sold in 1960. According to the graphs, the number of widgets sold in 1960 was 115,000; 115,000(3)=345,000.

The only year in which more than 345,000 widgets sold was 1980 (490,000 widgets sold).

18. **The correct answer is E.** The graph shows approximately 125, 100, 125, 150, and 225 hamburgers sold, Monday through Friday. The sum of these sales is approximately 725 hamburgers. Approximately 400 hamburgers were sold over the weekend, so the ratio is 725:400, which reduces to 29:16.

19. **The correct answer is A and D.** Supplementary angles total 180°. $\angle 1$ is adjacent to $\angle 2$ and forms a straight line, so the two angles are supplementary. $\angle 1 \cong \angle 3$ because they are corresponding angles. Since $\angle 6$ is adjacent and supplementary to $\angle 3$, it is also supplementary to $\angle 1$. In this case, angles represented by B, C, and E are all congruent to $\angle 1$.

20. **The correct answer is 1000.** The "9" is in the hundredths place, and the "3" is in the tens place. There are 1000 hundredths in a ten.

Section 5. Quantitative Reasoning

1. **The correct answer is C.** In order to calculate 15 percent of 90, multiply 90 by 0.15, the decimal equivalent of 15%. Likewise, to calculate 90 percent of 15, multiply 15 by 0.90, the decimal equivalent of 90 percent:

$$(0.15)(90) = 13.5$$
$$(0.90)(15) = 13.5$$

The quantities are equal.

2. **The correct answer is D.** Quantity A simplifies to n^{17}, while Quantity B simplifies to n^{10}. However, the greater quantity depends on the value of n. If the value is positive, then n^{17} is greater, but if n is negative, then n^{10} is the greater value. Since the quantities depend on the value assigned to the variable, the relationship cannot be determined from the information given.

3. **The correct answer is B.** By the Pythagorean Theorem, the rectangle measures 6 cm. by 8 cm. (a 6-8-10 triangle), making its perimeter 28 cm. The equilateral triangle contains three sides that each measure 10 cm, making its perimeter 30 cm and, therefore, greater than the perimeter of the rectangle.

4. **The correct answer is A.** To answer this question, first multiply the bottom equation by -3 to get $-9x-21y=-246$. Now you can add the two equations and eliminate one of the variables, as follows:

$$(9x-2y=16)$$
$$+(-9x-21y=-246)$$
$$-23y=-230$$
$$y=10$$

Substitute 10 for y in the first equation and solve for x:

$$9x-2(10)=16$$
$$9x-20=16$$
$$9x=36$$
$$x=4$$

Quantity A $(x+y)$ is equivalent to $4+10$, or 14, and Quantity B $=10$; therefore, Quantity A is greater than Quantity B.

5. **The correct answer is B.** To solve this problem, plot the points in the coordinate plane, as shown below:

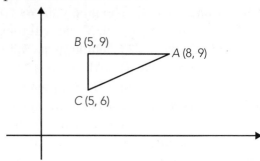

   AC is the hypotenuse of the right triangle that you just created, and AB is a side; the hypotenuse is always longer than either of the sides, so Quantity B (AC) is greater than Quantity A (AB).
6. **The correct answer is D.** Because you do not know the value of x, you cannot determine a relationship between the two quantities. For example, when $x=3$, the quantities are equal. However, when x is an integer greater than 3, Quantity B is greater.
7. **The correct answer is D.** The values of p and r are not given, so you cannot determine the relationship between Quantity A and Quantity B.
8. **The correct answer is B.** The problem can be solved by using two simultaneous equations: $s+d=3.40$ and $3s+2d=9.10$. Doubling the first equation and subtracting it from the second gives the result that s (the cost of a soda) is $1.10.
9. **The correct answer is C only.** Among the choices, only $\sqrt{8}$ is not an integer; it is an irrational number.
10. **The correct answer is B.** If a 17% discount is taken, then the customer is actually paying 83% of the original cost. Taking 83% of 180 (0.83×180), the discounted price would be approximately $149.
11. **The correct answer is D.** One way to quickly solve this problem would be to note that the distance between the points is 16 units, so the correct answer will be 4 units $\left(\frac{1}{4} \text{ of } 16\right)$ from Point Y and 12 units $\left(\frac{3}{4} \text{ of } 16\right)$ from Point Z. You could also try each of the answer choices.
12. **The correct answer is 400.** To solve this problem, note that the diameter of the circle is 20 cm, which means that each side of the square is 20 cm. The area of the square is 20 cm $\times$ 20 cm, which equals 400 cm^2.
13. **The correct answer is A.** To quickly solve this problem, note that when you divide a whole number by a fraction, the result is greater than the whole number. You could also solve each of the operations separately.
14. **The correct answer is D.** The soft wheels data is in the second table. Calculate the average of those three times: $(57.0+56.4+56.7) \div 3 = 56.7$

15. **The correct answer is B.** Since the car traveled at a constant speed, you can set up a proportion between the time and distance of the whole run and the time and distance of the partial run.

$$\frac{22.5 \text{ seconds}}{75 \text{ ft}} = \frac{11.25 \text{ seconds}}{x \text{ ft}}$$
$$75 \times 11.25 = 22.5x$$
$$843.75 = 22.5x$$
$$37.5 = x$$

Therefore, the car traveled 37.5 feet in 11.25 seconds.

16. **The correct answer is C.** The data in the tables reflects the amount of time the cars took to travel a constant distance. Therefore, the car that finished in the least amount of time traveled at the highest speed.

17. **The correct answer is C.** The first step is to calculate the average speed for all three trials: $22.8 + 23.2 + 22.5 \div 3 = 22.8$. Next, since the car traveled at a constant speed, you can set up a proportion between the time and distance of the whole run and the time and distance of the partial run: $22.8 \div 75 = 0.304$ sec/feet. Finally, multiply 0.304 by 100 to get 30.4 seconds.

18. **The correct answer is B.** To solve this problem, remember that 1/4 is equivalent to 0.25, and that 0.1 percent is equivalent to 0.001(0.1/100). Therefore, 1/4, or 0.25 of $0.001 = 0.00025$; do not get confused and simply find 1/4 of 0.1, (0.025) because the question asks for 1/4 of 0.1 *percent*.

19. **The correct answer is** $\frac{1}{15}$. Since there are 6 names in the hat, and 2 are men, the probability that the first name drawn is a man is $\frac{2}{6} = \frac{1}{3}$. Then, of the remaining 5 names in the hat, only 1 is a man, so the chances that he will be chosen are 1 in 5. To find the probability of both events occurring, take $\frac{1}{3} \times \frac{1}{5} = \frac{1}{15}$.

20. **The correct answer is C.** The quickest way to solve this problem is to note that, if you draw a line from C perpendicular to AD, you create a rectangle whose area is 16×8, or 128 square units. Because the trapezoid is slightly larger than the rectangle, the area must be slightly greater than 128. Only answer choice C works. You can also calculate the area of the small triangle you created when you drew the perpendicular line: $\frac{1}{2}(2 \times 8) = 8$; $128 + 8 = 136$.

4

GRE General Testing Strategies

CHAPTER GOALS

- Understand the importance of developing test-taking skills.
- Discover specific test-taking strategies that can help you raise your score.
- Find out how to eliminate stress and build confidence.
- Learn how to deal with the computerized testing format.
- Get last-minute tips for test day.

Now that you've assessed your strengths and weaknesses, it's time to take a look at some general test-taking strategies that should help you approach the GRE with confidence. This chapter discusses the importance of acquiring the skills necessary to maximize your GRE score. At the end of the chapter you'll find some tips on how to handle stress before, during, and after the GRE.

Later chapters in this book present strategies and techniques specific to each of the GRE sections.

Knowledge, Skills, and Abilities (KSA)

Cognitive psychologists, those who study learning and thinking, use the letters KSA to refer to the basic components of human performance in all human activities, from academics to athletics, from playing music to playing games. The letters stand for *Knowledge, Skills, and Abilities.*

> **GRE Tip**
> The GRE measures both knowledge and skills. Study to acquire knowledge, but practice to acquire skills.

As mentioned previously, the GRE measures a specific set of skills. Many thousands of students have successfully raised their GRE scores by acquiring the requisite skills through study and practice.

The human brain stores and retrieves factual knowledge a little differently from the way it acquires and executes skills. You learn factual information by studying, and you acquire skills through practice. There is some overlap between these actions; you will learn while you practice, and vice versa. In fact, research shows that repetition is important for both information storage and skills acquisition.

Repetition is also necessary to improve skills: Knowing *about* a skill, or understanding how the skill should be executed, is not the same as actually *having* that skill and being able to execute it. For instance, you might be told *about* a skill such as driving a car with a manual transmission, playing the piano, or typing on a computer keyboard. You might have a great teacher, have wonderful learning tools, and pay attention very carefully. You might *understand* everything perfectly. But, the first few times that you actually attempt the skill, you will probably make some mistakes. In fact, you will probably experience some frustration because of the gap between your understanding of the skill and your actual ability to perform the skill. Perfecting skills takes practice. When skills are repeated so many times that they can't be further improved, psychologists use the term *perfectly internalized skills,* which means that the skills are executed automatically, without any conscious thought. You need repetition to create the pathways in your brain that control your skills. Therefore, you shouldn't be satisfied with simply reading this book and then saying to yourself, "I get it." You will not reach your full GRE scoring potential unless you put in sufficient time practicing as well as understanding and learning.

We hope that you will internalize the skills that you need for top performance on the GRE so that you don't have to spend time and energy figuring out what to do during the introduction to the exam. We hope that you will be well into each section while some of your less-prepared classmates are still reading the directions and trying to figure out exactly what they are supposed to be doing. With sufficient practice you will develop your test-taking skills, and, specifically, good GRE-taking skills. While you practice, you should distinguish between practice that is meant to serve as a learning experience and practice that is meant to be a realistic simulation of what will happen on your actual GRE.

> **NOTE**
>
> During practice meant for learning, it is acceptable to "cheat." You should feel free to disregard the time limits to think about how the questions are put together; you can stop to look at the explanations in the back of the book. It is even acceptable to talk to others about what you are learning during your "learning practice."

Be sure to do some simulated testing practice, in which you time yourself carefully and try to control as many variables in your environment as possible. Research shows that you will have an easier time executing your skills and remembering information when the environment in which you are testing is similar to the environment in which you studied and practiced.

You must be realistic about how you spend your time and energy during the preparation process. The psychological term *cognitive endurance* refers to your ability to perform difficult mental tasks over an extended period of time. Just as with your physical endurance, you can build up your cognitive endurance through training. As you prepare yourself for the GRE, you should start with shorter practice sessions and work up to the point at which you can easily work for 40 minutes without noticeable fatigue. That is the longest period of time you will have to work on test day without a break.

Now, let's explore the skills and strategies important to ensuring your success on the GRE.

> **GRE Tip**
> You should not attempt any timed practice tests when you are mentally or physically exhausted. This will add unwanted tension to an already stressful situation.

Focus on the Easy Stuff

You will have to get familiar with the format of each section of the GRE so that you can recognize passages and questions that are likely to give you trouble. It is in your best interest to spend less time on the questions that you will probably answer incorrectly, and simply make an educated guess. Focus on the questions that you're sure you can answer correctly in order to maximize your GRE score. The only way to become competent in this strategy is to practice using the tests in this book, the online tests at **MHPracticePlus.com**, and the tests contained in the POWERPREP® software available from Educational Testing Service (ETS) (**www.gre.org**).

The writers of the GRE know that they are dealing with a group of test-takers who probably share certain characteristics. For example, they know that you probably have evidence that you are intelligent, or you would have self-selected out of the process by now. You probably also have evidence that you are tenacious, perhaps even stubborn. There will be some time-consuming questions in each section that are meant to lure you into wasting time that would be better spent answering some more reasonable questions.

Stay "On Point"

It is important to note that many incorrect GRE answers are incorrect because they are irrelevant. This applies to all the different question types in all the various sections. If you get very good at spotting answer choices that are outside the scope of a reading passage, for example, you'll go a long way toward improving your score. This can be more difficult than it sounds because some of the irrelevant choices will use terms, numbers, and ideas from the question or passage.

> **GRE Tip**
> A good way to check relevance is to ask yourself, "So what?" when evaluating the answer choices.

When your training is finished, you will be able to do this type of analysis on most of the questions and answer choices that you encounter on your GRE. You will be able to quickly and efficiently eliminate all of the answer choices that are irrelevant, or not "on point." This strategy will also help you to write better essays. Many students lose points either by introducing irrelevant information into their essays, or by going "off topic."

Simplify

The GRE contains relatively straightforward, simple ideas that sometimes appear difficult because of a complex sentence structure and an elevated vocabulary level. The best way to simplify the language that you encounter on the GRE is to paraphrase as you go. We suggest to our GRE tutoring students to think first of explaining the gist of what they are reading to an intelligent tenth grade student. After some time spent practicing, the simplification process becomes second nature and can be done quite quickly.

Guess Wisely

Because there is no penalty for wrong answers on the GRE, it is a good idea to learn how to make an educated guess. If you do not know how to solve a math problem, for example, you might still be able to eliminate at least one answer choice that is clearly incorrect; draw pictures and apply logic to assist you during this process. After you have eliminated the answer choices that you know cannot be correct, select the best answer or answers from those choices that remain.

There are specific suggestions in each chapter regarding the process of elimination and how to identify the question types on which you should probably guess and move on. As you practice, you'll also develop likes and dislikes, meaning that you will recognize certain question types that will always be tough for you. By test day you will have done enough timed practice tests that you will also develop a "feel" for how long you should be spending on each question. Be flexible. If a question is of a type that you can usually answer easily, do not spend more time on it than you should.

You also need to find out whether you are an answer-changer or not; if you change an answer, are you more likely to change it *to* the correct answer, or *from* the correct answer? You can only learn this about yourself by taking practice exams and paying attention to your tendencies.

Manage Stress

In graduate school, stress arises from sources such as family expectations, fear of failure, heavy workload, competition, and difficult subjects. The GRE is designed to create similar stresses. The psychometricians (specialized psychologists who study the measurement of the mind) who contribute to the design of standardized tests use artificial stressors to test how you will respond to the stress of graduate school. In other words, they are actually trying to create a certain level of stress in you.

The main stressor is the time limit. The time limits are set on the GRE so that many students cannot finish all of the questions in the time allowed. Use the specific strategies mentioned in Chapters 7 and 8 to help you select as many correct answers as possible in the time allowed.

Another stressor is the element of surprise that is present for most test-takers. If you practice enough, there should be no surprises on test day. For example, test takers who have not practiced sufficiently are more likely to encounter a question that is unlike any that they saw during their limited practice. A well-prepared test-taker, however, will know what to expect.

> **GRE Tip**
> Once you get a handle on the various question types, do most of your practice under timed conditions so that you learn how to pace yourself.

Relax to Succeed

Probably the worst thing that a test-taker can do is to panic. Research shows that there are very predictable results when a person panics. When you panic, you can usually identify a specific set of easily recognizable symptoms, including sweating, shortness of breath, muscle tension, increased pulse rate, tunnel vision, nausea, lightheadedness, and, in rare cases, even loss of consciousness. These symptoms are the result of chemical changes in the brain brought on by some stimulus. The stimulus does not have to be external. Therefore, we can panic ourselves just by thinking about certain things.

The stress chemical in your body called *epinephrine,* more commonly known as *adrenalin,* brings on these symptoms. Adrenalin changes the priorities in your brain activity. It moves blood and electrical energy away from some parts of the brain and over to others. Specifically, it increases brain activity in the areas that control your body and decreases blood flow to the parts of your brain that are involved in complex thinking. Therefore, panic makes a person stronger and faster—and also less able to perform the type of thinking that is important on a GRE exam. It is not a bad thing to have a small amount of adrenaline in your bloodstream brought about by a healthy amount of excitement about your exam. However, you should take steps to avoid panic before or during your GRE.

You can control your adrenaline levels by minimizing the unknown factors in the testing process. The biggest stress-inducing questions are as follows:

- *"What do the GRE writers expect?"*
- *"Am I ready?"*
- *"How will I do on test day?"*

If you spend your time and energy studying and practicing under realistic conditions before test day, then you will have a much better chance of controlling your adrenaline levels and handling the exam with no panic.

The goals of your preparation should be to learn about the test, acquire the skills that are being measured by the test, and learn about yourself and how you respond to the different parts of the test. You should also consider which question types you will answer with certainty on test day and which ones you will give an educated guess. You need to be familiar with the material that is tested on each section of your exam. As you work through this book, make an assessment of the best use of your time and energy. Concentrate on the areas that will give you the highest score in the amount of time that you have until you take the GRE. This will give you a feeling of confidence on test day even when you are facing very challenging questions.

> **GRE Tip**
> Preparation goals:
> 1. Learn about the test
> 2. Learn about yourself
> 3. Approach the test with confidence

Specific Relaxation Techniques

The following sections present various ways to help you be as relaxed and confident as possible on test day.

Be Prepared

The more prepared you feel, the less likely it is that you'll be stressed on test day. Study and practice consistently between now and your test day. Be organized. Have your supplies and lucky testing clothes ready in advance. Make a practice trip to the test center before your test day.

Know Yourself

Get to know your strengths and weaknesses on the GRE and the things that help you to relax. Some test-takers feel that being slightly anxious helps them to focus. Others folks do best when they are so relaxed that they are almost asleep. You will learn about yourself through practice.

Rest

The better rested you are, the better things seem. As you become fatigued, you are more likely to look on the dark side of things and worry more, which hurts your test scores. Our favorite Shakespeare quote refers to ". . . sleep that knits up the raveled sleeve of care."

In addition, consider doing something "mindless" the night before your GRE. You should be well prepared by then, so take the night off!

Eat Right

Sugar is bad for stress and brain function in general. Consuming refined sugar creates biological stress that has an impact on your brain chemistry. Keep sugar consumption to a minimum for several days before your test. If you are actually addicted to caffeine, then by all means consume your normal amount. Don't forget to eat regularly while you're preparing for the GRE. It's not a good idea to skip meals simply because you are experiencing some additional stress. It is also important to eat something before you take the GRE. An empty stomach might be distracting and uncomfortable on test day. Consider bringing a high-protein snack to eat during your break.

Breathe

If you feel yourself tensing up, slow down and take deeper breaths. This will relax you and get more oxygen to your brain so that you can think more clearly.

Take Mental Breaks

You cannot stay sharply focused on your GRE for the whole time in the testing center. You will certainly have distracting thoughts or times when you just can't process all the information. When this happens, close your eyes, clear your mind, and then start back on your test. This process should take only a minute or so. You could pray, meditate, or just visualize a place or person that helps you relax. Try thinking of something fun that you have planned to do after your GRE.

Have a Plan of Attack

Know how you are going to work through each part of the exam. There is no time to create a plan of attack on test day. Practice enough that you internalize the skills you need to do your best on each section, and you won't have to stop to think about what to do next.

Be Aware of Time

You should time yourself on test day. You should time yourself on some of your practice exams. We suggest that you use an analog (dial face) watch. You can turn the hands on your watch back from noon to allow enough time for the section that you are working on. Remember, all that matters during the test is your test. All of life's other issues will have to be dealt with after your test is finished. You might find this attitude easier to attain if you lose track of what time it is in the "outside world."

Listen to Music

Some types of music increase measured brain stress and interfere with clear thinking. Specifically, some rock, hip-hop, and dance rhythms, while great for certain occasions, can have detrimental effects on certain types of brain waves that have been measured in labs. Other music seems to help to organize brain waves and create a relaxed state that is conducive to learning and skills acquisition.

Some Strategies for the Computer-based Test

While all of the previously mentioned strategies will help on both the paper-based and computer-based tests, following are some specific guidelines for approaching the computer-based test with confidence:

- Take the POWERPREP® practice tests. This software includes tutorials that teach you how to use the computer features available to you on test day.
- Practice typing your Analytical Writing responses. Your goal on test day is to type a complete essay in the time allowed, so practice to improve your typing speed and accuracy.
- Within each Verbal and Quantitative section, you can skip around between questions, answering easier ones and leaving harder ones for last. Budget enough time for each question and work actively through the test material.
- Try to complete the entire test, even if you are running out of time. Most test takers get higher scores if they finish the test. Learn to pace yourself so that you have time to consider each question and can avoid making random guesses.

Refer to Chapter 1, "Overview of the GRE," for more information on the computer-based test.

What to Expect on Test Day

If you work through the material in this book and do some additional practice on released GRE exams, then you should be more than adequately prepared for the GRE. Use the following tips to help the entire testing process go smoothly.

> **GRE Tip**
> Remember that the Analytical Writing section is always first but the other sections can appear in any order. Refer to Chapter 1 for more information.

Take a Dry Run

Make sure that you know how long it will take to get to the testing center, where you will park, alternative routes, and so on. If you are testing in a place that is new to you, try to get into the building between now and test day so that you can absorb the sounds and smells, find out where the bathrooms and snack machines are, and so on.

Wake Up Early

You will have to be at the testing center by a specified time. Set two alarms if you have to so that you're not late. Leave yourself plenty of time to get fully awake and alert before you have to run out the door. If you have a family member who wants to feel like part of the process, you might want to have him or her act as your wake-up call. If you arrive at the testing center late, you might not be admitted.

Dress for Success

Wear loose, comfortable clothes in layers so that you can adjust to the temperature. Remember your watch. There might not be a clock in your testing room.

Fuel Up

Eat something without too much sugar in it on the morning of your test. Get your normal dose of caffeine, if any. (Test day is not the time to "try coffee" for the first time!)

Bring Supplies

Bring your ID and your admission ticket. If you need them, bring your glasses or contact lenses. You won't be able to eat or drink while the GRE is in progress, but you can bring a snack for the break time.

Warm Up Your Brain

Read a newspaper or something similar, or review some practice material so that the GRE isn't the first thing you read on test day.

Plan a Mini-Vacation

Most students find it easier to concentrate on their exam preparation and on their GRE if they have a plan for some fun right after the test. Plan something that you can look forward to as a reward for all the hard work and energy that you're putting into preparing for and taking the GRE.

What's Next?

Chapter 5 of this book includes an introduction to logic, which will be useful on almost all of the sections of the GRE General Test. Chapters 6 through 8 focus on the specific sections of the GRE, while Chapters 9 and 10 provide an in-depth review of both the quantitative and verbal content that is tested on the exam. Read these chapters carefully, note the particular strategies and techniques, and answer the practice questions included at the end of each chapter. The full-length Practice Tests (Chapters 11 through 13) can be found in Part IV of this book. Plan to take a full-length test approximately one week prior to the actual GRE. Read the explanations for the questions that you missed, and review Chapters 4 through 10 as necessary.

Remember, practice as much as you can under realistic testing conditions to maximize your GRE score.

5
Introduction to GRE Logic

> **CHAPTER GOALS**
> - Learn the structure of a logical argument.
> - Understand the logic of conditional statements.
> - Learn to recognize different kinds of logical fallacies.

A basic understanding of Informal Logic is important for GRE success because the GRE is, primarily, a test of your critical thinking skills. This chapter contains information that applies directly to the Analytical Writing section (especially the Analyze an Argument task) and Reading Comprehension question types on the GRE. It applies indirectly to the Quantitative (both Multiple-choice and Quantitative Comparison) question types.

Furthermore, because logic is the foundation of research and analysis in every field, the topics covered in this chapter will certainly be useful during graduate school and for the rest of your professional career.

Before we begin, let's talk briefly about logic and the question types to which it has a less obvious connection. As will be made clear in later chapters, even question types such as Quantitative and Sentence Equivalence questions that seem most grounded in specific content have a logic component. With sentence equivalence, of course a strong vocabulary is necessary. But it is not all that's needed (this distinction will be explained in detail later in this chapter).

If the makers of the GRE had simply wished to test your vocabulary, a synonyms section would have sufficed. Finding the best words to complete the sentence not only forces you to take an extra step, it also requires an understanding of the relationship between the question prompt and the answer choices. Similarly, Quantitative Comparison questions are not asking for an absolute answer, but rather a relative one: Which quantity is greater? Analyzing that relativity requires logic. If you are ever in doubt about the correct answer choice, know that the credited answer is always grounded in logic.

Now let's begin our discussion of Informal Logic.

Arguments

Logic is often defined as "the science of argument." In this context, an argument does not refer to a verbal skirmish, nor does it usually involve shouting. An argument is an orderly process of supporting a *conclusion* with *evidence*. The conclusion is the main point of the argument and the evidence is the information that supports it. An evidentiary statement is also called a *premise*. Breaking an argument down into these component parts is called *analysis*. The Reading Comprehension passages will all contain logical (sound) arguments. The Analysis of an Argument prompts will all contain logical flaws. By understanding how a logical argument is constructed, you can more easily navigate a Reading passage and more thoroughly criticize an Argument prompt.

Some of the words that commonly signal *evidence* are

- Since
- Because
- For
- As
- Due to
- In that

Some of the words that commonly signal *conclusion* are

- Therefore
- Hence
- Thus
- So
- Accordingly
- Consequently
- Ergo

The basic form of an argument is illustrated by the following time-honored example:

Socrates is a man.

Men are mortal.

Therefore, Socrates is mortal.

The first two statements are pieces of evidence; the last statement is the conclusion that follows naturally from them.

Context

The function that a statement serves within an argument is entirely dependent upon *context*. In other words, a mere raw assertion is neither evidence nor conclusion until it is placed in a context of surrounding statements.

Consider the following statement:

Steve wears glasses.

Is this statement evidence or conclusion? The truth is that it is neither evidence nor conclusion without context.

Consider the following two arguments, each of which includes the previous statement:

1. **Steve wears glasses.**

   People who wear glasses are smart.

   Therefore, Steve is smart.

2. **Steve is nearsighted.**

   Nearsighted people wear glasses.

   Therefore, Steve wears glasses.

Both arguments contain the original statement. However, in Argument 1 the statement is evidence. In Argument 2, it is the conclusion.

Chain of Reasoning

Sometimes arguments are linked together in chains, as shown in the following example that combines the two previous arguments:

Steve is nearsighted.

Nearsighted people wear glasses.

Therefore, Steve wears glasses

People who wear glasses are smart.

Therefore, Steve is smart.

In this example, the first conclusion drawn becomes what is known as a *subsidiary conclusion*. The subsidiary conclusion is then used as a piece of evidence to support another conclusion. The last conclusion in such a chain is sometimes referred to as the *ultimate conclusion*.

Sometimes competing evidence can also lead to a conclusion (e.g., "Steve likes to wear disguises. Glasses are effective disguises. Therefore, Steve wears glasses."). When this competing evidence is ignored or omitted by the writer, it's called an *alternative explanation*. Finding *alternative explanations* is useful in evaluating the Analytical Writing Argument task and answering some Reading Comprehension questions.

Assumptions

> **GRE Tip**
> Practice spotting assumptions in arguments that you encounter in daily life. This habit will help you to score higher on the GRE.

Many Reading Comprehension questions directly test your ability to recognize assumptions—they're a common question type. Assumptions also provide many of the flaws in the Argument writing prompts. Sometimes, one or more pieces of evidence are left unstated. Such unstated evidence is called an *assumption*; assumptions are also known as *suppressed premises*.

If you leave out the second piece of evidence in the sample argument, as shown next, you'll have an illustration of an argument that makes an essential assumption:

Socrates is a man.

Therefore, Socrates is mortal.

The only statement that would provide the necessary link between the stated evidence and the stated conclusion is "Men are mortal."

You need a bridge between the unlike terms in the two statements. "Socrates" is a term in both the single stated premise and the conclusion of the argument. The two other terms are "man" and "mortal." This recognition leads you to infer that the missing premise is "Man is mortal."

This is a process that is often performed intuitively. Recognizing key assumptions is very important for several exam question types; as mentioned previously, Reading Comprehension questions will ask about assumptions/inferences directly. The GRE also assumes that you will recognize them in the Argument essay prompt. After all, often the easiest way to attack an argument is to attack its assumptions. Finally, when writing your own Issues essay, be aware of your assumptions—not every reader will agree with you.

Validity, Truth, and Soundness

Validity refers to the strength of the structure of an argument, whereas *truth* refers to the factual verifiability of the evidence and the conclusion. An argument that is both valid and true is said to be *sound*.

Here is an example of an argument that is valid but *not* true:

All dogs can fly.

Ralph is a dog.

Therefore, Ralph can fly.

The argument is valid because *if* the evidence is true, *then* the conclusion follows logically. However, the evidence is clearly not true, and therefore, the conclusion is not true. Giving an example of a dog that cannot fly would disprove the argument and show that it is not sound. This is known as a *counterexample*. A counterexample is an example, real or hypothetical, that disproves evidence used in an argument.

Here is an example of an argument that is *not* valid but has a conclusion that is verifiably true:

Bluebirds are blue.

Some things that are blue can fly.

Therefore, bluebirds can fly.

Although it is true that bluebirds can fly, the argument is not valid because the evidence does not fully support the conclusion.

Conditionals

Statements in the form of **"if X, then Y"** are known as *conditionals*; if X occurs, then Y is certain to occur. In other words, X *implies* Y. In fact, another name for a conditional statement is an *implication*. This category, along with negation, is most useful for the Analytical Writing tasks. It will help you to understand exactly what can and cannot be understood from a sound argument.

> **NOTE**
> The "if" clause is known as the *antecedent*; the "then" clause is known as the *consequent*.

Consider the following example:

If it rains, then the flowers will grow.

"If it rains . . ." is the antecedent, and ". . . then the flowers will grow" is the consequent.

The sentence means that if the rain comes, then the flowers will certainly grow. Let's accept this as true.

However, if the flowers grow, you cannot be sure that the rain fell. For example, it could be that they were watered by hand.

So, "if the flowers are growing, then it has rained" does not necessarily follow from the previous statement. In fact, this is known as a *fallacy*. (Note that fallacy has the same root as the word *false*.) The fallacy of simply reversing a conditional statement is known as *affirming the consequent*.

In addition, you cannot simply negate the components of the statement by saying, "If it doesn't rain, the flowers will not grow." This is known as the fallacy of *denying the antecedent*.

> **NOTE**
>
> If you reverse the position of the terms and negate both terms, you arrive at a statement that always has exactly the same truth value as the original statement, as shown here:
>
> **If the flowers did not grow, then it did not rain.**
>
> This must be true because the original statement tells you that if it had rained, then the flowers would certainly have grown. This is known as the *contrapositive*.

There are two varieties of conditional statements, *sufficient conditions* and *necessary conditions*. They both include the concept of "If" and "Then," but they can create confusion.

Sufficiency

Consider the following statement:

If my car has gas in it, then it will run.

This is known as a *sufficient condition* because having gasoline in the car is sufficient to guarantee that it will run. The statement implies that there are no other problems with the car and you can rest assured that, as long as there is gas in the tank, this car will run.

The contrapositive of this implication would be: "If the car is not running, then it has no gas."

Necessity

Consider the following statement:

Only if my car has gas in it, will it run.

This is a *necessary condition* because the gas is necessary for the car to run but not sufficient to guarantee that it will certainly run. In other words, the car in this statement might not have an engine in it, and the statement would still be true.

The contrapositive of this statement would be: "If the car has no gas, then it will not run."

Negation

As you can see from the discussion of the previous contrapositive, it is important to be able to negate statements properly. If you negate clumsily, then your logic will fail.

> **NOTE**
> Understanding proper negation is important for several reasons, one of which involves a useful technique for some Reading Comprehension questions, which will be discussed later.

For example, try to negate the following statement:

All clocks are round.

You might be tempted to say:

No clocks are round.

But, this is clearly an incorrect statement. In fact, it is just as incorrect as the original statement.

However, suppose you say:

At least one clock is not round.

You have negated the original statement safely and correctly. In other words, you have negated a categorical statement with a single counterexample. Categorical statements are phrased absolutely using words like *all*, *none*, *always*, *every*, and so on. You have probably heard the phrase "Never say 'never'!" This is sound advice because categorical statements are inherently unreliable.

You might find yourself in a position where you must negate a statement such as the following:

Some birds can fly.

In this case, simply use a categorical statement:

No birds can fly.

Because the original statement is *not* categorical, you can use a categorical statement to negate it.

Fallacies

A *fallacy* is a statement or argument that is not logically sound. In other words, it lacks validity. Notice that fallacy looks and sounds a lot like the word *false*. This is not a coincidence. Both words derive from the Latin word *fallere*, which means "to deceive."

GRE Reading Comprehension questions include EXCEPT questions, in which the fallacy will be the *correct* answer (see Chapter 8). Fallacies are also important in the Analytical Writing section discussed in Chapter 6. Avoid fallacies when you Analyze an Issue and exploit them when you Analyze an Argument!

The sections that follow outline several fallacies that appear often on the GRE, either as examples of flawed arguments, or as incorrect answer choices.

- Slippery Slope
- Percent versus Number
- Sampling Error
- Correlation versus Causation
- Equivocation
- *Ad hominem* Arguments
- Appeal to Authority
- Appeal to Majority: The Quantity/Quality Fallacy
- Circular Argument
- Begging the Question
- *Reductio ad Absurdum*

Slippery Slope

Slippery slope arguments are often referred to as "domino arguments," and are more properly called *causal slippery slope arguments*.

Consider the following example:

> **If you eat one hot, fresh, glazed donut, then you will eat another one, and soon it will become a habit. Eventually, you will eat so many that you will gain a large amount of weight and suffer from the health problems that result from being significantly overweight. These problems include diabetes. So, if you eat that one hot, fresh, glazed donut, you will suffer from diabetes in the future.**

The reason that the conclusion does not necessarily follow from the evidence presented is that the evidence is made up of suppositions about the future. Although the suppositions are possible and plausible, they are not certain to occur. The mistake in this kind of argument is that the author is focusing on one possible set of outcomes and stacking them on top of one another to form what looks like an argument but really isn't.

This is not to say that all suppositions about the future are meaningless. If one has accurate data regarding the probability of certain outcomes, one can often make more informed decisions about a given course of action available now, in the present. However, the slippery slope argument is based on pure conjecture and not solid probability.

Percent versus Number

Often, the success of an argument is based on the distinction between percentage and raw number. Consider this example:

> **The gross revenue of Company X increased by more than $1 million when comparing last year to the year before. The gross revenue of Company Y increased by over $10 million during the same period. Clearly Company Y experienced a larger percentage of increase in gross revenue than Company X did.**

The reason that you cannot be convinced by this argument is that there is some very important information missing. You do not know the overall amount of gross revenue for either Company X or Company Y. Therefore, you cannot accept the conclusion that one or the other had a larger percentage of increase in gross revenue.

> **NOTE**
> Percent versus Number and Sampling Error fallacies have appeared in Quantitative Comparison questions. Be aware of them when you have to determine which given value is actually larger.

Sampling Error

Here is another fallacy that might trick you into a mistake on the Quantitative Comparison questions. Remember that for any statistical conclusion to be valid, it must be drawn from a proper random sample. Consider the following example:

> **All of the instructors at the community college wear glasses. I know that this is true because I have taken three auto repair classes at the community college and all of my instructors wore glasses.**

The reason that you should not be convinced by this argument is that all of the classes had something in common. They were not a random sample of classes.

They were all auto repair classes. In fact, you can easily suppose that the glasses that were worn by the instructors were safety glasses.

You might also question the sample size. Perhaps three instructors, even if they were randomly chosen, would not be considered a large enough group to fully represent the entire faculty of the community college.

Sampling error results from either an insufficient sample size or a nonrepresentative, or *skewed*, sample. Look for this type of fallacy in the Data Interpretation questions.

Correlation versus Causation

Correlation is finding two things that occur together, either simultaneously or consecutively. It is a mistake to conclude that one thing caused the other based only on the correlation. For example:

1. **It rained yesterday and today I have a cold. The rain must have caused my cold.**
2. **As the popularity of cell phones has increased, the prevalence of cheating on college campuses has increased. Cell phone availability must contribute to cheating by college students.**
3. **An Olympic gold medalist eats this brand of breakfast cereal. Therefore, if I eat the same brand of breakfast cereal, I, too, can become an Olympic champion.**

The reason these arguments are not convincing is that, in each case, something else could have caused the result.

In Example 1, the rain happened before the cold but that doesn't mean that it caused the cold. The cold might have some other cause entirely.

In Example 2, two phenomena are seen to be increasing together. There are four possibilities: (a) Cell phones cause cheating; (b) cheating increases cell phone use; (c) some third factor is causing both cell phone use to increase and cheating to increase; or (d) there is no connection at all and the observed correlation is simply a coincidence.

In Example 3, it should be clear that there are many other factors involved in Olympic success than the choice of a certain breakfast cereal. Even if the cereal does contribute in some measure to the athlete's success, it cannot be safely concluded that eating the cereal is a sufficient condition to guarantee any other individual the same kind of success.

Equivocation

Sometimes the author of an argument gets very tricky and uses the fact that words often have more than one meaning. Consider the following:

> **Hollywood gossip reporting is legitimate news reporting. It is well established that the press has a right to act in the public interest. Everyone would agree that all reporting that is in the public interest is legitimate. The public is obviously interested in gossip reporting based on the large audience that such reporting garners. Since the public is interested in gossip, such reporting is clearly in the public interest and therefore legitimate.**

The reason that you should not be persuaded by this argument is that it takes advantage of the flexibility of the English language and uses more than one meaning for the word *interest*. On one hand, when discussing "the public interest" in the first and second sentences, the meaning is closer to "in the best interest of the public" or "to provide a valuable service to the public." In the next two sentences, "interested" means merely "to pay attention to," or "to desire to observe." These two definitions are not interchangeable. As a result, the "argument" about Hollywood gossip is not sound because the same word is used to represent two different meanings. Therefore, the conclusion does not follow from the evidence presented.

Ad Hominem Arguments

The Latin term *ad hominem* means "against the person," and refers to arguments that are directed against the person who is making a given argument rather than against the validity or truth of the argument. Consider the following:

> **We should not accept Milton's conclusions regarding the soundness of our investment decisions since he is an adult who spends his off time playing video games and lives in his mother's basement.**

The reason this argument is not convincing is that it does not actually give you any reason to doubt Milton's conclusions other than some facts about Milton himself. The author of this argument is asking you to follow along on some rather large assumptions about adults who live in their mothers' basements and play video games as a hobby. You are supposed to conclude that there is no way that such a person could be correct about investment decisions. In other words, this is nothing more than an attack on Milton himself with no real logic or argumentation. If you listen closely to many political advertisements and debates, you will easily find many *ad hominem* arguments.

Appeal to Authority

Some purported arguments simply rely on the reputation of some third party rather than any convincing evidence. Consider the following examples:

1. My conclusions about foreign policy must be correct since they are in accord with the pronouncements of Winston Churchill.
2. Pacifism must be the correct course of action since Albert Einstein supported it.
3. Dr. Ligenfelder says that houses built of discarded tires are the best way to save energy so you cannot disagree with me when I say the same thing.

All three examples use a reference to some person who is an authority of some kind as their only evidence to support their argument. As with some other fallacies, you will often find appeal to authority included in popular advertising.

There is no real logic or argumentation. You are expected simply to accept the conclusions offered because someone who is famous, or has some kind of expertise, has reached the same conclusions.

In some cases, such as Example 2, the expert is speaking out on a topic that is not within his area of expertise. In Example 3, you don't even know what Dr. Ligenfelder's area of expertise is; you are expected to agree simply because the person making the assertion is called "Doctor."

Appeal to Majority: The Quantity/Quality Fallacy

Sometimes a position is supported only by the number of people who hold it. Consider the following:

1. Can 4 million voters be wrong?
2. The new game show is the most popular one on television; therefore, it must be the best thing on TV.

Of course, the implied conclusion in Example 1 is "No. They cannot be wrong." The problem is that, as you are aware, it is possible for any number of individuals to be wrong. So, there is no real evidence offered to provide support for the implied assertion that this particular group of 4 million voters is correct.

In Example 2, you are expected to accept the fact that more people watch this game show than any other game show as evidence of its quality. (Example 2 also asks you to assume that even if it is the best game show, it is therefore ". . . the best thing on TV." This is another fairly sizable assumption that is probably not warranted.)

Circular Argument

A circular argument is characterized by the conclusion appearing as a premise. Consider the following example:

> All newspaper reporters are biased. Only biased individuals would go into journalism so that they could influence the public's thinking on issues. Such a person tries to influence the public's thinking to create changes in our culture. Therefore, all newspaper reporters are biased.

This is a glaring example of a fairly common fallacy. This argument assumes the truth of its own conclusion and provides no support for the contention that newspaper reporters are biased.

Begging the Question

The fallacy of begging the question is characterized by an "if, then" implication with a clearly false consequent. Consider the following example:

> If this isn't the best pizza in the world, then pigs can fly. We all know that pigs can't fly, so clearly this is the best pizza in the world.

The author of this argument makes it seem that he is simply applying the contrapositive to an implication. However, the original implication contains a statement, "then pigs can fly," that is patently ridiculous, thereby ensuring that the conclusion "this is the best pizza in the world" appears to be inescapably true, even though no real evidence has been offered.

Reductio ad Absurdum

The Latin term *reductio ad absurdum* means "to reduce to the absurd." This technique is used to convince the listener that an argument seems ridiculous by pointing out the similarities between the original argument and an absurd argument. Consider the following:

> *Mother:* This copper bracelet must prevent arthritis since I have been wearing it for years and I do not have arthritis.
>
> *Son:* That is just like arguing that the brown roof on your house repels meteorites since you have not had any meteorite strikes since installing it.

The son in this case is using the technique of making an absurd argument using the same structure as his mother's argument, in order to show her that her argument must also be absurd. This technique is sometimes effective to illustrate the flaws in a given argument. However, its value is dependent on the subject matter content chosen for the counterexample and a structure that is perfectly parallel to the original argument. For this reason, it is included in this list of common fallacies.

What's Next?

As we mentioned at the beginning of this chapter, an understanding of logic is essential to success on several of the sections tested on the GRE. Some questions might ask you to analyze an argument, or ask you to identify assumptions or conclusions, while other questions will simply be easier for you to manage if your logic skills are sharp.

Refer to this chapter as necessary while working through the rest of this book. You might want to hang on to it as a reference source long after you have taken the GRE.

6
GRE Analytical Writing

> **CHAPTER GOALS**
> - Understand how the Analytical Writing section is scored.
> - Learn valuable writing techniques and strategies.
> - Practice writing Issue Task and Argument Task essays.
> - Study sample essays and compare them to your own responses.

The Analytical Writing section of the GRE is purely a skills test. This means that you are not tested on any knowledge whatsoever. Instead, you are given an opportunity to demonstrate your ability to reason clearly and write coherently and concisely.

There are two separate tasks within this section:

- "Analyze an Issue" (which we'll call the Issue Task)
- "Analyze an Argument" (which we'll call the Argument Task)

You are allowed 30 minutes for the Issue Task, and 30 minutes for the Argument Task, including reading and prewriting. Note that the essays are generally weighted equally by department admissions boards.

Breaking Down Analytical Writing

No specialized knowledge is required to complete either writing exercise. You are not tested on what you might know about a particular subject. Instead, you are given the opportunity to demonstrate your ability to reason clearly and write coherently and concisely. Graduate schools are looking for logical reasoning, clarity, organization, writing mechanics, and proper usage of the language.

In addition, how *well* you write is much more important than how *much* you write. The GRE software provides more "space" than you will ever be able to use. You should write enough to clearly support your position or analyze the given argument within the allotted time.

It's very important to note that the Argument Task has a very different purpose than the Issue Task; you're not being asked to write the same type of essay twice. If, after practicing, you still have trouble separating the two in your mind, consider how they might be used in graduate school. The Issue Task is similar to the writing you have done and will continue to do in greater depth: to propose a thesis and defend it. The Argument Task, however, reflects the processes used during research. As an undergraduate, you have probably had most of your academic resources vetted by your professors. As you will discover in graduate school, if you haven't already, not everything published is solid scholarship. Some theses are simply false. Others are justifiable, but are poorly defended by their authors. You will have to be able to evaluate published work and identify any logical flaws, if only to avoid introducing the same mistakes into your own papers. The Argument Task measures your readiness to perform this important part of academic research.

We'll discuss how to approach each task later in the chapter.

Scoring the Analytical Writing Sections

Each essay is scored on a scale of 0 to 6 by two readers. The readers might be college faculty members (often graduate students serving as teaching assistants) or a computer program referred to as an "automated engine." Therefore, your initial scoring might be done by two well-trained human beings, or by one such human and a computer. All readers, human or not, use the same *rubric*, or scoring guide. The process contains several safeguards to ensure fairness. For instance, the essays are randomly assigned to the readers, who have no way of learning the identity of the writer. Also, two readers grade each essay. If the two scores given to a single essay differ by more than one point, a third, senior, reader (always a human being) is called in to resolve the conflict.

Essays are scored *holistically*, which means that a reader simply assigns a single number grade to the essay without assigning any specific point value to the various factors considered in scoring. Although many factors can enter into the reader's decision, the most important factors are clear structure (logic) and analytical writing (also logic).

What the GRE Readers Are Looking For

Logical structure is far more important than mechanics such as spelling and grammar. However, you shouldn't take any chances with mechanics. If you aren't absolutely certain how to use a semicolon properly, don't use one. If you are unsure of the meaning of a word, do not use it. Instead, think of a simpler term with the same meaning and use it.

Here is a description of how the essays are scored at each level on both tasks. Essays that receive the following scores exhibit one or more of the characteristics listed:

- **Score of 0:** Response does not address the assigned task, is in a foreign language, is indecipherable, or contains no text (not attempted).

- **Score of 1: *Fundamentally deficient.*** The essay is extremely confusing or mostly irrelevant. There is little or no development of ideas. Contains severe and pervasive errors. Does not present a logical analysis of the argument.

- **Score of 2: *Seriously weak.*** Contains frequent problems in sentence structure or use of language. Errors obscure meaning. The essay lacks analysis or development of ideas.

- **Score of 3: *Shows some competence.*** Contains some analysis and development of ideas. The essay has limited organization with flawed control or numerous sentence structure or language errors. It is vague and lacks clarity.

- **Score of 4: *Competent.*** Main ideas are supported with relevant evidence and examples. The essay shows adequate organization and is reasonably clear. The argument is identified and important features are analyzed. There is adequate control of sentences and language, but the essay might include some errors that reduce overall clarity.

- **Score of 5: *Generally thoughtful analysis of complex ideas.*** Sound reasoning and well-chosen examples support conclusions. The essay is well organized and focused, and includes sentences of varying length and complexity. Any errors are minor and do not affect the meaning of the essay.

- **Score of 6: *Insightful, in-depth analysis of complex ideas.*** Compelling logic and very persuasive examples. Essay is well organized and focused and displays skill in structuring sentences; vocabulary is precise and relevant. If there are any errors, they do not affect the logic or meaning of the essay.

Writing Techniques

Following are the steps you should take when writing your essays. To write the best essay that you can in the time allotted, these steps should be performed one at a time.

> **GRE Tip**
> The planning stage is the most important stage of the essay-writing process. Even if you spend up to 10 minutes on this stage, you will still be able to write a well-crafted essay in the time allowed.

Carefully read the prompt. You should read the prompt more than once to be certain that you understand what you are reading. You must know what the task is before you begin. Rushing through this step can cost valuable points and make some of your hard work worthless.

Plan your essay. Your essay should start out with a clear statement of your position on the issue or a clear evaluation of the strength of the argument. The outline that you create does not have to include complete sentences. It does have to include the ideas that you will put into your final draft. You need to be sure that you have a clear picture of where you are going and how you will get there before you start to write on the answer document. Finally, don't underestimate the effect of stress on memory. You may think the order of your essay is obvious, but it's easy to forget even brilliant insights once you begin the actual writing.

Type your essay out in the space provided. Remember that graduate school admissions professionals will only look at what you've typed on the computer screen. Be sure to save time to review your work in order to make necessary corrections or improvements.

Writing Strategies

As noted earlier in this book, humans acquire skills through practice. Because the Analytical Writing section tests your writing skills, you should practice writing under test-like conditions. The best way to make sure that you are on track is to have someone with writing experience, someone you trust (such as your personal tutor), give you specific feedback on your practice essays. It is important to have someone else read and critique your essays because writers tend to develop blind spots when it comes to areas that need improvement in their own essays. It is always a good idea to get a fresh set of eyes to review your work. It will not take long for an experienced reader to give feedback that can be immensely valuable.

If you will be critiquing your own essays, put them away for a week or so after you write them and then take them out for another spin. You might find errors and lapses in logic that were not evident to you as you were writing. Be aware that this process will significantly increase the amount of time required for your overall preparation, so be sure to plan accordingly.

Consider the following strategies to help you write an effective essay.

Clearly State Your Position

Your essay should start out with a clear statement of your position on the issue. There should be no doubt in the reader's mind about which side you are on from the beginning of your essay. For the Argument Task, clearly identify important flaws in the prompt argument. Use the scratch paper with which you are provided to outline the structure of your essay. This is not the time for multitasking; do not simply read the prompt and then try to write your essay from the beginning to the end. It is very difficult to simultaneously create the logical structure of your essay, anticipate counterarguments, attempt to correctly apply the rules of grammar, punctuation, and spelling, and identify appropriate examples to plug into your essay structure.

> **GRE Tip**
> Make sure that you understand the issue or argument that is presented before you begin writing. Remember that responses that are off the topic are not acceptable.

Too often, GRE test-takers make broad, general statements in their essays without giving any specific support. Make sure that you provide clear, simple examples of the general statements that you make, and that your evaluations are logical and well supported. In your response to the Argument Task, be sure to include a cause and effect relationship between *your* evidence and *your* conclusion.

Present Your Ideas Logically

As we mentioned, many factors can enter into the reader's scoring decision, but the most important factors are critical thinking (logic) and analytical writing (also, logic). Remember that logic is far more important than mechanics such as spelling and grammar. Be sure to prewrite before you begin to type your essay. This strategy acquaints you with the stimulus and suggests patterns for presenting your thoughts. Carefully consider the prompt and make sure you understand it. Decide which course of action you will support, and jot down your ideas on the topic: this might simply be a list of ideas, reasons, and examples that you will use to explain and support your decision. Think of how best to organize the ideas in your essay. You can refer back to these notes as you type the essay into the space provided by the GRE software.

Review and Correct Your Essay

When you start to write your essay, remember that those who read it will consider it a first draft. Your essay will not be perfect; however, it should be an example of the best writing you can produce under the time constraints and testing conditions. Be sure to take a few minutes before the end of the time period to read over your essay, correcting any mistakes in grammar, usage, punctuation, and spelling.

The practice tests included later in this book contain additional essay prompts. Use these as well as the prompts in the GRE topic pool, which can be found at **www.gre.org,** to write several practice essays between now and test day. The following section also provides some sample prompts you can use to start practicing and honing your writing skills.

Issue Task

The Issue Task requires you to read a given issue, and then write a short essay supporting your position on that issue. Although you cannot be certain what the issue choice will be in advance, some examples of issue prompts are provided later in this chapter so that you can get an idea of the type of issue that is likely to appear. The topics presented are usually of general public interest. You are expected to think clearly and critically about the topic and create a thoughtful, well-reasoned essay supporting your position. There is never a "correct" answer. Your task is simply to write a good essay from whatever perspective you choose.

The Time Limit

The 30-minute time limit starts running from the moment that the issue is revealed to you on the computer screen. Use the scratch paper you are given to make a few notes about the positives and negatives of various sides to the issue and to outline your response before you begin to type.

The Issue

Issues are carefully chosen so that they aren't biased toward any one college major or profession. However, luck is a bit of a factor on this section of the GRE. If you happen to be presented with an issue that you know something about, you will probably feel more comfortable writing about it. But, be careful to respond to the issue presented. Don't answer a question that wasn't asked just because you happen to know something about the subject matter. Finally, don't assume your reader is an expert in the subject; if you use specialized examples, always explain their significance.

Your Response

There are many possible responses to any Issue prompt. You might agree or disagree in part, or in whole. You might attack the underlying assumptions in the statement that is given. You might decide to discuss the fact that the statement you are writing about has only limited applicability in certain situations. Whatever your decision, tell your reader the position you have taken. This will be your thesis statement. Everything in your essay should work to support your thesis. You should certainly use at least one example to support your position. You may choose to use more than one example, which is fine as long as the examples you select are relevant and you stay focused on your main idea. Make sure it's clear to your reader how your examples relate to your thesis. Do not create fictional examples and try to pass them off as factual. It is OK to use hypothetical situations in your discussion if that is appropriate. Just be sure to let your readers know that the situations are hypothetical.

The Response Format

Don't feel that you must develop a complete, traditional five-paragraph essay to succeed on this task. Remember: Everything in your essay should work to strengthen your argument. That includes the essay's structure. If you have the time and ability to write a strong five-paragraph essay, go right ahead. However, a solid three-paragraph essay is often sufficient. In fact, a very solid, effective strategy is to write just three paragraphs. The first paragraph would contain your thesis, and by extension, the position that you are arguing *for*. The second would address the position that you are arguing *against*. The third would be an effective concluding paragraph. Whatever form you choose, you should use relevant examples to support your argument.

Be sure to explain the connection between the examples that you use and your conclusion. Don't assume that the reader will agree with your viewpoint regarding the significance of a given fact. For instance, in a situation in which you suggest that private education is relevant to a given issue, a statement in your essay such as ". . . merely a public school . . ." would reveal prejudices held by the writer and might or might not actually contribute to a convincing essay. A safer course of action would be to go out of your way to adopt a neutral, convincing tone and try not to reveal very much at all about any personal axes that you might have to grind.

The four categories of information that should be included in an Issue essay are as follows:

1. Positive for your position.
2. Negative for your position.
3. Positive for the other side.
4. Negative for the other side.

While an effective essay uses facts from all four categories, you should not give all four categories equal time. Consider the solid three-paragraph construction mentioned above: Most of the first paragraph should focus on a positive for your position, followed by a "weak" negative. The second paragraph should be a "weak" positive for the other side, followed by a longer, answering negative. Write a strong concluding paragraph to tie everything together.

You can think of your side as "correct" and the other side as "incorrect." When you write a paragraph that is focused on the "correct" side of the issue, you should mention at least one aspect of your choice that might be seen as a negative by some people. Your essay will be much more persuasive if you do not ignore potential problems with your side of the debate. The negative can be obvious, but it should be weak enough that you can easily explain why it doesn't destroy your argument. In other words, you should be sure to mention plenty of positive information to overcome the potential down side that you are admitting to.

The Counterargument

The previous technique can be applied to the part of your essay in which you discuss the opposition's position. You should admit that the other side of the debate has at least one good point. Then, follow up with enough discussion of the pitfalls associated with the other side of the argument that your side still ends up looking like the clear winner. This is known as dealing with counterarguments, and it is the most effective way of presenting a written argument. Remember: The goal is not to be fair; it's to be persuasive.

An effective counterargument requires certain transition words to guide the reader through your pros and cons. Following are four basic categories of transition words, along with some examples of effective transition words and phrases:

Contrast: But, however, on the other hand, conversely, although

Similarity: Likewise, similarly

Evidence: Since, because, in light of, first, second, third

Conclusion: Therefore, thus, as a result, so, it follows that, in conclusion

> **NOTE**
>
> See Chapter 5, "Introduction to GRE Logic," for more examples of structural signal words.

Your Tone

Avoid being too familiar, or colloquial, in your response. Just as you can't assume your reader will agree with you about a given issue, you also can't assume he or she will share your sense of humor. Also, do not take any chances with vocabulary. If you are at all unsure of the meaning of a word, *do not* use it in your essay. If you are wrong, you'll end up sounding foolish or even offensive to your readers. While the GRE rewards sophisticated language, it's better to use simple vocabulary correctly than to misuse a fancy word.

> **NOTE**
>
> See Chapter 10, "Basic GRE Verbal Review," for help with common mistakes in vocabulary and grammar.

Now let's take a look at some sample Issue essays.

Sample Essay Prompt 1: Analyze an Issue

Following is a sample prompt, similar to the prompts you will encounter on the GRE. Carefully read the directions and write your essay using the strategies outlined previously. After you have written your essay, read the graded sample essays that follow. You can compare your essay to the samples to get a sense of how your essay stacks up. You should also compare the samples to one another to understand better what the GRE readers are looking for. Finally, try to show your essay to an English professor or other qualified person for an evaluation. Remember that many different essays can earn high scores.

<u>Directions</u>: You have 30 minutes to plan and compose a response that presents your perspective on the topic in the prompt below. You may accept, reject, or qualify the claim made in the prompt, as long as the ideas you present are relevant to the topic. A response to any other topic will earn a score of zero.

Use a word processor with the spell-checker and grammar checker turned off. You may cut, copy, and paste parts of your essay. Take a few minutes to plan your response and write an outline before you begin your essay. Be sure to develop your ideas fully and organize them coherently. Leave time to proofread your essay and make any revisions you think are necessary.

> "In raising a child, love is important, but discipline is most important of all."
>
> Discuss whether you agree or disagree with the statement. Use relevant reasons and examples to support your point of view. In developing and supporting your position, consider ways in which the statement might or might not hold true. Explain how those considerations affect your point of view.

Issue Task Sample Essay: Score of 6

The following essay received a score of 6 because it is well organized and focused, uses language effectively, and provides an insightful in-depth analysis of a complex issue.

> *The issue of proper child rearing is an important, yet rarely debated, social issue, with implications affecting both children and adults. One of the most important variables in a child-rearing philosophy is whether the philosophy values discipline or love more highly. A philosophy that values discipline above love is one in which love may be denied for the purpose of promoting discipline, particularly through withheld affection or through corporal punishment. Most of today's leading authorities recommend that discipline be valued above love for raising children, especially boys. However, most of these commentators, such as James Dobson, base their child-rearing philosophies not on sound research studying the happiness and social success of the children, but on one particular interpretation of religious texts. Studies have shown that these ideas about child-rearing, far from producing happy, competent adults, in fact do serious harm to*

children raised under their influence. Indeed, a child-rearing philosophy that values discipline above love fails both a philosophical and a pragmatic test.

From a practical perspective, a child-rearing technique can be considered successful if the child has generally positive memories of childhood, and goes on to be a valuable member of society, as measured through such traits as honesty, compassion, and initiative. Most discipline-based child-rearing philosophies fail on precisely these grounds. It needs little argument that most children do not have happy memories of physical discipline, but the denial of affection can also be a powerfully traumatic act: children who are told that they run the risk of losing a parent's love also grow up to be nervous, clingy adults, prone to pretending that problems do not exist, in lieu of risking the alienation of affection. Further, child-rearing research has come down strongly on the side of a care-based parenting method. Studies show that, contra Dobson et al, harsh punishment for disobedience does not create a powerful sense of self-discipline; instead, it promotes adults who are guided by punishment rather than conscience. To the contrary, children who are raised with compassion and love (though not without a due measure of discipline) tend to behave towards others in a compassionate and loving manner.

Philosophically, the discipline-based child-rearing philosophy also comes up short. Physical coercion as a valid means of achieving one's objectives is never a good lesson to teach. Moreover, some would argue that it is simply morally wrong to harm a child, whether it is with the intent of promoting discipline or not; since such behavior would not be tolerated in a non-discipline context, there is no reason to believe it acceptable in a discipline context, especially when there is no solid evidence that it has any beneficial effects. It is also unsatisfactory that strict-discipline parenting methodology presupposes the need to be even more strict and firm with male children than with female children. Without evidence for substantial behavioral differences between male and female prepubescent children, there is no reason to believe that their development would require radically different parenting strategies.

I do not wish to argue that discipline should be avoided. Completely lax parenting is just as bad as domineering parenting. However, parental discipline must always come second to love; parents must meet the physical and emotional needs of their children, even disobedient ones, under all circumstances. The good parent, having set boundaries, can make sure that the child is free to explore within them, and to deal adequately with the challenges beyond the home, simply by setting the positive example of treating the child with affection, care, and respect.

Issue Task Sample Essay: Score of 4

The following essay received a score of 4 because, although the ideas were supported with relevant examples, the essay lacks focus and includes errors that reduce its overall clarity.

I believe that love and discipline are both important, but discipline has to be more important. Too many children these days are raised without discipline. They do whatever they want, and don't pay attention to the effect they have on society. For a child to really grow up right, you have to set limits and make sure the child follows them, because otherwise they won't think that there ever are any limits. Nowadays we hear all kinds of stories from the media—in the papers, on television—about the things that kids do when they grow up unsupervised. All these things could have been prevented by a bit of discipline when that child was growing up.

Kids who grow up without discipline always wind up getting into trouble. Whether it's disrespecting their parents or their employers, to having no goals for themselves, to violent and unrestrained behavior, not having discipline leads to problems. Sometimes undisciplined children grow into violent adults, for instance, Lyle and Erik Menendez, who killed their parents solely to get the insurance money, clearly showed a profound lack of discipline. Their desire for material goods was not restrained by a proper sense of discipline that would have led them to work hard to get it. Thus, these two wild children did the unthinkable: they killed their parents in their undisciplined search for greater material happiness.

Another person who showed a remarkable lack of discipline in her life was Janet Jackson. Her crazy antics at the Super Bowl showed a remarkable lack of discipline, while it may be fun to flaunt yourself, someone with the proper upbringing that emphasizes the importance of discipline will know better than to expose herself on national television. She just wanted to jump-start her career without putting in the work. What she needed was more discipline.

In short, discipline is extremely important. A person who does not have will not go far in life, whether because of the mistakes they make or because they will lack ambition to achieve his or her goals, and if a person does not learn discipline in childhood, then when will they learn it? Therefore, the most important thing when raising a child is discipline, to prevent those kinds of mistakes in adulthood.

Issue Task Sample Essay: Score of 2

The following essay received a score of 2 because it lacks any serious development of the stimulus, and contains frequent errors that either distract from or obscure the author's intended meaning.

> Give a kid nothing but love all the time will turn them into spoiled brats. They'll think they never have to face any consequences for their actions and that they can get away with anything they want.
>
> The Bible says to spare the rod and spoil the child and I agree. My aunt raised my two cousins and never spanked them or hit them and they are both spoiled and mean. Every time I see them growing up, they take my toys and hit me and the other kids and they never get punished. My aunt always takes their side and blamed other kids for fights and problems.
>
> I'm not saying people should beat there kids, just that kids need discipline. It doesn't have to be spankings, it could be grounding them or taking away toys or something. But they need to know they can't just do anything they want.

Sample Essay Prompt 2: Analyze an Issue

Following is a sample prompt, similar to the prompts you will encounter on the GRE. Carefully read the directions and write your essay using the strategies outlined previously. After you have written your essay, read the graded sample essays that follow. You can compare your essay to the samples to get a sense of how your essay stacks up. You should also compare the samples to one another to understand better what the GRE readers are looking for. Finally, try to show your essay to an English professor or other qualified person for an evaluation. Remember that many different essays can earn high scores.

<u>Directions</u>: You have 30 minutes to plan and compose a response that presents your perspective on the topic in the prompt below. You may accept, reject, or qualify the claim made in the prompt, as long as the ideas you present are relevant to the topic. A response to any other topic will earn a score of zero.

Use a word processor with the spell-checker and grammar checker turned off. You may cut, copy, and paste parts of your essay. Take a few minutes to plan your response and write an outline before you begin your essay. Be sure to develop your ideas fully and organize them coherently. Leave time to proofread your essay and make any revisions you think are necessary.

> "Health care in the United States should be free for all citizens, fully financed by the government."

Issue Task Sample Essay: Score of 6

The following essay received a score of 6 because it is well organized and focused, uses language effectively, and provides an insightful in-depth analysis of a complex issue.

> *In the United States today an atmosphere of entitlement exists that could cause one to believe that free health care for all citizens is the best course of action. Government subsidized programs such as welfare and Medicaid continue to perpetuate the myth that all people, regardless of their actual need, should be entitled to unlimited government assistance simply by virtue of being born in America. While I agree that American citizens who evidence a legitimate need should receive help for such things as emergency health care, I do not believe that health care in the United States should be free for all citizens, fully financed by the government.*

History is replete with examples of failed states, which failed, for the most part, because they subverted the market and created a command economy, thus limiting the role of individual choice. The most recent example is the collapse of the Soviet Union, which proved that allocation of resources by a government bureaucracy is so inherently inefficient as to be literally fatal to a government and many of its individual citizens.

While I recognize that the proposal is limited to government-provided health care, it must be noted that the health care segment represents an overwhelmingly large portion of the total economy of the United States. Furthermore, the same weaknesses inherent in any centrally controlled economy will be found in a national system of health care.

It is a fundamental fact that human desires are limitless while resources are limited. When the market allocates resources via innumerable individual human decisions, it is likely that the highest overall satisfaction will be achieved. The proper role of government is to enforce procedural fairness so that no individual member of society gains an unfair advantage in bargaining. Once government steps into the process of actually allocating scarce resources, such as medicine, it must introduce a decision-making process that, by its nature, must be inefficient. Simply put, someone must decide who has access to which medicine, doctors, equipment, etc. If the government were to take over a system of payment, it would then take over such decisions.

I believe that such a government system would be disastrous. To paraphrase a political candidate from recent history: "It would combine the compassion of the Internal Revenue Service with the efficiency of the Department of Motor Vehicles."

Furthermore, the concept of health care is poorly defined. Would this free service be limited to "basic" health care or include sophisticated diagnostic services such as CAT scans and MRI's? Where would the lines be drawn? The opportunities for ridiculous waste are nearly limitless, as are the possibilities for abuse: Should the government health care system pay for multiple attempts at rehabilitation for unrepentant drug abusers?

There is also the potential slippery slope to consider. If government takes over payment for all health care, then it is conceivable that the government would be interested in limiting dangerous behaviors: for example, certain high-risk sports and activities such as motorcycle riding, as well as more mundane activities such as overeating. Could government health care regulations end up requiring a state-issued permit to consume a cheeseburger and a beer? Perhaps.

> *Because the unintended consequences would probably be far-reaching and overwhelmingly negative, I do not support the idea that health care should be government funded and free to all citizens.*

Issue Task Sample Essay: Score of 4

The following essay received a score of 4 because, although the ideas were supported with relevant examples, the essay lacks focus and includes errors that reduce its overall clarity.

> *In light of the current national debt situation, I disagree with the statement that health care in the United States should be free for all citizens, and that the government should finance health care. Many other countries around the world have government financed health care programs; the United States should see that these programs are not always very successful.*
>
> *For example, in a country like Canada, where health care is free to all citizens, the risk of heart disease is on the rise. Even though every citizen has access to free health care, it is not being taken advantage of. Studies show that people are not any healthier in a country, such as Canada, where health care is fully financed by the government. Many people think that if health care was free, the general population would be healthier. However, based on the previous example, it is not the case.*
>
> *In addition, government funded health care would put a financial strain on the government. We are already paying too much taxes, and that is the only place for the government to get the extra money it would need to pay for free health care. This, again, shows that each citizen should be responsible for their own health care, and not rely on the government to provide it. If we rely on the government for too much help, we learn, as a society, not to take care of ourselves, which may reduce our current status among the other countries of the world.*
>
> *Although some people may disagree, government financed health care is not the best action for the United States. As free citizens, we should be responsible for our own well-being.*

Issue Task Sample Essay: Score of 2

The following essay received a score of 2 because it seriously lacks any development of the stimulus and contains frequent errors that either distract from or obscure the author's intended meaning.

> If helth care in the US was free, then everyone could take advantage of it and Americans would be more healthy. There are many health problems that we face in the US, namely heart disease and obesity, that could be helped by free health care. Many other programs financed by the government are quite helpful. They should be available to all Americans, just like health care. Paying for programs for it's citizens is the job of the goverment.
>
> I think that the US government should pay for health care for all Americans because things like health care should be free for all Americans. Why do we live in America anyway? If programs aren't free for all? To me, that's what America is all about. We deserve the right to free health care; because we pay taxes. Other countries have free health care, and we, as the US, should do the same.

Argument Task

As with the Issue Task, the topic presented in the Argument Task is usually of general public interest. You are expected to think clearly and critically about the topic and create a logical analysis of the flaws in its presentation. To this purpose, you should read the prompt in the Argument Task even more carefully than you read the prompt in the Issue Task. You are being asked to critique an argument, not to present your own views on the subject. On the Argument Task, you are given only one argument. You are expected to analyze and critique how well its evidence supports its conclusion. It's important to remember that you must critique the argument as it's presented, as opposed to creating your own argument as you must on the Issue Task.

> **GRE Tip**
>
> If you haven't yet mastered the material in Chapter 5, "Introduction to GRE Logic," you should attempt to do so before tackling the rest of this chapter. Pay close attention to the sections on assumptions and fallacies.

The Time Limit

The 30-minute time limit starts running from the moment that the argument is revealed to you on the computer screen. Use the scratch paper you are given to take notes about the argument's logical development.

The Argument

The arguments are carefully chosen so that they aren't biased toward any one college major or profession. And you don't have to be a logic major to analyze an argument effectively. However, if you happen to be presented with a topic that you know something about, you will probably feel more comfortable in writing about it. In these situations, be careful not to focus too much on facts themselves. Your job is to criticize the way the facts are organized and presented. For example, you may disagree with your prompt, and think that public libraries are an excellent use of public funds. This is not the time to make that argument. Instead, focus on the ways the author has failed to be convincing. No matter what the topic, the argument will always have multiple flaws.

Your Response

As you've probably noticed, Argument Task essays are fundamentally different from most of the essays you have written as an undergraduate. Therefore, your mental approach must also be fundamentally different. First, *read* the prompt carefully. Make sure you understand exactly what the writer is saying, not what you might expect him to say. Next, *analyze* the structure of the argument, especially how the writer puts forth claims (i.e., evidence) and conclusions, and any assumptions that might link them. Then *consider the content*; you want to come up with alternative explanations and counterexamples. Would additional evidence strengthen or weaken the argument? What kind? Finally, you should also give some thought to the *implications* of the argument. That is, what would probably follow if the conclusion of the argument is accepted at face value?

When reading the Argument prompt, pay special attention to the structural signal words that indicate *evidence, conclusion, contrast,* and *continuation*. These terms usually blend into the background as you read. However, because structure is part of what you are analyzing and critiquing, you need to notice them. Take advantage of the printed format of the practice tests and circle the words as you read them. They'll provide handy signposts to understanding the argument. This habit will be useful on the actual exam.

Following are four basic categories of transition words, along with some examples of effective transition words and phrases:

Evidence: Since, because, in light of, first, second, third

Conclusion: Therefore, thus, as a result, so, it follows that, in conclusion

Contrast: But, however, on the other hand, conversely, although

Continuation: Similarly, next

> **NOTE**
>
> See Chapter 5, "Introduction to GRE Logic," for more examples of structural signal words.

The Response Format

Between assumptions and fallacies, an argument can have many different types of flaws. Keeping in mind your time constraints, you are free to focus on any or all of them. Thus, there are many possible responses to any Argument prompt. As with the Issue Task, don't feel the need to restrict yourself to a five-paragraph format. Remember: Everything in your essay should work to strengthen your argument. That includes the essay's structure. Many writers start a new paragraph for each new criticism. Others will group the criticisms by type of flaw. Whatever form you choose, explain clearly how each of your examples functions as a logical flaw. Don't assume your reader will make the connection without your help.

However you choose to structure your argument, your thesis statement should give your reader an overview of your criticism. To refer to our library example, you could say that while using public funds to support public libraries may be desirable in most cases, the given argument is fundamentally flawed for the following reasons. The rest of your essay would then develop those reasons. You should certainly use at least one criticism to support your position. You may choose to use more than one criticism, which is fine as long as the examples you select are relevant and you stay focused on your main idea. Make sure it's clear to your reader how your examples illustrate a flaw in the argument.

> **GRE Tip**
>
> One handy technique is to circle key function words as you read the prompt. Obviously, you won't be able to do this during the actual test, but it will train your mind to focus on structure while you practice your essays.

You don't need to know a lot of specialized logic vocabulary, although the concepts themselves are invaluable. Still, the GRE does reward the use and understanding of some terminology, including:

- **Argument:** an orderly process of supporting a conclusion with evidence
- **Analysis:** the process of breaking an argument down to its component parts in order to understand how they work together
- **Evidence:** the information that supports a conclusion
- **Conclusion:** the main point of an argument
- **Assumption:** unstated, or *assumed*, evidence
- **Alternative explanation:** competing evidence that also leads to the conclusion of the stated argument, but that has been ignored or omitted by the writer.
- **Counterexample:** an example, real or hypothetical, which disproves evidence used in an argument

Review Chapter 5, "Introduction to GRE Logic," if these terms aren't entirely familiar to you. You should also review the different types of logical flaws. You won't need to name the flaws in your essay, but being able to spot them quickly will be very handy on test day.

Your Tone

Despite the inherently negative content in an Argument essay, it's still important to adopt a neutral, convincing tone. Your reader should never get the impression that your criticism is personal.

Avoid being too familiar, or colloquial, in your response. Just as you can't assume your reader will agree with you about a given issue, you also can't assume he or she will share your sense of humor. Finally, do not take any chances with vocabulary. If you are at all unsure of the meaning of a word, *do not* use it in your essay. If you are wrong, you'll end up sounding foolish or even offensive to your readers.

> **NOTE**
>
> See Chapter 10, "Basic GRE Verbal Review," for help with common mistakes in vocabulary and grammar.

Now, let's take a look at some sample Argument essays.

Sample Essay Prompt 1: Analyze an Argument

Following is a sample prompt, similar to the prompts you will encounter on the GRE. Carefully read the directions and write your essay using the strategies outlined previously. After you have written your essay, read the graded sample essays that follow. You can compare your essay to the samples to get a sense of how your essay stacks up. You should also compare the samples to one another to understand better what the GRE readers are looking for. Finally, try to show your essay to an English professor or other qualified person for an evaluation. Remember that many different essays can earn high scores.

Directions: You have 30 minutes to read the prompt below and write an evaluation of the argument. An evaluation of any other topic will earn a score of zero.

Use a word processor with the spell-checker and grammar checker turned off. You may cut, copy, and paste parts of your essay. Take a few minutes to plan your response and write an outline before you begin your essay.

> "Funding for space exploration and colonization needs to be greatly expanded. At present, Earth is the only planet known to support life. A cataclysmic event could result in the extinction not only of human life, but of all life in the known universe. Moreover, as human society continues to progress, it will seek new frontiers to expand to and to gather resources from. For both of these reasons, we must ensure that humanity establishes a foothold on other worlds."
>
> Critique the reasoning used in the argument above. You are not being asked to discuss your point of view on the argument. You should identify and analyze the central elements of the argument, the underlying assumptions that are being made, and any supporting information that is given. Your critique can also discuss other information that would strengthen or weaken the argument or make it more logical.

Argument Task Sample Essay: Score of 6

The following essay received a score of 6 because it correctly identifies and supports its position, discusses the structure of the argument, and contains compelling logic and persuasive examples. Any errors are minor and do not affect the logic of the essay.

The argument presented, while interesting, makes several errors in reasoning that undermine its effectiveness. For this argument to be considered valid, it must state all of its premises more clearly. Further, it recommends a course of action based upon a chain of cause and effect, which is not internally supported. Last, it contains self-contradictory reasoning, which needs to be untangled before the argument will be truly convincing.

The most striking feature of this argument is its sweeping assumptions. The author of the argument attempts to argue that funding for space colonization must be increased, because of the possibility of a cataclysmic event wiping out all life on Earth. However, the author does not indicate why the continued survival of life in the general sense—or, more to the point, a relatively small group of individuals—would be important to the general masses presently on Earth, if life on this planet were to be wiped out. The author assumes that the need to spread and preserve life on a small scale is self-evident, when it is not. The author also assumes that human intervention would increase the chance of life surviving in the universe as a whole, without considering the possibility that Earth-bound life might have negative effects on what extraterrestrial life may already exist. And the author assumes that the probability of a cataclysmic event destroying life on earth is significant. The fossil record shows that life on earth has survived at least six cataclysmic events in the past; the argument does not specify the magnitude of future risks, nor does it estimate the extent to which those risks would be reduced.

Many of the more significant assumptions made in this argument are those which assume the effectiveness of the prescribed course of action. Supposing it is granted that Earth-bound life, particularly human life, needs to be spread to other planets; it does not follow that it is within our power to colonize other worlds, nor that increased funding for space exploration and colonization would let us achieve that goal. It is possible that current funding is sufficient; it is also possible that no amount of money would be enough to achieve an impossible goal. The funding could well be money wasted chasing a worthwhile cause, and without the author mentioning specific uses for the money, we cannot say otherwise. If the premise is that we need to preserve some form of terrestrial life in general, then it does not follow that humanity needs to establish a foothold on other worlds. It could easily be concluded that we should ensure some hardy form of terrestrial life, such as bacteria, be sent elsewhere.

Finally, one additional weakness bears consideration: the argument mentions the human need for more resources and more frontiers. However, the argument does not consider that catering to this aspect of human nature might well undermine the goal of the survival of Earth-bound life. One commonly-mentioned cataclysmic scenario is environmental destruction as a result of human activity; while spreading humanity to other planets might provide a reprieve from this scenario, there is no reason to think it would reduce the risk of further self-destruction. This is a conflict between the two premises that needs to be resolved. Were the argument to state all these assumptions directly as premises, and to use more specific examples, it would be more compelling. As it is, the chain of reasoning is hampered by generalities and by skipped steps that detract from its intellectual force.

Argument Task Sample Essay: Score of 4

The following essay received a score of 4 because it shows an adequate grasp of the argument and is reasonably clear. However, it includes some errors in logic and construction that reduce its overall clarity.

The argument presented above is generally a good one. However, there are some ways it could be improved. The author doesn't talk about where the money for space exploration will come from, and doesn't indicate how that money should be spent to ensure that humans can colonize space. Moreover, the argument is not convincing until we know how we will be able to get the resources gathered from other worlds to our own Earth.

While the author's argument is well-formed, he is a little lacking on the details. He rightly indicates that funding for space exploration needs to be increased. But who is going to pay for it? For this kind of colonization effort to work, we need to know there are practical sources for the money. Is every country going to pay? If poor countries pay less, do they get less? And whose going to spend the money? The author assumes that everything will go smoothly, but does not propose any way to monitor things to be sure.

In a similar vain, this argument would be much more convincing if the author detailed ways that the money could be spent to improve our current efforts to colonize space. While more money certainly couldn't hurt, we would be more inclined to believe the author if he gave us some practical examples of exactly how the money would be used to advance our goals of space exploration.

Last, the author mentions using colonies to provide resources for Earth society and to provide a new frontier for people to explore. These are great ideas, but will not have their full force unless the author explains how we can get large numbers of people to colonize other planets, and how we can bring those resources back to Earth to improve the standard of living of the people still here, a plan without specifics is not very effective when it comes to convincing an audience.

In short, this is a good start, but the author needs to provide more details of how the plan will work before it can be put into action. Until the specifics of how the money will be used, how the project will be overseen, and how space colonization will work, are provided, this proposal will not be as convincing as it otherwise could be.

Argument Task Sample Essay: Score of 2

The following essay received a score of 2 because it lacks analysis of the argument, is vague, and contains pervasive structural and grammatical errors.

This argument is just stupid. First, the author assumes we've just got all this money sitting around for space exploration. That's not true. And even if we did have alot of money, why not just use it to repair the damage they've done to our own planet. We could use the money for other energy and resources and then we wouldnt' need to look at space to meet our needs.

I think we should just start buying hibrid cares and stop using coal and stuff like that. Then no bodied need to go into space. I mean, man has walked on the moon for over 30 years and what have we gotten out of it? Like I said, this argument is just stupid.

Sample Essay Prompt 2: Analyze an Argument

Following is a sample prompt, similar to the prompts you will encounter on the GRE. Carefully read the directions and write your essay using the strategies outlined previously. After you have written your essay, read the graded sample essays that follow. You can compare your essay to the samples to get a sense of how your essay stacks up. You should also compare the samples to one another to understand better what the GRE readers are looking for. Finally, try to show your essay to an English professor or other qualified person for an evaluation. Remember that many different essays can earn high scores.

Directions: You have 30 minutes to read the prompt below and write an evaluation of the argument. An evaluation of any other topic will earn a score of zero.

In your assessment, analyze the line of reasoning used in the argument. Consider what, if any, questionable assumptions underlie the reasoning and how well any evidence given supports the conclusion. You can also discuss what sort of additional evidence would strengthen or refute the argument, what changes would make the conclusion more logically sound, and what additional information might be needed to better evaluate the argument. *Note that you are NOT being asked to present your views on the subject.*

Use a word processor with the spell-checker and grammar checker turned off. You may cut, copy, and paste parts of your essay. Take a few minutes to plan your response and write an outline before you begin your essay.

> "The following appeared in a letter to the editor of a local newspaper: 'Too much emphasis is placed on the development of math skills in high school. Many students who are discouraged by the difficulty of the content turn away from schoolwork merely because they lack basic math skills. But practice questions and content review on the Internet provide an important alternative for students at this crucial stage in their education, an alternative that the school board should not reject merely because of the expense involved. After all, many studies attest to the value of using Internet-based math review. Thus, allowing students to practice basic math skills and review relevant math content on the Internet can only make students more eager to study and learn math. Therefore, the school board should encourage schools to purchase computers and permit high school students to access the Internet.'"

Argument Task Sample Essay: Score of 6

The following essay received a score of 6 because it correctly identifies and supports its position, discusses the structure of the argument, and contains compelling logic and persuasive examples. Any errors are minor and do not affect the logic of the essay.

The argument is not persuasive for several reasons. It contains unexamined assumptions, fails to sufficiently address the issue of cost, and fails to consider potentially negative unintended consequences.

The argument begins by stating that, "Too much emphasis is placed on the development of math skills in high school." It then goes on to discuss a major expenditure that could only serve to place emphasis on math skills as educators seek to justify the expense of new equipment by focusing more energy and time on math. Furthermore, the author of the argument must be assuming that the students at this particular school will have access to the same Internet-based math review that was included in the studies that were cited. Additionally, the studies refer to "review" which may or may not be synonymous with "basic skill" acquisition.

In addition, the argument fails to make a valid comparison between the current methods of math instruction and the Internet method that is proposed. The argument states only that the Internet is an "important alternative" and neglects to provide any level of description of current methods.

Because the argument absolutely lacks even the most rudimentary cost-benefit analysis, it should not be considered valid. The expenditure should be justified by increased levels of achievement by students, or by increased efficiency, or both. There is simply insufficient evidence upon which the reader can base a decision.

The argument also ignores the fact that there are many distractions on the Internet as well as a large volume of content, including math review content, that may be unedited, unfiltered, and incorrect. The distractions alone should give one pause. At best, Internet access in the schools would provide a whole new level of supervision challenges for the faculty and staff. Students could easily be spending time communicating with each other, playing games, or viewing material that is completely irrelevant and perhaps even harmful to their development process.

All in all, the argument lacks merit due to its lack of completeness and its failure to provide a strong connection between the evidence provided and its conclusion.

Argument Task Sample Essay: Score of 4

The following essay received a score of 4 because it shows an adequate grasp of the argument and is reasonably clear. However, it includes some errors in logic and construction that reduce its overall clarity.

> The argument presented lacks any serious support, and fails to consider some problems that might come up if high school students use the Internet in school. The argument does not address any financial issues that might arise from encouraging schools to purchase more computers.
>
> First, because the argument doesn't say whether the Internet use would be monitored in any way, it is likely that students would abuse the privilege. Teenagers have too much access to the Internet in the home and would most likely just use the Internet at school to chat with friends and look at information that is not appropriate, like games or movies. This would not help a student to learn anything about math.
>
> Also, the argument does not cover the additional cost of putting computers in the schools. Although computers are relatively inexpensive these days, a high school would probably need to install many computers in order to give students access to the Internet. There is no evidence provided to support any additional cost to the schools. Many schools are facing budget crunches right now, and may not be able to afford computers or be able to pay for the cost of Internet access.
>
> Finally, if high school students had access to the Internet in school, it might take away from their other studies. There is no gurantee that students would learn the right math skills or if they would be able to spend enough time away from the computer to focus on other classes. Therefore, I believe that the argument is not sufficient and does not completely answer all of the questions necessary to make a good decision.

Argument Task Sample Essay: Score of 2

The following essay received a score of 2 because it lacks analysis of the argument, is vague, and contains pervasive structural and grammatical errors.

I support the argument that the Internet should be available to high schoolers, especially math students. Despite that putting computers into high schools will be expensive, it is a good investment. Not enough high school students focus on math, and being able to access the Internet and be exposed to different learning tools and practice tests will be a good thing.

Also, the school board should encourage schools to purchase computers, because many students don't have computers at home. So, they can't get online and learn important math skills. If they could access the Internet at school, in the classroom even, there time would be spent more effectively learning. Because math is an important skill to have—even if some people would disagree - being able to learn more math more easily should be supported.

The argument is a good one that the school board should encourage high schools to purchase computers and permit high schoolers to access the Internet. There are many good reasons for it.

Practice Writing Prompts

Use the following set of prompts to practice your analysis and writing skills. Limit your time to 30 minuets for the Issue Task and 30 minutes for the Argument Task. Use scratch paper to plan your response before you begin to write.

Because you have virtually unlimited space in which to type your answer on the computer version of the GRE General Test, we have not included any lined pages here. Using regular lined paper, practice writing a complete, well-supported essay in the time allotted. You may also type your responses using a word processor with the spell and grammar check functions turned off.

Issue Task Practice

Plan and compose a response that represents your perspective on the following topic. Support your views with reasons and examples drawn from personal experience, reading, observations, or academic studies. Take a few minutes to think about the issue and plan a response. Organize and fully develop your ideas; be sure to leave time to evaluate your response and revise as necessary.

Sample Prompt

> "When high-profile celebrities speak out in favor of a certain politician, that politician's reputation is generally damaged."

Argument Task Practice

Plan and write a critique of the argument presented. Analyze the line of reasoning in the argument and consider any questionable assumptions that underlie the thinking. Discuss the evidence provided and whether there might be evidence that strengthens or weakens the argument, as well as what changes would make the argument more logically sound. You are not being asked to present your views on the subject.

Sample Prompt

> "Sadly, widespread negative images of teenagers have been created in large part by popular movies. Consider the fact that, although they make up a mere 15 percent of the characters in dramatic roles in movies, teenagers are responsible for about one-fifth of all the crimes committed in dramatic films. In fact, in a recent survey of movie producers, only 35 percent of the movie roles for teenagers were viewed as positive ones."

What's Next?

Each of the practice tests in Part IV of this book includes an Issue Task and an Argument Task. Continue to practice your writing under timed conditions.

The remaining chapters in this section provide a comprehensive review of the GRE Quantitative and Verbal sections.

7
GRE Quantitative

CHAPTER GOALS

- Review the four types of GRE quantitative questions: Multiple-choice—Select One Answer, Multiple-choice—Select One or More Answers, Quantitative Comparison, and Numeric Entry.
- Study examples of each quantitative question type.
- Learn specific strategies for answering each quantitative question type.
- Practice answering sample GRE quantitative questions.

The GRE Quantitative section is designed to test your ability to reason mathematically, to understand basic math terminology, and to recall basic mathematic formulas and principles. You should be able to solve problems and apply relevant mathematics concepts in arithmetic, algebra, geometry, and data analysis. Keep in mind, though, that the GRE is primarily a critical thinking test, so your ability to apply reason and logic to solving the quantitative questions is more important than your ability to recall mathematic formulas and principles.

The GRE Quantitative sections include two kinds of Multiple-choice questions, each with several answer choices from which to choose, Quantitative Comparison questions, each with four possible answers (A–D), and Numeric Entry questions, for which you must come up with an answer on your own. Some of the Multiple-choice and Numeric Entry questions are part of question sets based on the data in charts or graphs.

GRE Tip

Be sure to practice the strategies and techniques covered in this chapter on the simulated exams found in Part IV of this book.

In this chapter, we will discuss the format of each question type and provide you with specific strategies for successfully answering the GRE quantitative questions. Chapter 9, "Basic GRE Math Review," provides an overview of the mathematical content tested on the GRE, so be sure to read that chapter to fill any gaps in your knowledge.

Multiple-choice Questions

The GRE includes two kinds of multiple-choice questions: Multiple-choice—Select One Answer and Multiple-choice—Select one or More Answers.

- **Multiple-choice—Select One Answer** questions each have five answer choices. Your task is to select the one correct choice.
- **Multiple-choice—Select One or More Answers** questions can have fewer than five answer choices or more than five answer choices. Your task is to select all the choices that answer the question correctly. The directions may tell you how many choices to select. If you are told how many, you should select exactly that number of choices.

Some GRE multiple-choice questions involve straightforward calculations, while others require you to evaluate a word-problem in a real-life setting. Still others may be part of question sets called Data Interpretation sets. All of the questions in a Data Interpretation set are based on the same data presented in tables, graphs, charts, or figures.

To solve GRE Multiple-choice questions, you typically will not be required to perform complex calculations. However, you will be given scratch paper for whatever figuring you wish to do, and you will also be provided with a calculator to assist you when necessary. (In the computer-based test, the calculator will appear on screen.)

Anatomy of a GRE Multiple-choice—Select One Answer Question

Before you start studying solution strategies, take a look at some typical Multiple-choice—Select One Answer questions.

1. If $5x-6=14$, then $8x=$
   - (A) $\dfrac{8}{5}$
   - (B) 4
   - (C) $\dfrac{64}{5}$
   - (D) 20
   - (E) 32

Use the following information to answer question 2.

State X Spending Changes

	1990–1995	1995–2000	2000–2005	2005–2010
Education	+8%	+9%	+1%	−3%
Transportation	+2%	+5%	−3%	−5%
Police	+3%	+4%	+0%	−2%
Health	+5%	+8%	+7%	+9%
Other	+2%	+7%	−10%	−8%

2. What was the change in total health spending, as a percent, from 1990 to 2010 (rounded to the nearest tenth)?
   - Ⓐ 29.0%
   - Ⓑ 29.2%
   - Ⓒ 30.7%
   - Ⓓ 31.5%
   - Ⓔ 32.3%

Anatomy of a GRE Multiple-choice—Select One or More Answers Question

Now look at some examples of typical GRE multiple-choice questions that ask you to consider selecting more than one answer.

3. If a and b are positive integers such that the greatest common factor of a^2b^2 and ab^3 is 45, then which of the following could b equal?

   Select all such integers.
   - Ⓐ 3
   - Ⓑ 5
   - Ⓒ 9
   - Ⓓ 15
   - Ⓔ 45

4. A colored marble is to be chosen at random from a bag of marbles. The probability that the marble chosen will be green is 4/9. Which two of the following could NOT be the total number of marbles in the bag?
   - Ⓐ 36
   - Ⓑ 64
   - Ⓒ 81
   - Ⓓ 110

General Strategies for Multiple-choice Questions

Remember the following general strategies when approaching GRE Multiple-choice questions. Note that these strategies might also be helpful in answering the other question types.

Draw Pictures

Visualize the problem by creating a figure or diagram. This strategy should not take a lot of time, and can prevent careless errors. Sometimes, you are given a figure or a table that you can work with; sometimes, you just have to make your own. Consider the following examples:

The greatest number of diagonals that can be drawn from one vertex of a regular 8-sided polygon is

(A) 1
(B) 2
(C) 3
(D) 4
(E) 5

The correct answer is E. To solve this problem, draw a diagram such as the one that follows:

(Vertex)

As you can see, if you draw a regular octagon (8-sided polygon), you can make only five diagonals from one vertex.

A square is inscribed in a circle. If the area of the inscribed square is 50, then the area of the circle is

(A) 5π
(B) $5\pi\sqrt{2}$
(C) 10π
(D) 25π
(E) 50π

The correct answer is D. To solve this problem, draw a diagram such as the one that follows:

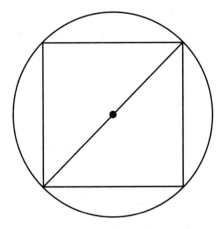

If the area of the square is 50, then one side of the square is $\sqrt{50}$, which is equivalent to $(\sqrt{25})(\sqrt{2})$, or $5\sqrt{2}$. The diagonal of an inscribed square is equal to the diameter of the circle. The diagonal creates two isosceles right triangles. Use the Pythagorean theorem: $(5\sqrt{2})^2 + (5\sqrt{2})^2 = c^2$. Simplify the equation to get $(50) + (50) = c^2$, and $c = 10$. If the diameter (d) is 10, then the radius (r) is 5. Since the area of a circle is πr^2, the area of this circle is 25π.

Apply Logic

Remember, most of the actual calculations for GRE Quantitative problems are fairly simple. In fact, the GRE test writers are just as likely to test your logical reasoning ability or your ability to follow directions as they are to test your ability to plug numbers into an equation. Consider the following examples:

If $b - c = 2$, and $a + c = 16$, then $a + b =$

(A) 8
(B) 14
(C) 16
(D) 18
(E) 32

The correct answer is D. To solve this problem, first recognize that $(b - c) + (a + c) = a + b$. This is true because the c values cancel each other out, leaving you with $b + a$, which is equivalent to $a + b$. Therefore, $a + b$ must equal $2 + 16$, or 18.

Which of the following equations correctly translates this statement: "Three less than twice a number is the same as eight more than half the number"?

Ⓐ $3 - 2x = 8 + \frac{x}{2}$
Ⓑ $2 - 3x = x - 4$
Ⓒ $2x - 3 = 4 - x$
Ⓓ $3x - 2 = \frac{1}{2}x + 8$
Ⓔ $2x - 3 = \frac{1}{2}x + 8$

$2x - 3 = \frac{1}{2}x + 8$

The correct answer is E. The first step in solving this problem is to recognize that "three less than" means to subtract 3 from some other quantity. Quickly review the answer choices to see that you only need to consider answer choices C and E. Likewise, the statement "eight more than" means to add 8 to some other quantity. Only answer choice E meets both of these criteria. The expression "three less than twice a number" is expressed mathematically as $2x - 3$, and "eight more than half the number" is expressed mathematically as $\frac{1}{2}x + 8$.

Answer the Question Asked

If the problem requires three steps to reach a solution and you only completed two of the steps, then it is likely that the answer you arrived at will be one of the choices. However, it will not be the correct choice! Consider the following examples:

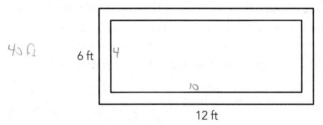

40 ft   6 ft   4
         10
         12 ft

The rectangular garden shown in the figure above has a stone border 2 feet in width on all sides. What is the area, in square feet, of that portion of the garden that excludes the border?

Ⓐ 4
✗ Ⓑ 16
Ⓒ 40
Ⓓ 56
Ⓔ 72

The correct answer is B. This problem asks for the area of the *middle* portion of the garden. To solve this problem, perform the following calculations, and remember that the border goes around the entire garden. First, subtract the border width from the length of the garden:

$12 - 2(2) = 8$

Next, subtract the border width from the width of the garden:

$6 - 2(2) = 2$

The area (length × width) of the portion of the garden that excludes the border is 8×2, or 16.

If you only accounted for the border along one length and one width of the garden, you would have gotten answer choice C. Answer choice D is the area of the border around the garden. Answer choice E is the area of the entire garden, including the stone border.

Which of the following is the slope of a line that is perpendicular to the line $3x + 5y = 10$?

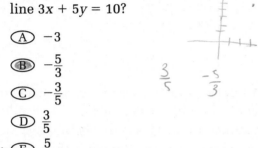

- Ⓐ -3
- Ⓑ $-\frac{5}{3}$
- Ⓒ $-\frac{3}{5}$
- Ⓓ $\frac{3}{5}$
- Ⓔ $\frac{5}{3}$

The correct answer is E. The first step in solving this problem is to put the equation in the standard form $y = mx + b$, where m is the slope:

$3x + 5y = 10$

$5y = -3x + 10$

$y = -\frac{3}{5}x + 2$

The slope of the given line is $-\frac{3}{5}$. However, you are asked for the slope of a line that is *perpendicular* to the given line. Perpendicular lines have negative reciprocal slopes, so the correct answer is $\frac{5}{3}$.

Don't Quit Early

Particularly for questions that ask you to consider selecting more than one answer choice, make sure you examine all the answer choices. Don't make the mistake of moving on to the next problem as soon as you have found one correct answer choice! Consider the following examples.

If $0 < pr < 1$, then which <u>two</u> of the following CANNOT be true?

- Ⓐ $p < 0$
- Ⓑ $r < 0$
- Ⓒ $p < -1$
- Ⓓ $r < -1$

The correct answer is C and D. At first glance, you might think that you don't have enough information to solve this problem. However, if you recognize that *pr* must be a positive fraction because it lies between 0 and 1, you can quickly solve the problem.

If both *p* and *r* were less than −1, then *pr* would be greater than 1, which breaks the rule in the question stem.

For which values of *x* is the following function undefined?

$$f(x) = \frac{x^2 - 9}{x^2 - 49}$$

Select all such values.

- [A] −7
- [B] −3
- [C] 3
- [D] 7

The correct answer is A and D. Don't let the term *function* scare you; this is not really a function question at all. To solve this problem, first recall that a fraction is undefined when the denominator is 0. This is true because you cannot divide a number by 0. Therefore, the correct answer will include the values of *x* for which $x^2 = 49$. Because both 7^2 and $-7^2 = 49$, answer choices A and D are correct.

Check the Choices

Take a quick look at the answer choices as you read the problem for the first time. They can provide valuable clues about how to proceed. For example, many answer choices will be in either ascending or descending order. If the question asks you for the least possible value, try the smallest answer choice first. If it does not correctly answer the question, work through the rest of the answer choices from smallest to largest. Remember that one of them is the correct choice. Consider the following examples:

If *x* is an integer and $y = 7x + 11$, what is the greatest value of *x* for which *y* is less than 50?

- (A) 7
- (B) 6
- (C) 5
- (D) 4
- (E) 3

The correct answer is C. Because the question asks for the greatest value of *x*, evaluate answer choice A first because it is the greatest value among the answer choices:

Answer choice A: $y = 7(7) + 11 = 60$. This is not less than 50, so eliminate answer choice A, and look at answer choice B.

Answer choice B: $y = 7(6) + 11 = 53$. This is not less than 50, so eliminate answer choice B, and look at answer choice C.

Answer choice C: $y = 7(5) + 11 = 46$. Because 5 is the greatest of the remaining answer choices and the result is less than 50, answer choice C must be correct.

Noah's Ark Fish Store sold 80 guppies and 48 bala sharks on Saturday. Which of the choices below could represent the ratio of bala sharks to guppies sold on Saturday?

(A) $\frac{12}{20}$
(B) 5:3
(C) $\frac{6}{5}$
(D) 25 to 15
(E) $\frac{20}{35}$

The correct answer is A. The first step in solving this problem is to note that the ratio is bala sharks to guppies, which can be expressed mathematically in the following ways: 48 to 80, 48:80, and $\frac{48}{80}$. Therefore, the correct answer must include a factor of 48 in the first position. Eliminate answer choices B, D, and E because 5, 25, and 20 are not factors of 48. Answer choice C cannot be correct because, although 6 is a factor of 48 and 5 is a factor of 80, the fraction $\frac{48}{80}$ is less than the fraction $\frac{6}{5}$ (note that the numerator is larger than the denominator in the second fraction). Therefore, the correct answer must be A; $\frac{12}{20} = \frac{48}{80}$.

Pick Numbers for the Variables

You can sometimes simplify your work on a given problem by using actual numbers as "stand-ins" for variables. This strategy works when you have variables in the question and the same variables in the answer choices. You can simplify the answer choices by substituting actual numbers for the variables. Pick numbers that are easy to work with and that meet the parameters of the information given in the question. If you use this strategy, remember that numbers on the GRE can be either positive or negative and are sometimes whole numbers and sometimes fractions. You should also be careful not to use 1 or 0 as your "stand-ins" because they can create "identities," which can lead to more than one seemingly correct answer choice. The word identity refers to an equality that remains true regardless of the values of any variables that appear within the equality. For example, any number multiplied by 0 is always 0.

In addition, it is sometimes necessary to try more than one number to see if the result always correctly responds to the question. If the numbers that you pick work for more than one answer choice, pick different numbers and try again, focusing on the remaining answer choices. Consider the following examples:

If x and y are both positive even integers, which of the following expressions must be even?

Select all such expressions.

- [A] x^y
- [B] $(x+1)^y$
- [C] $x^{(y+1)}$

The correct answer is A and C. The question states that both x and y are positive even integers. Therefore, you can pick any positive even integer and substitute that value for x and y in each of the choices, as follows:

Choice A: $2^2 = 4$, which is even; $4^2 = 16$, which is also even. Any positive even integer raised to another positive even integer will result in an even number; therefore, Choice A correctly answers the question.

Choice B: $(2+1)^2 = 3^2 = 9$, which is odd; $(4+1)^2 = 5^2 = 25$, which is also odd. When you add 1 to a positive even integer and raise the sum to a positive even integer, the result will be odd; therefore, Choice B does not correctly answer the question.

Choice C: $2^{(2+1)} = 2^3 = 8$, which is even; $4^{(2+1)} = 4^3 = 64$, which is also even. Any positive even integer raised to an odd power will result in an even number; therefore, Choice C correctly answers the question.

If a and b are positive consecutive odd integers, where $b > a$, which of the following is equal to $b^2 - a^2$?

(A) $2a$
(B) $4a$
(C) $2a + 2$
(D) $2a + 4$
(E) $4a + 4$

The correct answer is E. You are given that both a and b are positive consecutive odd integers, and that b is greater than a. Pick two numbers that fit the criteria: $a = 3$ and $b = 5$. Now substitute these numbers into $b^2 - a^2$, as follows:

$5^2 = 25$ and $3^2 = 9$; therefore, $b^2 - a^2 = 25 - 9$, or 16

Now substitute the value that you selected for a into the answer choices until one of them yields 16, as follows:

$2(3) = 6$; eliminate answer choice A.

$4(3) = 12$; eliminate answer choice B.

$2(3) + 2 = 8$; eliminate answer choice C.

$2(3) + 4 = 10$; eliminate answer choice D.

$4(3) + 4 = 16$; answer choice E is correct.

Read the Questions Carefully

Sometimes the questions include irrelevant data, so be sure you're working with the correct numbers! Also, it helps to write down key words and phrases in the question. When you are looking at ratio problems, for example, note whether the question is giving a part-to-part ratio or a part-to-whole ratio. The ratio of girls to boys in a class is a part-to-part ratio. The ratio of girls to students in a class is a part-to-whole ratio. Focusing on the right information will help you to quickly answer the question. Consider the following examples:

The ratio of two quantities is 4 to 5. If each of the quantities is increased by 3, which of the following could be the ratio of these two new quantities?

Indicate all answer choices that apply.

A. $\frac{7}{8}$

B. $\frac{11}{13}$

C. $\frac{23}{28}$

The correct answer is A, B, and C. To understand this problem, realize that, although the ratio of two quantities is 4 to 5, the actual values of the quantities might be very different. For different sets of values, increasing each by 3 will create different ratios. For instance, if the quantities were 4 and 5, increasing each by 3 would result in a ratio of 7 to 8. If the quantities were 8 and 10 (a ratio of 4 to 5), increasing each by 3 would result in a ratio of 11 to 13. If the quantities were 20 and 25 (a ratio of 4 to 5), increasing each by 3 would result in a ratio of 23 to 28. So answer choices A, B, and C are all correct.

What percent of 5 is 7?

- Ⓐ 35%
- Ⓑ 57%
- Ⓒ 71%
- Ⓓ 140%
- Ⓔ 157%

The correct answer is D. To solve this problem, note that 7 is greater than 5, which means that the correct answer must be greater than 100%; eliminate answer choices A, B, and C. To find what percent of 5 the number 7 is, you can simply divide 7 by 5 and multiply by 100%, as follows:

$$\frac{7}{5} = 1.4$$

$$(1.4)(100) = 140\%$$

Multiple-choice Practice Questions

1. Jim's Hardware store normally sells bulk nails at $1.09 a pound. There is a sale of 3 pounds of nails for $2.19. How much can be saved by purchasing 9 pounds of nails at the sale price?
    - Ⓐ $1.89
    - Ⓑ $3.24
    - Ⓒ $4.29
    - Ⓓ $6.57
    - Ⓔ $9.90

2. In $\triangle ABC$, $AB \cong AC$ and the measure of $\angle B$ is 34°. What is the measure of $\angle A$?
    - Ⓐ 34°
    - Ⓑ 56°
    - Ⓒ 68°
    - Ⓓ 73°
    - Ⓔ 112°

3. If $7y + 9$ represents an odd integer, which of the following represents the next smaller odd integer?
    - Ⓐ $7(y + 1)$
    - Ⓑ $7(y - 2)$
    - Ⓒ $7(y + 3)$
    - Ⓓ $7(y + 2)$
    - Ⓔ $7(y - 2) + 1$

4. What is the largest integer value of t that satisfies the inequality $\frac{24}{30} > \frac{t}{24}$?
   - (A) 8
   - (B) 10
   - (C) 18
   - (D) 19
   - (E) 30

5. The larger of two numbers exceeds twice the smaller number by 9. The sum of twice the larger and 5 times the smaller number is 74. If a is the smaller number, which equation below determines the correct value of a?
   - (A) $5(2a+9)+2a=74$
   - (B) $5(2a-9)+2a=74$
   - (C) $(4a+9)+5a=74$
   - (D) $2(2a+9)+5a=74$
   - (E) $2(2a-9)+5a=74$

6. If $W = XYZ$, then which of the following is an expression for Z in terms of W, X, and Y?
   - (A) $\frac{XY}{W}$
   - (B) $\frac{W}{XY}$
   - (C) WXY
   - (D) $W-XY$
   - (E) $W+XY$

7. What is $\frac{1}{5}$ of 16% of $24,000?
   - (A) $160
   - (B) $768
   - (C) $3,840
   - (D) $4,032
   - (E) $7,500

8. Which two of the following are NOT solutions of $(x-5)(x-3)(x-9)(x+9)=0$?
   - [A] -9
   - [B] -5
   - [C] -3
   - [D] 3
   - [E] 5
   - [F] 9

9. What is the least common multiple of 3, 4a, 5b, and 6ab?
   Ⓐ 15ab
   Ⓑ 60ab
   Ⓒ $60a^2b$
   Ⓓ 120ab
   Ⓔ $120a^2b$

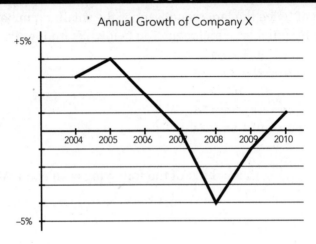

Annual Growth of Company X

10. What was the total percent change of Company X's value from the start of 2007 to the start of 2010?
    Ⓐ −4.86%
    Ⓑ −4.9%
    Ⓒ −4.96%
    Ⓓ −5%
    Ⓔ −5.1%

Answers and Explanations

1. **The correct answer is B.** The first step in solving this problem is to calculate the cost of 9 pounds of nails at the regular price:

   9 ($1.09) = $9.81

   Next, calculate the cost of 9 pounds of nails at the sale price:

   3($2.19) = $6.57

   Finally, subtract $6.57 from $9.81 to get a savings of $3.24.

2. **The correct answer is E.** A good way to solve this problem is to sketch triangle *ABC*, as shown below:

   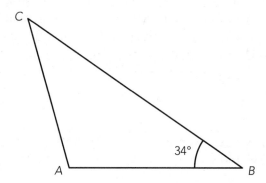

   You are given that *AB* is congruent to *AC*, and that the measure of angle *B* is 34°. This means that the measure of angle *C* is also 34°, and the measure of angle *A* is 180° − 34° − 34° = 112°.

3. **The correct answer is A.** To answer this question, note that odd numbers are every other number: 1, 3, 5, 7, . . . , etc. So an odd number plus or minus 2 would create another odd number. Therefore, $7y + 7$ would be the next *smaller* odd integer. Factor out a 7 to get $7(y + 1)$.

4. **The correct answer is D.** One way to solve this problem is to recognize that, in order for $\frac{24}{30}$ to be greater than $\frac{t}{24}$, t must be less than 24. This is true because any fraction with a denominator larger than or equal to its numerator will always be *less* than a fraction whose numerator is larger than or equal to its denominator. So, $\frac{t}{24}$ is only less than $\frac{24}{30}$ when t is less than 24. Because you are asked for the largest integer value of t and you know that t must be less than 24, the correct answer must be 19. You could also set the values equal to each other, cross-multiply and solve for t, as follows:

   $$\frac{24}{30} = \frac{t}{24}$$

   $$30t = 576$$

   $$t = 19.2$$

   The integer value that makes $\frac{24}{30}$ greater than $\frac{t}{24}$, therefore, is 19.

5. **The correct answer is D.** To solve this problem, first convert the information given into its mathematical equivalent, as follows (use b to represent the larger number):

    The larger of two numbers exceeds twice the smaller number by 9:
    $$b = 2a + 9$$

    The sum of twice the larger and five times the smaller number is 74:
    $$2b + 5a = 74$$

    Now, simply substitute the value of b into the second equation in order to solve for a:
    $$2(2a + 9) + 5a = 74$$

6. **The correct answer is B.** Don't let the fact that there are no numbers in this math problem confuse you! Simply remember that W, X, Y, and Z each represent some number, and perform the correct mathematical operations to isolate Z on one side of the equation, as follows:

    $$W = XYZ$$
    $$\frac{W}{XY} = Z$$

7. **The correct answer is B.** To solve this problem, first calculate 16% of 24,000, as follows:

    $$24{,}000 \times .16 = 3{,}840$$

    Next, calculate $\frac{1}{5}$ of 3,840, as follows:

    $$3{,}840 \times \frac{1}{5}$$
    $$= 3{,}840 \div 5 = 768$$

8. **The correct answer is B and C.** The solutions are the values of x that make the product of $(x-5)(x-9)(x-3)(x+9)$ equal to 0. Therefore, x can equal 5, 3, 9, or –9, but x cannot equal –5 or –3.

9. **The correct answer is B.** Each of the numbers in the values given must divide evenly into the least common multiple. Therefore, you can quickly eliminate answer choice A because 4 does not divide evenly into 15. Next, notice that each of the number values divides evenly into 60, which is less than 120, so eliminate answer choices D and E. Because ab is a smaller multiple than a^2b, and ab divides evenly into the product of all of the given values, answer choice B is the least common multiple of the given values.

10. **The correct answer is C.** The value did not change in 2007, lost 4% in 2008, and lost 1% in 2009. Thus the ending value was $0.96 \times 0.99 = 95.04\%$, a loss of $100\% - 95.04\% = 4.96\%$.

Quantitative Comparison Questions

Quantitative Comparison questions ask you to compare two quantities and determine whether one is larger than the other, if the quantities are equal, or if there is not enough information to determine a relationship between the two quantities. Some questions include additional information that is centered above the two quantities that concerns one or both of the quantities. Quantitative Comparison questions generally require more logic skills than math skills, so refer to Chapter 5, "Introduction to GRE Logic," for additional help.

You will be asked to select from answer choices A through D. If you decide that Quantity A is greater than Quantity B, select answer choice A. If you decide that Quantity B is greater than Quantity A, select answer choice B. If you decide that the quantities are equal, select answer choice C. If there is not enough information to determine a relationship between the two quantities, select answer choice D.

> **GRE Tip**
> Memorize the answer choices to Quantitative Comparison questions to save on time:
> A = Quantity A is greater
> B = Quantity B is greater
> C = Quantities are equal
> D = Not enough information

> **NOTE**
> Quantitative Comparison figures might not be drawn to scale. Rely on the information given, not on the appearance of the figures, to answer the questions.

The best way to handle the Quantitative Comparison questions is to simply determine the value of each quantity. It is often better to estimate values because you are really just trying to decide if one value is greater than the other. After you have calculated the values, you can easily determine the relationship, if one exists.

If one quantity is sometimes greater than or sometimes less than the other quantity, the relationship cannot be determined from the information. You should select answer choice D if *no one* can determine the relationship between the two values.

Anatomy of a GRE Quantitative Comparison Question

Before moving on to strategies, you should understand what a Quantitative Comparison question looks like. Consider the following example:

Quantity A	Quantity B
$-(3)^4$	$(-3)^4$

General Strategies for Quantitative Comparison Questions

Most of the strategies that apply to the Multiple-choice questions will work for the Quantitative Comparison questions, too. Use the following additional strategies when tackling more difficult Quantitative Comparison questions.

Memorize the Answer Choices

Don't spend time on test day trying to determine what A, B, C, and D mean. Remember that if Quantity A is greater, choose A; if Quantity B is greater, choose B; if the quantities are equal, choose C; if you can't determine a relationship, choose D. Take the time now to commit the answer choices to memory.

Simplify

You generally will not have to perform all of the calculations necessary to reach a definitive answer. You need to manipulate the quantities only until you know the relationship between them. Stop as soon as you know whether one is always greater than the other, or whether the quantities will always be equivalent. Consider the following example:

x is an integer less than 0.

Quantity A	Quantity B
3^{2x}	4^x

The correct answer is B. You are given that x is an integer, which means that it is a whole number. You also know that x is less than zero, which means it is a negative number. Choose several values for x that meet the previous criteria, and substitute those values into the two quantities:

When $x = -1$, Quantity A is 3^{-2}, which is equivalent to $\frac{1}{3^2}$, or $\frac{1}{9}$.

When $x = -1$, Quantity B is 4^{-1}, which is equivalent to $\frac{1}{4}$. Therefore, Quantity B is greater than Quantity A.

When $x = -2$, Quantity A is 3^{-4}, which is equivalent to $\frac{1}{3^4}$, or $\frac{1}{81}$.

When $x = -2$, Quantity B is 4^{-2}, which is equivalent to $\frac{1}{4^2}$, or $\frac{1}{16}$, and Quantity B is still greater than Quantity A.

In fact, because you will always multiply x by 2 in Quantity A, the denominator in Quantity A will always be greater than the denominator in Quantity B, and Quantity B will always be greater than Quantity A.

Use What You Know

You can often apply common sense to solving Quantitative Comparison problems. For example, if you are asked to compare the quantity $(399)^2$ to the quantity $(299)^3$, you can simply recognize that 399 is almost 400, and 400 squared is 1,600. Likewise, 299 is almost 300, and 300 cubed is 2,700. You don't actually have to perform the calculations in the question.

Be sure to read and evaluate the information (if any) that is given above the quantities to be compared. Sometimes you will only have to substitute values into equations in the column to reach an answer.

Consider the following example:

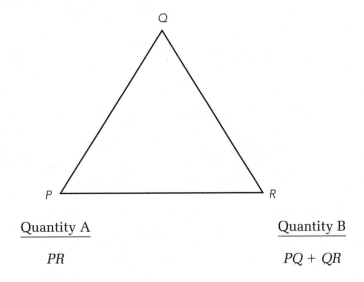

Quantity A	Quantity B
PR	PQ + QR

The correct answer is B. Any side of a triangle must be greater than the difference and less than the sum of the other two sides. Otherwise, you have either a triangle that falls in on itself, or two lines that lie on top of each other. Therefore, Quantity B, which is the sum of two sides of the triangle, is greater than Quantity A, which is the length of one side.

> **NOTE**
>
> Logical approximations are rewarded on the GRE; the test makers realize that you will not have time to perform detailed calculations for most of the questions.

Quantitative Comparison Practice Questions

	Quantity A	Quantity B
1.	The cost of p pens at a cost of $r + 29$ cents each	The cost of 7 notebooks at a cost of $(p + r)$ cents each

$$7x - 4 = 16 - 3x$$

	Quantity A	Quantity B
2.	x	4

	Quantity A	Quantity B
3.	$(-3)^7$	$(-3)^6$

$$x + y = 27$$
$$y + 12 = 23$$

	Quantity A	Quantity B
4.	x	y

A windmill makes one revolution every 8 seconds.

	Quantity A	Quantity B
5.	23	The number of revolutions made in 3 minutes

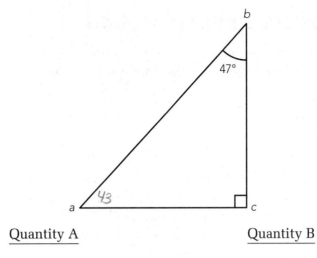

	Quantity A	Quantity B
6.	a	43

On Friday 120 people purchased lottery tickets. 34 more women than men purchased tickets.

	Quantity A	Quantity B
7.	The number of tickets purchased by women	The number of tickets purchased by men

George scored higher on his science midterm than Mark did.

	Quantity A	Quantity B
8.	George's score on the test	Three times Mark's score on the test

The area of square region *R* is 64.

	Quantity A	Quantity B
9.	32	The perimeter of *R*

	Quantity A	Quantity B
10.	15% of 30	$\sqrt{28}$

Answers and Explanations

1. **The correct answer is D.** The values of p and r are not given, so you cannot determine the relationship between Quantity A and Quantity B.
2. **The correct answer is B.** To solve this problem, simplify the equation:

    $10x = 20$
    $x = 2$

    Quantity B is greater than Quantity A.
3. **The correct answer is B.** A negative number raised to an odd power is negative. A negative number raised to an even power is positive. Therefore, Quantity A is negative and Quantity B is positive.
4. **The correct answer is A.** To solve this problem, simplify the second equation, as follows:

    $y + 12 = 23$
    $y = 11$

    Now substitute 11 for y in the first equation:

    $x + 11 = 27$
    $x = 16$

    Quantity A is greater than Quantity B.
5. **The correct answer is A.** To solve this problem, first determine that there are 180 seconds in 3 minutes. You are given that the windmill makes 8 revolutions in 3 minutes; divide 180 by 8 to get 22.5, which is less than 23. Therefore, Quantity A is greater than Quantity B.
6. **The correct answer is C.** Since the triangle is a right triangle, the two smaller angles must total 90°. $90 - 47 = 43$. So $a = 43$, and the quantities are equal.
7. **The correct answer is D.** Even though you can calculate how many women and men purchased tickets, you have no information about how many tickets each individual purchased. Therefore, you do not have enough information to determine the relationship between the quantities.
8. **The correct answer is D.** You are not given the relationship between the scores. For example, if George scored an 88 and Mark scored an 87, then Quantity B would be greater. However, if George scored a 90 and Mark scored a 30, then the two quantities would be equal. Therefore, the relationship cannot be determined from the information given.
9. **The correct answer is C.** You are given that the area of the square is 64, which means that each side must be $\sqrt{64}$, or 8 (remember, the area of a square is equal to s^2). Therefore, the perimeter of the square is 8×4, or 32, making the quantities equal.
10. **The correct answer is B.** To calculate 15% of 30, multiply 30 by .15:

    $30 \times .15 = 4.5$

    You can use logic to determine that Quantity B is greater:

    $\sqrt{25} = 5$, so $\sqrt{28}$ must be greater than 5.

Numeric Entry Questions

Questions of this type require you to enter your answer as an integer in a single answer box or as a fraction in two separate answer boxes. You will use the computer mouse and keyboard to make your entry.

Once you've calculated your answer, click on the answer box(es) to activate, then type your answer. To erase, simply backspace. For a negative sign, type a hyphen, and for a decimal point, type a period. You should apply the standard rules of rounding if the question asks for an approximate answer; otherwise, type in the exact answer. It is not necessary to reduce fractions to their lowest terms.

Anatomy of a GRE Numeric Entry Question

Before moving on to strategies, you should understand what a Numeric Entry question looks like. Consider the following example:

For the following question, write your answer in the box.

Solve the equation for x: $2(x - 3) + 9 = 4x - 7$

$x = \boxed{5}$

$2x - 6 + 9 = 4x - 7$
$2x + 3 = 4x - 7$
$2x = 10$

General Strategies for Numeric Entry Questions

You can apply many of the strategies discussed for Multiple-choice questions to Numeric Entry questions. In addition, keep the following in mind when answering this new question type:

- Read the questions carefully and be sure to provide the type of answer indicated. For example, if you are asked to type an answer to the nearest tenth, don't round your answer to the nearest whole number.

- If you are not asked to round or estimate your answer, type in an exact value. Make the necessary computations on your scratch paper—set up equations, draw pictures, and so on—to avoid making careless errors.

- You will not have any answer choices to guide you, so check your answer and make sure it is logical based on the information provided in the question.

… Part II: Preparing for the GRE General Test

Numeric Entry Practice Questions

1. If $3x + 4y = 17$ and $5x + 2y = 23$, what is the value of $x - y$?

2. If $-7 \leq x \leq 5$ and $-3 \leq y \leq 4$, what is the greatest possible value of $(y-x)(x+y)$?

3. A salesperson made a profit of $50 on the sale of a bicycle that cost the salesperson $180. What is the profit expressed as a percent of the salesperson's cost? Give your answer to the nearest tenth of a percent.

4. A rope 55 feet long is cut into two pieces. If one piece is 23 feet longer than the other, what is the length, in feet, of the shorter piece?

5. An integer from 10 through 99, inclusive, is to be chosen at random. What is the probability that the number chosen will have 0 as at least one digit? Give your answer as a simplified fraction.

Answers and Explanations

1. **The correct answer is 3.** In order to solve this system of equations, subtract the first equation from the second. The result is $2x - 2y = 6$. Factor out 2 to get $2(x - y) = 6$. Divide both sides by 2 to get $x - y = 3$.
2. **The correct answer is 99.** Because you are looking for the greatest value of $(y - x)(x + y)$, your goal is to make $x + y$ as big as possible and $y - x$ as big as possible. Therefore, from the range of values given, choose $x = 5$ and $y = 4$ to get $x + y = 9$, and $x = -7$ and $y = 4$ to get $y - x = 11$. The greatest value of $(y - x)(x + y)$ is $(9)(11) = 99$.

3. **The correct answer is 27.8.** One way to solve this problem is to set up a proportion, as follows:

   $50 is to $180 as x is to 100%

   $$\frac{50}{180} = \frac{x}{100}$$

   $180x = 5{,}000$

   $x = 27.777$, which should be rounded to 27.8, as per the instructions in the question.

4. **The correct answer is 16.** To solve this problem, set up an equation to determine the length of the shorter piece, substituting x for the unknown, shorter length:

   $$x + (x + 23) = 55$$
   $$2x + 23 = 55$$
   $$2x = 32$$
   $$x = 16$$

5. **The correct answer is $\frac{1}{10}$.** The first step in solving this problem is to determine how many integers between 10 and 99, inclusive, will have 0 as at least one digit, as follows:

   10, 20, 30, 40, 50, 60, 70, 80, 90

   There are 9 integers that will have 0 as at least one digit. Next, because there is a total of 90 numbers in the given range, the probability of choosing one of those 9 numbers is $\frac{9}{90}$, which simplifies to $\frac{1}{10}$.

What's Next?

If you require a review of the basic math concepts tested on the GRE, be sure to read Chapter 9, "Basic GRE Math Review," before you tackle the practice tests in Part IV.

8
GRE Verbal

CHAPTER GOALS

- Review the three types of GRE verbal questions: Sentence Equivalence, Reading Comprehension, and Text Completion.
- Study examples of each verbal question type.
- Learn specific strategies for answering each verbal question type.
- Practice answering sample GRE verbal questions.

The GRE Verbal section is designed to measure the skills required to carefully read and understand sentences and passages in standard written English. A GRE Verbal section includes questions of the following types: Sentence Equivalence, Reading Comprehension, and Text Completion. The questions appear in random order.

This chapter provides you with useful strategies and techniques, an overview of the question types, and a breakdown of the critical reading skills that will be tested. This chapter also includes some sample practice questions with explanations.

Sentence Equivalence Questions

The Sentence Equivalence questions on the GRE Verbal section are designed to test vocabulary in context as well as your ability to understand relationships among words and concepts. You should be able to answer many questions with only a general knowledge of vocabulary; however, some challenging questions might require you to make distinctions between more subtle meanings.

Questions in this section are composed of a sentence with one blank, followed by six answer choices. You must select the two choices that, when independently inserted in place of the blank, best fit the meaning of the sentence as a whole and produce two completed sentences that are alike in meaning. In other words, the two answer choices should be synonyms that perform equivalent roles in the sentence.

Because this section of the exam tests your ability to determine the relationship between words, both answer choices are equally important. There is no partial credit given if only one word is chosen or if only one choice is correct.

In general, the words that appear in Sentence Equivalence questions are limited to nouns, verbs, and adjectives. Answer choices will be either single words or short phrases. Some of the answer choices might be very similar to one another. Your job is to select the two best choices from among the six options. Keep in mind that a complete sentence is clear and concise, conveys a logical meaning, and is uniform in grammar and style.

> **NOTE**
>
> A strong vocabulary is the cornerstone of critical reading, and the best way to develop a large and varied vocabulary is to read extensively. In addition to reading more, you might want to review the Vocabulary List included as Appendix A at the end of this book.

Anatomy of a GRE Sentence Equivalence Question

Before moving on to the strategies that will help you to approach these questions with confidence, you should understand what a GRE Sentence Equivalence question looks like. Consider the following:

Question Stem It comes as no surprise that different cultures have certain behavioral norms; however, to an outsider, the specifics of these behaviors can often be _____.

Answer Choices
[A] explicit
[B] startling
[C] predictable
[D] unexpected
[E] derisive
[F] admirable

General Strategies for Sentence Equivalence Questions

The following are some general strategies that will help you to answer GRE Sentence Equivalence questions correctly:

- Carefully examine the context.
- Use the correct part of speech.
- Use prefixes, suffixes, roots, and cognates.
- Use connotation.
- Watch for idiom.
- Predict answer choices.
- Use the process of elimination.

Carefully Examine the Context

Use contextual clues within the sentence to give you an idea of the words or phrases that will best fit the blank. Pay attention to the logical flow of the sentence. You should quickly be able to pick up on the idea that the sentence is trying to convey, as well as any suggestions of tone or mood. Understanding the general meaning and nature of the sentence will help you to choose the most logical and stylistically appropriate answers.

When reading, pay attention to words or phrases in the structure of the sentence that indicate a relationship between ideas or tell you where the sentence is going. Consider the following examples:

> Due to recent studies touting the health benefits of regular exercise, health club memberships have increased dramatically in the past year.

The phrase "due to" implies a cause of action, or suggests that one thing provides evidence for another: *Recent studies promoting the health benefits of regular exercise have led to a dramatic increase in health club memberships.*

> **GRE Tip**
> Let the context of the sentences guide you. Make sure that you understand what is going on in the sentence, and pay attention to introductory and transition words and phrases in each sentence that might suggest a continuation, contrast, or comparison.

> Just as Traci's excellent grade in Physics is a result of her diligent study habits, so too is her medal-winning performance at the track meet proof of her adherence to a difficult training regime.

The phrase "just as" indicates a comparison between the first part of the sentence and the last part of the sentence: *Traci received a good grade in Physics because she studied hard, and she won a medal at the track meet because she trained hard.* The GRE might have left a blank for "adherence to" and asked you to select that phrase and one other with the same meaning from among the answer choices.

Transitional words often lead you to the correct answer. Even if you cannot immediately determine the best answers using context clues, you can still use transitional words to help you establish the nature and meaning of the sentence. Figure 8.1 shows some commonly used introductory and transitional words and phrases.

WORDS OR PHRASES THAT SUGGEST CONTINUATION	WORDS OR PHRASES THAT SUGGEST CONCLUSION
Furthermore Moreover In addition	Therefore Thus In other words

WORDS OR PHRASES THAT SUGGEST COMPARISON	WORDS OR PHRASES THAT SUGGEST CONTRAST	WORDS OR PHRASES THAT SUGGEST EVIDENCE
Likewise Similarly Just as Like	But Whereas Although Despite However	Because Since As a result of Due to

Figure 8.1 Common introductory and transitional words and phrases.

Use the Correct Part of Speech

It is important to remember that a single word can often be used interchangeably as a verb or a noun, or as a noun or an adjective, or it might simply have multiple definitions. For example, the word *bore* can be a:

- verb as in "to cause a loss of interest."
- verb as in "to drill a hole."
- verb as in the past tense of "to bear," which means to "support," "carry," or "have" something.
- noun meaning "a dull or boring person or thing."

The key to successfully answering a GRE Sentence Equivalence question will often be your ability to quickly switch between possible meanings and select a correct answer based upon your reactions to the answer choices.

Use Prefixes, Suffixes, Roots, and Cognates

Use your knowledge of *prefixes*, *suffixes*, and *roots* to help you to determine the relationship between the words that will best complete the sentence.

A *prefix* is a letter or group of letters attached to the front of a word to produce a derivative of that word. For example, the prefix *multi-* means "many," as in *multilingual*, which means "many languages."

A *suffix*, on the other hand, is a letter or group of letters added to the end of a word that serves to form a new word or functions as an inflectional ending. For example, the suffix "*-less*" means "without," as in *careless*.

Learn to recognize *roots*, or stems, that some words have in common. The root provides the basis from which certain words are derived. For example, the Latin root *gen* means "birth, class, or kin," as in *congenital*, which refers to a condition that is present at birth.

In addition, look for *cognates* from French, Spanish, or Italian (the modern versions of Latin) if you recognize them. Cognates are words in different languages that look or sound more or less the same and that have the same or similar meanings. For example, the word *amigo*, which means "friend" in Spanish, the word *ami*, which means "friend" in French, and the word *amicable*, which means "friendly" in English, all come from the Latin root word for "friend," *amicus*. These words are considered cognates.

Use Connotation

Each word in the English language expresses two things: a *definition* and a *connotation*. The definition of a word is its meaning. The connotation of a word is the positive, negative, or neutral feeling or emotion that the word suggests or that is associated with the word. While context is the part of a sentence that surrounds a particular word or passage and contributes to its meaning, *connotation* refers to the emotion that is suggested by the word itself. For example, the adjective *thrifty* has a positive connotation, whereas the adjective *cheap* has a negative connotation. The two words have similar definitions, but they have very different connotations. Using connotations might help you to determine the correct answer or at least eliminate a few wrong answers.

Watch for Idiom

Idiom refers to the common or everyday usage of a word or phrase. *Idiomatic usage* refers to the characteristic ways in which words or phrases are used in ordinary speech in writing. Learn to recognize idiomatic words and phrases because they might provide additional clues regarding the intended meaning of the sentence. Idiom is part of standard written English, and it must be considered when answering this type of GRE question. Ask yourself if the completed sentence "sounds" correct, and make sure that the sentence effectively combines words into phrases that express a logical idea. If you try inserting an answer choice, if any portion of the sentence becomes unclear, wordy, or awkward, eliminate that choice.

Predict Answer Choices

Before you look at the answer choices, try to predict a word or phrase that fits the blank based on the context. Remember that the incorrect answers have been specially designed to distract you. If you predict an answer before you look at the answer choices, you can begin to eliminate words and are less likely to get caught up in these confusing, incorrect choices. If your prediction matches one of the answer choices, it is most likely correct. Next, look for another word or phrase among the answer choices that is a synonym to your prediction, and that completes the sentence in the same way.

> **NOTE**
>
> Be careful to consider all of the choices before you confirm your answer, even if your predicted answer is among the choices. The difference between the best answer and the second-best answer is sometimes very subtle. When you think that you have the correct answer, read the entire sentence to yourself, using your choices in the blank. If the sentence makes sense, mark your answer on the computer screen and move on to the next question.

Use the Process of Elimination

This strategy is useful if you are unable to find the correct answer using any of the previously mentioned strategies. Look at each answer choice and determine whether you know something about each word or phrase, and use that information to eliminate answer choices that are clearly incorrect. The process of elimination can be time-consuming, so it should generally be saved for "last-ditch" efforts to select the correct answer. You will probably employ this strategy in conjunction with the others mentioned, eliminating answer choices that do not fit logically into the sentence.

Practice Sentence Equivalence Questions

Following are simulated GRE Sentence Equivalence questions with explanations.

Directions: For each question, select the two answer choices that, when used to complete the sentence, fit the meaning of the sentence as a whole and produce completed sentences that are alike in meaning.

1. Because the employee's motives were found to be _____, no disciplinary action will be taken against him for the mistake.
    - [A] absurd
    - [B] gratuitous
    - [C] improvised
    - [D] benign
    - [E] intentional
    - [F] harmless

2. Jennifer loves roses for the _____ of their petals and leaves, but I am most enthralled by their olfactory properties.
   - [A] aesthetics
   - [B] scent
   - [C] beauty
   - [D] usefulness
   - [E] enjoyment
   - [F] location

3. His penchant for learning history should prove to be _____ during his studies to become a history teacher.
   - [A] fickle
   - [B] practical
   - [C] exceptional
   - [D] futile
   - [E] advantageous
   - [F] gratuitous

4. We felt _____ once the committee issued its report that authenticated our actions.
   - [A] angered
   - [B] abused
   - [C] vindicated
   - [D] helpless
   - [E] ignorant
   - [F] justified

5. The political science of international relations is renowned for being a _____ subject; beyond a few governing principles, very little is graced with universal agreement.
   - [A] fractious
   - [B] divisive
   - [C] discerning
   - [D] lucrative
   - [E] pervasive
   - [F] significant

6. Before eating the main courses at a buffet, my mother likes to _____ her appetite with a garden salad.
   - [A] discern
   - [B] obscure
   - [C] whet
   - [D] obviate
   - [E] clear
   - [F] sharpen

7. Earth sheltering, the practice of using packed earth or soil to cover and insulate homes, is sometimes regarded with _____ by those who employ this technique, though practical considerations often temper their original enchantment.
   A disdain
   B enthrallment
   C apathy
   D agitation
   E fascination
   F disinterest

8. During a time of protracted economic duress, the wealthy can become poor, _____ both income from high-paying jobs and dividends earned on investments.
   A losing
   B regaining
   C denying
   D insuring
   E pursuing
   F forfeiting

9. Discussion of personal income is generally seen as _____ when among people who are not close friends, as it can easily be interpreted as either bragging, whining, or attempting to make the other party feel inferior.
   A complimentary
   B thoughtless
   C awkward
   D self-absorbed
   E haughty
   F inconsiderate

10. The elementary school students have a _____ understanding of fractions; some days they comprehend the math concepts, but other days they seem not to grasp them at all.
    A formidable
    B conducive
    C clear
    D tenuous
    E peripatetic
    F questionable

Answers and Explanations

1. **The best answer is D and F.** The context of the sentence indicates that the employee will not be disciplined as a result of his mistake, which suggests that the error was not intentional, and that the employee meant no harm. The words *benign* and *harmless* are synonyms, so they are the best choices based on the context of the sentence.
2. **The best answer is A and C.** Because the sentence indicates that Jennifer "loves roses," the words that best fit in the first blank should have a positive connotation. *Aesthetic* refers to "the appreciation of beauty," which makes the most sense in this sentence. Likewise, *beauty*, works well to complete the sentence in the same way.
3. **The best answer is B and E.** To have a "penchant" for something means to have a fondness for it. A fondness for history would be *practical* or helpful for future studies in the field. The word *advantageous* completes the sentence in the same way.
4. **The best answer is C and F.** *Vindicated* means "cleared of suspicion or doubt" and *authenticated* means "proved to be genuine." The context also indicates that the authors of the sentence would be *justified* in their beliefs because the committee authenticated their actions.
5. **The best answer is A and B.** While these two words are not true synonyms, they both provide a similar meaning for the overall sentence: something *fractious* is ornery or troublesome, while something *divisive* tends to divide people or cause division. Both fit with the latter half of the sentence, which points out the widespread lack of agreement in the field.
6. **The best answer is C and F.** The word *whet* means to "sharpen or stimulate," so it is the best choice based on the context. Likewise, *sharpen* is a synonym of *whet*, so it will complete the sentence in the same way.
7. **The best answer is B and E.** The sentence refers to "original enchantment," so the words should be synonyms of *enchantment*. Both *enthrallment* and *fascination* will complete the sentence in the same way.
8. **The best answer is A and F.** It makes sense that the wealthy would become poor by *losing* both income and dividends. Because *forfeiting* also implies *losing*, it will also be a good choice.
9. **The best answer is B and F.** Most of these choices would make sense in the context of the sentence. However, only one pair will yield two sentences with very similar meanings: *thoughtless* and *inconsiderate*, both of which draw attention to the way these actions might negatively influence others. *Inadvisable* is an accurate description, but focuses on pragmatics, rather than the negative social consequences. *Awkward* is also potentially accurate but has no mate among the choices, and it also fails to convey the potential offensiveness of the act. *Haughty* and *self-absorbed* do not make much sense in the context of the sentence.

10. **The best answer is D and F.** The words that best fit in the blank are defined by the information the follows the semicolon. *Tenuous* means "unsubstantial or vague," so it, along with *questionable*, is the best choice.

Reading Comprehension Questions

GRE Reading Comprehension questions are designed to measure your ability to read, understand, and analyze a written passage. Correctly answering a question requires you to recognize both what is stated and what is implied within the passage, and to establish the relationships and ideas expressed in the passage.

The GRE includes a balance of reading passages across different subject matter areas, such as humanities, social sciences, and natural sciences. Each passage will be approximately 150 words in length and will be followed by one to three questions. You should select the best possible answer, or combination of answers, for each question.

Anatomy of a GRE Reading Comprehension Question

Before you learn about strategies, you should understand what GRE Reading Comprehension questions look like. If you took the GRE prior to 2010, the current formats of these questions may be unfamiliar. In the revised GRE, Reading Comprehension questions have three formats:

1. Multiple-choice Questions—Select One Answer Choice
2. Multiple-choice Questions—Select One or More Answer Choices
3. Select-in-Passage Questions

While these variants add some complexity to the Reading Comprehension section, you will use essentially the same strategies to tackle questions in all three formats. Familiarity through practice will help you tremendously.

Multiple-choice Questions—Select One Answer Choice

These are the traditional multiple-choice questions with five answer choices, from which you must select one. Consider the following passage and sample question:

Passage Scientists know very little about the eating habits of our ancestors who lived over 2.5 million years ago. To solve this problem, scientists have started examining chimpanzees' hunting behavior and diet to find clues about our own prehistoric past. It is not difficult to determine why studying chimpanzees might be beneficial. Modern humans and chimpanzees are actually very closely related. Experts believe that chimpanzees share about 98.5 percent of our DNA sequence. If this is true, humans are more closely related to chimpanzees than they are to any other animal species.

Question Stem   The main purpose of the passage is to

Answer Choices
- Ⓐ explore biological and physiological similarities between humans and chimpanzees.
- Ⓑ examine the hunting behavior and diet of chimpanzees and compare them to human activity.
- Ⓒ discuss the health benefits of eating and hunting meat while simultaneously predicting the effect of this behavior on chimpanzee offspring.
- Ⓓ bring attention to the pioneering research of Dr. Jane Goodall in Tanzania.
- Ⓔ educate the public on the impact that tool use had in early human societies.

Multiple-choice Questions—Select One or More Answer Choices

These questions provide three answer choices and ask you to select all that are correct. One, two, or all three of the answer choices may be correct. To gain credit for these questions, you must select all the correct answers, and only those; there is no credit for partially correct answers. Consider the following passage and sample question:

Passage   Healthy knee joints contain healthy cartilage, a smooth tissue that covers the ends of the thigh and shin bones and the underside of the kneecap. Cartilage absorbs stress placed on the knee and allows the bones to move smoothly against one another. When cartilage becomes damaged, either through accident or illness, inflammation can occur. Bones can rub directly against each other, causing further damage. The result is stiffness and pain. Eventually, the patient can lose function and even basic mobility. At this point, the best option may be total knee replacement surgery. In this surgery, the ends of the thighbone and the shinbone and the underside of the kneecap are replaced with metal and plastic. These prosthetic surfaces mimic the function of cartilage and so allow for increased movement and decreased pain.

Question Stem   Which of the following statements about total knee replacement surgery is supported by the passage?
Select <u>all</u> statements that apply.

Answer Choices
[A] If successful, total knee replacement surgery restores full range of movement to damaged knees.
[B] Total knee replacement surgery is not always the best option following serious knee injury.
[C] Properly installed, a knee prosthesis is a permanent solution for chronic knee pain.

Select-in-Passage Questions

This kind of question asks you to click on the sentence in the passage that meets a certain description. To answer the question, you choose one of the sentences and click on it; clicking anywhere on the sentence will highlight it. Consider the following passage and sample question:

Passage   Thomas Malory's *Tale of Sir Tristram* is first and foremost a tale of knights-errant in the Arthurian world. Historically, knights-errant developed in the twelfth century because of a societal need to protect patrimony. Younger sons could not inherit family lands without seriously reducing the estate over successive generations. In fiction, if not in fact, these displaced young men became knights-errant: the young, adventurous knights who wander, seemingly homeless, throughout early medieval epics and tales. While scholarship refers primarily to men and tales of the late twelfth century, these texts form the basis for Malory's primary sources. Scholars have noted that chivalric ideals were taken extremely seriously in fifteenth-century England, even if they were beginning to have little relationship to the actual facts of political and social life. Malory's text is very much concerned with the exploration of these ideals; and the *Tale of Sir Tristram* focuses the reader's attention on the high point of Arthur's reign.

Question Stem   Select the sentence within the paragraph that explains the economic reasoning for denying estate inheritance to younger sons.

General Strategies for Reading Comprehension Questions

Regardless of the question format type, probably the biggest mistake that you could make is to read these passages as though you are studying for a college exam. The "open-book" aspect of the passage-based Reading Comprehension sections means that you should read in a way that helps your brain to work through the information efficiently. You should not read slowly and carefully as though you will have to remember the information for a long period of time. You should read loosely and dwell only on information that you are sure is important because you need it to answer a question. This type of reading should be very goal oriented; if the information you are looking at does not help to answer a question that the test writers find important, you should not linger over it. You will be helped by the length of Reading Comprehension passages in the current test format. Longer passages of 400 or 500 words have mostly been replaced by shorter passages of fewer than 200 words. Nevertheless, valuable time can still be lost if you dwell too long on individual passages.

Students who possess two key skills—paraphrasing and skimming—usually earn the best scores on this section. These skills, along with techniques on how to determine the main idea, read and answer the questions, and use the process of elimination, are discussed in more detail in the following sections.

> **GRE Tip**
> The computer-based test includes highlighted lines of text in place of line-number references for some questions. Be sure to read a line or two before and after the referenced text to guarantee you understand its context.

Paraphrase the Questions and Predict an Answer

After you have found the information in the passage that will provide the answer that you are looking for, try to answer the question in your mind. Put the question in your own words so that it makes more sense to you. Try to predict an answer for the question, and then skim the choices presented and look for your answer. You might have to be a little flexible to recognize it. If you can recognize a paraphrase of your predicted answer, select it. Developing this skill will help you to become more time efficient and will lead you to the correct answer more often than not.

Skim the Passage

Don't use context clues to help you determine the meaning of any unfamiliar terms the first time that you skim through a passage. When you come to a word or phrase that is unclear or unfamiliar, just read past it. There is a strong chance that you won't need to determine exactly what that one word or phrase means to answer the question(s) that accompany the passage. If you waste some of your precious time, you'll never get it back. With perseverance and practice, you will start to get comfortable with a less-than-perfect understanding of the passage.

Be sure to read actively. That is, think about things such as the tone and the purpose of the passage. This technique will help you to stay focused on the material and, ultimately, will allow you to select the best answer to the questions.

Determine the Main Idea

As you begin to read a passage, your first step should be to determine the main idea. This technique will help you to answer the "big picture" questions and assist you in locating information necessary to answer other question types. The main idea has three components:

- Topic ("What is the passage about?")
- Scope ("What aspect of the topic does the passage focus on?")
- Purpose ("Why did the author write the passage?")

If you can answer these three questions, you understand the main idea. Consider the following scenarios:

1. The world's tropical rain forests are being decimated at an alarming rate. Each day, thousands of acres of trees are destroyed in both developing and industrial countries. Nearly half of the world's species of plants and animals will be eliminated or severely threatened over the next 25 years due to this rapid deforestation. Clearly, it is imperative that something be done to curtail this rampant destruction of the rain forests.

2. Tropical rain forests are crucial to the health and welfare of the planet. Experts indicate that over 20 percent of the world's oxygen is produced by the Amazon rain forest alone. In addition, more than half of the world's estimated 10 million species of plants, animals, and insects live in the tropical rain forests. These plants and animals of the rain forest provide us with food, fuel wood, shelter, jobs, and medicines. Indigenous humans also inhabit the tropical rain forests.

The topic of both passages is tropical rain forests. However, the scope of each passage is very different. The first passage discusses destruction of the tropical rain forests, whereas the second passage introduces the diversity of the forests and indicates why the rain forests are important. The purpose of the first passage is a call to action, while the second passage is primarily informative.

As you read the passage for the main idea and for the author's purpose, avoid arguing with the author. If you disagree with any viewpoints expressed in a passage, do not let your personal opinions interfere with your selection of answer choices. In addition, you should not rely on any prior knowledge you might have about a particular topic. The questions will ask about information that is stated or implied in the passage, not information that you might recall about the topic being discussed.

The Reading Comprehension questions are not meant to test your knowledge about a particular subject. You should answer questions based only on the information presented in the passage, and not on any prior knowledge that you might have of the subject. You might be asked to draw a conclusion or make an inference, but you should do so based only on what the writer's words actually state or imply.

Read and Answer the Questions

Follow these tips as you read and answer the questions in the GRE Reading Comprehension section:

- Read the question and make sure that you understand it, paraphrasing if you need to.
- After you read the questions, take a moment to mentally summarize the main idea and the tone of the passage.

- Some of the questions on the GRE ask you to draw conclusions based on the information that you read. However, even these questions should be answered based on the information in the passage. There are always some strong hints or evidence that will lead you to an answer.

- Some of the questions contain references to specific lines of the passage. The trick for these questions is to read a little before and a little after the specific line that is mentioned. Remember that you must answer the questions based on the context of the passage, so be sure that you fully understand what that context is. At a minimum, read the entire sentence that contains the line that is referenced.

- One of the important skills rewarded by the GRE is the ability to sift through text and find the word or concept that you are looking for. This skill improves with practice. It is possible for an answer choice to be both true and wrong. The answer that you choose must respond correctly to the question being asked. Simply being true is not enough to make an answer correct. The best answer is always supported by details, inference, or tone.

> **NOTE**
>
> **Apply Logic**
> It is important that you know the difference between information that is stated directly in the passage, and inferences and assumptions. You might be asked questions based on factual information found in the reading passages. The reading passages might also include information about which you will be asked to make an inference.
>
> **Inference:** An inference is a conclusion based on what is stated in the passage. You can infer something about a person, place, or thing by reasoning through the descriptive language contained in the reading passage. In other words, the author's language implies that something is probably true.
>
> **Assumption:** An assumption, conversely, is unstated evidence. It is the missing link in an author's argument.

Use the Process of Elimination

Elimination is the process most test-takers use when answering exam questions. It is reliable but slow. However, it is still useful as a backup strategy for questions for which you cannot predict an answer or for which you find that your prediction is not a choice.

The process of elimination is a good tool, but it shouldn't be the only tool in your box. It can be hard to break the habit of always applying the process of elimination. You have likely developed this habit because on past exams you have been given too much time to answer questions. On the GRE, you will need to be more time efficient, which is why you should use the process of elimination only when other strategies fail to yield an answer. Eliminate any answer choices that are clearly incorrect, including answer choices that are outside the scope of the passage. Answer choices that fall outside the scope of the passage are very common in this section. For example, an answer choice might be too specific, too general, or have no relation to the content of the passage itself or for the question being asked.

Finally, always consider all of the choices before you confirm your answer, even if your predicted answer is among the choices. The difference between the best answer and the second-best answer is sometimes very subtle.

Reading Comprehension Question Content Types

Besides having different formats, GRE Reading Comprehension questions can also be divided into different content types based on the skill each one measures. The following subsections discuss the different types of Reading Comprehension questions that you are likely to encounter on the GRE. Specific approaches to each type are also included. You will begin to recognize the different types as you work through the sample questions and practice exams. The most common types measure these different skills:

- identify the main idea/primary purpose of a paragraph or passage
- locate a specific detail
- identify the purpose of a detail
- draw a conclusion/make an inference
- extrapolate from given information
- identify the structure of the passage
- identify facts or other data that would weaken the author's argument
- identify the answer choice that is *not* supported by the passage ("EXCEPT")

Main Idea/Primary Purpose

These questions can ask about the main idea of the whole passage or of a specific paragraph. They also often ask about the author's point of view or perspective and the intended audience. These questions might also ask you to determine the best title for the passage.

Questions that begin "The author of the passage would be most likely to agree with which of the following?" or "The primary purpose of the passage is to…" are main idea/primary purpose questions.

Strategy: Answer these questions according to your understanding of the three components of the main idea, which were listed previously (topic, scope, and purpose). It is also worth noting that the incorrect choices are usually either too broad or too narrow. You should eliminate the answer choices that focus on a specific part of the passage and also eliminate the answer choices that are too general and could describe other passages besides the one you are reading.

Specific Detail

These questions can be as basic as asking you about some fact that is easily found in the passage. Some questions even provide specific text from the passage.

Questions that begin "According to the author" or "According to the passage" might be specific detail questions.

Strategy: When you skim the passage, make sure that you establish the structure and purpose of the passage. If you have a clear idea of how the passage is organized, you should be able to refer quickly to the portion of the passage that contains the answer. Sometimes the answer choices are paraphrased, so don't just select the answers that contain words that appear in the passage. Make sure that the choice you select is responsive to the question being asked.

Purpose of Detail

These questions ask you to determine the author's purpose in mentioning a certain detail, or how a detail in the passage supports the main idea.

Questions that begin "The author mentions ―― in order to..." are most likely purpose of detail questions.

Strategy: Making a connection between the supporting details and the main idea of the passage helps you to answer these questions correctly. Think of the details as the building blocks of the author's thesis. This should provide you with some insight into why the author included these details in the passage. Refer specifically to any line references given in the questions.

Conclusion/Inference

These questions require you to put together information in the passage and use it as evidence for a conclusion. You have to find language in the passage that leads you to arrive at the inference that the question demands.

Questions that begin "According to the author" or "It can be inferred from the passage that..." might require you to locate language in the passage that supports a conclusion.

Strategy: Understanding the main idea of the passage, and particularly the author's tone, is key for these types of questions. Although you have to do a bit of thinking for these questions, you should be able to find very strong evidence for your answers. If you find yourself creating a long chain of reasoning and including information from outside the passage, stop and reconsider your selection.

Extrapolation

These questions ask you to go beyond the passage itself and find answers that are probably true based on what you know from the passage. They can be based on the author's tone or on detailed information in the passage. You are often required to reason by analogy or to discern relationships between a situation presented in the passage and other situations that might parallel those in the passage.

These questions might begin with "The author anticipates…" or "Which of the following best exemplifies —— as it is presented in the passage?"

Strategy: You need to be sensitive to any clues about the author's tone or attitude and any clues about how the characters in the passage feel. Eliminate any choices that are outside the scope of the passage. As with the inference questions, the GRE rewards short, strong connections between the passage and the correct answers.

Structure

These questions might ask you to describe the structure of the passage or how a particular detail functions within the passage as a whole.

Questions such as "The last paragraph performs which function?" or "Which of the following describes the organization of the passage?" are structure questions.

Strategy: You need to recognize the author's purpose in writing the passage and determine how the author develops the main thesis or argument. If the passage is purely informational, for example, the author might simply make a statement followed by some supporting details. Conversely, the author might offer comparisons between two different theories in order to persuade the reader that one theory is better. Pay attention to both the language and the connotation.

Weaken

These questions require you to select the answer choice that weakens the author's argument. Weakening does not necessarily mean to disprove completely; it merely means to make the conclusion of the argument somewhat less likely.

These questions take the form of "Which of the following, if true, would most weaken the author's argument in lines…?"

Strategy: The best approach to answering these questions correctly is to first make sure that you understand the author's argument or main point. To weaken the author's argument, you should usually attack the author's assumptions (unstated evidence). In some cases, the correct answer actually contradicts a statement made in the passage.

Except

Questions that require you to determine which answer choice is *not* supported by the passage fall into this category. For these questions, you will need to eliminate all but one of the possible answer choices.

These questions are often phrased as follows: "The author probably believes all of the following EXCEPT" or "All of the following are listed in the passage as examples of biodiversity EXCEPT."

Strategy: The best answer in these instances includes information that is not directly stated in the passage or cannot be inferred from information stated in the passage. For example, in the first sample question—"The author probably believes all of the following EXCEPT"—each incorrect answer choice will be something that the passage suggests the author does believe. Likewise, in the second sample question—"All of the following are listed in the passage as examples of biodiversity EXCEPT"—the incorrect answer choices will likely all be stated explicitly in the passage as examples of biodiversity. The process of elimination is a good strategy for EXCEPT questions.

Practice Reading Comprehension Questions

Following are two simulated GRE Reading Comprehension passages with questions and explanations.

Directions:

Multiple-choice Questions—Select One Answer Choice: These are the traditional multiple-choice questions with five answer choices from which you must select one.

Multiple-choice Questions—Select One or More Answer Choices: These questions provide three answer choices; select all that are correct.

Select-in-Passage: Choose the sentence in the passage that meets a certain description.

Questions 1 to 3 are based on the following passage.

Defined biologically, hair is primarily composed of keratin, a protein, which grows out through the skin from follicles deep within the dermis. This definition holds for all mammals. What sets humans apart is not in the hair, but in the follicle. Under the microscope, an individual human's hair follicles are anatomically indistinguishable, meaning that a hair follicle on your head is visually identical to one on your upper arm. Physiologically, however, the two follicles behave very differently. The first type, found in all mammals, produces terminal hair, the longer, darker, thicker hair generally found on the scalp, eyebrows, and eyelashes. The second type, particular to humans, produces the fine, unpigmented vellus hair found on most places of the human body, including the face and back. Vellus hair is usually very short and the follicles are not connected to sebaceous glands.

1. It can be inferred from the passage that
    - (A) mammals do not have sebaceous glands.
    - (B) animals such as monkeys cannot grow terminal hair.
    - (C) the hair of a horse is composed mainly of keratin.
    - (D) scientists cannot distinguish human hair from the hair of other mammals.
    - (E) terminal hair grows much faster than vellus hair.

2. The main purpose of the passage is to
   - Ⓐ introduce the idea that human hair is different from the hair of other mammals.
   - Ⓑ explain how terminal hair follicles change into vellus hair follicles.
   - Ⓒ describe the similarities between two types of human hair follicles.
   - Ⓓ compare the anatomy of human hair follicles with that of other types of hair follicles.
   - Ⓔ demonstrate that human hair growth contradicts the commonly held definition of biology.

3. Which of the following, if true, most weakens the author's argument that human hair is distinct from the hair of other mammals?
   - Ⓐ Scientific research shows that both vellus hair follicles and terminal hair follicles develop from a common follicle stem cell.
   - Ⓑ Keratin has been found to exist in cells other than hair cells.
   - Ⓒ Other animals, including insects and spiders, have been categorized as having hair-like filaments.
   - Ⓓ Vellus hair follicles have been identified on chimpanzees.
   - Ⓔ Hair follicle stem cells are also responsible for new skin growth after injury.

Questions 4 and 5 are based on the following passage.

By definition, tea is produced from the leaves of the *Camellia sinensis*, an evergreen plant grown mainly in the tropical and sub-tropical climates of Asia, though some varieties can also tolerate cooler, marine climates and are cultivated as far north as Great Britain and the coastal western United States. The most popular varieties of tea plant are the China and the Assam. The leaves of these plants are variously processed and blended with many different strains and fragrances to create the most popular tea varieties and flavors. While extracted oils, like bergamot, may be added to create signature flavors, such as Earl Grey, most recognized tea varieties are created through different methods of processing the tea leaves themselves. In fact, tea is traditionally classified based on the techniques with which it is produced and processed. For example, white teas are produced from wilted and unoxidized leaves. Oolongs are from wilted, bruised, and partially oxidized leaves. And black teas are produced from wilted, sometimes crushed, and fully oxidized leaves.

Consider each of the choices separately and select all that apply.

4. Which of these statements about teas does the information in this passage support?
   Select all such statements.
   A Tea plants can be cultivated across the northern hemisphere.
   B Tea leaves can be blended with various fragrances to create new flavors of tea.
   C Tea varieties are classified according to their individual processing method.

5. Select the sentence within the paragraph that identifies the most popular varieties of tea plants. *The most popular variety of tea plants are the China & the Assam.*

Answers and Explanations

1. **The best answer is C.** According to the passage, "hair is primarily composed of keratin, a protein, which grows out through the skin from follicles deep within the dermis. This definition holds for all mammals." Therefore, a horse has hair that is mainly composed of keratin. The other answer choices are not supported by the passage.

2. **The best answer is A.** The main purpose of this short passage is simply to introduce the idea that human hair is different from the hair of other mammals. Answer choices B, C, and D are too specific and beyond the scope of the passage. Answer choice E is not supported by information in the passage.

3. **The best answer is D.** The author argues that humans are unique in having vellus hair follicles in addition to terminal hair follicles. If another mammal were found also to have vellus hair follicles, humans would no longer be unique, and the author's argument would collapse. The other answer choices are outside the scope of the passage or are irrelevant to the author's argument.

4. **The best answer is B and C.** Choice B is implied in the author's assertion that the leaves of tea plants are blended with many different fragrances to create the most popular tea varieties and flavors. Choice C is supported by the statement that "tea is traditionally classified based on the techniques with which it is produced and processed." Therefore, both choices are supported by the passage, and both are necessary to receive credit for this question. Choice A refers to a far broader geographical area than is cited in the passage, and so is not supported as an answer choice.

5. **The best answer is:** ***The most popular varieties of tea plant are the China and the Assam.*** While the passages mentions many different tea varieties and flavors, this is the only sentence that specifically identifies varieties of tea plants. Therefore, it is the best answer choice.

Text Completion Questions

This question type includes a short passage, usually one or two sentences in length, containing one, two, or three numbered blanks. The blanks indicate that something has been omitted from the text. You are required to select words or phrases from corresponding columns of choices to fill all the blanks in a way that best completes the text.

For questions with one blank, you will be given five answer choices. Otherwise, you will be given a choice of three answers per blank, each of which functions independently. Selecting an answer choice for one blank does not affect your choice for the second or third blanks. A correct answer must include one choice for each blank. You will *not* be given partial credit.

Anatomy of a GRE Text Completion Question

Before moving on to strategies, you should understand what a Text Completion question looks like. Consider the following example:

Experts believe that humans have 10 trillion cells in their bodies that (i) _____ any number of essential genetic elements; scientists often marvel at what incredible (ii) _____ would ensue should the cells become jumbled or misunderstand their purpose.

Blank (i)	Blank (ii)
(A) govern	(D) order
(B) organize	(E) method
(C) dislocate	(F) chaos

General Strategies for Text Completion Questions

You can apply many of the strategies discussed for the other question types to Text Completion questions, particularly the strategies for Sentence Equivalence questions. In addition, keep the following things in mind when answering this new question type:

- The text is generally only one or two sentences, so read through it once to get a sense of the context.
- Pay attention to "clue" words in the text, such as transition words, that will help you to identify the structure of the text.
- Predict a word or phrase for the blanks based on the context clues.

- You do not have to complete the blanks in order; start with the blank that seems the most simple to fill, and then work on the others.
- Once you've made your selections, check the text for logic and grammar. Review Chapter 5, "Introduction to GRE Logic," Chapter 10, "Basic GRE Verbal Review," and Appendix A, "GRE Vocabulary List," for additional help.

Practice Text Completion Questions

Following are simulated GRE Text Completion questions with explanations.

<u>Directions:</u> The following passages each contain one to three blanks, indicating that something has been left out of the passage. Select one entry for each blank from the corresponding column of choices. Fill all of the blanks in the way that best completes the text.

1. Built over 50 years by two private companies and one city-owned corporation, the New York subway suffers from certain problems (i) _____ infrastructure, which has evolved over time rather than being (ii) _____ planned from the beginning.

Blank (i)	Blank (ii)
Ⓐ predictive of	Ⓓ querulously
Ⓑ relegated to	Ⓔ conscientiously
Ⓒ endemic to	Ⓕ sporadically

2. Primarily a fantasy writer, Ursula K. LeGuin is also a (i) _____ literary critic and philosophical commentator. Her fiction (ii) _____ this: Her stories are woven through with a wide range of complex themes, such as the importance of naming, the nature of identity, and courage in the face of the self, which draw from such (iii) _____ sources as the work of Carl Jung and the *Tao Te Ching*.

Blank (i)	Blank (ii)	Blank (iii)
Ⓐ conventional	Ⓓ stymies	Ⓖ relevant
Ⓑ recondite	Ⓔ pinpoints	Ⓗ eclectic
Ⓒ profound	Ⓕ underscores	Ⓘ vapid

3. Foucault turned the world of ideas on its head by boldly charging in to explore the subjects of prisons and sexuality, about which previous writers had done little more than (i) _____. But the *tour de*

force of this exploration was his habit of using these fields to draw (ii) _____ parallels to safe, sanitized everyday life.

Blank (i)	Blank (ii)
Ⓐ ruminate	Ⓓ trenchant
Ⓑ equivocate	Ⓔ presumptuous
Ⓒ politicize	Ⓕ probative

4. Computer technology has made checking dictionaries written in Chinese a much more (i) _____ task. Since the Chinese languages did not traditionally use a phonetic alphabet, looking up a word in a traditional dictionary could be incredibly (ii) _____. Computers have decreased that time remarkably.

Blank (i)	Blank (ii)
Ⓐ reliable	Ⓓ noisome
Ⓑ specious	Ⓔ noxious
Ⓒ accessible	Ⓕ vexatious

5. Sometimes the combination of several (i) _____ improvements creates an overall improvement much greater than would be predicted by merely adding the individual contributions together. For instance, Oliver Cromwell's New Model Army revealed the (ii) _____ relationship that could be achieved through organized discipline, regular pay, meritocracy, and, of course, (iii) _____ devotion to a Puritan cause.

Blank (i)	Blank (ii)	Blank (iii)
Ⓐ lackluster	Ⓓ salutary	Ⓖ sanctimonious
Ⓑ incremental	Ⓔ meretricious	Ⓗ saturnine
Ⓒ picayune	Ⓕ minatory	Ⓘ fervid

Answers and Explanations

1. **The best answers are C, *endemic to* and E, *conscientiously*.** Problems "endemic to" a certain situation are particularly characteristic of and commonly found within that situation. In this case, the infrastructure predates the problems, so they are not "predictive of" it, nor are they "relegated to," or placed into a minor role relating to, it. Good infrastructure systems are *conscientiously*, or thoroughly, planned from the beginning.

2. **The best answers are C, *profound*; E, *underscores*; and H, *eclectic*.** The point of the paragraph is that this author is an insightful thinker, and that her fiction reflects it, being inspired by diverse intellectual sources. *Profound* reflects the idea of insight. *Conventional* would not demonstrate insight, while *recondite* means "obscure," and is usually applied to things, rather than people. The second blank shows how her fiction illustrates, emphasizes, or *underscores* her insight; *stymies* means "bogs down," which does not apply, and *pinpoints* means "locates": The fiction is not used to locate her insight, it merely reflects it. The final blank should reflect the wide array of interesting intellectual works that share her themes: These are a broad selection, and therefore *eclectic*. *Relevant* would not work in the context of the sentence (relevant to what?), and *vapid* indicates a lack of substance, which one hopes does not apply to recognized philosophical works.
3. **The best answers are B, *equivocate* and D, *trenchant*.** The word *equivocate* means to "hesitate or dodge an issue, or to avoid discussion." *Trenchant* observations are insightful ones, precisely the sort that would make people uncomfortable with Foucault's comparisons. *Presumptuous* comparisons might be shocking, but would not constitute a *tour de force*.
4. **The best answers are C, *accessible* and F, *vexatious*.** The first sentence seems to be describing an improvement in the ease of use of Chinese dictionaries, while the second sentence states that formerly, these books were not easy to use. *Accessible*, or "convenient," is a fair way to describe a greatly simplified task, and *vexatious* or "vexing" is an apt description of a troublesome one.
5. **The best answers are B, *incremental*; D, *salutary*; and I, *fervid*.** The improvements themselves are all minor and build upon one another; in other words, they are *incremental*. However, together they create synergy, a healthful, or *salutary*, effect. Part of this effect was grounded on the troops' fanatical, *fervid*, devotion to their religious cause. *Lackluster* means "unimpressive," and *picayune* means "tiny"; both are a bit harsh for the kind of improvement referenced here. *Meretricious* means "vulgar or gaudy," and *minatory* means "threatening"; neither one describes the generally positive relationship. While the Puritans were not *saturnine*, or "gloomy," they may have seemed *sanctimonious*, or "morally fussy"; however, the real function of the sentence is to stress their fanatical, *fervid* devotion to their cause.

What's Next?

If you require a review of the rules that govern standard written English, be sure to read Chapter 10, "Basic GRE Verbal Review," before you tackle the practice tests in Part IV.

PART III

Content Area Review

CHAPTER **9**   BASIC GRE MATH REVIEW

CHAPTER **10**   BASIC GRE VERBAL REVIEW

9
Basic GRE Math Review

CHAPTER GOALS

- Review the math concepts tested on the GRE: numbers and operations, algebra and functions, geometry, word problems, and data analysis.
- Solve practice problems to test your mastery of each concept.

The GRE Quantitative questions are designed to measure your basic mathematical skills, as well as your ability to reason mathematically. You should be able to solve problems and apply relevant mathematics concepts in arithmetic, algebra, geometry, and data analysis. As you've already seen, the GRE Quantitative section includes Multiple-choice and Quantitative Comparison questions, as well as Numeric Entry questions. Each question type was covered previously in Chapter 7, "GRE Quantitative."

This chapter serves as a review of the mathematical concepts tested on the GRE. Familiarize yourself with the basic mathematical concepts included here and be able to apply them to a variety of math problems. You will have access to a calculator, but should not rely exclusively upon it. Recognize the underlying math concept being tested to more quickly answer the questions.

> **NOTE**
> The GRE is rarely a test of pure mathematics calculations; rather, it involves seeing relationships and patterns—a skill broadly applicable across all disciplines.

The following sections review the arithmetic concepts generally tested on the GRE.

Numbers and Operations

The GRE Quantitative section requires you to add, subtract, multiply, and divide whole numbers, fractions, and decimals. When performing these operations, be sure to keep track of negative signs and line up decimal points to eliminate careless mistakes. These questions might involve basic arithmetic operations, operations involving decimals, factoring, percents, ratios, proportions, sequences, number sets, number lines, absolute value, and prime numbers.

The Properties of Integers

The following are properties of integers commonly tested on the GRE:

- Integers include both positive and negative whole numbers.
- Zero is considered an integer.
- Consecutive integers follow one another and differ by 1. For example, 6, 7, 8, and 9 are consecutive integers.
- The value of a number does not change when multiplied by 1. For example, $13 \times 1 = 13$.

Real Numbers

The following are properties of real numbers commonly tested on the GRE:

- All real numbers correspond to points on the number line, as shown below:

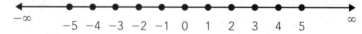

Figure 9.1 Number line.

- All real numbers except zero are either positive or negative. On a number line such as that shown above, numbers that correspond to points to the right of 0 are positive, and numbers that correspond to points to the left of 0 are negative.

- For any two numbers on the number line, the number to the left is always less than the number to the right.
- *Ordering* is the process of arranging numbers from smallest to greatest or from greatest to smallest. The symbol $>$ is used to represent "greater than," and the symbol $<$ is used to represent "less than." To represent "greater than or equal to," use the symbol $\geq$; to represent "less than or equal to," use the symbol $\leq$.
- If any number n lies between 0 and any positive number x on the number line, then $0 < n < x$; in other words, n is greater than 0 but less than x. If n is any number on the number line between 0 and any positive number x, including 0 and x, then $0 \leq n \leq x$. This means that n is greater than or equal to 0, and less than or equal to x.
- If any number n lies between 0 and any negative number x on the number line, then $-x < n < 0$; in other words, n is greater than $-x$ but less than 0. If n is any number on the number line between 0 and any negative number x, including 0 and $-x$, then $-x \leq n \leq 0$. This means that n is greater than or equal to $-x$, and less than or equal to 0.

Order of Operations (PEMDAS)

Following is a description of the correct order in which to perform mathematical operations. The acronym PEMDAS stands for Parentheses, Exponents, Multiplication, Division, Addition, Subtraction. It should help you to remember to do the operations in the correct order, as follows:

P—First, do the operations within the *parentheses*, if any.

E—Next, do the *exponents*, if any.

M/D—Next, do the *multiplication and/or division*, in order from left to right.

A/S—Next, do the *addition and/or subtraction*, in order from left to right.

For example, $\frac{2(4 + 1)^2 \times 3}{5} - 7$ would be solved in the following order:

$$= \frac{2(5)^2 \times 3}{5} - 7$$

$$= \frac{2(25) \times 3}{5} - 7$$

$$= \frac{50 \times 3}{5} - 7$$

$$= \frac{150}{5} - 7$$

$$= 30 - 7 = 23$$

Decimals

The following are properties of decimals that are commonly tested on the GRE:

- *Place value* refers to the value of a digit in a number relative to its position. Starting from the left of the decimal point, the values of the digits are ones, tens, hundreds, and so on. Starting to the right of the decimal point, the values of the digits are tenths, hundredths, thousandths, and so on.

- When *adding and subtracting decimals*, be sure to line up the decimal points.

$$\begin{array}{r} 236.78 \\ +113.21 \\ \hline 349.99 \end{array} \qquad \begin{array}{r} 78.90 \\ -23.42 \\ \hline 55.48 \end{array}$$

For example,

- When *multiplying decimals*, it is not necessary to line up the decimal points. Simply multiply the numbers, then count the total number of places to the right of the decimal points in the numbers being multiplied to determine placement of the decimal point in the product.

For example,
$$\begin{array}{r} 173.248 \\ \times \quad 0.35 \\ \hline 60.63680 \end{array}$$

- When *dividing decimals*, first move the decimal point in the divisor to the right until the divisor becomes an integer. Then move the decimal point in the dividend the same number of places.

    For example, $58.345 \div 3.21 = 5834.5 \div 321$. (The decimal point was moved two places to the right, in order to make the divisor an integer.)

- You can then perform the long division with the decimal point in the correct place in the quotient, as shown below:

$$\begin{array}{r} 18.17 \\ 321 \overline{\smash{)}5834.50} \\ -321 \\ \hline 2624 \\ -2568 \\ \hline 565 \\ -321 \\ \hline 2440 \\ -2247 \\ \hline 193 \end{array}$$

and so on

Fractions and Rational Numbers

The following are properties of fractions and rational numbers that are commonly tested on the GRE:

- The *reciprocal* of any number, n, is expressed as $\frac{1}{n}$. The product of a number and its reciprocal is always 1. For example, the reciprocal of 3 is $\frac{1}{3}$, and $3 \times \frac{1}{3} = \frac{3}{3}$, which is equivalent to 1. By the same token, the reciprocal of $\frac{1}{3}$ is $\frac{3}{1}$, or 3.

- To *change any fraction to a decimal*, divide the numerator by the denominator. For example, $\frac{3}{4}$ is equivalent to $3 \div 4$, or 0.75.

- Multiplying and dividing both the numerator and the denominator of a fraction by the same non-zero number will result in an *equivalent fraction*. For example, $\frac{1}{4} \times \frac{3}{3} = \frac{3}{12}$, which can be reduced to $\frac{1}{4}$. This is true because whenever the numerator and the denominator are the same, the value of the fraction is 1; $\frac{3}{3} = 1$.

- When *adding and subtracting like fractions*, add or subtract the numerators and write the sum or difference over the denominator. So, $\frac{1}{8} + \frac{2}{8} = \frac{3}{8}$, and $\frac{4}{7} - \frac{2}{7} = \frac{2}{7}$.

- To *simplify a fraction*, find a common factor of both the numerator and the denominator. For example, $\frac{12}{15}$ can be simplified into $\frac{4}{5}$ by dividing both the numerator and the denominator by the common factor 3.

- To *convert a mixed number to an improper fraction* (a fraction that includes both a whole number and a fraction, such as $3\frac{2}{5}$), multiply the whole number by the denominator in the fraction, add the result to the numerator, and place that value over the original denominator. For example, $3\frac{2}{5}$ is equivalent to $(3 \times 5) + 2$ over 5, or $\frac{17}{5}$.

- When *multiplying fractions*, multiply the numerators to get the numerator of the product, and multiply the denominators to get the denominator of the product. For example, $\frac{3}{5} \times \frac{7}{8} = \frac{21}{40}$.

- When *dividing fractions*, multiply the first fraction by the reciprocal of the second fraction. For example, $\frac{1}{3} \div \frac{1}{4} = \frac{1}{3} \times \frac{4}{1}$, which equals $\frac{4}{3}$, or $1\frac{1}{3}$.

- A *rational number* is a fraction whose numerator and denominator are both integers, and the denominator does not equal 0. Note that when the denominator is 0, the fraction is undefined; you cannot divide a number by 0.

Squares and Square Roots

The following are properties of squares and square roots that are commonly tested on the GRE:

- When a number is multiplied by itself, the product is called the *square* of the number. A square will always be a positive number. However, square roots can be negative; for example, when $x^2 = 25$, $x = 5$ or -5, because a negative times a negative yields a positive. The *principal square root* is the positive square root of any number.
- The principal square root of a number, n, is written as $\sqrt{n}$, or the non-negative value a that fulfills the expression $a^2 = n$. For example, "the principle square root of 5" is expressed as $\sqrt{5}$, and $(\sqrt{5})^2 = 5$.
- A number is considered a *perfect square* when the square root of that number is a whole number. For example, 25 is a perfect square because its principal square root is 5.

Exponents

The following are properties of exponents that are commonly tested on the GRE:

$$a^m \times a^n = a^{(m+n)}$$

- When multiplying the same base number raised to any power, add the exponents. For example, $3^2 \times 3^4 = 3^6$. Likewise, $3^6 = 3^2 \times 3^4$; $3^6 = 3^1 \times 3^5$; and $3^6 = 3^3 \times 3^3$.

$$(a^m)^n = a^{mn}$$

- When raising an exponential expression to a power, multiply the exponent and power. For example, $(3^2)^4 = 3^8$. Likewise, $3^8 = (3^2)^4$; $3^8 = (3^4)^2$; $3^8 = (3^1)^8$; and $3^8 = (3^8)^1$.

$$(ab)^m = a^m \times b^m$$

- When multiplying two different base numbers and raising the product to a power, the product is equivalent to raising each number to the power, and multiplying the exponential expressions. For example, $(3 \times 2)^2 = 3^2 \times 2^2$, which equals 9×4, or 36. Likewise, $3^2 \times 2^2 = (3 \times 2)^2$, or 6^2, which equals 36.

$$\left(\frac{a}{b}\right)^m = \frac{a^m}{b^m}$$

- When dividing two different base numbers and raising the quotient to a power, the quotient is equivalent to raising each number to the power, and dividing the exponential expressions. For example, $\left(\frac{2}{3}\right)^2 = \frac{2^2}{3^2}$, or $\frac{4}{9}$.

$a^0 = 1$, when $a \neq 0$

- When raising any number to the power of 0, the result is always 1.

$a^{-m} = \frac{1}{a^m}$, when $a \neq 0$

- When raising a number to a negative power, the result is equivalent to 1 over the number raised to the same positive power. For example, $3^{-2} = \frac{1}{3^2}$, or $\frac{1}{9}$.

Scientific Notation

When numbers are very large or very small, they are often expressed using *scientific notation*. To write a number in scientific notation, express it as a decimal greater than or equal to 1 but less than 10, multiplied by 10 raised to a power. The power depends on the number of places to the left or right that the decimal was moved.

For example, 667,000,000 written in scientific notation would be 6.67×10^8 because the decimal was moved 8 places to the left. The number 0.0000000298 written in scientific notation would be 2.98×10^{-8} because the decimal was moved 8 places to the right.

Mean, Median, and Mode

The following are properties of mean, median, and mode that are commonly tested on the GRE:

- The *arithmetic mean* is equivalent to the average of a series of numbers. Calculate the average by dividing the sum of all of the numbers in the series by the total count of numbers in the series. For example, a student received scores of 80%, 85%, and 90% on 3 math tests. The average score received by the student on those tests is 80 + 85 + 90 divided by 3, or 255 ÷ 3, which is 85%.
- The *median* is the middle value of a series of numbers when those numbers are in either ascending or descending order. In the series (2, 4, 6, 8, 10) the median is 6. To find the median in a data set with an even number of items, find the average of the middle two numbers. In the series (3, 4, 5, 6) the median is 4.5.
- The *mode* is the number that appears most frequently in a series of numbers. In the series (2, 3, 4, 5, 6, 3, 7) the mode is 3, because 3 appears twice in the series and the other numbers each appear only once in the series.

Ratio, Proportion, and Percent

The following are properties of ratios, proportions, and percents that are commonly tested on the GRE:

- A *ratio* expresses a mathematical comparison between two quantities. A ratio of 1 to 5, for example, is written as either $\frac{1}{5}$ or 1:5.

- When working with ratios, be sure to differentiate between part-to-part and part-to-whole ratios. In a part-to-part ratio, the elements being compared are parts of the whole. For example, if two components of a recipe are being compared to each other, it is a part-to-part ratio (2 cups of flour : 1 cup of sugar). Conversely, if one group of students is being compared to the entire class, it is a part-to-whole ratio (13 girls : 27 students).

- A *proportion* indicates that one ratio is equal to another ratio. For example, $\frac{1}{5} = \frac{x}{20}$ is a proportion. Consider the following example:

  If a 20% deposit that has been paid toward the purchase of a certain product is $150, how much more remains to be paid?

  If a 20% deposit equals $150, then 20% of the price of the product is $150. Calculate the price of the product, x, by setting up a proportion, as follows:

  $150 is to $x, as 20% is to 100%

  $$\frac{150}{x} = \frac{20}{100}; \text{ solve for } x$$
  $$20x = 15{,}000$$
  $$x = 750$$

  The total price of the product is $750, so $750 − $150, or $600, remains to be paid.

- A *percent* is a fraction whose denominator is 100. The fraction $\frac{25}{100}$ is equal to 25%, which can also be expressed as 0.25. To calculate the percent that one number is of another number, set up a ratio, as shown next:

  What percent of 40 is 5?

  5 is to 40 as x is to 100

  $$\frac{5}{40} = \frac{x}{100}$$

  Cross-multiply and solve for x:

  $$40x = 500$$
  $$x = \frac{500}{40} = 12.5$$

  5 is 12.5% of 40

- If a price is discounted by p percent, then the discounted price is $(100 - p)$ percent of the original price.

Absolute Value

Absolute value describes the distance of a number on the number line from 0, without considering which direction from 0 the number lies. Therefore, absolute value is always positive. For example, consider the distance from −10 to 0 on the number line and the distance from 0 to 10 on the number line; both distances equal 10 units.

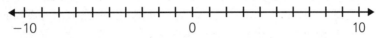

Figure 9.2 Absolute value.

The absolute value is indicated by enclosing a number within two vertical lines, as follows:

$|-3| = 3$ and $|3| = 3$

Simple Probability and Outcomes

Following are properties of probability and outcomes that are commonly tested on the GRE:

- *Probability* refers to the likelihood that an event will occur. For example, Jeff has three striped and four solid ties in his closet; therefore, he has a total of seven ties in his closet. He has three chances to grab a striped tie out of the seven total ties, because he has three striped ties. So, the probability that Jeff will grab a striped tie is 3 out of 7, which can also be expressed as 3:7 or $\frac{3}{7}$.

- Two specific events are considered independent if the *outcome* of one event has no effect on the outcome of the other event. For example, if you toss a coin, there is a 1 in 2, or $\frac{1}{2}$, chance that it will land on either heads or tails. If you toss the coin again, the outcome will be the same. To find the probability of two or more independent events occurring together, multiply the outcomes of the individual events. For example, the probability that both coin tosses will result in heads is $\frac{1}{2} \times \frac{1}{2}$, or $\frac{1}{4}$.

Factors and Multiples

The following are properties of factors and multiples that are commonly tested on the GRE:

- A *prime number* is any number that can be divided only by itself and 1. That is, 1 and the number itself are the only factors of a prime number. For example, 2, 3, 5, 7, and 11 are prime numbers. (Note that 2 is the only even prime number, since all other even numbers can be divided by 2.)

- *Factors* are all of the numbers that will divide evenly into one number. For example, 1, 2, 4, and 8 are all factors of 8.
- *Common factors* include all of the factors that two or more numbers share. For example, 1, 2, 4, and 8 are all factors of 8, and 1, 2, 3, and 6 are all factors of 6. Therefore, 8 and 6 have common factors of 1 and 2.
- *The Greatest Common Factor* (GCF) is the largest number that will divide evenly into any 2 or more numbers. For example, 1, 2, 4, and 8 are all factors of 8, and 1, 2, 3, and 6 are all factors of 6. Therefore, the Greatest Common Factor of 8 and 6 is 2.
- A number is a *multiple* of another number if it can be expressed as the product of that number and a second number. For example, $2 \times 3 = 6$, so 6 is a multiple of both 2 and 3.
- *Common multiples* include all of the multiples that two or more numbers share. For example,

    Multiples of 3 include $3 \times 4 = 12$; $3 \times 8 = 24$; $3 \times 12 = 36$.

    Multiples of 4 include $4 \times 3 = 12$; $4 \times 6 = 24$; $4 \times 9 = 36$.

    Therefore, 12, 24, and 36 are all common multiples of both 3 and 4.
- The *Least Common Multiple* (LCM) is the smallest number that any two or more numbers will divide evenly into. For example, the common multiples of 3 and 4 include 12, 24, and 36; 12 is the smallest multiple, and is, therefore, the Least Common Multiple of 3 and 4.
- The *Commutative Property of Multiplication* is expressed as $a \times b = b \times a$, or $ab = ba$. For example, $2 \times 3 = 3 \times 2$.
- The *Distributive Property of Multiplication* is expressed as $a(b + c) = ab + ac$. For example, $x(x + 3) = x^2 + 3x$.
- The *Associative Property of Multiplication* can be expressed as $(a \times b) \times c = a \times (b \times c)$. For example, $(2 \times 3) \times 4 = 2 \times (3 \times 4)$; they both equal 24.

Exercises: Numbers and Operations

These exercises are designed to help you apply the mathematics concepts just covered. They are not in GRE format, but should help you to identify your areas of strength and weakness.

Basic Operations

These questions will test your knowledge of operations using integers, real numbers, fractions, and decimals.

Chapter 9: Basic GRE Math Review **191**

Insert the correct operator in the blanks below.

1. 108 _/_ 9 = 12

2. 7 _/_ 2 = 3.5

3. $\frac{1}{4}$ _+_ $\frac{3}{8}$ = $\frac{5}{8}$

Answer the following questions.

4. When 5 consecutive odd integers, each greater than 34 are added, what is the smallest possible sum? 195
   35 + 37 + 39 + 41 + 43

5. What is the Lowest Common Denominator of $\frac{5}{8}$ and $\frac{3}{4}$? 8

Solve the following equations.

6. $\frac{(96-21)}{15} + 11 =$ _16_ $\frac{75}{15} = 5$

7. $3(27 + 2^{2^*} - 3) =$ _78_

8. $\frac{1}{3} + \frac{3}{7} =$ _16/21_

9. 231.2 − 198.7 = _32.5_

   231.2
   198.7
   32.5

10. $0.25 \times \frac{1}{5} =$ _1/20_

Squares and Square Roots

These questions will test your knowledge of operations using square roots.

Solve the following problems.

1. $7^2 =$ _49_

2. $\sqrt{36} \div \sqrt{4} =$ _3_

3. Express 3 × 3 as a square: _9 = 3^2_

4. $7^2 - 3^2 =$ _40_

5. $\sqrt{64} \times 2^2 =$ _32_

Exponents

These questions will test your knowledge of operations using exponents.

Fill in the blanks below with the correct number.

1. 2 raised to the power of __3__ = 8

2. 3^3 = __27__

3. $2^2 \times 2^3$ = __32__

4. 125 = $5^{\underline{3}}$

5. $(2^4)^2$ = __2^8 = 256__

Scientific Notation

These questions will test your knowledge of operations using scientific notation.

Fill in the blanks below with the correct number.

1. 423,700,000 = 4.237 × 10 to the power of __8__

2. 3.76×10^5 = __376,000__

3. $(2.50 \times 10^4) \div (1.25 \times 10^3)$ = __20__ (or 2×10^1)

4. 6.47×10^{-5} = __.0000647__

5. 9.832×10^4 = __98,320__

Mean, Median, and Mode

These questions will test your knowledge of operations involving mean, median, and mode.

Fill in the blanks below with the correct number.

1. Ann scored 88, 93, 84, and 99 on 4 tests. What is her mean test score?
   __91__

2. What is the mode of the data given below?

   7, 3, 6, 7, 5, 8, 9, 7

   __7__

3. What is the median of the data given below?

    8, 13, 9, 8, 15, 14, 10   10
    8 8 9 10 13 14 15

4. Jordan had 3 hits in his first 4 baseball games and 4 hits in his next 4 games. What is the average number of hits Jordan had in all of his games?
    3.5

5. What is the median of the data given below?

    80, 19, 82, 15, 72, 3   45.5
    3 15 19 72 80 82

Ratio, Proportion, and Percent

These questions will test your knowledge of operations involving ratio, proportion, and percent.

Answer the following questions.

1. __6__ is 30% of 20.

2. $\frac{x}{6} = \frac{39}{78}$ What is the value of x? 3

3. As an analyst for the Department of Natural Resources, you analyze samples of river water. A 2-liter sample of water contained about 24 of a particular organism and a 4-liter sample of water contained about 48 such organisms. At this rate, how many of the organisms would you expect to find in a 10-liter sample of water from the same river? 120

    $\frac{24 \text{ pts}}{2L} \cdot 10L$

4. If 20% of x equals 16, then $x = $ __80__
    $0.2x = 16$

5. Jim scored 95 points in 5 basketball games for his school. At this rate, how many points will he have scored by the end of the 12-game season?
    $\frac{95 \text{ pts}}{5 \text{ games}} \cdot 12 \text{ games} = 228 \text{ pts}$

Absolute Value

These questions will test your knowledge of operations involving absolute value.

Solve the following equations.

1. If $x = -8$, what is the value of $|x - 6|$? 14

2. Solve $|4x - 6| = 10$ for x. $|4x| = 10$
    $x = 2.5$ or -2.5 $|x| = \frac{5}{2}$

    $4x - 6 = 10$ and $4x - 6 = -6$
    $x = 4$ or $x = -1$

3. $|-15| \times |6| = $ __90__

4. Solve $|6x + 8| = |3x - 7|$ for x.

5. $\dfrac{-32}{|-8|} = \dfrac{-4}{\_\_\_}$

Simple Probability and Outcomes

These questions will test your knowledge of operations involving simple probability and outcomes.

Answer the following questions.

1. If you roll a single 6-sided die, what is the probability that you will roll an odd number?

2. A company knows that 2.5% of the CD players it makes are defective. If the company produces 300,000 CD players, how many will be defective?

3. When flipping a coin, what is the probability that it will land on tails four times in a row?

4. If the probability that Dave will go to class is 0.7, what is the probability that he will not go to class?

5. A bowl contains 20 marbles (8 blue, 6 red, 3 green, 2 yellow, and 1 orange). If you reach in and choose one marble at random, what is the probability that it will be red?

Factors and Multiples

These questions will test your knowledge of operations involving factors and multiples.

Answer the following questions.

1. A certain integer n is a multiple of both 5 and 9. Must n be a multiple of 15?

2. What are the common factors of 7 and 42?

3. What is the Greatest Common Factor of 48 and 72?

4. What is the Least Common Multiple of 30 and 40?

5. What is the greatest positive integer x such that 2^x is a factor of 12^{10}?

Chapter 9: Basic GRE Math Review **195**

Answers and Explanations

Basic Operations

1. In order for 12 to be the result of this operation, you must divide 108 by 9. Insert the ÷ symbol in the blank.

2. To reach an answer of 3.5, you must divide 7 by 2. Insert the ÷ symbol in the blank.

3. One way to solve this problem is to look for the Lowest Common Denominator (LCD). The smallest number that both 4 and 8 divide evenly into is 8, so the fraction $\frac{3}{8}$ does not need to be changed. The fraction $\frac{1}{4}$ is equivalent to $\frac{2}{8}$; $\frac{2}{8}$ plus $\frac{3}{8}$ equals $\frac{5}{8}$, so insert the + symbol in the blank.

4. To find the smallest possible sum, take the 5 consecutive odd integers that are the closest to 34 (remember, they all must be greater than 34). These numbers would be: 35, 37, 39, 41, and 43. Add them together: $35 + 37 + 39 + 41 + 43 = 195$.

5. The Lowest Common Denominator (LCD) is the smallest number into which all of the denominators will divide evenly. For this problem, you must find the smallest number into which 8 and 4 will divide evenly. Since 4 will divide evenly into 8 ($\frac{8}{4} = 2$), 8 is the LCD.

6. You must first complete the math within the parentheses ($96 - 21 = 75$). Next, do any multiplication or division in the problem, from left to right: $\frac{75}{15} = 5$. Finally, do any addition or subtraction in the problem, from left to right: $5 + 11 = 16$.

7. You must first do the operations within the parentheses ($27 + 2 - 3 = 26$). Now multiply the value from the parentheses by 3: $3 \times 26 = 78$.

8. You must first find the Lowest Common Denominator (LCD) for the two fractions involved. The denominators are 3 and 7. The smallest number into which both of these numbers can divide evenly is 21. Convert each denominator to 21 by multiplying $\frac{1}{3}$ by $\frac{7}{7}$ and $\frac{3}{7}$ by $\frac{3}{3}$. This gives you $\frac{7}{21} + \frac{9}{21}$, which equals $\frac{16}{21}$.

9. This is a simple subtraction problem. To solve this without a calculator, line up the decimal points and subtract (remembering to "borrow" and "carry"), as follows:

$$\begin{array}{r} 231.2 \\ -198.7 \\ \hline 32.5 \end{array}$$

10. First convert $\frac{1}{5}$ to its decimal equivalent, which is .2. Then multiply .25 by .2 to get .05. Another way to solve is to first convert .25 to its equivalent fraction, which is $\frac{1}{4}$. When multiplying the two fractions, you first multiply the numerators, and then the denominators, giving you $\frac{1}{20}$. Because this is equivalent to .05, either answer will be correct.

Squares and Square Roots

1. 7^2 simply means 7 times 7, which is 49.

2. Find the square roots before you do the division. The square root of 36 is 6, and the square root of 4 is 2. You then divide 6 by 2, which equals 3.

3. Three times 3 can be stated as "3 squared." The proper way to write this is 3^2.

4. Both numbers are raised to the power of 2 (they are squared.) You must first find these squares before you do your subtraction; 7 squared is 49, and 3 squared is 9. So, the answer is $49 - 9$, which equals 40.

5. This problem requires you to find a square root of a number as well as a number squared. The square root of 64 is 8 (64 is called a "perfect square" because its square root is a whole number), and 2 squared equals 4. The answer is 8 times 4, which is 32.

Exponents

1. The power that a number is raised to is equivalent to the number of times you multiply that number by itself: $2 \times 2 \times 2$ is equal to 8, so the answer is 2 raised to the power of 3 (2^3).

2. 3^3, or 3 to the third power, means you must multiply $3 \times 3 \times 3$, which equals 27.

Chapter 9: Basic GRE Math Review **197**

3. Remember to add the exponents when multiplying exponential values with the same base: $2^2 \times 2^3 = 2^5 = 32$.

4. $5^3 = 5 \times 5 \times 5$, which gives you 125.

5. When raising an exponent to another power, multiply the exponents ($4 \times 2 = 8$). So, the answer is 2^8, or 256.

Scientific Notation

1. When dealing with scientific notation, the power that 10 is raised to gives you the number of spaces you must move the decimal place, either to the right (for a positive value), or to the left (for a negative value). To turn 4.237 into 423,700,000, you must move the decimal place 8 spaces to the right. Therefore, 10 needs to be raised to the power of 8 (10^8).

2. To solve this problem, you must simply move the decimal point the number of times indicated by the power to which 10 is raised. Since you are given 10^5, you know that you must move the decimal point 5 spaces to the right, because the exponent is a positive number. This gives an answer of 376,000.

3. This problem can be set up as $\left(\frac{2.50}{1.25}\right) \times \left(\frac{10^4}{10^3}\right)$; $\frac{2.50}{1.25} = 2$. When dividing like bases, you subtract your exponents, so $10^4 \div 10^3 = 10^1$. You are left with 2×10^1. Since 10 to the first power is 10, the correct answer is 20.

4. You are given a negative value for the power to which 10 is raised (-5). This means that you must move the decimal point 5 spaces to the left to get the answer, which is .0000647.

5. Because 10 is raised to the fourth power, move the decimal point 4 places to the right to get 98,320.

Mean, Median, and Mode

1. The mean is the average, so simply add the test scores and divide by 4 (the total number of tests):

    $88 + 93 + 84 + 99 = 364$
    $364 \div 4 = 91$

2. The mode is the number that appears most frequently in a series of numbers. In this case, the mode is 7.

3. The median is the middle value in an ordered set of values. Therefore, the first step is to put the numbers in order, as follows:

   8, 8, 9, 10, 13, 14, 15

   As you can see, 10 is the middle value.

4. To calculate Jordan's average number of hits, first find his total number of hits:

   $3 \times 4 = 12$ and $4 \times 4 = 16$

   $12 + 16 = 28$

   Next, find the average:

   $28 \div 8 = 3.5$

5. The median is the middle value in an ordered set of values. Therefore, the first step is to put the numbers in order, as follows:

   3, 15, 19, 72, 80, 82

   Because the set includes an even number of values, take the average of the middle values:

   $19 + 72 = 91$
   $91 \div 2 = 45.5$

Ratio, Proportion, and Percent

1. To solve this problem, set up a proportion. You are looking for a number that is 30% of 20. The proportion will be $\frac{x}{20} = \frac{30}{100}$, because the unknown number is 30% of the whole (20). To solve, cross-multiply, leaving you with $100x = 600$. Divide both sides by 100, and you get the final answer: $x = 6$.

2. You are given a proportion to solve. To find the answer, cross-multiply, giving you $78x = 234$. Dividing both sides by 78 will give you the answer: $x = 3$.

3. To answer this question you must determine the ratio of organisms to liters of river water. The problem states that a 2-liter sample of water contained about 24 organisms and a 4-liter sample of water contained about 48 organisms. Upon closer examination of this information you will see that the ratio of organisms to water is the same in each sample. Therefore, you can set up a ratio using one sample:

   2 liters of water yields 24 organisms.

This can be expressed as 2 to 24, or 2:24, which can be reduced to 1:12. For every 1 liter of water you will see 12 organisms. Therefore, 10 liters of water will contain 120 organisms.

4. Set up a proportion. You are given that 20% of *x* is equal to 16, and you want to find the value of *x*. The proportion will look like this:

$$\frac{16}{x} = \frac{20}{100}$$

After cross-multiplying, you are left with $20x = 1,600$. After dividing both sides by 20, you have the answer: $x = 80$.

5. Use a proportion to solve this problem. You know that Jim scored 95 points in 5 games, and you want to find out how many points he will score in a total of 12 games. The proportion will look like this:

$$\frac{95}{5} = \frac{x}{12}$$

Cross-multiply to get $5x = 1,140$. Divide both sides by 5, and you get the answer: $x = 228$. If Jim continues to score at this rate, he will score a total of 228 points by the end of the season (12 games).

Absolute Value

1. First, substitute -8 for *x* and do the subtraction within the absolute value lines ($-8 - 6 = -14$). Absolute value is the numerical value of a real number without regard to its sign. Therefore, the absolute value of -14 is 14.

2. To solve this problem, set up two equations because *x* has two values:

   $4x - 6 = 10$, and $4x - 6 = -10$.
   Solve both for *x*.
   $4x = 16$, and $4x = -4$
   $x = 4$, and $x = -1$

3. In order to perform the multiplication in this problem, first find the absolute value of both numbers. The absolute values of -15 and 6 are 15 and 6, respectively. The answer is $15 \times 6 = 90$.

4. To find the possible answers for x in this problem, set up two equations:

$$6x + 8 = 3x - 7, \text{ and } 6x + 8 = -(3x - 7).$$

First, distribute the minus sign in the second equation, giving you $6x + 8 = -3x + 7$. Then solve both for x:

$$3x = -15, \text{ and } 9x = -1$$

$$x = -5, \text{ and } x = -\frac{1}{9}$$

5. First find the absolute value of the denominator. The absolute value of -8 is 8. Now perform the division: $-32 \div 8 = -4$.

Simple Probability and Outcomes

1. On a 6-sided die, there are 3 even numbers, and 3 odd numbers. Therefore, the probability that you will roll an odd number is 3 out of 6, or $\frac{3}{6}$. This can be reduced to $\frac{1}{2}$, or 0.5.

2. If 2.5% of the CD players produced by this company are defective, then the number of defective devices out of 300,000 can be determined by multiplication, as follows:

$$0.025 \times 300{,}000 = 7{,}500$$

3. When flipping a coin, there are only two possible outcomes: heads or tails. Therefore, each side has a probability of $\frac{1}{2}$, or .5, of landing facing up. The chances of the coin landing on tails four times in a row can be expressed as $\frac{1}{2} \times \frac{1}{2} \times \frac{1}{2} \times \frac{1}{2}$, or $\frac{1}{2^4} = \frac{1}{16}$.

4. The probability that Dave will go to class is 0.7, or 70%. Therefore, the probability that he will NOT go to class is $100\% - 70\%$, or 30%, which is equivalent to 0.3, so either answer will be correct.

5. There is a total of 20 marbles in the bowl, 6 of which are red. If one marble is selected at random, the probability that it will be red is $\frac{6}{20}$ $\left(\frac{\text{the number of red marbles}}{\text{the total number of marbles}}\right)$. This can be reduced to $\frac{3}{10}$.

Factors and Multiples

1. The first step in solving this problem is to find the Least Common Multiple (LCM) of 5 and 9. Because a multiple of 5 must have either a 5 or a 0 in the digits place, and 9 × 5 is the first multiple of 9 with a 5 in the digits place, 9 × 5 = 45 must be the LCM. Therefore, n must be a multiple of 15, since 45 (one possible value of n) is a multiple of 15.

2. Remember that common factors are all of the factors that two or more numbers share. The factors of 7 are 1 and 7 because 7 is a prime number. The factors of 42 include 1 (42 × 1 = 42) and 7 (6 × 7 = 42), so the common factors of 7 and 42 are 1 and 7.

3. The Greatest Common Factor (GCF) is the largest number that divides evenly into any two or more numbers. List the factors of 48 and 72, then select the largest factor that they have in common:

48	72
1	1
2	2
3	3
4	4
6	6
8	8
12	9
16	12
24	18
48	**24**
	36
	72

Based on this list, the GCF is 24.

4. The Least Common Multiple is the smallest number that any two or more numbers can divide evenly into. One way to solve this problem is to determine the multiples of 30, stopping at the first one that is also a multiple of 40:

$$30 \times 1 = 30$$
$$30 \times 2 = 60$$
$$30 \times 3 = 90$$
$$30 \times 4 = 120$$

Because 40 divides evenly into 120, 120 is the Least Common Multiple of 30 and 40.

5. To reach an answer, you first must find the smallest factors of 12, as follows:

$$12^{10} = (3 \times 2 \times 2)^{10}$$

Remember that the exponent applies to every value within the parentheses; thus, $(3 \times 2 \times 2)^{10} = 3^{10} \times 2^{10} \times 2^{10}$. When multiplying powers with the same base, you add the exponents:

$$3^{10} \times 2^{(10 + 10)} = (3^{10})(2^{20}); \ 2^{20} \text{ is a factor of } 12^{10}$$

Algebra and Functions

These questions might involve solving linear equations with one variable, polynomial equations and inequalities, factoring, and working with functions.

Linear Equations with One Variable

In a *linear equation with one variable*, the variable cannot have an exponent or be in the denominator of a fraction. An example of a linear equation is $2x + 13 = 43$. The GRE will most likely require you to solve for x in that equation. Do this by isolating x on the left side of the equation, as follows:

$$2x + 13 = 43$$
$$2x = 43 - 13$$
$$2x = 30$$
$$x = \frac{30}{2}, \text{ or } 15$$

Polynomial Operations and Factoring Simple Quadratic Expressions

Following are properties of polynomial operations and factoring simple quadratic expressions that are commonly tested on the GRE:

- A *polynomial* is the sum or difference of expressions such as $2x^2$ and $14x$. The most common polynomial takes the form of a simple quadratic expression, such as $2x^2 + 14x + 8$, with the terms in decreasing order of the exponents. The standard form of a simple quadratic expression is $ax^2 + bx + c$, where a, b, and c are whole numbers. When the terms include both a number and a variable, such as x, the number is called the *coefficient*. For example, in the expression $2x$, 2 is the coefficient of x.

- The GRE will often require you to evaluate, or solve a polynomial, by substituting a given value for the variable, as follows:

    For $x = -2$, $2x^2 + 14x + 8 = ?$

    Substitute -2 for x and solve:

    $$2(-2)^2 + 14(-2) + 8$$
    $$= 2(4) + (-28) + 8$$
    $$= 8 - 28 + 8 = -12$$

- You will also be required to add, subtract, multiply, and divide polynomials. To *add or subtract polynomials*, simply combine like terms, as in the following examples:

1. $(2x^2 + 14x + 8) + (3x^2 + 5x + 32)$
   $= 5x^2 + 19x + 40$

and

2. $(8x^2 + 11x + 23) - (7x^2 + 3x + 13)$
   $= x^2 + 8x + 10$

- To *multiply polynomials*, use the distributive property to multiply each term of one polynomial by each term of the other polynomial. Following are some examples:

  1. $(3x)(x^2 + 4x - 2)$
     $= (3x^3 + 12x^2 - 6x)$

  and

  2. $(2x^2 + 5x)(x - 3)$

Remember the *FOIL* Method whenever you see the type of multiplication in Example 2: multiply the *F*irst terms, then the *O*utside terms, then the *I*nside terms, then the *L*ast terms.

$(2x^2 + 5x)(x - 3) =$

*F*irst terms: $(2x^2)(x) = 2x^3$

*O*utside terms: $(2x^2)(-3) = -6x^2$

*I*nside terms: $(5x)(x) = 5x^2$

*L*ast terms: $(5x)(-3) = -15x$

Now put the terms in decreasing order:

$2x^3 + (-6x^2) + 5x^2 + (-15x)$
$= 2x^3 - x^2 - 15x$

Systems of Equations

The GRE will include questions that contain two equations and two unknowns. To solve a *system of equations* like this, follow the steps below:

$4x + 5y = 21$
$5x + 10y = 30$

If you multiply the top equation by -2, you will get:

$-8x - 10y = -42$
$5x + 10y = 30$

Now, you can add the two equations together.

$-8x - 10y + 5x + 10y = -42 + 30$
$-3x = -12$

Notice that the two *y*-terms cancel each other out. Solving for *x*, you get $x = 4$. Now, choose one of the original two equations, substitute 4 for *x*, and solve for *y*:

$$4(4) + 5y = 21$$
$$16 + 5y = 21$$
$$5y = 5$$
$$y = 1$$

Inequalities

Inequalities can usually be solved in much the same way equations are solved. For example, to solve for *x* in the inequality $2x > 8$, simply divide both sides by 2 to get $x > 4$.

When an inequality is multiplied by a negative number you must switch the sign. For example, follow these steps to solve for *x* in the inequality $-2x + 2 < 6$:

$$-2x + 2 < 6$$
$$-2x < 4$$
$$-x < 2$$
$$x > -2$$

Functions

A *function* is a set of ordered pairs in which no two of the ordered pairs have the same *x*-value. In a function, each input (*x*-value) has exactly one output (*y*-value). An example of this relationship would be $y = x^2$. Here, *y* is a function of *x* because for any value of *x*, there is exactly one value of *y*. However, *x* is not a function of *y* because for certain values of *y*, there is more than one value of *x* (if $y = 25$, then $x = 5$ and $x = -5$).

The *domain* of a function refers to the *x*-values, while the *range* of a function refers to the *y*-values. If the values in the domain correspond to more than one value in the range, the relation is not a function.

Consider the following example:

For the function $f(x) = x^2 - 3x$, what is the value of $f(5)$?

Solve this problem by substituting 5 for *x* wherever *x* appears in the function:

$$f(x) = x^2 - 3x$$
$$f(5) = (5)^2 - (3)(5)$$
$$f(5) = 25 - 15$$
$$f(5) = 10$$

Exercises: Algebra and Functions

These exercises are designed to help you apply the mathematics concepts just covered. They are not in GRE format, but should help you to identify your areas of strength and weakness.

Linear Equations with One Variable

These questions will test your knowledge of linear equations involving one variable.

Solve the following equations.

1. $3x - 17 = 46$. Solve for x.   21
   $3x = 63$
2. $\frac{x}{4} = -6$. Solve for x.   -24
3. If $x = 15$, then $4x - \underline{} = 42$ 18
   $60 - v = 42$
4. Two trains running on parallel tracks are 600 miles apart. One train is moving east at a speed of 90 mph, while the other is moving west at 75 mph. How long will it take for the two trains to pass each other?
   $90(x) + 75(x) = 600$ 3.63 hrs
5. $3(x - 4) = 5x - 20$. Solve for x.   4
   $3x - 12 = 5x - 20$
   $2x = 8$

Polynomial Operations and Factoring Simple Quadratic Equations

These questions will test your knowledge of operations involving polynomial operations and factoring simple quadratic equations.

Solve the following equations.

1. For $x = 4$, $3x^2 - 5x + 9 = \underline{37}$
   $48 - 20 + 9$
2. $(5x^3 + 3x - 12) - (2x^3 - 6x + 17) = \underline{3x^3 + 9x - 29}$
3. $(4x^2 + 2x)(x - 6) = \underline{4x^3 - 22x^2 - 12x}$
   $4x^3 - 24x^2 + 2x^2 - 12x$

Answer the following questions.

4. What are the solution sets for $x^2 + 2x - 48$?
   $(x + 8)(x - 6)$
5. $(x - 4)$ and $(2x + 3)$ are the solution sets for what equation?
   $2x^2 - 5x - 12$

Systems of Equations

These questions will test your knowledge of operations involving systems of equations.

Solve the following systems of equations.

1. $x - 2y = 14$
   $x - 4y = -8$

   [handwritten: $-x+2y=-14$, $x-4y=-8$, $-2y=-22$, $y=11$, $x-22=14$, $x=36$]

2. $4x - 2y = 6$
   $-6x + 5y = 7$

   [handwritten: $12x-6y=18$, $-12x+10y=14$, $4y=32$, $y=8$, $4x-16=6$, $x=5.5$]

3. $3x - y = 18$
   $4x = 24 - 6y$

   [handwritten: $18x=108+6y$, $4x=24-6y$, $22x=132$, $x=6$, $y=0$]

4. $8(y + x) = 12$
   $4x - 3y = -22$

   [handwritten: $8y+8x=12$, $6y-8x=44$, $14y=56$, $y=4$, $x=-2.5$]

5. $4x - y = 63$
   $3y + x = 6$

   [handwritten: $12x-3y=189$, $x+3y=6$, $13x=195$, $x=15$, $y=-3$]

Linear Inequalities with One Variable

These questions will test your knowledge of operations involving linear inequalities with one variable.

Answer the following questions.

? 1. For $-5 \leq x < 15$, $x = $ _____

2. For which values of x is $6x - 3 > 4x + 5$?

   [handwritten: $6x > 4x+8$, $2x > 8$, $x > 4$]

3. If $x = 7$, then is $3x + 7$ greater than or less than $5x - 6$?

   [handwritten: 28, 29, Less than]

4. For which values of x is $2x - 5 < -3x + 20$?

   [handwritten: $2x < -3x+25$, $5x < 25$, $x < 5$]

? 5. Solve for x: $-4 \leq x + 3 < 18$

   [handwritten: $-7 \leq x < 15$]

Functions

These questions will test your knowledge of operations involving functions.

Answer the following questions.

1. For the function $f(x) = x^2 - 4x + 8$, what is the value of $f(6)$?

   $36 - 24 + 8 = 20$

2. If $f(x) = x^2$, find $f(x + 1)$.

   $x^2 + 2x + 1$

3. If the function $f(x) = x + 2$, and the function $g(x) = 3x$, what is the function $g(f(x))$?

   $g(f(x)) = 3(x+2) = 3x + 6$

4. For the function $f(x) = \dfrac{x^4 - 3x}{2}$, what is the value of $f(2)$?

   5

5. For the function $f(x) = x^2 + x$, what is the value of $f(-5)$?

   20

Answers and Explanations

Linear Equations with One Variable

1. To solve this problem, first isolate the unknown number on one side. To do this, add 17 to both sides to get $3x = 63$. Next, divide both sides by 3 to isolate the x on the left side: $x = 21$.

2. To solve this problem, multiply both sides by 4 to get rid of the fraction and isolate the x on the left side: $x = -24$.

3. You are given the value of x, and asked to calculate a missing number in the equation. Because $x = 15$, then $4x = 60$. The equation is now $60 - $ (some number) $= 42$. The difference between 60 and 42 is 18.

4. This is a standard Rate × Time = Distance problem. Since the two trains start 600 miles apart, the combined distance traveled by both trains must equal 600. Using the $R \times T = D$ formula, you know that (Rate of Train 1 × Time of Train 1) + (Rate of Train 2 × Time of Train 2) = 600. You are given that the rate of travel is 90 mph for the first train and 75 mph for the second train, and the distance traveled is 600 miles; therefore, you must solve for T, as follows:

$$90T + 75T = 600$$

$$165T = 600$$

$$T = \text{(approximately) } 3.64 \text{ hours}$$

5. To solve this problem, first do the multiplication on the left side of the equation to get $3x - 12 = 5x - 20$. Next, put the like terms together. To do this, subtract $3x$ from both sides, and add 20 to both sides to get $8 = 2x$. Divide both sides by 2 to get $x = 4$.

Polynomial Operations and Factoring Simple Quadratic Equations

1. To solve the equation, substitute 4 for x:

    $3(4^2) - 5(4) + 9 =$

    $3(16) - 20 + 9 =$

    $48 - 20 + 9 = 37$

2. To add or subtract polynomials, combine like terms (remember to keep track of the negative signs!):

    $(5x^3 + 3x - 12) - (2x^3 - 6x + 17)$

    $(5x^3 - 2x^3) + (3x + 6x) - (17 - 12)$

    $3x^3 + 9x - 29$

3. Use the Distributive Property to multiply each term of one polynomial by each term of the other (remember to use the FOIL method).

    $(4x^2 + 2x)(x - 6)$

    First terms: $(4x^2)(x) = 4x^3$

    Outside terms: $(4x^2)(-6) = -24x^2$

    Inside terms: $(2x)(x) = 2x^2$

    Last terms: $(2x)(-6) = -12x$

    Now place the terms in decreasing order of the exponents:

    $4x^3 - 22x^2 - 12x$

4. Find two numbers whose product is -48 and sum is 2. 8 and -6 are the only possible numbers. Therefore, the solution sets are $(x - 6)$ and $(x + 8)$.

5. The solution sets are given, so multiply the two sets together to find the original equation, using the FOIL method:

    $(x - 4)(2x + 3)$

    $= 2x^2 + 3x - 8x - 12$

    $= 2x^2 - 5x - 12$

Systems of Equations

1. When solving systems of equations, the best thing to do first is to isolate one of the variables. In this problem, you can do so by changing the sign on the bottom equation:

   $$x - 2y = 14$$
   $$-x + 4y = 8$$

   Add the two equations together (note that the x terms cancel out):

   $$2y = 22$$
   $$y = 11$$

   Choose one of the original equations and substitute 11 in for y. Solve for x:

   $$x - 2(11) = 14$$
   $$x - 22 = 14$$
   $$x = 36$$

   It is a good idea to test your answers by substituting x and y values into both of the original equations.

2. This problem is a little trickier than the first, as you cannot simply change the sign of one of the equations to isolate one of the variables. In this situation, you have to make the coefficients the same through multiplication. Since you know that 4 and 6 both go into 12, use the x term. Multiply the top equation by 3, and the bottom by 2:

   $$12x - 6y = 18$$
   $$-12x + 10y = 14$$

   Add the two equations together (note that the x terms cancel out):

   $$4y = 32$$
   $$y = 8$$

   Finally, choose one of the original equations, substitute 8 for y, and solve for x.

   $$4x - 2(8) = 6$$
   $$4x - 16 = 6$$
   $$4x = 22$$
   $$x = \frac{22}{4}, \text{ or } \frac{11}{2}$$

3. The first step is rearranging the equations to align like terms:

    $3x - y = 18$

    $4x + 6y = 24$

   Multiply the top equation by 6 and add the equations:

   $$18x - 6y = 108$$
   $$\underline{4x + 6y = 24}$$
   $$22x = 132$$
   $$x = 6$$

   Now choose one of the original equations, substitute 6 in for x, and solve for y:

   $3(6) - y = 18$

   $18 - y = 18$

   $-y = 0$

   $y = 0$

4. First, distribute the 8 to get $8y + 8x = 12$. You can then multiply the second equation by -2 to isolate one of the variables, and rearrange the equations to line up the like terms:

   $8x + 8y = 12$

   $-8x + 6y = 44$

   Add the equations together (note that the x terms cancel out):

   $14y = 56$

   $y = 4$

   Now choose one of the original equations, substitute 4 for y, and solve for x.

   $8x + 8(4) = 12$

   $8x + 32 = 12$

   $8x = -20$

   $x = -\frac{20}{8}$

   $x = -\frac{5}{2}$

5. Line up the like terms in both equations:

   $4x - y = 63$

   $x + 3y = 6$

Multiply the top equation by 3 and add the equations:

$$12x - 3y = 189$$
$$x + 3y = 6$$

Note that the *y* terms cancel out:

$$13x = 195$$
$$x = 15$$

Now substitute 15 for *x* in one of the equations.

$$x + 3y = 6$$
$$15 + 3y = 6$$
$$3y = -9$$
$$y = -3$$

Linear Inequalities with One Variable

1. The inequality states that -5 is less than or equal to *x* AND *x* must be less than 15 ($\leq$ means "less than or equal to" and $<$ means "less than"). Therefore, *x* could be any number between and including -5 and 15.

2. Solve this problem algebraically, as follows:

   $$6x - 4x > 5 - (-3)$$
   $$2x > 8$$
   $$x > 4$$

   x must be greater than 4 for this inequality to be true.

3. The value of *x* is given, so substitute 7 for *x* and calculate the value of both sides:

   $$3(7) + 7 = 28 \text{ and } 5(7) - 6 = 29$$

   The less than sign ($<$) is used because $28 < 29$.

4. The first step in solving this problem is to isolate the variable on one side of the inequality:

   $$-5 - 20 < -3x - 2x$$
   $$-25 < -5x$$
   $$5 > x$$

   It is important to remember that when dealing with inequalities, multiplying or dividing by a negative number involves reversing the sign. In this case, both sides were divided by -5, so the sign changes from $<$ to $>$.

5. To solve this problem, subtract the 3 from both sides of the inequality:

$$-4 - 3 \leq x < 18 - 3$$
$$-7 \leq x < 15$$

x is greater than or equal to -7, and it is less than 15.

Functions

1. To solve, substitute 6 for x in the function:

    $f(6) = 6^2 - 4(6) + 8$
    $f(6) = 36 - 24 + 8$
    $f(6) = 20$

2. To solve, substitute $(x + 1)$ for x in the function:

    $f(x + 1) = (x + 1)^2$
    $(x + 1)(x + 1)$
    $x^2 + x + x + 1$
    $x^2 + 2x + 1$

3. The problem gives $g(x) = 3x$ and $f(x) = x + 2$ and asks for $g(f(x))$. The function $g(f(x))$ means that all of the x values in $g(x)$ are replaced with $f(x)$, as follows:

    $g(f(x)) = 3(f(x))$
    $g(f(x)) = 3(x + 2)$
    $g(f(x)) = 3x + 6$

4. To solve, substitute 2 for x in the function:

    $f(2) = \frac{2^4 - 3(2)}{2}$
    $f(2) = \frac{16 - 6}{2}$
    $f(2) = \frac{10}{2}$
    $f(2) = 5$

5. To solve, substitute -5 for x in the function:

    $f(-5) = (-5)^2 + (-5)$
    $f(-5) = 25 - 5$
    $f(-5) = 20$

Geometry

These questions might involve coordinate geometry; parallel and perpendicular lines; triangles, rectangles, and other polygons; circles; area, perimeter, volume, and angle measure in degrees.

Coordinate Geometry

The following are properties of coordinate geometry that are commonly tested on the GRE:

- The (x,y) *coordinate plane* is defined by two axes at right angles to each other. The horizontal axis is the *x*-axis, and the vertical axis is the *y*-axis.
- The *origin* is the point $(0,0)$, where the two axes intersect, as shown in the following figure:

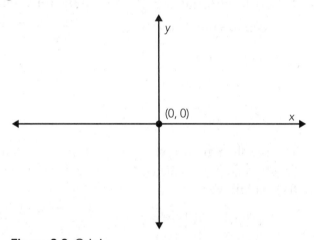

Figure 9.3 Origin.

- The *slope* of a line is calculated by taking the change in *y*-coordinates divided by the change in *x*-coordinates from two given points on a line. The formula for slope is $m = \frac{(y_2 - y_1)}{(x_2 - x_1)}$ where *m* is the slope and (x_1,y_1) and (x_2,y_2) are the two given points. For example, the slope of a line that contains the points $(3,6)$ and $(2,5)$ is equivalent to $\frac{(6-5)}{(3-2)}$, or $\frac{1}{1}$, which equals 1.
- A positive slope means that the graph of the line will go up and to the right. A negative slope means that the graph of the line will go down and to the right. A horizontal line has slope 0, while a vertical line has an undefined slope, because it never crosses the *y*-axis. The figure shown next illustrates the possible slopes of line *l*:

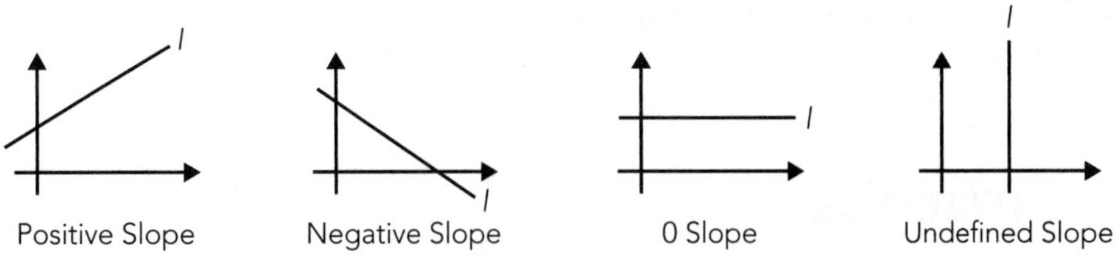

Positive Slope   Negative Slope   0 Slope   Undefined Slope

Figure 9.4 Different slopes.

> **NOTE**
> The slope of a vertical line is undefined because there is no change in the x-coordinate of any of the points on the line. This will make the denominator 0 in the formula for determining slope.

- The *slope-intercept (standard) form* of the equation of a line is $y = mx + b$, where m is the slope of the line and b is the y-intercept (that is, the point at which the graph of the line crosses the y-axis).
- Two lines are *parallel* if and only if they have the same slope. For example, the two lines with equations $2y = 6x + 7$ and $y = 3x - 14$ have the same slope (3).
- Two lines are *perpendicular* if and only if the slope of one of the lines is the negative reciprocal of the slope of the other line. In other words, if line *a* has a slope of 2, and line *b* has a slope of $-\frac{1}{2}$, the two lines are perpendicular.
- To find the distance between two points in the (x,y) coordinate plane, use the Distance Formula $\sqrt{([x_2 - x_1]^2 + [y_2 - y_1]^2)}$, where (x_1,y_1) and (x_2,y_2) are the two given points. For example, if you are given the points (2,3) and (4,5), you would set up the following equation to determine the distance between the two points:

$$\sqrt{(4-2)^2 + (5-3)^2}$$
$$= \sqrt{2^2 + 2^2}$$
$$= \sqrt{8} = 2\sqrt{2}$$

- To find the midpoint of a line given two points on the line, use the *Midpoint Formula* $\left(\frac{[x_1 + x_2]}{2}, \frac{[y_1 + y_2]}{2}\right)$. For example, you would set up the following equation to determine the midpoint of the line between the two points (2,3) and (4,5):

$$\frac{(2 + 4)}{2}$$
$$= \frac{6}{2} = 3;$$ the x-value of the midpoint is 3
$$\frac{(3 + 5)}{2}$$
$$= \frac{8}{2} = 4;$$ the y-value of the midpoint is 4

Therefore, the midpoint of the line between the points (2,3) and (4,5) is (3,4).

Triangles

The following are properties of triangles that are commonly tested on the GRE:

- In an *equilateral* triangle, all three sides have the same length, and each interior angle measures 60 degrees.
- In an *isosceles* triangle, two sides have the same length, and the angles opposite those sides are congruent.
- In a *right* triangle, one of the angles measures 90 degrees. The side opposite the right angle is the hypotenuse, and it is always the longest side.
- The sum of the interior angles in any triangle is always 180 degrees.
- The *perimeter* (P) *of a triangle* is the sum of the lengths of the sides.
- The *area* (A) *of a triangle* is equivalent to $\frac{1}{2}$(base)(height). The height is equal to the perpendicular distance from an angle to a side. Following are examples of the height of a given triangle:

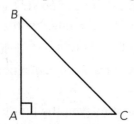

In right triangle *ABC*, the height is simply the distance from *A* to *B*.

Figure 9.5 Triangle height (right triangle).

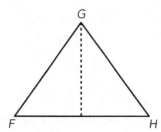

In triangle *FGH*, the height is the perpendicular line drawn from angle *G* to the midpoint of side *FH*. The height is **not** the distance from *F* to *G* or from *G* to *H*.

Figure 9.6 Triangle height.

- The *Pythagorean theorem* states that $c^2 = a^2 + b^2$, where *c* is the hypotenuse (the side opposite the right angle) of a right triangle and *a* and *b* are the two other sides of the triangle.

- The following are angle measures and side lengths for *Special Right Triangles*:

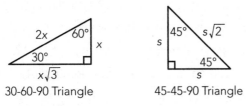

30-60-90 Triangle   45-45-90 Triangle

Figure 9.7 Special right triangles.

Quadrilaterals, Lines, Angles

The following are properties of quadrilaterals, lines, and angles that are commonly tested on the GRE:

- A *quadrilateral* is any four-sided object.
- In a *parallelogram*, the opposite sides are of equal length, and the opposite angles are equal, as shown below:

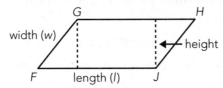

Figure 9.8 Parallelogram.

You can write the following equations for the parallelogram above:

$GH = FJ$

$GF = HJ$

$\angle F = \angle H$

$\angle G = \angle J$

- The *area* (A) *of a parallelogram* is equivalent to (base)(height). The *height* is equal to the perpendicular distance from an angle to a side. In the parallelogram shown above, the height is the distance from angle G to the bottom side, or base, or the distance from angle J to the top side, or base. The height is **not** the distance from G to F or the distance from H to J.
- A *rectangle* is a polygon, or multisided figure, with four sides (two sets of congruent, or equal sides) and four right angles, as shown below. All rectangles are parallelograms.

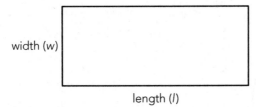

Figure 9.9 A rectangle.

- The sum of the angles in a rectangle is always 360 degrees, because a rectangle contains four 90-degree angles.
- The *perimeter* (P) *of both a parallelogram and a rectangle* is equivalent to $2l + 2w$, where l is the length and w is the width.
- The *area* (A) *of a rectangle* is equivalent to $(l)(w)$.
- The lengths of the diagonals of a rectangle are congruent, or equal in length. A *diagonal* is a straight line between opposite angles, as shown below:

Figure 9.10 Diagonals of a rectangle.

- A *square* is a special rectangle where all four sides are of equal length. All squares are rectangles.
- The length of each diagonal of a square is equivalent to the length of one side times $\sqrt{2}$. For example, a square with a side length of x would have diagonals equal to $x\sqrt{2}$.
- A *line* is generally understood to be a straight line.
- A *line segment* is the part of a line that lies between two points on the line.
- Two distinct lines are said to be *parallel* if they lie in the same plane and do not intersect.
- Two distinct lines are said to be *perpendicular* if their intersection creates right angles.
- When two parallel lines are cut by a *transversal*, each parallel line has four angles surrounding the intersection that are matched in measure and position with a counterpart at the other parallel line. The vertical (opposite) angles are congruent, and the adjacent angles are *supplementary* (they total 180°). See the figure below.

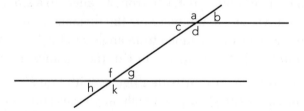

Figure 9.11 Parallel lines cut by a transversal.

- You can write the following equations regarding the parallel lines cut by a transversal shown:

    Vertical angles: $a = d = f = k$

    Vertical angles: $b = c = g = h$

    Supplementary angles: $a + b = 180°$

    Supplementary angles: $c + d = 180°$

    Supplementary angles: $f + g = 180°$

    Supplementary angles: $h + k = 180°$

- An *acute angle* is any angle less than 90 degrees.
- An *obtuse angle* is any angle that is greater than 90 degrees and less than 180 degrees.
- A *right angle* is an angle that measures exactly 90 degrees.
- Two angles are *complementary* if the sum of their measures is 90 degrees.

Some Other Polygons

The following are properties of other polygons (multisided objects) that are commonly tested on the GRE:

- A *pentagon* is a five-sided figure, as shown below.

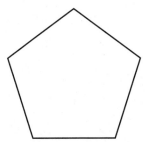

Figure 9.12 A pentagon.

- The sum of the interior angles of a pentagon is $(5 - 2)(180°)$, or $540°$.
- A *hexagon* is a six-sided figure, as shown below.

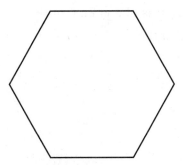

Figure 9.13 A hexagon.

- The sum of the interior angles of a hexagon is (6 − 2)(180°), or 720°.
- An *octagon* is an eight-sided figure, as shown below.

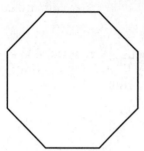

Figure 9.14 An octagon.

- The sum of the interior angles of an octagon is (8 − 2)(180°), or 1,080°.

Circles

The following are properties of circles that are commonly tested on the GRE:

- The *radius (r) of a circle* is the distance from the center of the circle to any point on the circle.
- The *diameter (d) of a circle* is twice the radius.

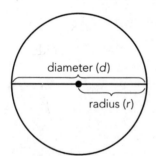

Figure 9.15 A circle.

- The *area (A) of a circle* is equivalent to πr^2. So, the area of a circle with a radius of 3 is $3^2\pi$, or 9π.
- The *circumference (C) of a circle* is equivalent to $2\pi r$ or πd. So, the circumference of a circle with a radius of 3 is $2\pi 3$, or 6π.
- The *equation of a circle* centered at the point (h,k) is $(x - h)^2 + (y - k)^2 = r^2$, where r is the radius of the circle.
- The complete *arc* of a circle has 360°.

Three-Dimensional Figures

The following are properties of three-dimensional figures that are commonly tested on the GRE:

- The formula for the *volume* (V) of a rectangular solid is V = *lwh*, where *l* = length, *w* = width, and *h* = height, as shown in the following figure:

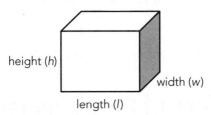

Figure 9.16 A rectangular solid.

- The *surface area* of a rectangular solid is the sum of the area (*l* × *w*) of each of the six faces of the solid. Think of each face as a square or a rectangle.

Exercises: Geometry

These exercises are designed to help you apply the mathematics concepts just covered. They are not in GRE format, but should help you to identify your areas of strength and weakness.

Coordinate Geometry

These questions will test your knowledge of operations involving the equation and the slope of a line and distance and midpoint formulas.

Answer the following questions.

1. What is the y-intercept of the line with the equation 2y = 4x + 6?
   3
2. What is the slope of the line with the equation 3y = −2x + 5?
   −2/3
3. What is the slope of the line x = 4?
   Undefined
4. What is the equation of a line parallel to y = 4x − 12 that crosses the y-axis at 3?
   y = 4x + 3
5. What is the equation of a line perpendicular to 3x = 2 − y with the y-intercept 8?
   y = ⅓x + 8

6. What is the distance between the points (3,−4) and (9,4)?

7. Solve for y if the distance between the two points (2,8) and (−6,y) is 17.

8. What is the midpoint between the two points (12,5) and (10,−7)?

9. Solve for x if the midpoint between the two points (x,1) and (−2, −3) is (5,−1).

10. What is the distance between the points (0,5) and (5,0)?

Properties and Relations of Plane Figures

These questions will test your knowledge of operations involving plane figures.

Answer the following questions.

1. What is the hypotenuse of a right triangle with a base of 9 cm and an area of 54 cm²?

2. What is the area of a circle with a circumference of 14π inches?

3. If one of the angles of a parallelogram measures 35°, what is the sum of the remaining angles?

4. A trapezoid has one base of 8 ft, a height of 3 ft, and an area of 30 ft². What is the length of the other base?

5. A polygon with four sides and four right angles has one side of 6 mm. If the area of the polygon is 42 mm², would the polygon be considered a square or a rectangle?

Angles, Parallel Lines, and Perpendicular Lines

These questions will test your knowledge of operations involving angles, parallel lines, and perpendicular lines.

Answer the following questions.

1. What is the measure of the angle that is supplementary to a 40° angle?

2. What is the measure of the angle that is complementary to a 25° angle?

3. In the figure below, line n is parallel to line m, and line p is parallel to line o. What is the measure of angle a?

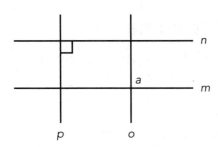

4. In the figure below, line x is parallel to line y. What is the measure of angle a? 137°

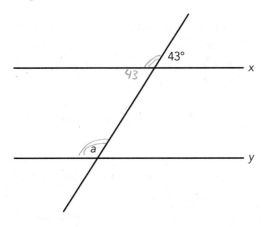

5. In the figure below, line t is parallel to line u, and line v is perpendicular to line u. What is the measure of angle a? 55°

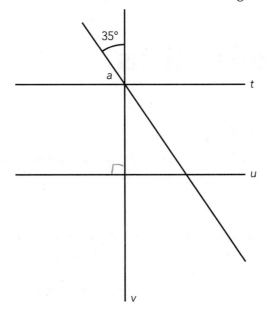

Perimeter, Area, and Volume

These questions will test your knowledge of operations involving perimeter, area, and volume.

Answer the following questions.

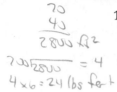

1. You are applying fertilizer to your backyard. The rectangular yard measures 40 feet wide and 70 feet long. You use 6 pounds of fertilizer to treat 700 square feet. The fertilizer comes in 8-pound bags. How many bags of fertilizer will you need to complete the job?

2. John is building a circular fence around his circular pool. The pool is 26 feet in diameter. If John wants to have 2 feet of space between the edge of the pool and the fence, what is the approximate area that will be encompassed by the fence? ($\pi = 3.14$)

3. Tiffany inflates a beach ball. If the diameter of the ball is 0.6 m, what is its volume?

4. A cylindrical can of pineapple juice contains 350 cm³ of liquid. If the can is $\frac{14}{\pi}$ cm tall, what is its diameter?

5. If a square prism has an edge of 5 inches, what is the volume of the square?

Answers and Explanations

Coordinate Geometry

1. First, rearrange the equation into the slope-intercept form by isolating y on the left side; divide both sides by 2:

   $$y = 2x + 3$$

   You know that in the slope intercept formula, $y = mx + b$, b is the y-intercept. Because $b = 3$, the correct answer is 3.

2. Rearrange the equation into the slope intercept form by isolating y on the left side; divide both sides by 3:

   $$y = -\frac{2}{3}x + \frac{5}{3}$$

You know that in the slope intercept formula, $y = mx + b$, m is the slope. Because $m = -\frac{2}{3}$, the correct answer is $-\frac{2}{3}$.

3. This equation represents a vertical line; the y-intercept is 0, so the line is parallel to the y-axis. A vertical line has an undefined slope, because the denominator is 0.

4. For two lines to be parallel, their slopes must be equal; therefore, in the standard equation $y = mx + b$, $m = 4$. You are given that the line crosses the y-axis at 3, so the y-intercept (b) must be 3. If you substitute 4 for m and 3 for b in the standard equation, you get $y = 4x + 3$.

5. First, rearrange the equation into slope-intercept form, by subtracting $3x$ and $-y$ from both sides:

$$y = -3x + 2$$

For two lines to be perpendicular, their slopes must be negative reciprocals. The negative reciprocal of -3 is $\frac{1}{3}$. The problem also states that the perpendicular line has a y-intercept of 8. If you substitute $\frac{1}{3}$ for m and 8 for b in the standard equation, you get $y = \frac{1}{3}x + 8$.

6. Use the Distance Formula to solve this problem. Substitute the given values of x and y into the formula to solve for the distance, as follows:

$$\text{Distance} = \sqrt{(3-9)^2 + (-4-4)^2}$$
$$\text{Distance} = \sqrt{(-6)^2 + (-8)^2}$$
$$\text{Distance} = \sqrt{36 + 64}$$
$$\text{Distance} = \sqrt{100}$$
$$\text{Distance} = 10$$

7. Use the Distance Formula to solve this problem. Because you are given the distance between the points, your equation will look like this:

$$17 = \sqrt{(-6-2)^2 + (y_2 - 8)^2}$$

Square both sides and solve for y_2:

$$289 = (-8)^2 + (y_2 - 8)^2$$
$$289 = (64) + (y_2 - 8)^2$$
$$225 = (y_2 - 8)^2$$
$$15 = y_2 - 8$$
$$23 = y_2$$

8. Use the midpoint equation to solve this problem. First solve for the x-coordinate, which is half the distance between 12 and 10:

$$x_m = \frac{(x_2 + x_1)}{2}$$

$$x_m = \frac{(10 + 12)}{2}$$

$$x_m = \frac{22}{2}$$

$$x_m = 11$$

Do the same for y_m, which is half the distance between 5 and −7:

$$y_m = \frac{(y_2 + y_1)}{2}$$

$$y_m = \frac{(5 + -7)}{2}$$

$$y_m = \frac{-2}{2}$$

$$y_m = -1$$

Therefore, the midpoint is (11,−1)

9. You only have to solve for the x-coordinate because you are given the y-coordinate:

$$x_m = \frac{(x_2 + x_1)}{2}$$

$$5 = \frac{(-2 + x_1)}{2}$$

$$10 = -2 + x_1$$

$$12 = x_1$$

10. Use the Distance Formula to solve this problem. Substitute the given values of x and y into the formula to solve for the distance, as follows:

$$\text{Distance} = \sqrt{(x_2 - x_1)^2 + (y_2 - y_1)^2}$$
$$\text{Distance} = \sqrt{(5 - 0)^2 + (0 - 5)^2}$$
$$\text{Distance} = \sqrt{(5)^2 + (5)^2}$$
$$\text{Distance} = \sqrt{(25 + 25)}$$
$$\text{Distance} = \sqrt{50}, \text{ which can be reduced to } 5\sqrt{2}$$

Properties and Relations of Plane Figures

1. The area of a triangle and the length of one of the legs of a right triangle are given. However, you need the length of both legs to use the Pythagorean theorem to determine the hypotenuse. Since you have the

area, start there. For a triangle, A = $\frac{1}{2}$ (base) × (height). You are given the base and area, so solve for the height:

$$54 = \frac{1}{2}(9) \times (\text{height})$$
$$\text{height} = 12$$

Now you know the lengths of the two legs of the right triangle and can use the Pythagorean theorem ($a^2 + b^2 = c^2$) to determine the hypotenuse:

$$9^2 + 12^2 = c^2$$
$$81 + 144 = c^2$$
$$225 = c^2$$
$$15 = c$$

2. The equation for the area of a circle is A = πr^2. The equation for the circumference of a circle is $C = 2\pi r$. Since you are given the circumference, you can use that to find the radius, r, and then use the radius to find the area:

$$14\pi = 2\pi r$$
$$14 = 2r$$
$$r = 7$$

Now substitute r into the equation for area:

$$\text{Area} = \pi(7^2)$$
$$\text{Area} = 49\pi$$

3. A parallelogram's angles add up to 360°. So simply subtract 35° from 360°: 360° − 35° = 325°.

4. The equation for the area of a trapezoid is A = $\frac{1}{2}$ (base$_1$ + base$_2$) (height). Substitute the given variables into the equation and solve for the missing base:

$$30 = \frac{1}{2}(8 + \text{base}_2)(3)$$
$$20 = (8 + \text{base}_2)$$
$$\text{base}_2 = 12 \text{ ft}$$

5. A square is a special kind of rectangle. All of its sides are equal in length. Since the area of a rectangle is area = $l \times w$, the area of a square would be area = s^2 (side squared) because length and width are equal. For this problem, the given side is 6 mm. If the figure were a square, the area would be 36 mm². However, the area is said to be 42 mm². Therefore the shape is a rectangle and not a square.

Angles, Parallel Lines, and Perpendicular Lines

1. Supplementary angles add together to total 180°. Therefore, the supplementary angle to a 40° angle is a 140° angle.

2. Complementary angles add together to total 90°. Therefore, the complementary angle to a 25° angle is a 65° angle.

3. The answer is 90°. You are given that the angle formed by the intersection of line p and line n is a right angle, which is 90°. Since line o is parallel to line p, it will make the same angles as any line crossing line p. The same rule applies for line m and line n. Therefore, all of the angles on the diagram are equal to 90°.

4. The answer is 137°. The transversal crosses two parallel lines, so the angles made at the intersections will be identical. 43° corresponds to the supplementary angle of a on line y. Since 43° and a are supplementary angles, they must add up to 180°. Therefore, the answer is 137°.

5. The answer is 55°. Since line v is perpendicular to line t, it forms four right angles. Another line, which is unnamed in the diagram, dissects one of the right angles. Angle a is one side and 35° is the given measurement for the other side. These two angles are complementary because they must add up to 90°: 35° + 55° = 90°.

Perimeter, Area, and Volume

1. The question asks you to determine the number of bags of fertilizer that will cover your rectangular backyard. According to information in the problem, 6 pounds of fertilizer can cover 700 square feet. Calculate the area of the backyard. The area of a rectangle is determined by multiplying the length (70 feet) by the width (40 feet):

    70 × 40 = 2,800

    The area of the backyard is 2,800 square feet. The problem states that 6 pounds of fertilizer can cover 700 square feet. Calculate the number of times that 700 will go into 2,800:

    2,800 ÷ 700 = 4

    You will need 4 times 6 pounds of fertilizer to treat 2,800 square feet:

    4 × 6 = 24

Since you will need a total of 24 pounds of fertilizer to treat the backyard, and each bag of fertilizer weighs 8 pounds, divide 24 by 8 to find the number of bags of fertilizer you will need:

$24 \div 8 = 3$

You will need 3 bags of fertilizer to treat a backyard that measures 2,800 square feet.

2. If the pool has a diameter of 26 feet, and the fence needs to be 2 feet away from the edge of the pool, the diameter of the area enclosed by the fence would be 26 + 2 + 2 = 30 feet. Draw a picture to help visualize the problem:

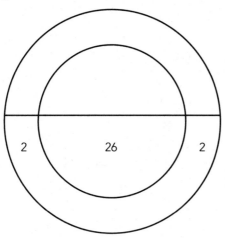

The area of a circle is πr^2. The radius is half of the diameter, so $r = 15$. Substitute 15 for r and 3.14 for π and solve:

Area = $(3.14)(15)^2$

Area = 706.5 ft^2

3. A beach ball is a sphere, and the equation for the volume of a sphere is $\left(\frac{4}{3}\right)\pi r^3$. The diameter is given as 0.6 m, so the radius is half of that, 0.3 m. Substitute that value into the equation and solve:

Volume = $\left(\frac{4}{3}\right)\pi(0.3^3)$

Volume = $\left(\frac{4}{3}\right)\pi(0.027)$

Volume = $0.036\pi \text{ m}^3$ or approximately 0.113 m^3

4. The equation for the volume of a cylinder is $\pi r^2 h$. The question is asking for diameter, so first solve for r, then double it.

$$350 = \pi r^2 \left(\frac{14}{\pi}\right)$$
$$r^2 = 25 \text{ cm}$$
$$r = 5 \text{ cm}$$

Since the radius is 5 cm, the diameter is 10 cm.

5. The equation for the volume of a square prism is s^3. Since you are given a side (s) of 5, simply substitute 5 for s. The answer is 125 in^3.

Word Problems and Data Analysis

The GRE might test any of the previous concepts as word problems or data analysis questions. This section will give you some strategies for approaching these questions.

Word Problems

The following are concepts that are commonly tested in word problems (story problems) on the GRE:

- When solving word problems, translate the verbal statements into algebraic expressions. For example:

    "greater than," "more than," and "sum of" means addition (+)

    "less than," "fewer than," and "difference" means subtraction (−)

    "of" and "by" means multiplication (×)

    "per" means division (÷)

- Distance = Rate × Time. So, if you know that Jordan travels 50 miles per hour (Rate), you can calculate how long (Time) it would take him to travel 100 miles (Distance) as follows:

$$100 = 50 \times \text{Time}$$
$$\frac{100}{50} = \text{Time}$$
$$2 = \text{Time}$$

- To calculate simple annual interest, multiply the principal × interest rate × time. For example, if you invest $10,000 at 6.0% for 1 year, you would earn $10,000 × 0.06 × 1, or $600 in interest during that year.
- If interest is compounded, interest must be computed on the principal as well as on interest that has already been earned.
- Apply logic and critical thinking to more easily solve word problems.

Data Analysis

Some of the information presented on the GRE will be in the form of charts, tables, and graphs.

Carefully read the labels on the tables, charts, or graphs. Make sure that you understand the relationships between the data represented in the tables, charts, or graphs before you answer the question.

For example, in the pie graph shown next, you should recognize that Miscellaneous funding, $x\%$, is less than 50% and less than 20% of the Total funding. A question might ask you to calculate the value of *x* as a percentage, and you might be able to quickly eliminate some incorrect answer choices. You should also remember that there are 360 degrees in a circle, because a question might ask you to calculate the value of *x* as the number of degrees it represents on the graph.

SOURCES OF SCHOOL FUNDING, 1997

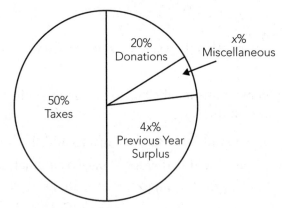

Figure 9.17 Sample pie graph.

Frequency distribution is often a more convenient way to express a set of measurements. A frequency distribution table or graph shows the frequency of occurrence of each value in the set. Following is an example of a frequency distribution table:

Rank	Degree of Agreement	Number of Students
1	Strongly agree	23
2	Somewhat agree	31
3	Somewhat disagree	12
4	Strongly disagree	7

Exercises: Word Problems and Data Analysis

These exercises are designed to help you apply the mathematics concepts just covered. They are not in GRE format, but should help you to identify your areas of strength and weakness in these areas.

Translating Word Problems

These questions will test your ability to locate relevant mathematical information in word problems.

Place an X next to the correct expression in the questions below.

1. Tom had 6 books. He gave 2 to his sister and then purchased 3 more books at the bookstore. Which of the following mathematical expressions is equivalent to the number of books that Tom now has?

    ✓ $6 - 2 + 3$
    ___ $6 + 2 - 3$
    ___ $6(2 + 3)$
    ___ $6(2 - 3)$

2. Juan walked 3 more miles than Rebecca. Rebecca walked 4 times as far as William. William walked 2 miles. Which of the following mathematical expressions is equivalent to the number of miles Juan walked?

    ___ $3 \times 4 \times 2$ *2(4) + 3*
    ___ $(2 + 4) \times 3$
    ✓ $4(2) + 3$
    ___ $4 + 3 + 2$

3. Tina goes to the store to purchase some CDs and DVDs. CDs cost $15 and DVDs cost $18. Which of the following expressions gives the total amount of money, in dollars, Tina will pay for purchasing 2 of the CDs and D of the DVDs?   *2(15) + D(18)*

    ___ $15 + D$
    ✓ $30 + 18D$
    ___ $18 + D + 30$
    ___ $D(18 + 15)$

4. Mark is older than Frank, but younger than David. If m, f, and d represent the ages, in years, of Mark, Frank, and David, respectively, which of the following is true?

    ___ $d < f < m$ *David   Mark   Frank*
    ✓ $f < m < d$ *d   m   f*
    ___ $d < m < f$
    ___ $f < d < m$

5. Kathy was twice as old as Jim 2 years ago. Today, Jim is j years old. In terms of j, how old was Kathy 2 years ago?

   ✓ $2(j - 2)$ K = 2(J-2)

   ___ $2j - 2$

   ___ $2(j + 2)$

   ___ $j(2 + 2)$

Data Analysis

These questions will test your ability to interpret and analyze data presented in charts, tables, and graphs.

Answer the following questions.

Medals awarded to the 10 highest-ranked countries in the Winter Olympics in Torino, Italy, in 2006 were as shown:

Country	Gold Medals	Silver Medals	Bronze Medals
Germany	11	12	6
United States	9	9	7
Austria	9	7	7
Russian Federation	8	6	8
Canada	7	10	7
Sweden	7	2	5
Korea	6	3	2
Switzerland	5	4	5
Italy	5	0	6
France	3	2	4

1. How many more medals did Germany win than Korea?

   29/11   18 more

2. What is the ratio of bronze to gold medals earned by Italy and France combined?

   Bronze: 10   Gold: 8   5:4

3. What percentage of all of the medals earned by the top 5 of these countries were silver medals (rounded to the nearest percent)?

   Total: 123

   Silver: 44   36%

Answers and Explanations

Translating Word Problems

1. You are given that Tom started out with 6 books. After he gave 2 books to his sister he was left with 6 − 2 books. He then purchased 3 more books, so he now has 6 − 2 + 3 books.

2. To solve this problem, start with William and work backward. William walked 2 miles, and Rebecca walked 4 times as far as William. Therefore, Rebecca walked 4(2) miles. Juan walked 3 more miles than Rebecca, so Juan walked 4(2) + 3 miles.

3. The first step is to calculate the total cost of the CDs: 2(15) = 30. You are given that, in addition to the 2 CDs, Tina also purchases D of the DVDs, each of which cost $18. Therefore, her cost for the DVDs was 18D. Now simply add the terms together to get 30 + 18D.

4. You are given that Mark, m, is older than Frank, f. Therefore, $f < m$. You are also given that Mark, m, is younger than David, d. Therefore, $d > m$. Mark's age is between Frank and David's ages, so $f < m < d$

5. You are given that Jim is j years old today; therefore, 2 years ago Jim would have been $j − 2$ years old. At that time, Kathy was twice as old as Jim, or $2(j − 2)$.

Data Analysis

1. Germany won a total of 29 medals, while Korea won a total of 11 medals. Therefore, Germany won 18 more medals than Korea.

2. In total, Italy and France earned 10 bronze and 8 gold medals. Therefore, the ratio of bronze medals to gold medals is 10:8, which simplifies to 5:4.

3. The top 5 countries were awarded 123 medals in all, 44 of which were silver medals. Therefore, the percentage of silver medals is $\frac{44}{123}$, or approximately 36%.

What's Next?

In our experience, those test-takers who internalize the basic math concepts will perform better on the GRE. When you can quickly recognize the concept being tested with a particular question, you can approach the question with confidence. Work through the simulated tests in Part IV and refer to this chapter as needed to review any math concepts with which you continue to struggle.

10
Basic GRE Verbal Review

CHAPTER GOALS

- Review the grammar and punctuation rules tested on the GRE.
- Review a list of commonly misused words and learn to avoid usage errors.

The GRE Essay tasks—both the Issue and Argument tasks discussed in Chapter 6—require effective writing skills. In addition, each of the question types in the Verbal section—Reading Comprehension, Sentence Equivalence, and Text Completion—requires a basic understanding of the rules that govern standard written English. This chapter provides an overview of the rules of grammar and punctuation that you should understand for success on the GRE.

Grammar Rules

You should have a firm grasp of the following concepts:

- Subject/Verb Agreement
- Nouns and Pronouns
- Verbs and Verb Forms
- Sentence Construction

Subject/Verb Agreement

A well-constructed sentence contains a subject and a verb and expresses a complete thought. The *subject* indicates who or what the sentence is about. The *verb* tells you what is happening with the subject or the state of the subject. Subjects and verbs are linked and must agree, meaning that they must match in form, according to person (first, second, or third) and number (singular or plural). Some complex sentences on the GRE try to conceal the subject, making identification of proper subject/verb agreement more of a challenge.

Person. A main verb must agree with the subject in person:

> *First Person*—**I am** eating lunch. **We left** the movie early.
>
> *Second Person*—**You are** eating lunch.
>
> *Third Person*—**She is** eating lunch. **He mowed** the lawn Tuesday. **It snows** often here in winter. **Someone is** paying for this mistake.

Number. A singular subject requires a singular verb.

> **Earth is** round.
>
> **One** of the boys **has** a dog.
>
> **Everyone thinks** that I will win.

A plural subject requires a plural verb.

> The **girls are** waiting for the bus.
>
> **Patricia and Janet enjoy** suspense novels.
>
> **Do football players like** classical music?

Voice. Voice defines whether the subject performs the action of the verb or receives the action of the verb. The active voice is usually the preferred mode of writing.

> *Active voice* means that the subject is acting, as in the following sentence:
>
> The **dog licked** my brother.
>
> *Passive voice* means that the subject is being acted upon, as in the following sentence:
>
> My brother **was licked** by the dog.

> **NOTE**
>
> Passive voice often appears as a present or past form of the verb *to be* (*am, are, is, was, were*) + past participle (*shot, laughed [at], interviewed, impressed*).

Tense. Verb *tense* provides you with information about when the action took place. Actions take place in the present, in the past, or in the future, as shown below:

> *Simple Present*: The action takes place continuously or regularly (this tense has the sense that that action has taken place in the past and will continue taking place in the future): Robin **works** at the mall after school.
>
> *Present Perfect*: The action began in the past and is ongoing: Robin **has worked** at the mall for the last two years.

Present Progressive: The action is ongoing *or* the action will take place in the near future: Robin **is working** today until six o'clock. Robin **is working** for her father this summer.

Simple Past: The action happened in the past: Robin **worked** at the mall last year.

Past Perfect: The action took place before another specified action: Robin **had worked** at the mall before taking a job at the theater.

Past Progressive: The action was ongoing in the past (and was interrupted): Robin **was working** when the tornado hit.

Future Tense: The action will take place in the future: Robin **will work** Tuesdays and Thursdays next semester.

Future Perfect: The action takes place in the past relative to a time in the future: Robin **will have worked** at the mall for two years as of next week.

Future Progressive: The action is ongoing relative to a time in the future: Robin **will be working** 40 hours per week by the end of the summer.

Nouns and Pronouns

English nouns can be categorized as *proper nouns*, which name specific people, places, objects, or ideas, or *common nouns*, which name nonspecific people, places, objects, or ideas. Proper nouns begin with an uppercase letter, and common nouns do not.

Pronouns take the place of either a proper or a common noun. Generally, a pronoun begins with an uppercase letter only if the pronoun begins a sentence. (The exception is *I*, which is always capitalized.) You should be able to determine and correctly apply pronoun case, as follows:

Nominative Case (renames the subject): *I, you, he, she, it, they, we*
   Mandy recently graduated from college; **she** now has a degree in nursing.

> **NOTE**
>
> **Use the *nominative* case of a personal pronoun with a compound subject.** If the subject consists of one or more nouns it is a compound subject.
>
>   Alan and **I** worked together on the project.
>
>   **She** and Pamela have been friends for a long time.
>
> **Use the *nominative* case for a pronoun that is the subject of an incomplete clause.** Completing the clause will lead you to the correct pronoun case.
>
>   No one in the classroom was as surprised as **I** (was).
>
>   He worked longer today than **she** (worked).

Possessive Case (shows possession): mine, ours, yours, his/hers, theirs

That one is John's plane ticket, and this one is **mine**.

> **NOTE**
>
> **English possessive determiners** (*my, our, your, his/her/its, their*—sometimes called possessive adjectives) must match the person and number of the possessor and not the noun phrase to which they are linked:
>
> > Richard likes **his** hot dogs with lots of relish. (The word *his* is third-person singular to match with Richard, NOT third-person plural [*their*] to match with hot dogs.)
>
> **Use a *possessive* determiner before a gerund.** A *gerund* is a verb ending in *–ing* that can function as a noun.
>
> > **Her** singing has often been admired.
> >
> > **His** studying for the exam shocked the class.

Objective Case (renames the object of a verb or preposition): me, us, you, him, her, it, them

The monkey made faces at **him** through the bars of the cage.

> **NOTE**
>
> **Use the *objective* case when the pronoun is the object of a verb.**
>
> > A large dog chased **me** down the road. (What/who was chased? Me.)
> >
> > The teacher gave **him** and **her** passing grades. (To what/whom did the teacher give passing grades? To him and her.)
>
> **Use the *objective* case when the pronoun is the object of a preposition.** A *preposition* is a word such as *from* or *before* that establishes a relationship between an object and some other part of the sentence, often expressing a location in place or time.
>
> > Matt received the greatest support from **you** and **me**.
> >
> > The paper fluttered to the ground before **him**.

Relative Pronouns are used to identify people, places, and objects in general. The relative pronouns **who, whom,** and **whose** refer to people. The relative pronouns **which, what, that,** and **whose** refer to places and objects.

Indefinite Pronouns are used to represent an indefinite number of persons, places, or things. Indefinite pronouns are treated as singular pronouns. Following are some examples of indefinite pronouns:

Everyone gather around the campfire!

There will be a prize for **each** of the children.

One of my sisters always volunteers to drive me to school.

Some are friendlier than others.

Be sure to maintain consistency in pronoun person and number. It is not grammatically correct to use the plural pronoun *their* to represent neutral gender. This is an example of a major difference between standard written English and the English that we ordinarily use when speaking.

A **small child** should always be with **his or her** parent or guardian.

NOT A small child should always be with **their** parent or guardian.

Ambiguous or Misleading Pronouns

The noun that a pronoun renames or to which it refers is called its *antecedent*. If the antecedent is not clear, the pronoun can be ambiguous or misleading. To make the meaning clear, you may need to substitute the noun that the pronoun replaced. See the following examples:

Ambiguous Pronoun: Matt asked Phil if **he** could play first base.

- Who is going to play first base, Matt or Phil?

Correct Sentence: Matt asked Phil if **Phil** could play first base.

Ambiguous Pronoun: When Leanne hit the car door with her bicycle, she badly damaged **it**.

- In this sentence, it is unclear what was damaged, the car door or the bicycle.

Correct Sentence: When Leanne hit the car door with her bicycle, she badly damaged the **car door**.

Every pronoun must have a clear antecedent. A pronoun that lacks an antecedent can be confusing. To make the meaning clear, you may need to supply an antecedent. Here is an example:

Pronoun Lacking Antecedent: The two species are somehow related, but the nature of **it** has been a subject of intense debate.

- What is the antecedent of *it*? To make the meaning clear, you need to provide an antecedent.

Correct Sentence: The two species are somehow related, but the nature of **the relationship** has been a subject of intense debate.

Verbs and Verb Forms

A *verb* describes the action that is taking place in the sentence. All verbs have five principle forms:

Bare Form: I like to **write**. (In this sentence, tense is carried on *like*.)

Simple Present: I **write**.

Simple Past: I **wrote**.

Gerund: I am **writing**. (In this sentence, tense is carried on *am*.)

Past Participle: I have **written**. (In this sentence, tense is carried on *have*.)

Simple Past versus Past Participle. The *simple past* and *past participle* forms of verbs can sometimes be confusing. Most past participles are formed by adding *–ed* to the word, as shown in the examples below:

Simple Present Tense: We **move** often.

Past Participle Tense: We have **moved** again this year.

Remember that there are many irregular past participles in English—for example, *written, eaten, came, gone,* and so on.

Some verbs have *irregular simple past-tense* forms, as shown in the examples below:

Simple Present Tense: I **see** my best friend every day.

Simple Past Tense: I **saw** my best friend yesterday.

Simple Present Tense: My little sister **eats** her breakfast quickly.

Simple Past Tense: My little sister **ate** her breakfast quickly.

Remember that the perfect and progressive tenses include so-called helping or *auxiliary* verbs, as shown in the examples below:

Present Perfect: They **have** already **passed** Calculus II.

Past Perfect: I **had seen** my best friend the day before.

Present Progressive: My little sister **is eating** her breakfast quickly.

Past Progressive: The winds **were howling** loudly as the vinyl siding began flying off the house.

Sentence Construction

A well-written sentence is clear, balanced, and properly punctuated. Refer to the next sections for more information on how to construct a sentence.

Parallel Construction

Parallel construction, or *parallelism*, allows a writer to show order and clarity in a sentence or a paragraph by putting grammatical elements that have the same function in the same form. Parallelism creates a recognizable pattern within a sentence and adds unity, force, clarity, and balance to writing. All words, phrases, and clauses used in parallel construction must share the same grammatical form. We have included some examples of sentences that include faulty parallelism, followed by revised versions of each sentence:

Non-Parallel Construction: Patricia enjoyed **running** and **to ride** her bike.

- In this sentence, the verb forms do not match. The first of the two verbs is a gerund (*running*), and the second verb is in the infinitive form (*to ride*), which is composed of the particle *to* and the bare form of the verb.

Correct Sentence: Patricia enjoyed **running** and **riding** her bike.

Non-Parallel Construction: **The distance** from Los Angeles to Detroit is greater than Detroit to New York City.

- In this sentence, "The distance" links only with the first portion of the comparative construction "from Los Angeles to Detroit."

Correct Sentence: **The distance** from Los Angeles to Detroit is greater than **the distance** from Detroit to New York City.

Run-on Sentences

A *run-on sentence* is a sentence that is composed of more than one main idea, and does not use proper punctuation or connectors. Following are examples of run-on sentences along with suggested corrections:

Run-on Sentence: Janet is an actress **she** often appears in major network television shows.

Correct Sentence: Janet is an actress **who** often appears in major network television shows.

Run-on Sentence: My nephew loves to play **football, you** can find him on the practice field almost every day.

Correct Sentence: My nephew loves to play **football. You** can find him on the practice field almost every day.

Run-on sentences are often created by substituting a comma for a semicolon or a period. This is called a *comma splice*, and it is incorrect.

Sentence Fragments/Incomplete Sentences

A *sentence fragment* has end punctuation (so it appears as a sentence) but lacks one or more crucial features of a sentence (subject, verb, or predicate). Following are examples of sentence fragments along with suggested corrections:

Sentence Fragment: My car is difficult to start in the winter. Because of the cold weather.

Correct Sentence: My car is difficult to start in the winter because of the cold weather.

Sentence Fragment: John is a heavy eater. Two hot dogs for lunch and four for dinner.

Correct Sentence: John is a heavy eater who normally consumes two hot dogs for lunch and four for dinner.

Sentence fragments may lack a verb, as shown in the examples below:

Incomplete Sentence: Yesterday, the **winning** float in the parade.

- The sentence as it is written is incomplete; there is no main verb. The sentence should be revised so that the **winning float** either performs an action or has an action performed upon it.

Revised Sentence: Yesterday, the **winning float** in the parade **received** its prize.

Incomplete Sentence: **Releasing** personal information by many school districts to third parties.

- The sentence as it is written is incomplete; the gerund **releasing** is being used as a noun in this sentence. Add a verb with tense.

Revised Sentence: Many school districts **prohibit releasing** personal information to third parties.

Misplaced Modifiers

A sentence must contain at least one main clause. A complex sentence may contain more than one main clause, as well as one or more *relative clauses*. *Relative clauses* follow the nouns that they modify. In order to maintain clarity within a sentence, it is important to place a relative clause near the object that it modifies. A *modifier* is a word, phrase, or clause that modifies, or changes, the meaning of another word or part of the sentence. Often, a modifier helps explain or describe who, when, where, why, how, and to what extent. Misplaced modifiers can inadvertently change the meaning of the sentence. We have included some examples of sentences that contain misplaced modifiers, followed by revised versions of each sentence:

Misplaced Modifier: Cassie had trouble deciding which college to attend **at first.**

- The meaning of this sentence is obscured by the placement of the modifying clause **at first.** It is unlikely that the writer intended to suggest that Cassie was considering attending more than one college.

Correct Sentence: **At first**, Cassie had trouble deciding which college to attend.

Misplaced Modifier: **As a teacher**, the school board hired Mrs. Smith to coach our team.

- This sentence as it is written suggests that the school board, and not Mrs. Smith, is a teacher.

Correct Sentence: The school board hired Mrs. Smith, **a teacher**, to coach our team.

> **GRE Tip**
> Make sure that each sentence is clear so that you know exactly "who" is doing "what," "how" something happens, and so on.

Punctuation Rules

A properly punctuated sentence helps the reader understand the organization of the writer's ideas. You should be able to identify and correct errors involving the following punctuation marks:

- Commas [,]
- Apostrophes [']
- Colons [:] and Semicolons [;]
- Parentheses [( )] and Dashes [—]
- Periods [.], Question Marks [?], and Exclamation Points [!]

Commas

A comma is used to indicate a separation of ideas or of elements within a sentence.

Use a comma with a coordinating conjunction to separate independent clauses within a sentence. There are seven basic coordinating conjunctions in English:

1. Jenny sings in the choir, **and** she plays the guitar in a rock band.

2. Amanda enjoys her job, **but** she is looking forward to her vacation.

3. Either I will study mathematics, **or** I will study chemistry.

4. His mother doesn't eat meat, **nor** does she eat dairy products.

5. Jordan will be playing football this year, **for** he made the team.

6. Frank earned a promotion, **so** we decided to celebrate.

7. I just completed my workout, **yet** I'm not tired.

Use a comma to separate elements that introduce and modify a sentence.

Yesterday, I painted the entire garage.

Before deciding on a major at college, Rana discussed her options with her parents.

Use commas before and after a parenthetical expression. A parenthetical expression is a phrase that is inserted into the writer's train of thought. Parenthetical expressions are most often set off using commas.

Stephanie's decision, **in my opinion,** was not in her best interest.

The new park, **of course,** is a popular tourist destination.

Use a comma to separate an appositive from a clause. An appositive is a noun or phrase that renames the noun that precedes it.

My brother, **a well-respected scientist,** made an important discovery.

Mr. Smith, **the fifth-grade math teacher,** was a favorite among the students.

Use commas to set off interjections.

Well, it's about time that you got here.

Say, did you pass your history test?

Use commas to separate coordinate adjectives. If two adjectives modify a noun in the same way, they are called coordinate adjectives. Coordinate adjectives can also be joined with the coordinating conjunction *and*.

We walked the **long, dusty** road to the abandoned farm.

OR We walked the **long and dusty** road to the abandoned farm.

Cows are **gentle, friendly** creatures.

OR Cows are **gentle and friendly** creatures.

Use commas to set off nonrestrictive phrases and clauses. A nonrestrictive phrase can be omitted from a clause without changing the meaning of the clause. Nonrestrictive clauses are useful because they can modify the nouns that they follow.

My sister's dog, **a brown and white terrier,** barks at me whenever I visit.

Katie celebrated her birthday, **which was in June,** with a party and a chocolate cake.

Use a comma to separate elements in a list or series.

Jill decided to purchase a **leash, a collar, and a water dish** for her dog.

Skippy **packed his suitcase, put on his jacket, and left the house**.

Use commas in dates, addresses, place names, numbers, and quotations.

> Mary is leaving for Jamaica on **Monday, February 19, 2009**.
>
> The Library of Congress is located at **101 Independence Avenue, Washington, D.C, U.S.A.**
>
> Forecasted annual earnings are currently **$42,521,000**.
>
> **"My sister is a nurse,"** Becky said proudly.
>
> John replied**, "So where are we exactly?"**
>
> **"You'll soon regret this,"** Luc cautioned under his breath**, "for things are not as they seem."**

Do <u>not</u> use a comma:
   to separate a subject from a verb;

> My cousin Mary walked down to the corner.
>
> *NOT* My cousin **Mary, walked** down to the corner.

to separate an adjective from the word it modifies;

> The pretty girl sat in front of me on the bus.
>
> *NOT* The **pretty, girl** sat in front of me on the bus.

to separate two independent clauses; this is known as a comma splice.

> I plan to attend a liberal arts college. My parents want me to get a well-rounded education.
>
> *NOT* I plan to attend a liberal arts **college, my** parents want me to get a well-rounded education.
>
> This sentence could be fixed by adding a conjunction, for example: "I plan to attend a liberal arts college, *as* my parents want me to get a well-rounded education."

Apostrophes

An apostrophe is used to form the possessive in nouns, to show the omission of letters in contractions, and to indicate plurals of letters and (as a matter of preference) numerals.

Use an apostrophe with s to form the possessive of singular nouns, plural nouns that do not end in s, or indefinite pronouns that do not end in s.

> My **friend's** house is at the end of the street.
>
> The **Women's** Society meets every Thursday at the high school.
>
> **Someone's** bicycle is leaning against the building.

Use an apostrophe to form the possessive of plural nouns ending in s.

The **horses'** stalls were filled with straw.

I did not enjoy the **brothers'** rendition of my favorite song.

Use an apostrophe with the last noun in a series to indicate joint possession.

Frank and **Ruth's** anniversary is in September.

Roger, Clark, and **Mike's** proposal will certainly beat any other trio's (proposal).

Add an apostrophe to all nouns to indicate individual possession.

Brian's, Jason's, and Michael's computers were stolen.

Add an apostrophe to indicate contractions.

It's raining outside again. (It's = It is)

We're running against each other in the election. (We're = We are)

If **you're** going to the movie with me we should leave now. (you're = you are)

My cousin **should've** taken the bus. (should've = should have)

Didn't Kevin know that classes had begun? (Didn't = Did not)

Regrettably, I **won't** be able to attend the party. (won't = will not)

That'll break his heart! (That'll = That will)

Add an apostrophe to form the plural of letters and numbers.

Did you dot your *i*'s and cross your *t*'s?

There are a total of four **7's** in my phone number.

Do not use apostrophes with possessive pronouns.

The car with the flat tire is **ours**.

NOT The car with the flat tire is **our's**.

Yours is the dog that barks all night.

NOT **Your's** is the dog that barks all night.

My car has a dent in **its** door.

NOT my car has a dent in **it's** door.

Colons and Semicolons

A *colon* is used before a list or after an independent clause that is followed by information that directly modifies or adds to the clause. An independent clause can stand alone as a complete sentence. A *semicolon* is used to join closely related independent clauses when a coordinate conjunction is not used, with conjunctive adverbs to join main clauses, to separate items in a series that contains commas, and to separate coordinate clauses when they are joined by transitional words or phrases.

Use a colon before a list.

> We are required to bring the following items to camp: a sleeping bag, a pillow, an alarm clock, clothes, and personal care items.

Use a colon after an independent clause that is followed by information that directly modifies or adds to the clause.

> Jennifer encountered a problem that she had not anticipated: a power outage.
>
> My sister suggested a great location: the park down the street from our house.

Colons can be used before direct quotations, after salutations in business correspondence, and between titles and subtitles.

> Captain John Paul Jones said: "I have not yet begun to fight."
>
> Dear Mr. Smith:
>
> *Blaze: A Story of Courage*

Use a semicolon to join closely related independent clauses when a coordinate conjunction is not used.

> Jane starts a new job today; she is very excited.
>
> I don't understand the directions; my teacher must explain them to me.

Use a semicolon with conjunctive adverbs to join independent clauses.

> Martha is interested in taking the class; **however,** it does not suit her schedule.
>
> My brother is very tall; **in fact,** he is the tallest person in our family.

Use semicolons in a series to separate elements containing commas.

> The art museum contained some fragile, old oil paintings; bronze, plaster, and marble statues; and recently completed modern art pieces.
>
> My first meal at college consisted of cold, dry toast; runny, undercooked eggs; and very strong, acidic coffee.

Use a semicolon to separate coordinate clauses when they are joined by transitional words or phrases. When a sentence contains more than one clause, each of which is considered to be equally as important as the other, the clauses are called coordinate clauses. They are typically joined by a coordinating conjunction. When the coordinating conjunction is not used, a semicolon should be.

> My sister and I enjoyed the play; **afterward,** we stopped for an ice cream cone.

OR My sister and I enjoyed the play, **and afterward,** we stopped for an ice cream cone.

Betty often misplaces her keys; **perhaps** she should get a key locator.

OR Betty often misplaces her keys, **so perhaps** she should get a key locator.

Parentheses and Dashes

Parentheses are used to enclose supplemental information that is not essential to the meaning of the sentence. *Dashes* are used to place special emphasis on a word or phrase within a sentence.

Use parentheses to enclose explanatory or secondary supporting details.

In addition to serving as Class Treasurer (**a challenging job**), she was also a National Merit Scholar.

Alan visited the Football Hall of Fame (**after years of begging his parents**) during his summer vacation.

Use dashes in place of parentheses to place special emphasis on certain words or phrases.

Dr. Evans—**a noted scientist and educator**—spoke at our commencement ceremony.

The homecoming float—**a cobbled mess of wire and nails**—meandered dangerously down the street.

End Punctuation

Periods, *question marks*, and *exclamation points* are considered end punctuation, which means that they should be used at the end of a sentence.

Use a period to end most sentences.

Scott enrolled in classes at the university.

Mary wanted to know what John made for dinner.

Use a question mark to end a direct question.

Do you think it will rain today?

What is the shortest route to the stadium?

Use an exclamation point to end an emphatic statement.

Please don't leave your vehicle unattended!

Wow! What a huge trout!

Rhetoric

Rhetoric refers to the effective and persuasive use of language. Rhetorical skills, then, refer to your ability to make choices about the effectiveness and clarity of a word, phrase, sentence, or paragraph. Good writing involves effective word choice as well as clear and unambiguous expression. The best-written sentences are relevant based on the context of the paragraph, avoid redundancy, and clearly and simply express the intended idea.

Commonly Misused Words

Following is a list of some of the words that are commonly misused in writing, along with definitions and examples of the proper use of each word. When practicing your essay-writing skills, remember that appropriate word choice will garner more points.

Accept, Except

Accept is a verb that means "to agree to receive something."

Example: I could not pay for my purchases with a credit card because the store would only *accept* cash.

Except is either a preposition that means "other than, or but," or a verb meaning "to omit or leave out."

Example: *Except* for a B+ in history, Kate received all A's on her report card.

Affect, Effect

Affect is usually a verb meaning "to influence."

Example: Fortunately, Kylie's sore ankle did not *affect* her performance in the game.

Effect is usually a noun that "indicates or achieves a result." Effect is also sometimes used as a transitive verb meaning "to bring into existence," but it is generally not used in this way on the GRE.

Example: Studies have shown that too much exercise can have a negative *effect* on a person's health.

Among, Between

Among is used with more than two items.

Example: Jackie's performance last night was the best *among* all of the actors in the play.

Between is usually used with two items.

Example: Simon could not decide *between* the two puppies at the pound, so he adopted them both.

Assure, Insure, Ensure

Assure means "to convince" or "to guarantee" and usually takes a direct object.

Example: If we leave two hours early, I *assure* you that we will arrive at the concert on time.

Insure means "to guard against loss."

Example: Before he could leave for his trip, Steve had to *insure* his car against theft.

Ensure means "to make certain."

Example: Our company goes to great lengths to *ensure* that every product that leaves the warehouse is of the highest quality.

Because, Since

Because means "for the reason that."

Example: My sister was late for school *because* she missed the bus.

Since implies "time," either continuous or not, in addition to "reason."

Example: *Since* he lost the election, he has remained sequestered in his home.

It is important to note that in your writing, you should be aware of the subtle difference in meaning.

Compare to, Compare with

Compare to means "assert a likeness."

Example: The only way to describe her eyes is to *compare* them *to* the color of the sky.

Compare with means "analyze for similarities and differences."

Example: For her final project, Susan had to *compare* bike riding *with* other aerobic activities and report her findings.

Complement, Compliment

A *complement* is "something that completes or adds to" something else. *Complement* can also be used as a verb meaning "to complete."

Example: My favorite place to dine is on the terrace; the breathtaking views are the ideal *complement* to a romantic dinner.

A *compliment* is "flattery or praise." *Compliment* can also be used as a verb.

Example: Larry was thrilled when the award-winning author *complimented* him on his writing style.

Farther, Further

Farther refers to distance.

Example: At baseball camp, Jack learned that with the correct stance and technique, he could throw the ball *farther* this year than he could last year.

Further indicates "additional degree, time, or quantity." It can also be used as a verb.

Example: I enjoyed the book to a certain degree, but I felt that the author should have provided *further* details about the characters.

Example: Kim *furthered* her education by taking summer classes.

Fewer, Less

Fewer refers to units or individuals that can be counted.

Example: Trish received all the credit, even though she worked *fewer* hours on the project than did the other members of the group.

Less refers to mass or bulk that can't be counted.

Example: When it comes to reading, Mike is *less* inclined to read for pleasure than is Stephanie.

Imply, Infer

Imply means "to suggest."

Example: His sister did not mean to *imply* that he was incorrect.

Infer means "to deduce," "to guess," or "to conclude."

Example: She *inferred* from the professor's remarks that he admired Russian novels.

Its, It's

Its is the possessive form of "it."

Example: In the summer, my family enjoys drinking white tea for *its* refreshing, light flavor.

It's is the contraction of "it is."

Example: Fortunately for the runners, *it's* a sunny day.

Lay, Lie

Lay means "to put" or "to place," and requires a direct object to complete its meaning.

Example: To protect your floor or carpet, you should always *lay* newspaper or a sheet on the ground before you begin to paint a room.

Lie means "to recline, rest, or stay," or "to take a position of rest." This verb cannot take a direct object. The past tense of *lie* is *lay*, so use extra caution if you see these words on the GRE.

Example: On sunny days, our lazy cat will *lie* on the porch and bask in the warmth of the sunlight.

Example: Yesterday, our lazy cat *lay* in the sun for most of the afternoon.

Like, Such As

Like indicates similarity.

Example: Kate and Allie were very close, *like* two peas in a pod.

Such as indicates an example or examples.

Example: Composers *such as* Mozart and Bach are among my favorites.

Number, Amount

Number is used when the items can be counted.

Example: The *number* of students enrolled at Valley College has increased during the last 5 years.

Amount denotes quantity.

Example: A small *amount* of rain has fallen so far this year.

Precede, Proceed

Precede means "to go before."

Example: When I go to an expensive restaurant, I expect a salad course to *precede* the main course.

Proceed means "to move forward."

Example: As a result of failed negotiations, the labor union announced its plan to *proceed* with a nationwide strike.

Principal, Principle

Principal is a noun meaning "the head of a school or an organization."

Example: A high school *principal* is responsible not only for the educational progress of his students, but also for their emotional well-being.

Principal can also mean "a sum of money."

Example: I hope to see a 30 percent return on my invested *principal* within the first two years.

Principal can also be used as an adjective to mean "first" or "leading."

Example: Our *principal* concern is the welfare of our customers, not the generation of profits.

Principle is a noun meaning "a basic truth or law."

Example: A study of basic physics will include Newton's *principle* that every action has an opposite and equal reaction.

Set, Sit

The verb *set* takes an object.

Example: I *set* the bowl of pretzels in the middle of the table so that everyone could reach it.

The verb *sit* does not take an object.

Example: When I dine alone, I always *sit* by the window so that I can watch all the people who pass by the restaurant.

Than, Then

Than is a conjunction used in comparison.

Example: Rana made fewer mistakes during her presentation *than* she thought she would make.

Then is an adverb denoting time.

Example: Mandy updated her resume and *then* applied for the job.

That, Which

That is used to introduce an essential clause in a sentence. Commas are not required before the word "that."

Example: I usually take the long route because the main highway *that* runs through town is always so busy.

Which is best used to introduce a clause containing nonessential and descriptive information. A comma is required before *which* if is used in this way. *Which* can also be used to introduce an essential clause in order to avoid repeating the word *that* in the sentence.

Example: The purpose of the Civil Rights Act of 1991, *which* amended the original Civil Rights Act of 1964, was to strengthen and improve federal civil rights laws.

Example: I gave Mandy that book *which* I thought she might like.

There, Their, They're

There is an adverb specifying location.

Example: Many people love to visit a big city, but few of them could ever live *there*.

Their is a possessive pronoun.

Example: More employers are offering new benefits to *their* employees, such as day-care services and flexible scheduling.

They're is a contraction of "they are."

Example: *They're* hoping to reach a decision by the end of the day.

To, Too, Two

To has many different uses in the English language, including the indication of direction and comparison. It is also used as an infinitive in verb phrases.

Example: Mary is driving *to* the beach tomorrow.

Example: Jill's painting is superior *to* Alan's painting.

Example: I try *to* run three miles every day.

Too generally means "in addition," or "more than enough."

Example: It is important that we consider Kara's opinion, *too*.

Example: Yesterday, I ran *too* far and injured my foot.

Two is a number.

Whether, If

> *Whether* should be used when listing alternatives.
>
> **Example: Traci could not decide *whether* to order the fish or the chicken.**
>
> *If* should be used when referring to a future possibility.
>
> **Example: *If* Traci orders the fish, she will be served more quickly.**

Your, You're

> *Your* is a possessive pronoun.
>
> **Example: Sunscreen protects *your* skin from sun damage.**
>
> *You're* is a contraction of "you are."
>
> **Example: When *you're* at the beach, always remember to wear sunscreen.**

What's Next?

Now that you have reviewed the grammar rules included in this chapter, you might decide to focus on improving your own speaking and writing where applicable. We've found that the GRE test-takers who do the best on the GRE Verbal and Writing sections are those who have internalized the rules and can simply recognize correct English by its "sound." You should practice using proper English in your daily life to supplement the practice testing that you'll do; this will pay off in ways far beyond an improved GRE score.

PART IV

Practicing for the GRE General Test

CHAPTER **11**   **GRE PRACTICE TEST 1**

CHAPTER **12**   **GRE PRACTICE TEST 2**

CHAPTER **13**   **GRE PRACTICE TEST 3**

11
GRE Practice Test 1

CHAPTER GOALS

- Take a full-length GRE under actual test conditions.
- Check your results using the Answer Key.
- Review the explanations for each question, focusing particularly on questions you answered incorrectly or did not answer at all.
- Build your test-taking confidence.

The simulated GRE in this chapter contains 80 multiple-choice questions and two essay tasks, divided into six main sections. You should allow approximately 3 hours and 30 minutes to complete the entire test. To make this simulated test as much like the actual GRE as possible, you should complete the test sections in the time indicated at the beginning of each section, and in the order in which the sections appear. You may skip around within a section, but complete each section before you move on to the next one.

Within each section there are several different types of questions. Make sure that you read and understand all directions before you begin.

- Circle your answers on the test so that you can compare your answers to the correct answers listed in the Answer Key on page 304.
- When asked to select a sentence in a passage that meets a certain description, circle or underline the sentence you choose.
- Carefully review the explanations for any question that you answered incorrectly.

We suggest that you make this practice test as much like the real test as possible. Find a quiet location, free from distractions, and make sure that you have pencils and a timepiece. Review the Scoring Guidelines in Chapter 2, but remember that your score on the actual GRE will be dependent on many factors, including your level of preparedness and your fatigue level on test day. The Practice Test begins on the next page.

GRE Diagnostic Test 1

SECTION **1**   **ANALYTICAL WRITING**

SECTION **2**   **VERBAL REASONING**

SECTION **3**   **VERBAL REASONING**

SECTION **4**   **QUANTITATIVE REASONING**

SECTION **5**   **QUANTITATIVE REASONING**

ANSWERS AND EXPLANATIONS

SECTION 1

Analytical Writing

PART 1. ANALYZE AN ISSUE

30 minutes

You will have 30 minutes to organize your thoughts and compose a response that represents your point of view on the issue. Do not respond to any issue other than the one presented; a response to any other issue will receive a score of 0.

Issue Topic

"Leaders should focus more on the needs of the majority than on the needs of the minority."

Discuss whether you agree or disagree with the statement. Use relevant reasons and examples to support your point of view. In developing and supporting your position, consider ways in which the statement might or might not hold true. Explain how those considerations affect your point of view.

Analytical Writing

PART 2.   ANALYZE AN ARGUMENT

30 minutes

You will have 30 minutes to organize your thoughts and compose a response that critiques the given argument. Do not respond to any argument other than the one given; a response to any other argument will receive a score of 0.

Argument Topic

The following appeared as part of an article in a health and fitness magazine.

"Several volunteers participated in a study of consumer responses to the new Exer-Core exercise machine. Every day for a month, they worked out on the machine for 30 minutes in addition to maintaining their normal fitness regimen. At the end of that month, most of the volunteers reported a significant improvement in both their stamina and muscle condition. Therefore, it appears that the Exer-Core exercise machine is truly effective in improving a person's overall general health and fitness."

Critique the reasoning used in the argument above. You are not being asked to discuss your point of view on the argument. You should identify and analyze the central elements of the argument, the underlying assumptions that are being made, and any supporting information that is given. Your critique can also discuss other information that would strengthen or weaken the argument or make it more logical.

SECTION 2

Verbal Reasoning

30 Minutes
20 Questions

This section consists of three different types of questions: Reading Comprehension, Text Completion, and Sentence Equivalence. To answer the questions, select the best answer from the answer choices given. Reading Comprehension questions appear in sets; Text Completion and Sentence Equivalence questions are independent. The questions will be presented in random order. Read the following directions before you begin the test.

Reading Comprehension Questions

Directions:
Multiple-choice Questions—Select One Answer Choice: These are the traditional multiple-choice questions with five answer choices from which you must select one.

Multiple-choice Questions—Select One or More Answer Choices: These questions provide three answer choices; select all that are correct.

Select-in-Passage: Choose the sentence in the passage that meets a certain description.

Text Completion Questions

Directions: Select one entry from the corresponding column of choices for each blank. Fill all blanks in the way that best completes the text.

Sentence Equivalence Questions

Directions: Select the two answer choices that, when used to complete the sentence, fit the meaning of the sentence as a whole and produce completed sentences that are alike in meaning.

Questions 1 to 3 are based on the following passage.

During the mid-twentieth century the United States began a policy toward Native Americans called "readjustment." This policy stemmed from the rise of the civil rights movement. Because of the movement, there was greater awareness that all Americans needed to be able exercise the rights guaranteed by the United States Constitution. Readjustment recognized that life on reservations prevented Native Americans from exercising those rights. Reservations had created segregation that caused

GO ON TO NEXT PAGE

just as much damage as the racially segregated schools still prevalent throughout the nation during the period. The readjustment movement advocated the end of the federal government's involvement in Native American affairs and encouraged the assimilation of Native Americans into mainstream American society. The belief was that if it were beneficial for African American children to be placed in schools with white children, it would also be beneficial for Native Americans to become integrated into white society. The policy, however, failed to recognize the emergence of a new generation of Native American leadership and efforts to develop tribal institutions and reaffirm tribal identity. The new leadership did not desire assimilation, but instead wanted more segregation. The Native American community was vying to reassert its distinct identity and separate itself from mainstream America.

For Question 1, select one answer choice.

1. According to the passage, the readjustment policy sought to
   - Ⓐ discourage assimilation of Native Americans
   - Ⓑ decrease the responsibility of tribal leaders
   - Ⓒ encourage desegregation among Native Americans
   - Ⓓ increase government involvement in Native American affairs
   - Ⓔ increase segregation among tribal institutions

2. Select the sentence that suggests the U.S. government believed that all minorities had equivalent educational needs.

   The belief was that if it were beneficial...

For Question 3, select one answer choice.

3. The passage suggests that the author would be most likely to agree with which of the following statements?
   - Ⓐ Readjustment was a well-intentioned, though flawed, attempt to redress historical wrongs.
   - Ⓑ Integration into predominantly white classrooms is the only option for minority schoolchildren.
   - Ⓒ In the mid-twentieth century, tribal leaders refused to allow Native American children to attend mainstream schools.
   - Ⓓ Tribal leaders did not understand the benefits of integration.
   - Ⓔ In the mid-twentieth century, government leaders never visited actual tribal reservations.

Question 4 is based on the following passage.

Eli Whitney's cotton gin famously changed the face of the agricultural industry by greatly increasing productivity. Although the gin was enormously popular, Whitney himself struggled to make a profit from it. After receiving a patent for his invention, Whitney and his business partner opted to produce as many cotton gins as possible and to charge farmers a user fee instead of selling them outright. Farmers considered this fee unnecessary and exorbitant, and began manufacturing copies of the cotton gin instead. Because of a loophole in the patent law, the many lawsuits brought by Whitney and his partner against the farmers were fruitless. The duo finally agreed to license their cotton gins at a reasonable price. However, due to the costs of their legal battles, they were unable to make the fortune that Whitney had previously predicted.

For Question 4, select one answer choice.

4. According to the passage, which one of the following was an obstacle in implementing widespread use of Whitney's cotton gin?
   - (A) Whitney's reluctance to seek a patent for his cotton gin
   - (B) The high fees being charged to farmers for the use of Whitney's cotton gin
   - (C) The negative impact of Whitney's cotton gin on the economy of the south
   - (D) Whitney's inability to profit from his invention
   - (E) Whitney's reliance on a loophole in the patent law

For Questions 5 to 7, select one entry from the corresponding column of choices for each blank. Fill all blanks in the way that best completes the text.

5. Many reformist criminal justice experts tend to believe that the key to long-term success with prisoners is through (i) _____ into the community itself, rather than just through the traditional, yet often unproductive, attempt at extended (ii) _____.

Blank (i)	Blank (ii)
(A) imprisonment	(D) inclusion
(B) isolation	(E) justice
(C) reintegration	(F) punishment

6. The teacher's directions regarding how to write our research paper were very (i) _____ and vague, so when she returned the papers and had graded them all extremely harshly, the class was (ii) _____ that she hadn't given us a better understanding of her expectations.

Blank (i)	Blank (ii)
(A) meticulous	(D) indignant
(B) ambitious	(E) agitated
(C) indefinite	(F) fortuitous

GO ON TO NEXT PAGE

7. The emergence of social networks on the Internet is being hailed by some as an innovation (i) _____ and (ii) _____ the concept of community; yet others criticize such institutions as (iii) _____ substitutions for old-fashioned human interactions.

Blank (i)	Blank (ii)	Blank (iii)
Ⓐ revolutionizing	Ⓓ expanding	Ⓖ gregarious
Ⓑ promoting	Ⓔ maculating	Ⓗ orthodox
Ⓒ obliterating	Ⓕ assuaging	Ⓘ inadequate

Questions 8 to 11 are based on the following passage.

It sounds like the premise for a science fiction novel, but scientists are today developing a drug that could eliminate traumatic events from our memories. Thus far the research is focused on altering memories immediately following one particular type of trauma, car accidents, with promising results. But the potential applications of the research are far more wide reaching and morally ambiguous. On one hand, such a drug could provide a breakthrough in the treatment of post-traumatic stress disorder in war veterans and rape victims. On the other hand, by relegating our memories to oblivion, such a drug could fundamentally change our sense of self and personal history. It is unclear how the human brain stores memories, and much is unknown about why painful memories of traumatic events come back to haunt some and not others. But one thing is certain—as research into the technology of altering memories continues, so will the ethical debates on whether this pharmaceutical innovation falls outside the spectrum of appropriate medical interventions.

For Question 8, select one answer choice.

8. The main point of the passage is to
   Ⓐ describe the premise of a science fiction novel
   Ⓑ propose a remedy for traumatic brain injuries
   Ⓒ question certain medical research
   Ⓓ admit to the failings of pharmaceutical innovation
   Ⓔ reject the concept of drug trials

For Question 9, consider each of the choices separately and select all that apply.

9. Which of the following can be inferred from the passage regarding research into the memory-altering drug?
   A It is currently applicable to many types of traumatic situations.
   B Research is ongoing, and the treatment remains controversial.
   C Our sense of self as well as our personal history is essentially static.

10. Select the sentence that mentions a specific moral dilemma resulting from the use of a memory-altering drug.

On the other hand, by relegating...

For Question 11, consider each of the choices separately and select all that apply.

11. It can be inferred from the passage that
    [A] scientists have discovered a means by which human memories can be completely eliminated
    [B] only drugs that affect memory are morally ambiguous
    [C] ethical debates are a predictable result of certain types of scientific research

Question 12 is based on the following passage.

Transportation has continued to change dramatically with each generation. The last commercial innovation was electric trains, like France's TGV, which were first introduced in the early 1980s and are capable of reaching speeds of more than 185 miles an hour. The next trend in trains will most likely be the "maglevs," or magnetic levitation trains, which are designed to hover over their tracks by resting on magnetic fields and which are driven by motors with no moving parts. Once these trains are up and running, they are expected to reach speeds of more than 400 miles per hour.

For Question 12, select one answer choice.

12. Which of the following would most likely be found at the beginning of this passage?
    (A) A discussion of different transportation methods that have been used throughout history
    (B) A statistical analysis of transportation trends in several countries
    (C) A series of portraits of the types of trains utilized throughout the history of the United States and Europe
    (D) An account of the technological challenges involved in engineering faster trains
    (E) An essay on historical transportation models

For Question 13, select one entry from the corresponding column of choices for each blank. Fill all blanks in the way that best completes the text.

13. Lamarck's theory of evolution, which argued that acquired characteristics could be inherited, was eventually (i) _____ by the world scientific community, yet it continued to be embraced in the former USSR, because it was (ii) _____ consistent with the official Party beliefs, which stated that individual men could (iii) _____ their nature.

Blank (i)	Blank (ii)	Blank (iii)
Ⓐ evinced	Ⓓ ideologically	Ⓖ defeat
Ⓑ spurned	Ⓔ erratically	Ⓗ transform
Ⓒ compartmentalized	Ⓕ idiosyncratically	Ⓘ expunge

Questions 14 and 15 are based on the following passage.

In Rembrandt's day, many of his fellow painters portrayed their characters much like the idealized gods of Greek and Roman mythology. Rembrandt differed by painting people in a more realistic and humble manner. He used himself, his family members, and even beggars as models. He viewed these individuals as being just as worthy of immortalization in art as mythological figures. He also fittingly enhanced his work by the use of *chiaroscuro*, a painting technique where light striking the foregrounded figures dramatically contrasts with a darkened background. Rembrandt reflected his paintings by remaining true to his singular artistic vision and casting his own light on the darkness of conformity.

For Question 14, select one answer choice.

14. The author of the passage is primarily concerned with
    Ⓐ defining the technical methods Rembrandt used in painting his various works
    Ⓑ providing a brief memoir of Rembrandt's motivations as a painter
    Ⓒ explaining how Rembrandt differentiated himself from other painters of his time
    Ⓓ cataloging the individuals Rembrandt used as models in his works
    Ⓔ contrasting the works of contemporary painters to the works of Rembrandt

For Question 15, consider each of the choices separately and select all that apply.

15. The passage supports which of the following statements about Rembrandt?
    - [A] Most of Rembrandt's contemporaries avoided the use of humble models for their paintings.
    - [B] Rembrandt achieved enhanced artistic effect through the use of a unique method.
    - [C] Rembrandt saw artistic value in subject matter outside the mainstream.

For Questions 16 through 20, select the two answer choices that, when used to complete the sentence, fit the meaning of the sentence as a whole and produce completed sentences that are alike in meaning.

16. Joanna's _____ lack of enthusiasm about the job made the interviewer extremely apprehensive to hire her; the company was searching for motivated employees who enjoyed what they did.
    - [A] covert
    - [B] manifest
    - [C] furtive
    - [D] feigned
    - [E] deceptive
    - [F] obvious

17. The American Civil War began after the Confederate States of America seceded from the Union, in essence dividing the United States into two _____ countries.
    - [A] concordant
    - [B] allied
    - [C] distinct
    - [D] discrete
    - [E] united
    - [F] banded

18. Despite the capricious impulses that often impelled him to action in his social life, he was actually quite _____ when it came to making business decisions.
    - [A] logical
    - [B] garrulous
    - [C] pragmatic
    - [D] guileless
    - [E] reclusive
    - [F] pretentious

GO ON TO NEXT PAGE

19. The fear inspired by the media's coverage of unprovoked shark attacks is _____; there are actually more fatalities each year from lightning strikes than from shark attacks.
    - [A] pompous
    - [B] exaggerated
    - [C] candid
    - [D] subdued
    - [E] excessive
    - [F] inevitable

20. Agriculturists have traditionally considered crop rotation to be _____; it helps to preserve soil nutrients, control disease, and deter weed growth.
    - [A] aesthetic
    - [B] didactic
    - [C] pedantic
    - [D] incidental
    - [E] crucial
    - [F] indispensable

STOP.
This is the end of Section 2. Use any remaining time to check your work.

SECTION 3

Verbal Reasoning

30 Minutes
20 Questions

This section consists of three different types of questions: Reading Comprehension, Text Completion, and Sentence Equivalence. To answer the questions, select the best answer from the answer choices given. Reading Comprehension questions appear in sets; Text Completion and Sentence Equivalence questions are independent. The questions will be presented in random order. Read the following directions before you begin the test.

Reading Comprehension Questions

Directions:
Multiple-choice Questions—Select One Answer Choice: These are the traditional multiple-choice questions with five answer choices from which you must select one.

Multiple-choice Questions—Select One or More Answer Choices: These questions provide three answer choices; select all that are correct.

Select-in-Passage: Choose the sentence in the passage that meets a certain description.

Text Completion Questions

Directions: Select one entry from the corresponding column of choices for each blank. Fill all blanks in the way that best completes the text.

Sentence Equivalence Questions

Directions: Select the two answer choices that, when used to complete the sentence, fit the meaning of the sentence as a whole and produce completed sentences that are alike in meaning.

GO ON TO NEXT PAGE

For Questions 1 through 5, select the two answer choices that, when used to complete the sentence, fit the meaning of the sentence as a whole and produce completed sentences that are alike in meaning.

1. It comes as no surprise that different cultures have certain behavioral norms; however, to an outsider, the specifics of these behaviors can often be _____.
    - A explicit
    - B startling
    - C predictable
    - D unexpected
    - E derisive
    - F admirable

2. Specific concerns frequently motivate the topics of scientific research, but the results are often _____.
    - A surprising
    - B specialized
    - C unanticipated
    - D beneficial
    - E spectacular
    - F expensive

3. Many people believe that strong individual initiative characterized the Industrial Revolution and see inventors as the _____ of that age.
    - A aberration
    - B legends
    - C personification
    - D misrepresentation
    - E liberators
    - F symbols

4. Buried thousands of years ago inside various sediments, recently discovered fossils are _____ time capsules, filled with information for scientists who study organisms from the remote past.
    - A impenetrable
    - B resplendent
    - C veritable
    - D inconsequential
    - E broken
    - F truly

5. The advertising executives were in _____ over continuing their latest successful, yet highly controversial, ad campaign; they could not decide on a course of action.

   A agreement
   B a quandary
   C harmony
   D a revolution
   E accord
   F a predicament

Questions 6 and 7 are based on the following passage.

Ernest Hemingway's novel, *The Sun Also Rises*, has frequently been treated as a novel of the Lost Generation—a group of young American expatriate writers living in Paris who came of age during World War I and established their reputations in the 1920's. They considered themselves "lost" because their inherited values could not operate in the postwar world and they felt spiritually alienated from a country that they considered hopelessly provincial and emotionally barren. More broadly, the Lost Generation represented the World War I American generation. This approach to *The Sun Also Rises* has become something of a critical cliché. Hemingway described the novel as less about the life of postwar expatriates than about the rhythms of nature as an expression of eternity.

For Question 6, consider each of the choices separately and select all that apply.

6. The passage suggests that Hemingway's novel is thought to display which of the following qualities?

   A An attempt to reconcile nature with the philosophical concept of eternity.
   B A description of the post-World War I expatriate experience.
   C A diatribe against the organized religion of Hemingway's day.

For Question 7, select one answer choice.

7. The passage addresses which of the following issues related to Hemingway's depiction of the Lost Generation?

   A Contemporary Parisians were frequently at odds with expatriate Americans because their wartime experiences were radically different.
   B Organized religion was ill-equipped to address the needs of post-war America.
   C Post-war Americans sometimes lived abroad as a response to their feelings of alienation in their home country.
   D Members of the Lost Generation frequently felt lost because they were unable to afford passage home.
   E Literary tropes such as nature and eternity are more compelling than the stories of individual characters.

GO ON TO NEXT PAGE

Question 8 is based on the following passage.

Advocates of the Raw Food Diet claim that raw food is the optimal fuel for the human body, since the digestive system evolved before humans started cooking with fire. Nutrition experts are in disagreement about the benefits and the pitfalls of a raw diet. Proponents of the Raw Food Diet believe that raw food contains enzymes that aid its own digestion, and that they help populate the digestive tract with beneficial flora that stimulates the human immune system. Opponents of the Raw Food Diet point out that raw food may contain harmful bacteria and parasites, and that certain products, such as kidney beans and buckwheat, are unsafe to consume in their raw form and that ignorance in such matters could result in poisoning. Additionally, critics are concerned that the structure of some foods, like tomatoes and carrots, makes it virtually impossible to access the available nutrients without cooking. Opponents also criticize raw food advocates as promoting data that is anecdotal, rather than scientific, in nature.

For Question 8, select one answer choice.

8. The primary purpose of the passage is to
   - (A) compare the Raw Food Diet to other alternative diets
   - (B) provide recipes and suggest specific products for people interested in exploring the Raw Food Diet
   - (C) provide an overview of the Raw Food Diet, highlighting some of the common arguments for and against it
   - (D) argue for the need of healthy alternatives to mainstream nutrition
   - (E) warn the readers against restrictive diets such as the Raw Food Diet

Questions 9 and 10 are based on the following passage.

Since 1875, when Alexander Graham Bell first discovered how to send the human voice along wires, the telephone has been one of the world's most utilized and essential methods of communication. The first telephone exchange in America was established in 1878 and served a total of 21 people. At that time, operators would answer a call and connect two parties by completing an electrical circuit. Little could those operators envision that, one century later, calls would be transmitted along optical fibers and, soon after, would become totally wireless and portable. The idea of orbiting satellites picking up millions of calls and relaying them across the planet would have been unimaginable.

For Question 9, consider each of the choices separately and select all that apply.

9. It can be inferred from the passage that
   - [A] satellites transmit telephone calls
   - [B] early telephone users were frustrated by the technology's inefficiencies
   - [C] wireless telephones are preferable to land-based lines

10. Select the sentence that establishes the scope of the earliest telephone communications.

    The first telephone exchange in America was established in 1878...

For Question 11, select one entry from the corresponding column of choices for each blank. Fill all blanks in the way that best completes the text.

11. Many modernists believe that form follows function, and therefore, their furniture designs have asserted the (i) _____ of human needs as the furniture's form was (ii) _____ human use.

Blank (i)	Blank (ii)
(A) importance	(D) dictated by
(B) universality	(E) refined by
(C) variability	(F) reflected in

Questions 12 to 14 are based on the following passage.

As concerns over man's impact on the global environment increase, many interesting innovations are being considered. For example, "green roofs" – plant-filled roof top gardens – are one substantial way to confront the country's ecological problems, and there seems to be very little in the way of a downside. For one thing, a green roof acts as a sponge for rainwater, absorbing the majority of water from a typical rainstorm. Only three to five inches of soil for a green roof is sufficient for this to occur, which keeps the weight of the roof to a minimum. Because the plantings on the roof absorb the rainwater, drainage and sewage systems have a decreased volume of water pumping through them, keeping these systems from becoming over-stressed. And while the soil and plants are absorbing rainwater, they are also taking in pollutants for their own nourishment by storing carbon and then emitting necessary oxygen back into the atmosphere.

GO ON TO NEXT PAGE

For Questions 12 to 14, select one answer choice.

12. The second and third sentences are characterized, respectively, by
    - Ⓐ warning and justification
    - Ⓑ generalization and specification
    - Ⓒ invocation and definition
    - Ⓓ authority and reverence
    - Ⓔ confession and resolution

13. The author's main point in the passage is that
    - Ⓐ green roofs are expensive to install and maintain
    - Ⓑ green roofs are both innovative and eco-friendly
    - Ⓒ global warming concerns have led to many new inventions
    - Ⓓ plant-filled roof gardens emit oxygen into the atmosphere
    - Ⓔ green roofs are the definitive cure for global warming

14. The author references the absorption capabilities of green roofs primarily in order to illustrate
    - Ⓐ a preoccupation with style over design practicality
    - Ⓑ the inefficiencies of installing plantings to a building's roof
    - Ⓒ how green roofs lead to more efficient and less-stressed home systems
    - Ⓓ the increased public interest in environmental friendliness in the construction industry
    - Ⓔ how global warming has accelerated society's interest in environmentally friendly structures

For Questions 15 and 16, select one entry from the corresponding column of choices for each blank. Fill all blanks in the way that best completes the text.

15. The availability of carbon dioxide is an essential (i) _____ for plant life, while oxygen is equally (ii) _____ for animal life.

Blank (i)	Blank (ii)
Ⓐ choice	Ⓓ optional
Ⓑ luxury	Ⓔ harmful
Ⓒ condition	Ⓕ necessary

16. People frequently state that books about recent catastrophes are morally (i) _____ attempts to profit from the misfortune of others, but an alternate opinion suggests that our desire for such material, together with the venerable tradition to which they belong, (ii) _____ their suffering.

Blank (i)	Blank (ii)
Ⓐ repugnant	Ⓓ legitimizes
Ⓑ treacherous	Ⓔ safeguards
Ⓒ fortuitous	Ⓕ honors

Question 17 is based on the following passage.

The Homestead Act of 1862 has been called one of the most important pieces of legislation in the history of the United States. Signed into law by Abraham Lincoln, this Act turned over vast amounts of the public domain to private citizens. 270 million acres, or 10% of the area of the United States was claimed and settled under this act. The Act provided that any head of a family who was a citizen, or declared his intention of becoming a citizen, could claim 160 acres of land. The claimants needed to pay a small registration fee and reside on the land for five years. Claimants were also required to build a home and grow crops on the land. If after five years, the original settler were still on the land, it would become his property, free and clear.

For question 17, select one answer choice.

17. Which of the following, if true, would most undermine the validity of the author's statements about the significance of the Homestead Act?
    Ⓐ Most settlers had moved on from their claim sites before the end of five years.
    Ⓑ Most settlers chose to grow non-food crops.
    Ⓒ Some congressmen thought there should be no registration fee for settlers.
    Ⓓ Some non-citizen claimants were unable to become citizens.
    Ⓔ Some of the land was unsuited to growing wheat.

Question 18 is based on the following passage.

Human fascination with space began hundreds of years ago. That interest has not waned, and today, the Hubble Telescope orbits 375 miles above Earth, working non-stop to unlock the secrets of the universe. The Hubble uses state-of-the-art instruments to provide amazing views of the universe that cannot be matched by ground-based telescopes. The reason for this is that, from the ground, we look at stars and other objects in space through Earth's atmosphere. Our atmosphere is full of clouds, dust, and pollution, which cause everything we see to shimmer and shake. This effect creates difficulty for scientists on the ground to make steady, accurate measurements of objects moving in space. With assistance from the Hubble Telescope, astronomers can pinpoint the location of faraway stars and galaxies, and measure the speeds and distances of astronomical objects with far greater precision. Astronomers may even one day tell us exactly when the universe began.

For Question 18, select one answer choice.

18. The author suggests that "steady, accurate measurements" can be difficult to attain because
    - Ⓐ scientists frequently introduce unnecessary complications to simple situations
    - Ⓑ Earth-based telescopes are insufficiently precise due to atmospheric dust and pollution
    - Ⓒ due to Earth's constant rotation, it is nearly impossible to pinpoint exact distances in outer space
    - Ⓓ most telescopes require regular repair missions when their cameras aren't functioning properly
    - Ⓔ astronomers are not yet able to tell us exactly when the universe began

Questions 19 and 20 are based on the following passage.

Recently, a group of researchers from Tokyo developed a device that allows them to identify individuals of the endangered Ganges River dolphin species. Ganges River dolphins are rare in that, unlike the majority of their counterparts, they live in fresh water rivers and lakes rather than salt water oceans. The species is blind and uses clicks to send out sonar pulses for guidance and to find food. The Tokyo researchers' new underwater acoustic device measures these pulses, which are as unique as a human fingerprint, thus allowing the identification and tracking of individual dolphins. Scientists estimate that, in the last few decades, the number of Ganges River dolphins has dropped by 50 percent due to a lethal combination of fishing nets, hunters, pollution, and human construction. With this new technology, scientists hope to get a better idea of how many of these dolphins still exist, as well as their migration patterns and feeding habits. In turn, this information may help scientists protect and conserve this unique species.

For Question 19, consider each of the choices separately and select all that apply.

19. The passage suggests that Ganges River dolphins exhibit which of the following characteristics?
    - [A] an ability to navigate waterways without using sight
    - [B] an ability to live in freshwater environments
    - [C] a tolerance for human interaction

20. Select the sentence within the paragraph that explains how scientists hope to help preserve the Ganges River dolphin.

STOP.
This is the end of Section 3. Use any remaining time to check your work.

SECTION 4

Quantitative Reasoning

35 Minutes
20 Questions

This section includes four types of questions: Multiple-choice Questions (Select One Answer Choice *and* Select One or More Answer Choices), Numeric Entry Questions, and Quantitative Comparison Questions. Read the following directions before you begin the test.

General Information:

Numbers: All of the numbers used in this section are real numbers.

Figures: Assume that the position of all points, angles, etc. are in the order shown and the measures of angles are positive.

Straight lines can be assumed to be straight.

All figures lie in a plane unless otherwise stated.

The figures given for each question provide information to solve the problem. The figures are not drawn to scale unless otherwise stated. To solve the problems, use your knowledge of mathematics; do not estimate lengths and sizes of the figures to answer questions.

Multiple-choice Questions

Select One Answer Choice

Directions: These questions are multiple-choice questions that ask you to select only one answer choice from a list of five choices.

Select One or More Answer Choices

Directions: Select one or more answer choices according to the specific question directions.

If the question does not specify how many answer choices to select, select all that apply.

The correct answer may be just one of the choices or as many as all of the choices, depending on the question.

No credit is given unless you select all of the correct choices and no others.

If the question specifies how many answer choices to select, select exactly that number of choices.

Numeric Entry Questions

Directions: Enter your answer in the answer box(es) below the question.

Equivalent forms of the correct answer, such as 2.5 and 2.50, are all correct. Fractions do not need to be reduced to lowest terms.

Enter the exact answer unless the question asks you to round your answer.

Chapter 11: GRE Practice Test 1 291

Quantitative Comparison Questions

Directions: Some questions give you two quantities, Quantity A and Quantity B. Compare the two quantities and choose one of the following answer choices:

- **A** if Quantity A is greater;
- **B** if Quantity B is greater;
- **C** if the two quantities are equal;
- **D** if you cannot determine the relationship based on the given information.

Note: Information and/or figures pertaining to one or both of the quantities may appear above the two columns. Any information that appears in both columns has the same meaning for both Quantity A and Quantity B.

You will also be asked Data Interpretation questions, which are grouped together and refer to the same table, graph, or other data presentation. These questions ask the examinee to interpret or analyze the given data. The types of questions may be Multiple-choice (both types) or Numeric Entry.

Each of Questions 1 to 7 presents two quantities, Quantity A and Quantity B. Compare the two quantities. You may use additional information centered above the quantities if such information is given. Choose one of the following answer choices:

- Ⓐ if Quantity A is greater;
- Ⓑ if Quantity B is greater;
- Ⓒ if the two quantities are equal;
- Ⓓ if you cannot determine the relationship based on the given information.

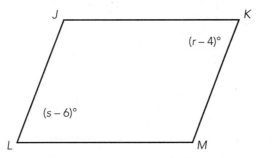

JKML is a parallelogram.
Both *r* and *s* are positive integers.

Quantity A	Quantity B
1. *r*	*s*

Ⓐ   Ⓑ   Ⓒ   Ⓓ

GO ON TO NEXT PAGE

	Quantity A	Quantity B	
2.	$1 - \dfrac{1}{8}$	$1 - \dfrac{1}{12}$	Ⓐ Ⓑ Ⓒ Ⓓ

	Quantity A	Quantity B	
3.	$-(4)^2$	$(-4)^2$	Ⓐ Ⓑ Ⓒ Ⓓ

x and *y* are each greater than 1

	Quantity A	Quantity B	
4.	$(4x)(7y)$	$28xy$	Ⓐ Ⓑ Ⓒ Ⓓ

Mike is 3 years younger than Tom
Mark is 8 years older than Tim
Tom is 9 years older than Tim

	Quantity A	Quantity B	
5.	Mark's age	Mike's age	Ⓐ Ⓑ Ⓒ Ⓓ

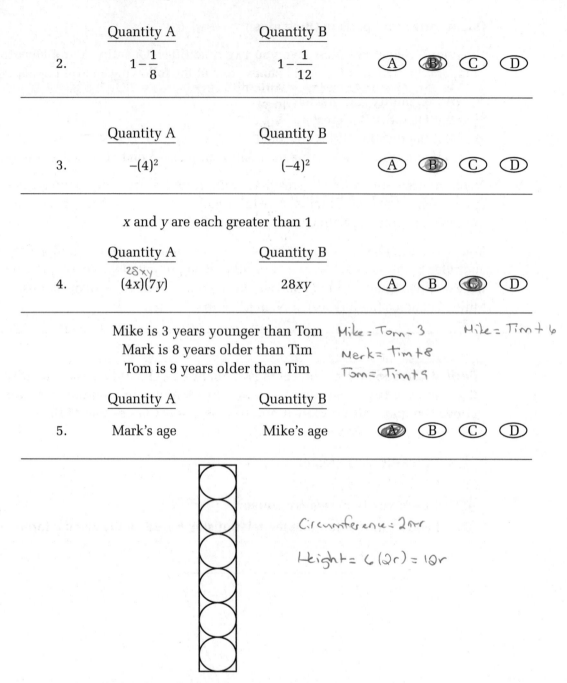

Six racquetballs of identical size are stacked one on top of the other so that they fit exactly inside a closed right cylindrical can, as shown.

	Quantity A	Quantity B	
6.	The sum of the circumferences of three of the balls	The height of the stack of 6 balls	Ⓐ Ⓑ Ⓒ Ⓓ

There are 17 dogs in a kennel. 5 of the dogs are female.

Quantity A	Quantity B
7. Fraction of male dogs at the kennel	Ratio of female to male dogs

(A) (B) (C) (D)

8. In an office supply shop, pens that normally sell for 89 cents each are on sale at 2 for $1.29. How much can be saved by purchasing 12 of these pens at the sales price?
   (A) $2.40
   (B) $2.94
   (C) $3.04
   (D) $4.80
   (E) $7.74

9. If the average (arithmetic mean) of 7 consecutive numbers is 16, what is the sum of the least and greatest of the 7 integers?
   (A) 13
   (B) 14
   (C) 16
   (D) 19
   (E) 32

For Question 10, write your answer in the box.

10. If $3x+4y=17$ and $5x+2y=23$, what is the value of $x-y$?

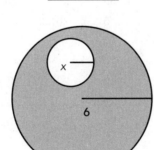

11. In the figure above, a small circle, with radius x, is inside a larger circle, with radius 6. What is the area, in terms of x, of the shaded region?
    (A) $6\pi - 2\pi x$
    (B) $6\pi - \pi x^2$
    (C) $12\pi - 2\pi x$
    (D) $36\pi - 2\pi x$
    (E) $36\pi - \pi x^2$

GO ON TO NEXT PAGE

For Question 12, select all the answer choices that apply.

12. If |4−3x| < 5, which of the following is a possible value of x?

    Select all such values.
    - [A] 1
    - [B] 2
    - [C] 3

13. The number 0.001 is how many times greater than the number $(0.0001)^2$?
    - (A) 10
    - (B) 10^3
    - (C) 10^5
    - (D) 10^7
    - (E) 10^9

Refer to the following information for Questions 14 to 17.

PROFILE OF CONGRESS IN YEAR X
(total membership: 535)

House of Representatives		Senate	House of Representatives		Senate
Party			**Profession**		
276	Democratic	54	272	Lawyer	74
159	Republican	46	75	Business Executive	12
435	Total	100	32	Educator	4
			9	Farmer or Rancher	2
Sex			16	Career Government Official	3
406	Male	95	5	Physician	1
29	Female	5	26	Other	4
Age			**Ethnic Group**		
29	Youngest	32	22	Black American	4
74	Oldest	79	3	Asian American	3
44	Average (arithmetic mean)	56	2	Hispanic American	1

14. In the Senate, if 20 male senators were replaced by 20 female senators, the ratio of male senators to female senators would be
    - (A) 4 to 1
    - (B) 3 to 1
    - (C) 3 to 2
    - (D) 2 to 1
    - (E) 1 to 1

15. Approximately what percent of the members of Congress belong to the Democratic Party?
    - Ⓐ 54%
    - Ⓑ 62%
    - Ⓒ 70%
    - Ⓓ 72%
    - Ⓔ 76%

For Question 16, select all the answer choices that apply.

16. Which of the following can be inferred from the information given in the chart?

    Indicate all such statements.
    - Ⓐ More than 75 percent of the lawyers in Congress are members of the House of Representatives.
    - Ⓑ There are more female educators in the Senate than in the House of Representatives.
    - Ⓒ On average, members of the Senate are older than members of the House of Representatives.

17. Approximately what fraction of the members of House of Representatives is Farmers or Ranchers?
    - Ⓐ $\dfrac{11}{159}$
    - Ⓑ $\dfrac{11}{276}$
    - Ⓒ $\dfrac{9}{435}$
    - Ⓓ $\dfrac{9}{276}$
    - Ⓔ $\dfrac{9}{2}$

GO ON TO NEXT PAGE

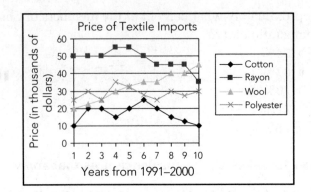

18. Based on the graph shown, what was the average yearly decrease in the price of polyester between 1994 and 1998, inclusive?

    (A) $1,250
    (B) $2,500
    (C) $3,750
    (D) $5,000
    (E) $6,250

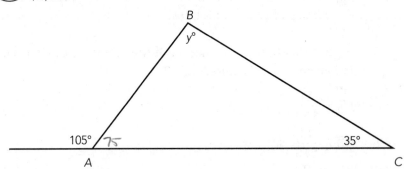

19. In triangle *ABC*, what is the value of *y*?

    (A) 35°
    (B) 50°
    (C) 65°
    (D) 75°
    (E) 80°

For Question 20, write your answer in the box.

20. WINK, Inc. is made up of 450 employees who work a total of 13,500 hours per week. If the number of weekly work hours per person has a normal distribution and the standard deviation equals 7 hours, how many employees work more than 37 hours per week?

STOP.
This is the end of Section 4. Use any remaining time to check your work.

SECTION 5

Quantitative Reasoning

35 Minutes
20 Questions

This section includes four types of questions: Multiple-choice Questions (Select One Answer Choice *and* Select One or More Answer Choices), Numeric Entry Questions, and Quantitative Comparison Questions. Read the following directions before you begin the test.

General Information:

Numbers: All of the numbers used in this section are real numbers.

Figures: Assume that the position of all points, angles, etc. are in the order shown and the measures of angles are positive.

Straight lines can be assumed to be straight.

All figures lie in a plane unless otherwise stated.

The figures given for each question provide information to solve the problem. The figures are not drawn to scale unless otherwise stated. To solve the problems, use your knowledge of mathematics; do not estimate lengths and sizes of the figures to answer questions.

Multiple-choice Questions

Select One Answer Choice

Directions: These questions are multiple-choice questions that ask you to select only one answer choice from a list of five choices.

Select One or More Answer Choices

Directions: Select one or more answer choices according to the specific question directions.

If the question does not specify how many answer choices to select, select all that apply.

The correct answer may be just one of the choices or as many as all of the choices, depending on the question.

No credit is given unless you select all of the correct choices and no others.

If the question specifies how many answer choices to select, select exactly that number of choices.

GO ON TO NEXT PAGE

Numeric Entry Questions

Directions: Enter your answer in the answer box(es) below the question.

Equivalent forms of the correct answer, such as 2.5 and 2.50, are all correct. Fractions do not need to be reduced to lowest terms.

Enter the exact answer unless the question asks you to round your answer.

Quantitative Comparison Questions

Directions: Some questions give you two quantities, Quantity A and Quantity B. Compare the two quantities and choose one of the following answer choices:

  A if Quantity A is greater;
  B if Quantity B is greater;
  C if the two quantities are equal;
  D if you cannot determine the relationship based on the given information.

Note: information and/or figures pertaining to one or both of the quantities may appear above the two columns. Any information that appears in both columns has the same meaning for both Quantity A and in Quantity B.

You will also be asked Data Interpretation questions, which are grouped together and refer to the same table, graph, or other data presentation. These questions ask the examinee to interpret or analyze the given data. The types of questions may be Multiple-choice (both types) or Numeric Entry.

Each of Questions 1 to 7 presents two quantities, Quantity A and Quantity B. Compare the two quantities. You may use additional information centered above the quantities if such information is given. Choose one of the following answer choices:

  Ⓐ if Quantity A is greater;
  Ⓑ if Quantity B is greater;
  Ⓒ if the two quantities are equal;
  Ⓓ if you cannot determine the relationship based on the given information.

x is an integer (positive or negative)

Quantity A	Quantity B
$\dfrac{7}{(4+6^x)}$	$\dfrac{7}{(6+4^x)}$

✗ 1.   Ⓐ Ⓑ̃ Ⓒ ✗Ⓓ

s is equal to -4 and 10

	Quantity A	Quantity B	
2.	$(s-3)^2$	49	Ⓐ Ⓑ ⓒ Ⓓ

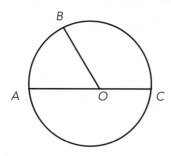

	Quantity A	Quantity B	
3.	$\angle AOB$	$\angle BOC$	Ⓐ Ⓑ Ⓒ Ⓓ

	Quantity A	Quantity B	
4.	$r-145$	$300-r$	Ⓐ Ⓑ Ⓒ Ⓓ

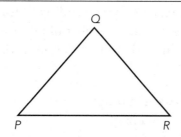

	Quantity A	Quantity B	
5.	PR	$QR-PQ$	Ⓐ Ⓑ Ⓒ Ⓓ

	Quantity A	Quantity B	
6.	$(x+3)(x+2)$	x^2+6	Ⓐ Ⓑ Ⓒ Ⓓ

$$\frac{9w+6v-3z}{3}=3w$$

	Quantity A	Quantity B	
7.	$2v$	z	Ⓐ Ⓑ Ⓒ Ⓓ

GO ON TO NEXT PAGE

8. A certain brownie recipe states that the brownies should be baked in a rectangular pan with an area of 32 square inches (disregard the depth of the pan). If Jaime wants to use the recipe to make a pan of brownies of the same depth but with an area of 48 square inches, by what factor should she multiply the recipe ingredients?

   (A) 3
   (B) $2\frac{1}{2}$
   (C) 2
   (D) $1\frac{1}{2}$
   (E) $\frac{2}{3}$

For Question 9, select all the answer choices that apply.

9. If $x=6y$, then which of the following expressions is a multiple of x? Select all such expressions.

   [A] $3y$
   [B] $12y$
   [C] $30y$

10. The cost, in dollars, of manufacturing x microwaves is $6{,}000+300x$ dollars. The amount received when selling these x microwaves is $700x$ dollars. What is the least number of microwaves that must be manufactured and sold so that the net profit is $2400?

    (A) 15
    (B) 17
    (C) 19
    (D) 21
    (E) 23

11. On the number line, 2.3 is halfway between which of the following numbers?

    (A) −2.3 and 2.3
    (B) −1.6 and 6.2
    (C) −.3 and 4.3
    (D) .24 and 6.84
    (E) .5 and 3

For Question 12, write your answer in the box.

12. The perimeter of a rectangular plot of land is 110 meters. If the length of one side of the plot is 35 meters, what is the area of the plot, in square meters?

    [700] m²

13. The average (arithmetic mean) of c and d is 12, and the average of c, d, and e is 10. What is the value of e?
    - (A) 6
    - (B) 10
    - (C) 12
    - (D) 18
    - (E) 20

Questions 14 to 17 are based on the following graphs.

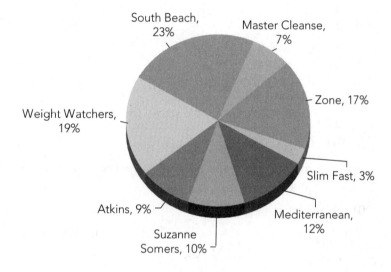

Types of Diets in 1995 (total dieters: 135 million)

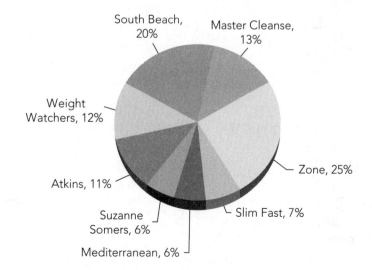

Types of Diets in 2000 (total dieters: 210 million)

GO ON TO NEXT PAGE

14. In 1995, approximately how many million people were on the Zone Diet?
    - (A) 12.2
    - (B) 17.0
    - (C) 23.0
    - (D) 24.3
    - (E) 35.7

15. What is the ratio of the number of people on the Slim Fast diet in 1995 to the number of people on the Mediterranean diet in 2000?
    - (A) $\dfrac{3}{28}$
    - (B) $\dfrac{1}{4}$
    - (C) $\dfrac{1}{3}$
    - (D) $\dfrac{9}{28}$
    - (E) $\dfrac{27}{98}$

16. Approximately what is the percent increase in the number of Master Cleanse dieters from 1995 to 2000?
    - (A) 200%
    - (B) 157%
    - (C) 189%
    - (D) 187%
    - (E) 129%

17. What is the approximate measure of the central angle representing Atkins dieters in 1995?
    - (A) 9°
    - (B) 15°
    - (C) 32°
    - (D) 91°
    - (E) 324°

18. If $A=(x-y)-z$ and $B=x-(y-z)$, then $A-B=$
    - (A) $-2z$
    - (B) $-2y$
    - (C) 0
    - (D) $2z$
    - (E) $2y$

For Question 19, write your answer in the box.

19. If $-7 \leq x \leq 5$ and $-3 \leq y \leq 4$, what is the greatest possible value of $(y-x)(x+y)$?

    (4+7)(5+4)　　　　[99]　　　　(-3-5)(-3-7)
    (11)(9)　　　　　　　　　　　　　(-8)(-10)

20. A square is inscribed in a circle. If the area of the inscribed square is 50, what is the area of the circle?
    - (A) 5π
    - (B) $5\pi\sqrt{2}$
    - (C) 10π
    - (D) 25π
    - (E) 50π

    $\sqrt{50} = 5\sqrt{2}$

    $d = \sqrt{2(5\sqrt{2})^2}$

    $d = 10 \quad r = 5$

STOP.
This is the end of Section 5. Use any remaining time to check your work.

GRE Practice Test 1 Answers and Explanations

Answer Key

Section 2. Verbal Reasoning

1. C
2. "The belief was...to become integrated into white society."
3. A
4. B
5. C, F
6. C, D
7. A, D, I
8. C
9. B
10. "On the other hand...sense of self and personal history."
11. C
12. C
13. B, D, H
14. C
15. A, B, C
16. B, F
17. C, D
18. A, C
19. B, E
20. E, F

Section 3. Verbal Reasoning

1. B, D
2. A, C
3. C, F
4. C, F
5. B, F
6. A, B
7. C
8. C
9. A
10. "The first telephone exchange... served a total of 21 people."
11. A, D
12. B
13. B
14. C
15. C, F
16. A, F
17. A
18. B
19. A, B
20. "With this new technology...and feeding habits."

Section 4. Quantitative Reasoning

1. B
2. B
3. B
4. C
5. A
6. A
7. A
8. B
9. E
10. 3
11. E
12. A, B
13. C
14. B
15. B
16. A, C
17. C
18. A
19. E
20. 72

Section 5. Quantitative Reasoning

1. D
2. C
3. D
4. D
5. A
6. D
7. C
8. D
9. B, C
10. D
11. B
12. 700
13. A
14. C
15. D
16. C
17. C
18. A
19. 99
20. D

Answer Explanations

Section 1. Analytical Writing Parts 1 and 2

Because grading the essay is subjective, we've chosen not to include any "graded" essays here. Your best bet is to have someone you trust, such as your personal tutor, read your essays and give you an honest critique. Make the grading criteria mentioned in Chapter 6, "GRE Analytical Writing," available to whoever grades your essays. If you plan on grading your own essays, review the grading criteria and be as honest as possible regarding the structure, development, organization, technique, and appropriateness of your writing. Focus on your weak areas and continue to practice in order to improve your writing skills.

Section 2. Verbal Reasoning

1. **The best answer is C.** According to the passage, reservations caused harmful segregation. Readjustment was intended to reintegrate Native Americans into mainstream society.
2. **The best answer is:** *The belief was that if it were beneficial for African American children to be placed in schools with white children, it was also beneficial for Native Americans to become integrated into white society.* This sentence implies that the U.S. government believed that the needs of African American children and Native American children could both be met by putting them in schools with white children. Since the response was the same, it implies that the government believed that the needs were equivalent.
3. **The best answer is A.** The passage states that government leaders failed to take into account the wishes of tribal leaders. This failure was a logical flaw in the government's plan to better the lives of Native Americans.
4. **The best answer is B.** According to the passage, farmers considered Whitney's fee to be exorbitant and they refused to use his gin.
5. **The best answer is C and F.** Because it is difficult to imprison or isolate into a community, "reintegration" is the best choice for Blank (i). The contrasting conjunction "rather than" indicates that the second word will have a negative meaning to contrast with the positive meaning of "reintegration." Therefore, "punishment" is the best choice for Blank (ii).
6. **The best answer is C and D.** The first blank should be filled by a synonym for "vague." Since "indefinite" has the meaning of "not clearly defined or inexact," it is the best choice for Blank (i). The teacher then acts in a way that the students feel is unfair. "Indignant" implies anger as a result of injustice, so it is the best choice for Blank (ii).
7. **The best answer is A, D, and I.** The first two choices should be positive. Since the networking sites are described as innovative, "revolutionizing" is the best choice for Blank (i). Likewise, "expanding" also conveys the

idea of positive growth and change. The second clause of the sentence contradicts this positive view of social networking sites. Consequently, "inadequate" is the best choice for Blank (iii).

8. **The best answer is C.** This passage presents the pros and cons of a new medical treatment. By emphasizing the differences between the two sides and by failing to offer any resolution, the author puts the treatment into question. Consequently, choice C is the best answer.

9. **The best answer is B only.** According to the passage, many of the details of the treatment are still open to debate. We know only that research is ongoing.

10. **The best answer is:** *On the other hand, by relegating our memories to oblivion, such a drug could fundamentally change our sense of self and personal history.* This sentence makes clear the potential negative consequences of using the treatment.

11. **The best answer is C only.** According to the passage, one thing is certain: debate will continue in this field. Therefore, it is implied that ethical debates are a predictable result of certain types of medical research.

12. **The best answer is C.** The passage focuses solely on trains, which narrows the choices to C and D. Because the structure of the passage is historical, choice C is the best option.

13. **The best answer is B, D, and H.** The actions of the scientific community are contrasted with the embracing done by the Soviets. Therefore, "spurned" is the best choice for Blank (i). For Blank (ii), "ideologically" refers to a system of ideas, which matches "Party beliefs." Finally, Lamarck's theory was about the process of evolution, which implies change or transformation over time.

14. **The best answer is C.** According to the passage, Rembrandt's works differ from those of his contemporaries in several important ways. Explaining those differences is the main point of the passage.

15. **The best answer is A, B, and C.** All of the choices are supported by the passage. Choice C is implied; Rembrandt presumably knew what his contemporaries were painting and chose different subject matter. This suggests that he saw artistic value in these other models.

16. **The best answer is B and F.** Joanne's lack of motivation was apparent enough to make the interviewer apprehensive about hiring her. Choices B and F are synonyms for "apparent" and are the best choices for the sentence.

17. **The best answer is C and D.** The Civil War divided the country. "Distinct" and "discrete" both have the meaning of clear division into separate parts.

18. **The best answer is A and C.** The word "despite" indicates that the choices should be antonyms for "capricious." "Logical" and "pragmatic" both work.

19. **The best answer is B and E.** According to the sentence, people should be more afraid of lightning than of shark attacks. This implies that public fear of attack is out of proportion to risk. Therefore, "exaggerated" and "excessive" are the best answer choices.

20. **The best answer is E and F.** The sentence's second clause lists the benefits of crop rotation. Therefore, the choices to fill in the blank should be positive. Only choices E and F are strongly positive.

Section 3. Verbal Reasoning

1. **The best answer is B and D.** The conjunction "however" indicates that the answer choices should contrast with "no surprise." Both "startling" and "unexpected" do just that.
2. **The best answer is A and C.** "Specific concerns" suggests that the topics of scientific research are known in detail. The conjunction "but" implies a contrasting idea, like "surprising" or "unanticipated."
3. **The best answer is C and F.** The sentence equates inventors with strong individual initiative. The synonyms "personification" and "symbols" both preserve that meaning.
4. **The best answer is C and F.** The way the fossils were preserved (in rock) and the fact that they have only recently been discovered, indicate that they are excellent resources for scientists. Choices C and F are synonyms that convey that idea.
5. **The best answer is B and F.** Because the executives could not decide on a course of action, the logical conclusion is that something was stopping them. Only choices B and F indicate problems that could stop a decision from being made.
6. **The best answer is A and B.** According to the passage, literary critics believe *The Sun Also Rises* is a description of American expatriate experiences, while Hemingway described the book as being about nature and eternity. Therefore, choices A and B are best.
7. **The best answer is C.** According to the passage, the Lost Generation specifically referred to Americans living abroad who felt spiritually alienated from their home country.
8. **The best answer is C.** The passage defines the Raw Food Diet primarily through the arguments of its proponents and opponents. Since the passage contains very little else, choice C is the best answer.
9. **The best answer is A.** The last sentence supports choice A. The passage doesn't indicate that early users were frustrated by inefficiency (as opposed to being amazed that it worked at all), nor does it give a preference for land-based vs. wireless technology.
10. **The best answer is: *The first telephone exchange in America was established in 1878 and served a total of 21 people.*** This sentence establishes scope by showing the limited circle of early users.
11. **The best answer is A and D.** The phrase "form follows function" means that how something is used, its function, is more important than how it looks, i.e. its form. Therefore, human needs are "important" and the form of furniture is controlled, or "dictated," by its intended use.

12. **The best answer is B.** The passage begins with an assertion that green roofs are a viable solution to the country's ecological problems. It then continues with specific ways by which green roofs would help.
13. **The best answer is B.** According to the passage, green roofs are an example of an interesting innovation that will help with our ecological problems. Therefore, choice B is the best answer. The remaining choices are either too specific or too broad.
14. **The best answer is C.** The passage focuses on specific examples of how the green roofs would work. The other answer choices are outside the scope of the passage.
15. **The best answer is C and F.** If something is "essential," it is unlikely to be either a choice or a luxury. Therefore, "condition" is the best answer for Blank (i). Blank (ii) must echo this idea, because of the adverb "equally." Consequently, "necessary" is the best choice for Blank (ii).
16. **The best answer is A and F.** It is generally considered unethical to take advantage of someone who is suffering. Therefore, "repugnant" is the best choice for Blank (i). ("Treacherous" would imply that the writers of the books had caused the misfortune.) The conjunction "but" indicates the contrasting view that the books are not unethical; instead, they "honor" the suffering of others.
17. **The best answer is A.** According to the passage, the Homestead Act of 1862 is one of the most important pieces of legislation in the history of the United States. However, claimants were supposed to reside on their property for five years in order to own it. If the majority of claimants left their land before the end of the five-year period, that would call into question the effectiveness of the Act.
18. **The best answer is B.** The sentence just before the one describing "steady, accurate measurements" explains that Earth's atmosphere is full of particles that cause distortion for telescopes. The passage also makes clear that all Earth-based telescopes are affected by Earth's atmosphere.
19. **The best answer is A and B.** The passage states that the Ganges River dolphins are blind, therefore they are able to navigate without sight. Also, they live in fresh-water rivers and lakes. Human contact is said to have caused a 50 percent decline in Ganges River dolphin numbers, so they do not exhibit a tolerance for human interaction.
20. **The best answer is:** *"With this new technology, scientists hope to get a better idea of how many of these dolphins still exist, as well as their migration patterns and feeding habits."* In this sentence, the author specifies the information the new technology can provide. This is the information that could help save the Ganges River dolphin.

Section 4. Quantitative Reasoning

1. **The correct answer is B.** Opposite angles of a parallelogram are congruent, or equal. Therefore, $(s-6)=(r-4)$. Select one variable and solve:

$$s-6=r-4$$
$$s=r+2$$

If $s=r+2$, then s must be greater than r, and Quantity B is greater than Quantity A.

2. **The correct answer is B.** Because $\frac{1}{12}$ is less than $\frac{1}{8}$, subtracting $\frac{1}{12}$ from 1 will result in a larger number than will subtracting $\frac{1}{8}$ from 1. Therefore, Quantity B is greater Quantity A.

3. **The correct answer is B.** To solve this problem, pay attention to the location of the negative sign. Quantity A $=-(4\times 4)=-16$. Quantity B $=(-4\times -4)=16$.

4. **The correct answer is C.** To easily solve this problem, recognize that $(4x)(7y)=28xy$. Therefore, no matter what value you assign to either x or y, the quantities will be the same.

5. **The correct answer is A.** To solve this problem set up 3 equations:
$$\text{Mike}=\text{Tom}-3$$
$$\text{Mark}=\text{Tim}+8$$
$$\text{Tom}=\text{Tim}+9$$

Substitute (Tim+9) for Tom in the first equation:
$$\text{Mike}=\text{Tim}+9-3=\text{Tim}+6.$$

If Mike=Tim+6 and Mark=Tim+8, then Mark=Mike+2. Therefore, Mark's age is greater Mike's age, and Quantity A is greater than Quantity B.

6. **The correct answer is A.** To solve this problem, let x be the radius of each racquetball. The height of the six racquetballs, then, is $12x$, because the diameter is equal to $2x$. The racquetballs are circles, so the circumference of each racquetball is $2\pi x$. Quantity A, the sum of the circumferences of three racquetballs, is $6\pi x$. The value of π is approximately 3.14, so $6\pi x$ will be greater than $12x$, and Quantity A is greater than Quantity B.

7. **The correct answer is A.** The number of male dogs is $17-5$ or 12. The fraction of male dogs in the kennel is $\frac{12}{17}$. The ratio of female to male dogs is $\frac{5}{12}$. Therefore, Quantity A is greater than Quantity B.

8. **The correct answer is B.** Normally, 12 pens would cost 12($0.89), or $10.68. At the sales price, 12 pens cost 6($1.29), or $7.74. This gives you a savings of $10.68−$7.74, or $2.94.

9. **The correct answer is E.** To solve this problem, first set the least of the seven values to x. When the least of the seven numbers is x, the remaining numbers are $x+1$, $x+2$, $x+3$, $x+4$, $x+5$, and $x+6$, because the numbers are consecutive. Because the average of the seven numbers is 16, then [x+ $(x+1)+(x+2)+(x+3)+(x+4)+(x+5)+(x+6)$] divided by $7=16$. Solve for x:
$$\frac{(7x+21)}{7}=16$$
$$7x+21=112$$
$$7x=91$$
$$x=13$$

The smallest number, x, is 13, and the largest number is x+6. Therefore the largest number is equal to 13+6, or 19, and the sum of these two numbers is 13+19, or 32.

10. **The correct answer is 3.** In order to solve this system of equations, subtract the first equation from the second. The result is 2x−2y=6. Factor out 2 to get 2(x−y)=6. Divide both sides by 2; x−y=3.

11. **The correct answer is E.** To solve this problem, first calculate the area of the larger circle: $A=\pi r^2=\pi 6^2=36\pi$. Next, calculate the area of the smaller circle: $A=x^2\pi$. Finally, subtract the area of the smaller circle from the area of the larger circle: $36\pi-x^2\pi$.

12. **The correct answer is A and B.** This problem tests your knowledge of absolute values and inequalities. |4−3x| <5 can be written as two separate inequalities: 4−3x<5 *and* 4−3x>−5. Because the original inequality was a "less than," the word in between the two new inequalities must be AND. Solve both inequalities as follows:

$$4-3x<5$$
$$-3x<1$$
$$-x<\frac{1}{3}$$

When you multiply both sides of an inequality by a negative number, you must reverse the inequality sign.

$$x>-\frac{1}{3}$$

Now move on to the next inequality.

$$4-3x>-5$$
$$3x>-9$$
$$x<3$$

Answer choices A and B are both greater than $-\frac{1}{3}$ and less than 3.

13. **The correct answer is C.** To solve this problem, first square the value 0.0001:

$$(0.0001)^2=0.00000001$$

This value is equivalent to 1×10^{-8}, because the decimal point is moved 8 places to the left. On the other hand, 0.001 is equivalent to 1×10^{-3}, because the decimal point is moved 3 places to the left. Thus, because $\frac{10^{-3}}{10^{-8}}=10^5$, 0.001 is 10^5 times greater than $(0.0001)^2$.

14. **The correct answer is B.** If 20 male senators were replaced by 20 female senators, then there would be 75 male senators (95−20) and 25 female senators (5+20). The ratio would be 75 to 25, which can be reduced to 3 to 1.

15. **The correct answer is B.** There are a total of 330 Democrats in Congress (276 in the House of Representatives and 54 in the Senate). There are a total of 535 members of Congress. So 330/535, or approximately 62% of the members of Congress belong to the Democratic Party.

16. **The correct answer is A and C.** According to the table, there are 346 lawyers in Congress, and 272 of them are in the House of Representatives. $\frac{272}{346}$ is approximately 0.79, or 79%, so Statement A can be inferred. Because

the educators are not divided into groups of male or female, you cannot determine if there are more female educators in one branch of Congress over another. Therefore, Statement B cannot be inferred. According to the table, members of the House of Representatives range in age from 29 to 74 (average age=44), while members of the Senate range in age from 32 to 79 (average age=56). Therefore, Statement C can be inferred.

17. **The correct answer is C.** To solve this problem, first note that there are 435 total members of the House of Representatives. According to the graph, 9 of these people are Farmers or Ranchers.
18. **The correct answer is A.** To find the average yearly decrease, first find the total decrease over the 4 years. In 1994 the total price of polyester was approximately $35,000, and in 1998, it was approximately $30,000. So the difference is $5,000. Now, to find the average, divide by 4 years: 5,000÷4=1,250.
19. **The correct answer is E.** To solve this problem, first calculate the value of the third angle in the triangle. Because the angle is adjacent to a 105°, its measure must be 65°. Therefore, y must equal 180−65−35=80.
20. **The correct answer is 72.** Based on the given information, you know that the average is 13,500÷450, or 30 hours. One standard deviation above the mean is 37 hours. The bell curve of a normal distribution puts the mean at 50%. One standard deviation in either direction is 34% away from the mean. So, one standard deviation is 84% of the employees. Since 84% of the employees work 37 hours, 16% work more than 37 hours. 16% of 450 employees=72.

Section 5. Quantitative Reasoning

1. **The correct answer is D.** Quantity B is larger when $x>1$; quantities A and B are equal when $x=1$. Because the value of x is not specified, you cannot determine a relationship between the quantities.
2. **The correct answer is C.** To solve this problem, substitute the given values into the equation for Quantity A:
   If $s=10$, then $(s-3)^2=(10-3)^2=49$
   If $s=-4$, then $(s-3)^2=(-4-3)^2=49$
   Therefore, both quantities are equal.
3. **The correct answer is D.** Even though you know that AC is a straight line, you don't know where B falls in arc AOC, because you are not given a value for either of the angles, and you do not know where BO intersects AC.
4. **The correct answer is D.** To solve this problem, pick values for r and substitute them into each equation. For example, when $r=200$, $r-125=75$, and $300-r=100$. In this case, Quantity B is greater. However, when $r=300$, $r-145=155$, and $300-r=0$ and Quantity A is greater. You cannot determine a relationship between the two quantities.

5. **The correct answer is A.** The sum of the lengths of the two sides of a triangle is always greater than the length of the third side; thus, $QR<PR+PQ$ and $QR-PQ<PR$. Therefore, Quantity A (PR) is greater than Quantity B ($QR-PQ$).
6. **The correct answer is D.** To solve this problem, you should first expand Quantity A using the FOIL method:

    Multiply the First terms: x^2
    Multiply the Outside terms: $2x$
    Multiply the Inside terms: $3x$
    Multiply the Last terms: 6

    Now add the terms together: x^2+5x+6. Quantity B is x^2+6. Because the value of x could be either positive or negative, Quantity A could be either greater than or less than Quantity B. Therefore, you cannot determine a relationship between the two quantities.
7. **The correct answer is C.** To solve this problem, multiply both sides of the given equation by 3 to get $9w+6v-3z=9w$. Next, subtract $9w$ from both sides to get $6v-3z=0$. Now you can solve for z in terms of v, as follows:

    $$6v=3z$$
    $$2v=z$$

    Both quantities are equal.
8. **The correct answer is D.** Because 48 square inches is 1½ times 32 square inches, Jaime should multiply the recipe ingredients by 1½.
9. **The correct answer is B and C.** In this case, a multiple of x has to also be a multiple of 6. Therefore, both $12y$ and $30y$ are correct.
10. **The correct answer is D.** The first step in solving this problem is to set up an equation based on the net profit. Net profit is equivalent to revenue minus cost. In this problem, revenue is equal to $700x$, and cost is equivalent to $6,000+300x$. You are also given that net profit is 2400 and asked to calculate the number of microwaves, x. The equation is, therefore, as follows:

    $$700x-(6,000+300x)=2,400$$
    $$700x-6,000-300x=2,400$$
    $$400x=8,400$$
    $$x=21$$

11. **The correct answer is B.** In order to solve this problem, find the distance between the first number in the answer and 2.3, and see if that matches the distance between 2.3 and the second number. The only pair for which this is true is −1.6 and 6.2; the distance between −1.6 and 2.3 is 3.9, and the distance between 2.3 and 6.2 is 3.9.
12. **The correct answer is 700.** To solve this problem, first calculate the width of the plot:

    $$P=2w+2l$$
    $$110=2w+2(35)$$
    $$110-70=2w$$
    $$40=2w$$
    $$20=w$$

    The area is $l\times w=35\times 20=700$.

13. **The correct answer is A.** First, set up equations to represent the given averages:

    $$\frac{c+d}{2} = 12 \text{ and } \frac{c+d+e}{3} = 10$$

    Next, simplify the first equation: $c+d=24$
    Now, substitute this value into the second equation and solve for e:

    $$\frac{24+e}{3} = 10$$
    $$24+e = 30$$
    $$e = 6$$

14. **The correct answer is C.** In 1995 the total number of dieters was 135 million. 17% of these people were on the Zone Diet: $0.17 \times 135 = 22.95$, or approximately 23 million people.

15. **The correct answer is D.** In 1995, 3% of 135 million people were on the Slim Fast diet: $0.03 \times 135 = 4.05$. In 2000, 6% of 210 million people were on the Mediterranean diet: $0.06 \times 210 = 12.6$. So the ratio is 4.05 : 12.6, or 405 : 1,260. This reduces to 9:28 or $\frac{9}{28}$

16. **The correct answer is C.** In 1995, 0.07×135, or 9.45 million people were on the Master Cleanse diet. In 2000, 0.13×210, or 27.3 million people were on it. The difference between the two numbers is 17.85. So the fraction is the difference over the original, or $\frac{17.85}{9.45}$, which simplifies to 1.88888 or 1.89.

17. **The correct answer is C.** According to the circle graph, Atkins dieters represent 9% of the total number of dieters in 1995. There are 360° in a circle, so the approximate measure of the central angle representing Atkins dieters in 1995 is 360(0.09) = 32.4, which rounds to 32.

18. **The correct answer is A.** To solve this problem, first set it up: $(x-y)-z-(x-(y-z))$. Now simply perform the subtraction (pay attention to the negative signs!) to get $-2z$.

19. **The correct answer is 99.** The goal would be to make $x+y$ as big as possible and $y-x$ as big as possible. The biggest $x+y$ can be is 9 (5+4). The biggest $y-x$ can be is 11 (4−(−7)). $9 \times 11 = 99$.

20. **The correct answer is D.** If the area of the square is 50, then one side of the square is $\sqrt{50}$ or $5\sqrt{2}$. The diagonal of an inscribed square is equal to the diameter of the circle. The diagonal creates 2 isosceles right triangles. Use the Pythagorean Theorem: $(5\sqrt{2})^2 + (5\sqrt{2})^2 = c^2$. Simplify the equation and you get $c=10$. If the diameter is 10, then the radius is 5. Since the area of a circle is πr^2, the area of this circle is 25π.

12
GRE Practice Test 2

CHAPTER GOALS

- Take a full-length GRE under actual test conditions.
- Check your results using the Answer Key.
- Review the explanations for each question, focusing particularly on questions you answered incorrectly or did not answer at all.
- Build your test-taking confidence.

The simulated GRE in this chapter contains 80 multiple-choice questions and two essay tasks, divided into six main sections. You should allow approximately 3 hours and 30 minutes to complete the entire test. To make this simulated test as much like the actual GRE as possible, you should complete the test sections in the time indicated at the beginning of each section, and in the order in which the sections appear. You may skip around within a section, but complete each section before you move on to the next one.

Within each section there are several different types of questions. Make sure that you read and understand all directions before you begin.

- Circle your answers on the test so that you can compare your answers to the correct answers listed in the Answer Key on page 357.
- When asked to select a sentence in a passage that meets a certain description, circle or underline the sentence you choose.
- Carefully review the explanations for any question that you answered incorrectly.

We suggest that you make this practice test as much like the real test as possible. Find a quiet location, free from distractions, and make sure that you have pencils and a timepiece. Review the Scoring Guidelines in Chapter 2, but remember that your score on the actual GRE will be dependent on many factors, including your level of preparedness and your fatigue level on test day. The Practice Test begins on the next page.

GRE Diagnostic Test 2

SECTION **1**   **ANALYTICAL WRITING**

SECTION **2**   **VERBAL REASONING**

SECTION **3**   **VERBAL REASONING**

SECTION **4**   **QUANTITATIVE REASONING**

SECTION **5**   **QUANTITATIVE REASONING**

ANSWERS AND EXPLANATIONS

SECTION 1

Analytical Writing

PART 1. ANALYZE AN ISSUE

30 minutes

You will have 30 minutes to organize your thoughts and compose a response that represents your point of view on the issue. Do not respond to any issue other than the one presented; a response to any other issue will receive a score of 0.

Issue Topic

"It is primarily through our personal relationships that we define ourselves."

Discuss whether you agree or disagree with the statement. Use relevant reasons and examples to support your point of view. In developing and supporting your position, consider ways in which the statement might or might not hold true. Explain how those considerations affect your point of view.

Analytical Writing

PART 2. ANALYZE AN ARGUMENT

30 minutes

You will have 30 minutes to organize your thoughts and compose a response that critiques the given argument. Do not respond to any argument other than the one given; a response to any other argument will receive a score of 0.

Argument Topic

Magnolia trees were once common in neighborhoods in the Midwest, but they have become increasingly rare. Black squirrels eat Magnolia tree seedpods. Few neighborhoods in the Midwest had any black squirrels until fifty years ago. At that time, black squirrels were introduced to certain college campuses throughout the Midwest. Biologists removed the black squirrels from ne neighborhood, and the Magnolia tree population soon increased. Therefore, removing black squirrels from neighborhoods in the Midwest is clearly the way to restore the Magnolia tree population to its former levels.

Critique the reasoning used in the argument above. You are not being asked to discuss your point of view on the argument. You should identify and analyze the central elements of the argument, the underlying assumptions that are being made, and any supporting information that is given. Your critique can also discuss other information that would strengthen or weaken the argument or make it more logical.

SECTION 2

Verbal Reasoning

30 Minutes
20 Questions

This section consists of three different types of questions: Reading Comprehension, Text Completion, and Sentence Equivalence. To answer the questions, select the best answer from the answer choices given. Reading Comprehension questions appear in sets; Text Completion and Sentence Equivalence questions are independent. The questions will be presented in random order. Read the following directions before you begin the test.

Reading Comprehension Questions

Directions:
Multiple-choice Questions—Select One Answer Choice: These are the traditional multiple-choice questions with five answer choices from which you must select one.

Multiple-choice Questions—Select One or More Answer Choices: These questions provide three answer choices; select all that are correct.

Select-in-Passage: Choose the sentence in the passage that meets a certain description.

Text Completion Questions

Directions: Select one entry from the corresponding column of choices for each blank. Fill all blanks in the way that best completes the text.

Sentence Equivalence Questions

Directions: Select the two answer choices that, when used to complete the sentence, fit the meaning of the sentence as a whole and produce completed sentences that are alike in meaning.

Questions 1 to 3 are based on the following passage.

Responsibilities pertaining to property and land use are agreed upon within a signed, binding contract. And while it is fathomable that a disagreement with the owner of an adjacent property may occur, particular difficulty arises in defining the party liable for necessary maintenance when said disagreement is over the deterioration of a naturally occurring, communally-owned parcel, such as a beach.

GO ON TO NEXT PAGE

In California, the coastal city of Encinitas is slowly watching its shoreline wash away. The beach has a massive sand deficit with over 100,000 cubic yards of sand lost on an annual basis. The sand erosion is a natural occurrence, but beachfront property owners and the city government are attempting to fight mother nature with a sand replenishment project. This involves dredging up 2 million cubic yards of sand from the ocean bottom at a cost of $25 million.

For Question 1, select one answer choice.

1. Which of the following most logically completes the passage?
   - (A) Everyone knows that $25 million is a lot of money.
   - (B) However, local oceanographers claim that dredging the ocean floor will have catastrophic consequences for native sea-life.
   - (C) Because sand erosion occurs naturally, many city residents claim that replenishment is unnecessary.
   - (D) While the property owners and the government are in agreement over the value of the project, neither side is willing to assume the costs.
   - (E) The dredging project would be repeated every five years.

2. Select the sentence that shows the scope of the problem in Encinitas.

For Question 3, select one answer choice.

3. The passage suggests that the author would be most likely to agree with which of the following statements?
   - (A) The situation in Encinitas is unusual for coastal cities.
   - (B) Binding contracts do not necessarily preclude all conflicts over property.
   - (C) Sand erosion must necessarily be prevented by all means possible.
   - (D) Current contract law is irreparably flawed.
   - (E) Beachfront property owners should always work with the local government in order to achieve a favorable outcome in property disputes.

Question 4 is based on the following passage.

In the world of art, distinguishing the authentic piece from the forgery is not an easy feat and often requires the use of multiple experts. Millions of dollars can be at stake, yet even experts can be fooled. However, a recent discovery has introduced a new resource for galleries and other groups seeking to establish the origins of their paintings: mathematicians. Math experts were able to analyze digital images of authenticated paintings where they found consistent differences in paint texture. This consistency suggests that each artist has a unique style of brush stroke that cannot be completely duplicated.

For Question 4, select one answer choice.

4. In the first two sentences of the passage, the author suggests which of the following?
   - (A) It is nearly impossible to determine whether a painting is authentic or fake without the use of math.
   - (B) Even if multiple experts from various fields analyze a painting, it is not always possible to determine its authenticity.
   - (C) New discoveries in art always lead to a greater degree of truth.
   - (D) Art can be difficult to analyze, but mathematical models can help to find the truth.
   - (E) Mathematicians have a great degree of expertise in analyzing art.

For Questions 5 to 7, select one entry from the corresponding column of choices for each blank. Fill all blanks in the way that best completes the text.

5. Since many people who casually tan indoors develop skin cancer and many (i) _____ indoor tanners do not, scientists believe that individuals differ in their (ii) _____ the development of melanoma.

Blank (i)	Blank (ii)
(A) habitual	(D) proximity to
(B) frequent	(E) susceptibility to
(C) chronic	(F) concern about

6. Despite claims that his artistic style can be traced to (i) _____ source, the style actually draws upon several traditions and methodologies and could justifiably be termed (ii) _____.

Blank (i)	Blank (ii)
(A) a fraudulent	(D) eclectic
(B) a schematic	(E) derivative
(C) a particular	(F) consistent

GO ON TO NEXT PAGE

7. When President Thomas Jefferson's relentless passion to know all about the flora and the (i) _____ of the Western section of the country grew too overwhelming, he enjoined explorers Lewis and Clark to (ii) _____ their journey into this vast, mysterious (iii) _____.

Blank (i)	Blank (ii)	Blank (iii)
Ⓐ flowers	Ⓓ dictate	Ⓖ uncharted territory
Ⓑ fauna	Ⓔ aggrandize	Ⓗ promised land
Ⓒ forests	Ⓕ chronicle	Ⓘ familiar ground

Questions 8 to 11 are based on the following passage.

The evolution of culture is dependent upon the development of the tools of civilization. Civilized cultures exhibit a high degree of ingenuity. It is the concept of humans as toolmakers and modifiers that differentiates us from other animals and, some would say, makes us civilized. A monkey might use a stick to remove termites from a log, but that stick will never be reworked into a fork or other eating utensil. Monkeys have never devised a spoken language, written a book, composed a melody, built a house, or paved a street. To claim that birds build nests and beavers construct dams is to miss the mark. Man once lived in caves, but our imagination and creativity have allowed us to progress toward true civilization.

For Question 8, select one answer choice.

8. Which generalization about modern civilization is supported by the passage?
   Ⓐ Modern civilization is not due to man's achievement.
   Ⓑ Modern civilization is a result of prolific human creativity.
   Ⓒ Modern civilization cannot be viewed as successful.
   Ⓓ Modern civilization is a result of man copying the behavior of certain animals.
   Ⓔ Modern civilization came about through luck.

For Question 9, consider each of the choices separately and select all that apply.

9. Which of the following can be inferred from the passage regarding man's imagination?
   A Great imagination is a necessary prerequisite to great art.
   B Architecture is the result of an imaginative act and results in more than simple habitation.
   C True communication is solely the purview of man.

10. Select the sentence that suggests that some specialists overstate the complexity of animal behavior.

For Question 11, consider each of the choices separately and select all that apply.

11. Based on the attitudes displayed in the passage, with which of the following statements would the author most likely disagree?
    - [A] High culture is the necessary result of a stable civilization.
    - [B] Flexibility is almost as important as ingenuity in the development of a civilized culture.
    - [C] Sophisticated social structures in the animal world can be seen as precursors to civilized culture in humans.

Question 12 is based on the following passage.

The basic concept of cellular phones began in 1947, when researchers looked at crude mobile (i.e. police car) phones and realized that, by using small cells, or ranges of service areas, with frequency reuse, they could increase the traffic capacity of mobile phones substantially. However, at that time, the technology to accomplish this was nonexistent. Dr. Martin Cooper, a former general manager for the systems division at Motorola, is considered the inventor of the first modern portable handset. Cooper made the first call on a portable cell phone in April 1973. He made the call to his rival, Joel Engel, Bell Laboratories head of research. Bell Laboratories had introduced the idea of cellular communications back in 1947. However, Motorola was the first to incorporate the technology into a portable device that was designed for use outside of an automobile.

For Question 12, select one answer choice.

12. Which of the following can be inferred from the passage regarding mid-twentieth century police car technology?
    - (A) Mid-twentieth century police car technology had no influence on the development of truly portable telephones.
    - (B) Mid-twentieth century police car technology was hailed as a revolutionary development.
    - (C) Mid-twentieth century police car technology was considered by many politicians to be crucial to America's war against communism.
    - (D) Mid-twentieth century police car technology was not completely understood by Bell Laboratories.
    - (E) Mid-twentieth century police car technology allowed officers a degree of mobility in communication not available to the general public.

For Question 13, select one entry from the corresponding column of choices for each blank. Fill all blanks in the way that best completes the text.

13. Economic predictions can be reasonably accurate when the assumption that the future will be much like the past is (i) _____; however, in times of major (ii) _____ in the economy, forecasts can be dangerously wrong.

Blank (i)	Blank (ii)
Ⓐ contradicted	Ⓓ spirals
Ⓑ entertained	Ⓔ surges
Ⓒ satisfied	Ⓕ shifts

Questions 14 and 15 are based on the following passage.

We had been anticipating this maiden voyage for a full nine months, since the initial purchase of 109 acres of northern, forested property. The property included a large, deep, somewhat murky pond that we were eager to investigate. In late April, the wait for decent weather was over, even though the sky still held intermittent steel gray clouds and the thermometer registered a mere 54° F. We could wait no longer; Buck's Pond was begging to be explored. Four adults and a precocious Golden Retriever gingerly climbed into the over-sized five-person canoe and, surprisingly, remained dry as the helmsman shoved us off the sandy launch. A bit of wind created ripples on the surface of the water, but we could only remark that this same breeze would be aiding us on our way back to shore; there was no room for any negative thoughts to mar our excitement and enthusiasm for this long-awaited adventure.

For Question 14, select one answer choice.

14. The author implies that the journey across Buck's Pond was
    Ⓐ relatively simple and required little exertion
    Ⓑ somewhat risky and uncertain
    Ⓒ difficult and required the strength of four adults
    Ⓓ a disappointment to the four weary travelers
    Ⓔ undertaken during hazardous weather conditions

For Question 15, consider each of the choices separately and select all that apply.

15. The passage indicates that the author would agree with which of the following statements?
    Ⓐ It is ill-advised to commence water explorations in winter.
    Ⓑ Ponds are small bodies of water that are always easily traversed.
    Ⓒ New adventures are never a cause of excitement and enthusiasm.

For Questions 16 through 20, select the two answer choices that, when used to complete the sentence, fit the meaning of the sentence as a whole and produce completed sentences that are alike in meaning.

16. With its rebellious approach to the subject, her book has been more widely debated than most; throughout the country, the media have brought the author's _____ opinions to the public's attention.
    - A authoritative
    - B popular
    - C controversial
    - D articulate
    - E conclusive
    - F polemical

17. Judged by almost any standard, the seahorse remains one of nature's more _____ creatures, with the male of the species giving birth to offspring.
    - A unique
    - B feckless
    - C novel
    - D lackluster
    - E industrious
    - F mettlesome

18. After numerous rejections, the actress was _____, certain that she would never act in a Broadway play.
    - A speculative
    - B optimistic
    - C despondent
    - D resilient
    - E insipid
    - F melancholy

19. After a slump in sales, the board of directors decided to _____ with another corporation, forming one of the largest conglomerates in the country.
    - A unite
    - B capitulate
    - C dissipate
    - D merge
    - E alternate
    - F disperse

GO ON TO NEXT PAGE

20. The topic of teaching evolution in schools, still a rather _____ issue, has been a subject of debate for years.
    - [A] ephemeral
    - [B] controversial
    - [C] abbreviated
    - [D] contentious
    - [E] inexplicable
    - [F] settled

STOP.
This is the end of Section 2. Use any remaining time to check your work.

SECTION 3

Verbal Reasoning

30 Minutes
20 Questions

This section consists of three different types of questions: Reading Comprehension, Text Completion, and Sentence Equivalence. To answer the questions, select the best answer from the answer choices given. Reading Comprehension questions appear in sets; Text Completion and Sentence Equivalence questions are independent. The questions will be presented in random order. Read the following directions before you begin the test.

Reading Comprehension Questions

<u>Directions:</u>
Multiple-choice Questions—Select One Answer Choice: These are the traditional multiple-choice questions with five answer choices from which you must select one.

Multiple-choice Questions—Select One or More Answer Choices: These questions provide three answer choices; select all that are correct.

Select-in-Passage: Choose the sentence in the passage that meets a certain description.

Text Completion Questions

<u>Directions:</u> Select one entry from the corresponding column of choices for each blank. Fill all blanks in the way that best completes the text.

Sentence Equivalence Questions

<u>Directions:</u> Select the <u>two</u> answer choices that, when used to complete the sentence, fit the meaning of the sentence as a whole <u>and</u> produce completed sentences that are alike in meaning.

GO ON TO NEXT PAGE

For Questions 1 through 3, select the two answer choices that, when used to complete the sentence, fit the meaning of the sentence as a whole and produce completed sentences that are alike in meaning.

1. While most addictions in today's culture center on recreational drugs or alcohol, some experts believe that more than six percent of the 189 million Internet users in the United States are _____ being on the web to the point of not being able to imagine going 24 hours without accessing the computer.
   - A fed up with
   - B compulsive about
   - C tired of
   - D obsessed with
   - E afraid of
   - F disgusted with

2. Although the act is often referred to as "book burning," occasionally other items are thrown into the flames in an act of extreme _____, including a variety of supposedly offensive graphic novels and records.
   - A revolution
   - B celebration
   - C censorship
   - D liberation
   - E suppression
   - F freedom

3. When Henry David Thoreau wrote, "If a man does not keep pace with his companions, perhaps it is because he hears a different drummer," it was his way of declaring that _____ and solitude were perfectly acceptable habits for a fulfilling life.
   - A poverty
   - B minimalism
   - C duplicity
   - D exorbitance
   - E infamy
   - F simplicity

> **Questions 4 and 5 are based on the following passage.**

We packed early. An 8 a.m. international flight, especially one to be taken with children, demands strict attention to detail and advance preparation. But with that chore finished, it was time to spend one last afternoon in Paris. We chose to see the Louvre. We planned our visit strategically: the *Mona Lisa*, of course, followed by the *Venus De Milo*. The Napoleon buff in our party insisted on seeing the Jacques-Louis David's seemingly life-sized painting of the emperor's coronation, while the children were thrilled by the Egyptian mummies. I think we walked for miles.

Despite the frenetic pace, we saw only a fraction of the museum before it was time to head home—home being a tiny, sixth-floor apartment in the 10th arrondissement. Sitting amongst our suitcases, we flipped through our souvenirs and swapped stories with our host until bedtime. Lifting a glass toward our window view of a sparkling Eiffel Tower, we toasted each other—and a beautiful day in Paris.

For Question 4, consider each of the choices separately and select all that apply.

4. Which of the following is implied about the visit to the Louvre?
   - [A] The Louvre is the largest, most comprehensive art museum in the world.
   - [B] The visit was exhausting and inappropriate for small children.
   - [C] The visit encompassed diverse tastes.

For Question 5, select one answer choice.

5. In the passage, the author is primarily concerned with
   - (A) emphasizing the immense diversity of art to be found at the Louvre museum
   - (B) describing the challenges of international travel with children
   - (C) complaining about inadequate accommodations in Europe
   - (D) giving an account of her last day in Paris
   - (E) bragging about her foreign vacation

Question 6 is based on the following passage.

Thousands of years ago, royalty of diverse cultures were often buried in extremely lavish tombs that they themselves commissioned in preparation for their inevitable deaths. About 2,200 years ago, a Chinese emperor named Qin Shihuang had such a tomb prepared. At the age of thirteen, Qin Shihuang had succeeded his father as emperor. The boy was very aggressive and ambitious. He assumed full power at the age of 22 by ridding himself of his rival, a man who had controlled the throne while Qin Shihuang was a minor. Qin Shihuang's goal was to unify and subjugate all of the Chinese states using his powerful political, economic, and military strength. Despite an ongoing quest for immortality, Qin Shihuang died while traveling at the age of 49. Although he has been dead for centuries, historians can continue to learn of his life by studying the artifacts found in the extravagant tomb in which he was laid to rest.

For Question 6, select one answer choice.

6. According to the passage, Qin Shihuang can best be described as
   - Ⓐ benevolent
   - Ⓑ modest
   - Ⓒ spontaneous
   - Ⓓ insightful
   - Ⓔ ruthless

Questions 7 and 8 are based on the following passage.

The Earthquake Country Alliance (ECA) recently released its guidelines for protective action in case of an earthquake. Operating under the slogan, "Drop, Cover, and Hold on," the EAC urges individuals experiencing an earthquake to drop to the ground, seek the cover of a sturdy table, and hold on. The EAC's most important message is stay put. Individuals should not try to leave the room, even if better cover could be found elsewhere. The secondary message includes what *not* to do. Persons caught in an earthquake are now told not to seek shelter in doorways. Structurally, doorways are no safer than the rest of the building, and they provide no protection from falling debris. Similarly, individuals should avoid the so-called "triangle of life" on the side of furniture or automobiles.

For Question 7, select one answer choice.

7. Based on the passage, the author would most likely disagree with which of the following statements?
   - Ⓐ Seeking out the "triangle of life" is an ineffective protective measure in the event of an earthquake.
   - Ⓑ In the event of an earthquake, individuals should always seek shelter in the dining room under the table.
   - Ⓒ In the past, people were told to seek shelter from earthquakes by standing in doorways.

8. Select the sentence that summarizes the current safety message from the Earthquake Country Alliance.

For Questions 9 and 10, select one entry from the corresponding column of choices for each blank. Fill all blanks in the way that best completes the text.

9. In a (i) _____ model, the political process centers on competing interest groups that are able to (ii) _____ the government and, by doing so, help to influence or impact many of its decisions.

Blank (i)	Blank (ii)
Ⓐ democratic	Ⓓ overthrow
Ⓑ pluralist	Ⓔ impede
Ⓒ despotic	Ⓕ access

10. Pathological liars are seldom disturbed by the use of a polygraph, since their overall _____ response to lying is often drastically reduced and as such, is undetectable.

Ⓐ cognitive
Ⓑ operational
Ⓒ physiological
Ⓓ qualitative
Ⓔ correlative

Questions 11 to 13 are based on the following passage.

Sometimes an object in nature is so rare that it escapes mention in nature books. Such is the case with the delightful Kirtland's warbler. The Kirtland's warbler is a plump, yellow-breasted bird that can be found nesting almost exclusively in the upper half of Michigan's Lower Peninsula. Although this bird does migrate to the Bahamas during the winter months, Michigan is its natural habitat. Unfortunately, reduced numbers have caused the Kirtland's warbler to be designated an endangered species. The remaining Kirtland's warblers now enjoy living among the jack pine trees located in protected Michigan forests. The male warblers generally return north before the female birds. Often, they return as early as May. When they arrive, the male warblers stake out their territories and choose a nesting area. At the completion of their own long journey from the Bahamas, the female warblers begin to collect leaves and grass to build their nests. Oddly, the Kirtland's warbler nests on the ground and not in the nearby jack pine trees themselves. During the nesting process, the male warbler provides food for his mate while the female Kirtland's warbler lays four to five speckled eggs. The eggs hatch in two to three weeks and both the male and female warblers tend to their chicks.

GO ON TO NEXT PAGE

For Questions 11 to 13, select one answer choice.

11. The passage implies that the author is
    - (A) disinterested in the fate of Kirtland's warbler
    - (B) a proponent of Kirtland's warbler
    - (C) a native of Michigan who travels to the Bahamas
    - (D) reluctant to discuss the migratory patterns of Kirtland's warbler
    - (E) annoyed that Kirtland's warbler is not mentioned in nature books

12. In the first two sentences of the passage, the author is mostly likely suggesting that
    - (A) Kirkland's warblers do not merit mention in nature books
    - (B) birds that migrate are considered native to the place where they build their nests
    - (C) many bird species are so rare that they escape mention in nature books
    - (D) most bird species in Michigan are well documented in scientific literature
    - (E) Kirkland's warblers are little known because of their limited numbers

13. Which of the following most logically completes the passage?
    - (A) Male and female warblers generally eat small insects.
    - (B) Most native species of birds only lay three to four eggs.
    - (C) Other Michigan-native birds species also nest on the ground.
    - (D) Five weeks after the eggs hatch, the fledglings are able to survive on their own.
    - (E) While the birds nest on the ground, the jack pine trees offer unique protection.

For Questions 14 to 16, select one entry from the corresponding column of choices for each blank. Fill all blanks in the way that best completes the text.

14. Queen Isabella was a strong and (i) _____ ruler, serving as a role model for noble women in Spain who had, until her reign, been politically (ii) _____.

Blank (i)	Blank (ii)
(A) domineering	(D) disregarded
(B) powerful	(E) lauded
(C) aberrant	(F) vilified

15. During a European broadcast in 2002, television viewers were (i) _____ by a border collie's ability to correctly retrieve specific toys at the request of its owner and, subsequently, researchers discovered that the dog had the (ii) _____ level of a three-year-old child.

Blank (i)	Blank (ii)
Ⓐ awestruck	Ⓓ maturation
Ⓑ appalled	Ⓔ cognitive
Ⓒ duped	Ⓕ education

16. The author spends so much time on this intricate description of scenery that the reader becomes lost in this _____, and the point of the entire article is overlooked or forgotten.

Ⓐ rabble
Ⓑ vocabulary
Ⓒ opulence
Ⓓ digression
Ⓔ machination

Question 17 is based on the following passage.

In 1979, Margaret Thatcher became Prime Minister of Great Britain. Her accession was one of the most important steps in finally making the Chunnel a reality. Thatcher had made it part of her political platform, finally giving the project full political weight. Still, it was not until two years later, when Thatcher met with French President François Mitterand for one of their routine economic meetings, that she and he organized a committee to take a new and serious look at building the Chunnel. Both political leaders felt that the underwater tunnel would be advantageous to their respective countries by bringing important financial support to local businesses as well as providing jobs to counteract growing unemployment. Both Thatcher and Mitterand also knew that it would enhance their image worldwide and leave behind a legacy of their respective times in office.

GO ON TO NEXT PAGE

For Question 17, select one answer choice.

17. Which of the following sentences can be inferred from this passage about the Chunnel?
    - Ⓐ At one time, the idea of the Chunnel was not necessarily a viable one.
    - Ⓑ The Chunnel was originally Prime Minister Margaret Thatcher's idea.
    - Ⓒ French President François Mitterand often agreed with Margaret Thatcher's ideas.
    - Ⓓ The Chunnel was an overhead bridge that would connect England and France.
    - Ⓔ Construction of the Chunnel was going to be challenging to the European economy.

Question 18 is based on the following passage.

Making snow angels usually falls under the category of children's winter recreation, but in early 2007, the process took on a whole new meaning. Almost 9,000 people gathered on the state Capitol grounds in Bismarck, North Dakota, to set a new world's record for the most people making snow angels at one time. They were determined to break Michigan's record of 3,784. Participants ranged from families with children to snowplow drivers. One woman was there to mark her 99th birthday! Kids of all ages flapped their arms in the snow and a young baby even made a snow angel by having her car seat spun in circles.

For Question 18, select one answer choice.

18. In the context in which it appears, "mark" most nearly means
    - Ⓐ memorialize
    - Ⓑ remember
    - Ⓒ identify
    - Ⓓ define
    - Ⓔ celebrate

Questions 19 and 20 are based on the following passage.

Although it is almost always taken for granted, sleep is an essential part of most creatures' lives. For giraffes, two hours a day is enough. For bats, however, that number is closer to 20! For human adults, the need averages between seven and eight hours a night, and if they do not get it, they can suffer in their ability to concentrate and to think logically. While humans sleep, a number of things occur. First, their bodies are resting and reenergizing for the next day. Second, their brains are sorting through information and retaining some details while discarding others. Some experts believe this process helps to strengthen individuals' memories. Third, humans dream.

Dreams have lent an ineffable quality to sleep. While modern scientists believe that dreams are the brain's method for sifting through life's daily events, this was not always the case. Long ago, philosophers and sages gave prophetic significance to dreams. Even the ever-practical ancient Romans thought that dreams could be messages sent directly from one of their gods.

For Question 19, consider each of the choices separately and select all that apply.

19. The author of the passage most likely mentions the Romans' beliefs about dreaming because
    - [A] it demonstrates that some dreams originate from deities
    - [B] it supports the idea that some cultures give dreams different kinds of significance
    - [C] it correlates to how the culture felt about the power of dreaming and sleepwalking

20. Select the sentence within the passage that illustrates a possible minimum level of sleep necessary for full functionality in the animal world.

STOP.
This is the end of Section 3. Use any remaining time to check your work.

SECTION 4

Quantitative Reasoning

35 Minutes
20 Questions

This section includes four types of questions: Multiple-choice Questions (Select One Answer Choice *and* Select One or More Answer Choices), Numeric Entry Questions, and Quantitative Comparison Questions. Read the following directions before you begin the test.

General Information:

Numbers: All of the numbers used in this section are real numbers.

Figures: Assume that the position of all points, angles, etc. are in the order shown and the measures of angles are positive.

Straight lines can be assumed to be straight.

All figures lie in a plane unless otherwise stated.

The figures given for each question provide information to solve the problem. The figures are not drawn to scale unless otherwise stated. To solve the problems, use your knowledge of mathematics; do not estimate lengths and sizes of the figures to answer questions.

Multiple-choice Questions

Select One Answer Choice

Directions: These questions are multiple-choice questions that ask you to select only one answer choice from a list of five choices.

Select One or More Answer Choices

Directions: Select one or more answer choices according to the specific question directions.

If the question does not specify how many answer choices to select, select all that apply.

The correct answer may be just one of the choices or as many as all of the choices, depending on the question.

No credit is given unless you select all of the correct choices and no others.

If the question specifies how many answer choices to select, select exactly that number of choices.

Numeric Entry Questions

Directions: Enter your answer in the answer box(es) below the question.

Equivalent forms of the correct answer, such as 2.5 and 2.50, are all correct. Fractions do not need to be reduced to lowest terms.

Enter the exact answer unless the question asks you to round your answer.

Quantitative Comparison Questions

Directions: Some questions give you two quantities, Quantity A and Quantity B. Compare the two quantities and choose one of the following answer choices:

    A if Quantity A is greater;
    B if Quantity B is greater;
    C if the two quantities are equal;
    D if you cannot determine the relationship based on the given information.

Note: Information and/or figures pertaining to one or both of the quantities may appear above the two columns. Any information that appears in both columns has the same meaning for both Quantity A and Quantity B.

You will also be asked Data Interpretation questions, which are grouped together and refer to the same table, graph, or other data presentation. These questions ask the examinee to interpret or analyze the given data. The types of questions may be Multiple-choice (both types) or Numeric Entry.

Each of Questions 1 to 7 presents two quantities, Quantity A and Quantity B. Compare the two quantities. You may use additional information centered above the quantities if such information is given. Choose one of the following answer choices:

  Ⓐ if Quantity A is greater;
  Ⓑ if Quantity B is greater;
  Ⓒ if the two quantities are equal;
  Ⓓ if you cannot determine the relationship based on the given information.

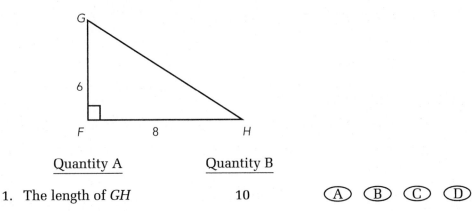

Quantity A	Quantity B	
1. The length of *GH*	10	Ⓐ Ⓑ Ⓒ Ⓓ

GO ON TO NEXT PAGE

	Quantity A	Quantity B	
2.	The average (arithmetic mean) of 11, 13, 15	The average (arithmetic mean) of 12, 14, 16	Ⓐ Ⓑ Ⓒ Ⓓ

r, s, and *t* are negative numbers.

	Quantity A	Quantity B	
3.	$r+s+t$	rst	Ⓐ Ⓑ Ⓒ Ⓓ

$$3x+4=28$$

	Quantity A	Quantity B	
4.	x	21	Ⓐ Ⓑ Ⓒ Ⓓ

$$a<0$$

	Quantity A	Quantity B	
5.	$1-a$	$a-1$	Ⓐ Ⓑ Ⓒ Ⓓ

$$0<x<1$$

	Quantity A	Quantity B	
6.	$(8.5+x)$ rounded to the nearest whole number	9	Ⓐ Ⓑ Ⓒ Ⓓ

	Quantity A	Quantity B	
7.	5 multiplied by a	a divided by 5	Ⓐ Ⓑ Ⓒ Ⓓ

8. If 65 percent of the people who purchase a certain model of a car are male, what is the ratio of the number of males who purchase the model to the number of females who purchase the model?

   (A) $\frac{13}{10}$

   (B) $\frac{13}{7}$

   (C) $\frac{7}{13}$

   (D) $\frac{7}{10}$

   (E) $\frac{7}{5}$

9. Which of the following is the sum of two positive integers whose product is 36?

   (A) 1
   (B) 11
   (C) 15
   (D) 17
   (E) 19

For Question 10, write your answer in the boxes.

10. There are six members on a committee, four of whom are women and two of whom are men. The members agree to randomly pull two names out of a hat to serve as Chair and Secretary for the group, respectively. What is the probability that both of the men are chosen? Give the probability as a fraction.

11. If the degree measures of the angles of a triangle are in the ratio 2 : 3 : 4, what is the degree measure of the smallest angle?

    (A) 15°
    (B) 20°
    (C) 40°
    (D) 45°
    (E) 60°

GO ON TO NEXT PAGE

For Question 12, select all the answer choices that apply.

12. If 4 more than twice n is a negative number and 6 more than n is a positive number, which of the following numbers could be the value of n?

    Select all such numbers.
    - [A] −5
    - [B] −4
    - [C] −3

13. If $a+c=13$ and $b-c=6$, then $a+b=$?
    - (A) 7
    - (B) 13
    - (C) 19
    - (D) 22
    - (E) 26

Refer to the following table for Questions 14 and 15.

Recommended Maintenance Schedule for a Certain Auto (Given in Miles)

Parts/Procedure	Primary Driving Condition	
	City	Highway
Motor Oil	3,000	4,500
Transmission Fluid	25,000	50–75,000
Power Steering Fluid	30,000	30,000
Main Belt	50,000	50,000
Radiator Hoses	50,000	50,000

14. The Recommended Maintenance Schedule is the same for which of the following parts, regardless of city or highway conditions?

    Select all such parts that apply.
    - [A] Motor Oil
    - [B] Transmission Fluid
    - [C] Power Steering Fluid
    - [D] Main Belt
    - [E] Radiator Hoses

15. If you drive primarily under city driving conditions, which of the following would be an appropriate mileage at which to change the motor oil?
    - (A) 4,500
    - (B) 4,000
    - (C) 3,800
    - (D) 3,200
    - (E) 2,400

Refer to the following graph for Questions 16 and 17.

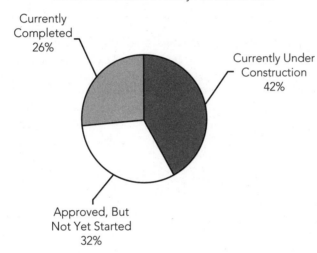

16. When construction is completed in Daisy Hill Subdivision there will be a total of 50 homes. Approximately how many homes have not yet been completed?
    - (A) 24
    - (B) 26
    - (C) 32
    - (D) 37
    - (E) 44

17. When construction is completed in Daisy Hill Subdivision there will be a total of 50 homes. What is the approximate ratio of new homes currently completed to new homes currently under construction?
    - (A) 1:2
    - (B) 13:21
    - (C) 5:8
    - (D) 21:25
    - (E) 4:3

GO ON TO NEXT PAGE

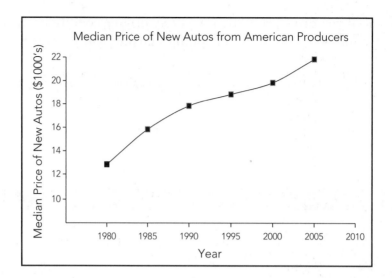

18. According to the graph above, what was the percent increase in the median price of a new automobile from American automakers from 1985–2005?
    (A) 20%
    (B) 37.5%
    (C) 50%
    (D) 62.5%
    (E) 94%

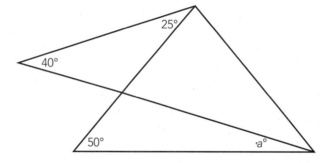

19. In the figure above, what is the value of a?
    (A) 15°
    (B) 25°
    (C) 30°
    (D) 45°
    (E) 115°

For Question 20, write your answer in the box.

20. A gift box has edges of 2 inches, 3 inches, and 7 inches. What is the surface area of the box, in square inches?

   ☐

STOP.
This is the end of Section 4. Use any remaining time to check your work.

SECTION 5

Quantitative Reasoning

35 Minutes
20 Questions

This section includes four types of questions: Multiple-choice Questions (Select One Answer Choice *and* Select One or More Answer Choices), Numeric Entry Questions, and Quantitative Comparison Questions. Read the following directions before you begin the test.

General Information:
Numbers: All of the numbers used in this section are real numbers.

Figures: Assume that the position of all points, angles, etc. are in the order shown and the measures of angles are positive.

Straight lines can be assumed to be straight.

All figures lie in a plane unless otherwise stated.

The figures given for each question provide information to solve the problem. The figures are not drawn to scale unless otherwise stated. To solve the problems, use your knowledge of mathematics; do not estimate lengths and sizes of the figures to answer questions.

Multiple-choice Questions

Select One Answer Choice

Directions: These questions are multiple-choice questions that ask you to select only one answer choice from a list of five choices.

Select One or More Answer Choices

Directions: Select one or more answer choices according to the specific question directions.

If the question does not specify how many answer choices to select, select all that apply.

The correct answer may be just one of the choices or as many as all of the choices, depending on the question.

No credit is given unless you select all of the correct choices and no others.

If the question specifies how many answer choices to select, select exactly that number of choices.

GO ON TO NEXT PAGE

Numeric Entry Questions

Directions: Enter your answer in the answer box(es) below the question.

Equivalent forms of the correct answer, such as 2.5 and 2.50, are all correct. Fractions do not need to be reduced to lowest terms.

Enter the exact answer unless the question asks you to round your answer.

Quantitative Comparison Questions

Directions: Some questions give you two quantities, Quantity A and Quantity B. Compare the two quantities and choose one of the following answer choices:

> **A** if Quantity A is greater;
> **B** if Quantity B is greater;
> **C** if the two quantities are equal;
> **D** if you cannot determine the relationship based on the given information.

Note: Information and/or figures pertaining to one or both of the quantities may appear above the two columns. Any information that appears in both columns has the same meaning for both Quantity A and Quantity B.

You will also be asked Data Interpretation questions, which are grouped together and refer to the same table, graph, or other data presentation. These questions ask the examinee to interpret or analyze the given data. The types of questions may be Multiple-choice (both types) or Numeric Entry.

Each of Questions 1 to 7 presents two quantities, Quantity A and Quantity B. Compare the two quantities. You may use additional information centered above the quantities if such information is given. Choose one of the following answer choices:

Ⓐ if Quantity A is greater;
Ⓑ if Quantity B is greater;
Ⓒ if the two quantities are equal;
Ⓓ if you cannot determine the relationship based on the given information.

$$(x+4)(x-2)<0$$

	Quantity A	Quantity B	
1.	2	x	Ⓐ Ⓑ Ⓒ Ⓓ

A briefcase that costs a retailer $120 is sold to a customer at 10% above the retailer's cost.

	Quantity A	Quantity B	
2.	$130	The price that the customer paid for the briefcase	Ⓐ Ⓑ Ⓒ Ⓓ

C is the circumference of a circle with diameter D and radius R. ($R > 0$)

	Quantity A	Quantity B	
3.	$\dfrac{R}{C}$	$\dfrac{D}{C}$	Ⓐ Ⓑ Ⓒ Ⓓ

$3a - b = 20$
a and b are integers.
$b < 1$

	Quantity A	Quantity B	
4.	−1	The greatest possible value of b	Ⓐ Ⓑ Ⓒ Ⓓ

2x ╲ 130°

	Quantity A	Quantity B	
5.	3x	100°	Ⓐ Ⓑ Ⓒ Ⓓ

$p = -\dfrac{1}{2}$
$q = -p$

	Quantity A	Quantity B	
6.	$8p^3$	$8q$	Ⓐ Ⓑ Ⓒ Ⓓ

The average of p, r, s, and 10 is 4.

	Quantity A	Quantity B	
7.	$\dfrac{p+r+s}{3}$	2	Ⓐ Ⓑ Ⓒ Ⓓ

GO ON TO NEXT PAGE ▶

8. If the average (arithmetic mean) of two numbers is 16 and one of the numbers is x, what is the other number in terms of x?
   - Ⓐ $16-x$
   - Ⓑ $16-2x$
   - Ⓒ $16+x$
   - Ⓓ $32-x$
   - Ⓔ $32-2x$

9. $173.28 \times \dfrac{1}{100} = ?$
   - Ⓐ 0.017328
   - Ⓑ 0.17328
   - Ⓒ 1.7328
   - Ⓓ 17.328
   - Ⓔ 17,328

10. Mandy and Jordan each bought some notebooks and a three-ring binder. Mandy paid $5.85 for 3 notebooks and 1 binder. Jordan paid $4.65 for 2 notebooks and 1 binder. What is the price of one of the notebooks?
    - Ⓐ $2.70
    - Ⓑ $2.25
    - Ⓒ $1.80
    - Ⓓ $1.20
    - Ⓔ $0.75

11. Which of the following is *not* a divisor of 336?
    - Ⓐ 6
    - Ⓑ 7
    - Ⓒ 8
    - Ⓓ 9
    - Ⓔ 12

For Question 12, write your answer in the box.

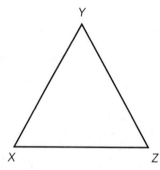

12. In the figure above, $XY = YZ$. If angle $Y = 40°$, then angle $X = ?$

13. $\sqrt{(33-9)(17+7)} = ?$

    Ⓐ 5
    Ⓑ 12
    Ⓒ 24
    Ⓓ 33
    Ⓔ 41

Questions 14 to 17 are based on the following information.

Mandy has a garden that is shaped like a right triangle, as shown below.

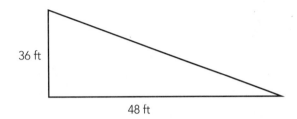

14. Suppose Mandy created another garden with the same dimensions adjacent to the short side of her current garden, as shown below:

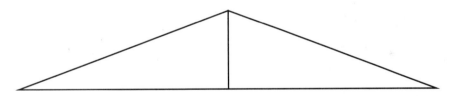

What is the total area of Mandy's gardens in square feet?
    Ⓐ 864
    Ⓑ 1,728
    Ⓒ 3,456
    Ⓓ 41,472
    Ⓔ 82,944

15. A bag of fertilizer costs $8.25 and will cover approximately 300 square feet. Which of the following is closest to the cost, in dollars, of fertilizing the original garden?
    Ⓐ $20.00
    Ⓑ $25.00
    Ⓒ $30.00
    Ⓓ $40.00
    Ⓔ $50.00

GO ON TO NEXT PAGE

16. To determine how much fencing to buy to enclose her original garden, Mandy calculates the garden's perimeter. What is the perimeter, in feet?
    - Ⓐ 60
    - Ⓑ 108
    - Ⓒ 132
    - Ⓓ 144
    - Ⓔ 168

17. Mandy wants to extend each of the side lengths of her original garden by 2 feet. What will the total area of her garden be, in square feet?
    - Ⓐ 176
    - Ⓑ 782
    - Ⓒ 864
    - Ⓓ 950
    - Ⓔ 1,900

For Question 18, select all the answer choices that apply.

18. A certain highway has Exits 1, 2, 3, and 4 in that order.
    Which of the following statements individually provide(s) sufficient additional information to determine the distance from Exit 2 to Exit 3?

    Select all such statements.
    - A̲ The distance from Exit 1 to Exit 3 is 7 miles, and the distance from Exit 3 to Exit 4 is 4 miles.
    - B̲ The total distance from Exit 1 to Exit 4 is 23 miles, the distance from Exit 1 to Exit 2 is 3 miles, and the distance from Exit 3 to Exit 4 is 9 miles.
    - C̲ The total distance from Exit 1 to Exit 4 is 23 miles, and the distance from Exit 2 to Exit 4 is 20 miles.

For Question 19, write your answer in the box.

19. The average of a set of six integers is 38. When a seventh number is included in the set, the average of the set increases to 47. What is the seventh number? ☐

20. What is the area, in square inches, of a circle with a diameter equal to 12 inches?
    - Ⓐ 144
    - Ⓑ 36
    - Ⓒ 12π
    - Ⓓ 36π
    - Ⓔ 144π

STOP.
This is the end of Section 5. Use any remaining time to check your work.

GRE Practice Test 2 Answers and Explanations

Answer Key

Section 2. Verbal Reasoning

1. D
2. "The beach has...on an annual basis."
3. B
4. B
5. A, E
6. C, D
7. B, F, G
8. B
9. A, B
10. "To claim that birds...is to miss the mark."
11. A, C
12. E
13. C, F
14. B
15. A
16. C, F
17. A, C
18. C, F
19. A, D
20. B, D

Section 3. Verbal Reasoning

1. B, D
2. C, E
3. B, F
4. C
5. D
6. E
7. B
8. "Operating under the slogan...and hold on."
9. B, F
10. C
11. B
12. E
13. D
14. B, D
15. A, E
16. D
17. A
18. E
19. B
20. "For giraffes, two hours a day is enough."

Section 4. Quantitative Reasoning

1. C
2. B
3. D
4. B
5. A
6. C
7. D
8. B
9. C
10. $\frac{1}{15}$ or equivalent fraction
11. C
12. A, B, C
13. C
14. C, D, E
15. D
16. D
17. B
18. B
19. A
20. 72

Section 5. Quantitative Reasoning

1. A
2. B
3. B
4. A
5. B
6. B
7. C
8. D
9. C
10. D
11. D
12. 70
13. C
14. B
15. B
16. D
17. D
18. B
19. 101
20. E

Answer Explanations

Section 1. Analytical Writing Parts 1 and 2

Because grading the essay is subjective, we've chosen not to include any "graded" essays here. Your best bet is to have someone you trust, such as your personal tutor, read your essays and give you an honest critique. Make the grading criteria mentioned in Chapter 6, "GRE Analytical Writing," available to whoever grades your essays. If you plan on grading your own essays, review the grading criteria and be as honest as possible regarding the structure, development, organization, technique, and appropriateness of your writing. Focus on your weak areas and continue to practice in order to improve your writing skills.

Section 2. Verbal Reasoning

1. **The best answer is D.** The passage's main idea is that conflict often arises over who has pay to improve communally-owned property. Only choice D links this idea to the situation in Encinitas.
2. **The best answer is:** *"The beach has a massive sand deficit with over 100,000 cubic yards of sand lost on an annual basis."* This sentence defines the problem with the beach in Encinitas. The last sentence is inappropriate because it outlines the scope of a potential solution.
3. **The best answer is B.** The solution here is to remember the scope of the passage and the main idea: that conflict often arises over who has to pay to improve communally-owned property. Choice B best fits those constraints.
4. **The best answer is B.** The first two sentences tell the reader that even multiple experts can be fooled into believing that a forged painting is authentic. This thought best matches choice B.
5. **The best answer is A and E.** The first blank sets up a contrast with "casually," which, here, has the sense of "habitual." The second blank requires a synonym for "likeliness to" develop melanoma. "Susceptibility" is the best choice.
6. **The best answer is C and D.** The conjunction "despite" indicates that the two blanks will contrast with each other. In this case, the first blank's phrase, "a particular," means something singularly known or identifiable, which contrasts with the sense of multiple, broad-ranging sources conveyed by "eclectic."
7. **The best answer is B, F, and G.** The stock phrase "flora and fauna" refers to plant and animal life. Jefferson wanted to know about the American west, so he asked Lewis and Clark to "chronicle," or record, their discoveries. The land was mysterious and unexplored, so "uncharted territory" is the best answer for Blank (iii).
8. **The best answer is B.** Choice B is the best option because the last sentence in the paragraph states that imagination and creativity have allowed true civilization.

9. **The best answer is A and B.** The author lists accomplishments, which include writing books, composing melodies, and building houses, that separate humans from animals. He then implies that great buildings are more than simply shelter (e.g. nests). Imagination and creativity are the qualities that allowed humans to achieve these accomplishments. These points support choices A and B.

10. **The best answer is:** ***To claim that birds build nests and beavers construct dams is to miss the mark.*** The author suggests that some scientists would argue that building nests or dams is fundamentally equivalent to human activities, but that the argument is not valid.

11. **The best answer is A and C.** The only necessary point argued by the author is the need for ingenuity to achieve high culture. He nowhere argues that stability plays a role. In fact, it's equally possible that the author might think that instability could spur invention. Equally, the author makes no link between animal behavior and human creativity. In fact, he states that people who do so "miss the mark."

12. **The best answer is E.** According to the passage, early mobile phones were found in police cars. Portable phones were not available for another 25 years, which is after the timeframe of the question.

13. **The best answer is C and F.** The conjunction "however" tells the reader that the two clauses of the sentence contrast with each other. For the first blank, that contrast will be with "wrong." Therefore, "satisfied" is the best choice. For the second blank, the phrase "the future will be much like the past" implies stability. While all three choices connote a degree of instability, only "shifts" matches the neutral tone of the sentence. Therefore, it is the best choice for Blank (ii).

14. **The best answer is B.** The description of the pond as "large, deep, and somewhat murky" combined with the uncertain weather implies that the journey had risk and unknown elements.

15. **The best answer is A only.** The exploration party waited until late April because of the weather. This implies that the author would agree that water explorations would be difficult in winter. Be wary of answer choices containing words such as "never" and "always."

16. **The best answer is C and F.** The answer choices should continue the idea introduced by the adjective "rebellious," which implies contrary, argumentative behavior. "Controversial" and "polemical" both share this meaning, and are equivalent words in this sentence.

17. **The best answer is A and C.** In the animal kingdom, males do not usually give birth. Therefore, the best answer choices will reflect this unusualness.

18. **The best answer is C and F.** After numerous rejections, the actress became certain she would never act in a Broadway play. This conclusion would naturally produce negative feelings. Choice C and F have similar meanings in this context, and both connote negative feelings.

19. **The best answer is A and D.** The two companies must come together if they are to form one company. Therefore, "unite" and "merge" are the best choices.
20. **The best answer is B and D.** The topic has been a subject of debate; therefore, "controversial" and "contentious," both of which imply argumentation, are excellent answer choices.

Section 3. Verbal Reasoning

1. **The best answer is B and D.** The answer choices must be consistent with addiction. Choices B and D match that idea. The other choices do not fit the context of the sentence.
2. **The best answer is C and E.** The main idea of this sentence is to broaden the definition of 'book burning' beyond books to include graphic novels and records. Book burning is, by definition, an act of censorship, or the suppression of ideas. Therefore, C and E are excellent choices.
3. **The best answer is B and F.** While "poverty" (choice A) might be a lifestyle Thoreau would approve of, it has no synonym among the other answer choices, so it cannot be a correct answer. "Minimalism" and "simplicity" do create sentences with similar meanings—and both fit the context— therefore, they are the best choices.
4. **The best answer is C only.** According to the passage, the tour of the Louvre included statuary, paintings, and mummies. These diverse elements best support choice C.
5. **The best answer is D.** While the passage does mention the points made in choices A and B, only choice D properly captures the scope of the passage.
6. **The best answer is E.** The adjectives used to describe Qin Shihuang include "aggressive" and "ambitious." He is also said to have attempted to "subjugate" all of the Chinese states by force. All of these descriptions support choice E.
7. **The best answer is B.** The EAC's primary message is that individuals should stay put during an earthquake. This means they should not leave the room that they are in, even if a better cover is in a nearby dining room.
8. **The best answer is:** *Operating under the slogan, "Drop, Cover, and Hold on," the EAC urges individuals experiencing an earthquake to drop to the ground, seek the cover of a sturdy table, and hold on.* This sentence clearly expresses the new safety guidelines promoted by the Earthquake Country Alliance.
9. **The best answer is B and F.** For Blank (i), you need a system that discusses the role of interest groups. Since "democratic" implies the participation of individual people and "despotic" implies tyrannical rule by one, "pluralist" is the best choice. According to the sentence, the interest groups are able to influence government decisions. Therefore, "access" is the best choice for Blank (ii), as the other choices are either contrary to the meaning of the clause or are too strong in tone.

10. **The best answer is C.** Polygraph tests measure a person's bodily reactions to questions in order to determine if that person is lying. In other words, the test measures the body's "physiological" response. If pathological liars can reduce that response, their lies would not be detected by polygraph machines.
11. **The best answer is B.** The passage is a generally scientific description of the Kirkland's warbler. The tone is mostly neutral, with a slightly positive bent. This tone and main subject matter support answer choice B. Note that while the bird is a native of Michigan, nothing in the passage indicates that the author must also be one.
12. **The best answer is E.** Choice E restates the main idea of the first two sentences. The difference between A and E is primarily that of tone. The author is slightly positive about the birds (e.g., "the delightful Kirkland's warbler), which would eliminate choice A. Choice C is too general, while choice B refers to information later in the passage.
13. **The best answer is D.** The passage concludes with a timeline of the warblers' nesting behaviors. Choice D continues that timeline to the point where the hatchlings are ready to leave the nest. Therefore, it is the best choice to end the passage.
14. **The best answer is B and D.** Isabella's position as a role model implies that a neutral or positive word like "powerful" should fill the first blank. Her strength and power contrast with the previous political position of noble women in Spain, so "lauded" can be eliminated. "Vilified" is too strongly negative for the tone of the sentence; therefore, "disregarded" is the best choice.
15. **The best answer is A and E.** Because the dog was tested on its ability to identify toys by name, the second blank should logically be filled by a word meaning intelligence (i.e. "cognitive"). Because the dog was found truly to have an unexpectedly high intelligence level, "awestruck" is the appropriate choice for the first blank.
16. **The best answer is D.** The focus of the criticism is the length of the description, not the difficulty of the words used in it. Therefore, the critic's complaint is with the author's "digression," which means to stray from the topic or to ramble. Indeed the author strays so much that the critic claims the main topic is overlooked or forgotten.
17. **The best answer is A.** According to the passage, the idea of the Chunnel existed before Thatcher's appointment to Prime Minister. However, it was not acted upon for years. Something must have delayed its construction. Therefore, it is implied that the idea of a Chunnel was not always considered viable.
18. **The best answer is E.** It is implied that the 99th birthday was happening in the present, not something in the past to be remembered. It can also be assumed to be a positive occasion, not a neutral one. For these reasons, "celebrate" is the best choice.

19. **The best answer is B only.** The author mentions the ancient Romans as an example of the types of people who gave prophetic significance to dreams. There is no indication that the author agrees with Roman beliefs.
20. **The best answer is:** *"For giraffes, two hours a day is enough."* The author describes a range of average sleep needs in the animal kingdom. Giraffes need for only two hours a day is given as an example of the lower end of the spectrum. Therefore, it is a possible minimum level of sleep necessary for functionality in the animal world.

Section 4. Quantitative Reasoning

1. **The correct answer is C.** Because the triangle in this problem is a right triangle, use the Pythagorean Theorem to compute the length of the hypotenuse, c, as follows:
$$c^2 = 6^2 + 8^2$$
$$c^2 = 36 + 64 = 100$$
Thus $c = 10$, and Quantity A and Quantity B are equal.

   If you recognized that the triangle is a 3-4-5 triangle you could have quickly arrived at the correct answer.

2. **The correct answer is B.** To solve this problem, compute the averages of both lists of numbers. For Quantity A, the average of 11, 13, and 15 is $\frac{11+13+15}{3}$, or $\frac{39}{3}$, which equals 13. For Quantity B, the average of 12, 14, and 16 is $\frac{12+14+16}{3}$, or $\frac{42}{3}$ which equals 14. Therefore, Quantity B is greater than Quantity A.

   Another way to solve this problem is to note that all of the numbers in Quantity B are greater than those in Quantity A. Therefore, the average of Quantity B will be greater than the average of Quantity A.

3. **The correct answer is D.** To solve this problem, try some test values for r, s, and t. Because it is given in the problem that they are negative numbers, $r<0$, $s<0$, and $t<0$. Let $r=-1$, $s=-2$ and $t=-4$. The sum is -7 ($-1+-2+-4$), but the product is -8 ($-1\times-2\times-4$), making the product *less* than the sum. Now, let $r=-0.5$, $s=-1$ and $t=-2$. The sum is -3.5 ($-0.5+-1+-2$), but the product is -1 ($-0.5\times-1\times-2$), making the product *greater* than the sum. Therefore, you cannot determine the relationship based on the given information.

4. **The correct answer is B.** To determine the relationship, solve the equation $3x+4=28$ for x. First, subtract 4 from both sides. Then divide both sides by 3 to get $x=8$. Thus, Quantity B (21) is greater than Quantity A (8).

5. **The correct answer is A.** Given that $a<0$, the quantity $1-a$ would be greater than 1, because subtracting a negative number has the effect of adding a positive number. The quantity $a-1$ is such that a number is being subtracted from a negative number, increasing the magnitude in the negative direction, thus the quantity is less than -1. Therefore, Quantity A is greater than Quantity B.

6. **The correct answer is C.** Because $0<x<1$, then $8.5<(8.5+x)<9.5$. Using the rules for rounding (.5 or higher rounds up), the quantity $(8.5+x)$ will always round to 9 when $0<x<1$. Therefore, quantities A and B are equal.

7. **The correct answer is D.** While it may seem obvious that $5a$ would be greater than $\frac{a}{5}$, consider the case when $a<0$. For example $5(-5)=-25$ while $-\frac{5}{5}=-1$. Thus when $a>0$, $5a$ is greater than $\frac{a}{5}$. However, when $a<0$, $5a$ is less than $\frac{a}{5}$. Therefore, you cannot determine the relationship between Quantity A and Quantity B based on the given information.

8. **The correct answer is B.** Because 65 percent of the people are male, then the rest of the 100 percent must be female; therefore, 100−65, or 35 percent of the people are female. If 100 people purchased this particular model of car, then the ratio of males to females would be $\frac{65}{35}$, which reduces to $\frac{13}{7}$.

9. **The correct answer is C.** To solve this problem, consider the pairs of positive integers whose product is 36: 1 and 36; 2 and 24; 3 and 12; 4 and 9; and 6 and 6. The only pair whose sum is an answer choice is 3+12, or 15.

10. **The correct answer is $\frac{1}{15}$ or any equivalent fraction.** Since there are 6 names in the hat and 2 are men, the probability that the first name drawn is a man is $\frac{2}{6}=\frac{1}{3}$. Of the remaining 5 names in the hat, only 1 is a man, so the chances that he will be chosen are 1 in 5. To find the probability of both events occurring, take $\frac{1}{3}\times\frac{1}{5}=\frac{1}{15}$.

11. **The correct answer is C.** If the degree measures of the angles of a triangle are in the ratio 2 : 3 : 4, then the smallest angle will constitute $\frac{2}{2+3+4}$, or $\frac{2}{9}$ of the sum of the three angles of the triangle. Because all triangles are composed of three angles whose sum is 180°, the degree measure of the smallest angle is $\frac{2}{9}$ of 180°, or 40°.

12. **The correct answer is A, B, and C.** To solve this problem, first translate the words into their mathematical equivalents:

    4 more than twice n translates to $4+2n$. You are given that this quantity is a negative number, which translates to $4+2n<0$.

    6 more than n translates to $6+n$. You are given that this quantity is a positive number, which translates to $6+n>0$.

    Solve each inequality as follows:
    $$4+2n<0$$
    $$n<-2$$
    $$6+n>0$$
    $$n>-6$$

    So, n could be any number less than −2 and greater than −6.

13. **The correct answer is C.** Given that $a+c=13$ and $b-c=6$, the quantity $a+b$ can be determined by substitution. If $a+c=13$, then $c=13-a$. Substituting $c=13-a$ into $b-c=6$ yields the following:
$$b-(13-a)=6$$
$$b-13+a=6$$
$$b+a=6+13$$
$$a+b=19$$

14. **The correct answer is C, D, and E.** Based on the chart, power steering fluid, the main belt, and radiator hoses are recommended for replacement at the same mileage, regardless of city or highway conditions.

15. **The correct answer is D.** Based on the chart, for city driving conditions it is recommended that motor oil be changed every 3,000 miles. Because the question suggests some highway driving, the answer choice that is closest to, but slightly more than 3,000 miles is correct.

16. **The correct answer is D.** According to the graph, 26% of the homes have been completed, leaving 74% unfinished. To solve the problem, calculate 74% of 50: $50(0.74)=37$.

17. **The correct answer is B.** According to the graph, 26% of the homes have been completed, which means that $50(0.26)=13$ homes have been completed. The graph shows that 42% of the homes are currently under construction: $50(0.42)=21$. Therefore, the ratio is 13:21.

18. **The correct answer is B.** According to the graph, the median price increased by $6,000 from 1985 to 2005 ($22,000–$16,000). Therefore, the percent increase is $\frac{\$6,000}{\$16,000}=0.375$, or 37.5%.

19. **The correct answer is A.** To solve this problem, recall the relationships between opposite angles. You are given the angle measures of two angles in one of the triangles in the figure: 40° and 25°. Therefore, the third angle must measure $180°-40°-25°=115°$. The angle opposite this angle will also measure 115°. You now know two of the angle measures for the triangle containing angle a, and can calculate the value of angle a: $180°-50°-115°=15°$.

20. **The correct answer is 72.** To calculate the surface area, first calculate the area of each side of the box:

    2 sides will have an area of $2\times3=6$ inches.
    2 sides will have an area of $2\times7=14$ inches.
    2 sides will have an area of $3\times7=21$ inches.

    Therefore, the surface area of the box is $2(6)+2(14)+2(21)=72$.

Section 5. Quantitative Reasoning

1. **The correct answer is A.** To solve this problem, find the interval of x for which $(x+4)(x-2)<0$. The expression $(x+4)(x-2)$ is equal to zero when

$x=-4$ and $x=2$. It would then make sense to try a few test values for x to see when $(x+4)(x-2)$ is *less than* 0.

For $x<-4$, $(x+4)(x-2)>0$.
For $-4<x<2$, $(x+4)(x-2)<0$.
Finally, for $x>2$, $(x+4)(x-2)>0$.

Thus the interval of x for which $(x+4)(x-2)<0$ is $-4<x<2$, which means that x must be a value greater than -4 and less than 2. Therefore Quantity A (2) is greater than Quantity B ($-4<x<2$), because x is less than 2.

2. **The correct answer is B.** To solve this problem, first calculate the cost to the customer. You are given that the briefcase costs a retailer $120, and that this briefcase is sold to a customer at 10% above the retailer's cost. Therefore, the markup is 10% of $120, or (0.10)(120), which equals $12. Thus the total price a customer would pay is $120+$12, or $132, making the Quantity B greater than Quantity A.

3. **The correct answer is B.** In a circle, the diameter, D, is twice the radius, R. Therefore, $\frac{D}{C}$ is equal to twice $\frac{R}{C}$. Thus, Quantity B is greater than Quantity A.

4. **The correct answer is A.** Each of the given parameters—that $3a-b=20$, that a and b are integers, and that $b<1$—is significant in determining the maximum value of b. Because it is given that that a and b are integers and that $b<1$, b can only have one of the following values: 0, –1, –2, –3, –4, and so on. One way to determine the maximum value of b would be to test the possible values, starting with the greatest, in the equation $3a-b=20$ to find a value of b such that a is an integer. For $b=0$, $a=\frac{20}{3}$, which is not an integer. For $b=-1$, $a=\frac{19}{3}$, which is not an integer. For $b=-2$, $a=\frac{18}{3}$, or 6, which *is* an integer. Thus, the maximum value of b is –2, and Quantity A is greater than Quantity B.

5. **The correct answer is B.** Because the angles are supplementary, their sum is 180°. Thus, $2x+130°=180°$. It follows that $2x=50°$ and $x=25°$. The quantity $3x$ is then equal to 75°, which is less than 100°. Therefore Quantity B is greater than Quantity A.

6. **The correct answer is B.** Given that $p=-\frac{1}{2}$, $8p^3 = 8\left(-\frac{1}{2}\right)^3$, or $8\left(-\frac{1}{8}\right)$, which equals –1. Also, given that $q=-p$, $q=-\left(-\frac{1}{2}\right)$, or $\frac{1}{2}$. Therefore, $8q = 8\left(\frac{1}{2}\right)$, or 4, and Quantity B is greater than Quantity A.

7. **The correct answer is C.** If the average of 4 numbers is 4, then their sum is 16. This means that $p+r+s=6$, which makes Quantity A equal to 2.

8. **The correct answer is D.** If the average of two numbers, x and some other number we'll call y, is 16, then $\frac{x+y}{2}=16$. Thus $x+y=32$ and $y=32-x$.

9. **The correct answer is C.** Multiplying 173.28 by $\frac{1}{100}$ is the same as dividing 173.28 by 100, which will have the effect of reducing the quantity. You can eliminate answer choice E. When dividing by 100, the decimal point is moved two places to the left. Thus, $173.28 \times \frac{1}{100} = 1.7328$.

10. **The correct answer is D.** To solve this problem, set up a system of equations and solve for n:

$$3n+b=5.85$$
$$2n+b=4.65$$
$$n=1.20$$

11. **The correct answer is D.** To solve this problem, simply divide 336 by each of the answer choices and see which one does not come out evenly. The number 336 can be evenly divided by 6, 7, 8, and 12, but not 9.

12. **The correct answer is 70.** To solve this problem, recognize that the angles opposite the congruent sides will also be congruent. The total of these angles must be 180−40=140, so both angle X and angle Z will equal 70°.

13. **The correct answer is C.** To solve this problem, first add the values in the parentheses: $\sqrt{(33-9)(17+7)} = \sqrt{(24)(24)}$. Recall that $xx=x^2$. Thus, $\sqrt{(24)(24)} = \sqrt{(24^2)}$, which equals 24.

14. **The correct answer is B.** To solve this problem, recall that the formula for the area of a triangle is ½(b)(h). The base of this new, larger garden is 2×48=96, and the height is still 36. Therefore, the area is ½(96)(36)=1,728 square feet.

15. **The correct answer is B.** To solve this problem, first calculate the total area. Recall that the formula for the area of a triangle is ½(b)(h). Therefore, the area to be covered by the fertilizer is ½(48)(36)=864 square feet. Next, determine the number of bags of fertilizer needed: 864÷300=2.88. Mandy will need at least 3 full bags of fertilizer, so she will spend $8.25×3=$24.75, or about $25 on fertilizer for her garden.

16. **The correct answer is D.** The perimeter is the distance around the garden, so you must calculate the length of the hypotenuse, using the Pythagorean Theorem:

$$a^2+b^2=c^2$$
$$36^2+48^2=c^2$$
$$1,296+2,304=c^2$$
$$3,600=c^2$$
$$60=c$$

Now, simply add the sides: 36+48+60=144.

17. **The correct answer is D.** To solve this problem, recall that the formula for the area of a triangle is ½(b)(h). Mandy is adding 2 feet to the length of each of the sides of her garden, so the new base is 50 and the new height is 38. Therefore, the total area will be ½(50)(38)=950 square feet.

18. **The correct answer is B.** To answer this question, you need information about the distance between all four exits; therefore, Statement (A) alone is not sufficient. Statement (B) gives you sufficient information to calculate the distance between Exit 2 and Exit 3: the entire distance is 23 miles, the distance between Exit 1 and Exit 2 is 3 miles, the distance between Exit 3 and Exit 4 is 9 miles, which means that the distance between Exit 2 and Exit 3 is $23-3-9=11$. Statement (C) does not provide sufficient information to determine the distance from Exit 2 to Exit 3.
19. **The correct answer is 101.** If the average of the six integers is 38, then the total must be $6 \times 38 = 228$. If the average of the seven integers is 47, then the total must be $7 \times 47 = 329$. You are adding the seventh integer to the set, so the value of the seventh integer will be $329 - 228 = 101$.
20. **The correct answer is E.** A circle with diameter 12 inches has a radius of 6 inches. The area of a circle is $A = \pi r^2$, where r is the radius. Therefore, the area of the circle is $\pi 6^2 = 36\pi$.

13
GRE Practice Test 3

CHAPTER GOALS

- Take a full-length GRE under actual test conditions.
- Check your results using the Answer Key.
- Review the explanations for each question, focusing particularly on questions you answered incorrectly or did not answer at all.
- Build your test-taking confidence.

The simulated GRE in this chapter contains 80 multiple-choice questions and two essay tasks, divided into six main sections. You should allow approximately 3 hours and 30 minutes to complete the entire test. To make this simulated test as much like the actual GRE as possible, you should complete the test sections in the time indicated at the beginning of each section, and in the order in which the sections appear. You may skip around within a section, but complete each section before you move on to the next one.

Within each section there are several different types of questions. Make sure that you read and understand all directions before you begin.

- Circle your answers on the test so that you can compare your answers to the correct answers listed in the Answer Key on page 411.
- When asked to select a sentence in a passage that meets a certain description, circle or underline the sentence you choose.
- Carefully review the explanations for any question that you answered incorrectly.

We suggest that you make this practice test as much like the real test as possible. Find a quiet location, free from distractions, and make sure that you have pencils and a timepiece. Review the Scoring Guidelines in Chapter 2, but remember that your score on the actual GRE will be dependent on many factors, including your level of preparedness and your fatigue level on test day. The Practice Test begins on the next page.

GRE Diagnostic Test 3

SECTION 1   **ANALYTICAL WRITING**

SECTION 2   **VERBAL REASONING**

SECTION 3   **VERBAL REASONING**

SECTION 4   **QUANTITATIVE REASONING**

SECTION 5   **QUANTITATIVE REASONING**

                    ANSWERS AND EXPLANATIONS

SECTION 1

Analytical Writing

PART 1.   ANALYZE AN ISSUE

30 minutes

You will have 30 minutes to organize your thoughts and compose a response that represents your point of view on the issue. Do not respond to any issue other than the one presented; a response to any other issue will receive a score of 0.

Issue Topic

"Despite the fact that cures have been found for several debilitating diseases, drug research should be curtailed due to ethical concerns."

Discuss whether you agree or disagree with the statement. Use relevant reasons and examples to support your point of view. In developing and supporting your position, consider ways in which the statement might or might not hold true. Explain how those considerations affect your point of view.

Analytical Writing

PART 2. ANALYZE AN ARGUMENT

30 minutes

You will have 30 minutes to organize your thoughts and compose a response that critiques the given argument. Do not respond to any argument other than the one given; a response to any other argument will receive a score of 0.

Argument Topic

A recent study indicated that sales of sports cars in Pine River have increased by 35 percent over the past five years, yet there are no currently operating car dealerships that specialize in selling sports cars. Furthermore, the majority of households in Pine River are one-income households, and a nationwide study has shown that members of such households are more likely to purchase sports cars. Therefore, a new Pine River car dealership specializing in selling sports cars will be quite popular and profitable.

Critique the reasoning used in the argument above. You are not being asked to discuss your point of view on the argument. You should identify and analyze the central elements of the argument, the underlying assumptions that are being made, and any supporting information that is given. Your critique can also discuss other information that would strengthen or weaken the argument or make it more logical.

SECTION 2

Verbal Reasoning

30 Minutes
20 Questions

This section consists of three different types of questions: Reading Comprehension, Text Completion, and Sentence Equivalence. To answer the questions, select the best answer from the answer choices given. Reading Comprehension questions appear in sets; Text Completion and Sentence Equivalence questions are independent. The questions will be presented in random order. Read the following directions before you begin the test.

Reading Comprehension Questions

Directions:
Multiple-choice Questions—Select One Answer Choice: These are the traditional multiple-choice questions with five answer choices from which you must select one.

Multiple-choice Questions—Select One or More Answer Choices: These questions provide three answer choices; select all that are correct.

Select-in-Passage: Choose the sentence in the passage that meets a certain description.

Text Completion Questions

Directions: Select one entry from the corresponding column of choices for each blank. Fill all blanks in the way that best completes the text.

Sentence Equivalence Questions

Directions: Select the two answer choices that, when used to complete the sentence, fit the meaning of the sentence as a whole and produce completed sentences that are alike in meaning.

Questions 1 to 3 are based on the following passage.

Thousands, perhaps even millions, of people around the world are afflicted with a neurological condition called *synesthesia*. The word synesthesia comes from the Greek words *syn*, which means "together," and *aisthesis*, which means "perception or sensation." Those affected by the disorder experience an involuntary, simultaneous joining of two senses; for example, some *synesthetes*—people with synesthesia—perceive words as colors. Researchers do not know the causes of synesthesia, nor

GO ON TO NEXT PAGE

do they fully understand the mechanisms of the disorder. However, some scientists believe that synesthesia results from crossed connections in the brain; synapses that are traditionally associated with one sensory system have somehow crossed over into another sensory system, which leads to a juxtaposition of two, typically unrelated senses. Synesthetic perceptions are idiosyncratic, and are as varied as the perceivers themselves. Theoretically, the number of types of synesthesia is bound only by the sensory pairings themselves, such as the color/sound pairing mentioned previously. Researchers estimate that there could be as many as 35 different broad pairings—sound/touch, taste/hearing, and so on—each characterized by many permutations and unique features. Indeed the variations could be endless, with each synesthete perceiving a slightly different color or sensation, for example. Although the perceptions vary among individuals, according to Dr. Richard Cytowic, a leading synesthesia expert, the lifelong inter-sensory associations of the synesthetes remain stable, no matter what senses are joined in a given synesthete.

For Question 1, select one answer choice.

1. The primary purpose of the passage is to
    - Ⓐ describe a medical condition that might be difficult to recognize even though it is clearly defined
    - Ⓑ propose a radical new treatment for a medical condition that was once thought untreatable
    - Ⓒ question the accuracy of the current definition of a well-known medical condition
    - Ⓓ reject one explanation of a complex phenomenon in favor of another
    - Ⓔ admit several weaknesses in the current theoretical approach to a complex medical condition

2. Select the sentence that best describes the scope of the sensory disorder.

For Question 3, select one answer choice.

3. According to the passage, each of the following statements regarding synesthesia is true EXCEPT
    - Ⓐ researchers have not yet fully explained the mechanisms behind synesthesia
    - Ⓑ synesthetic perceptions are unique to the individual synesthete
    - Ⓒ the term 'synesthesia' derives from a combination of Greek root words
    - Ⓓ the various permutations of synesthesia suggest that individuals experience shifting inter-sensory associations
    - Ⓔ researchers have so far failed to catalog all of the various sensory pairings experienced by synesthetes

Question 4 is based on the following passage.

In many Western European nations, the law is seen as rigid and not open to interpretation. This rigidity grants a consistency to questions of law that many would argue is absent in other, more flexible systems. The European construction of law provides litigants with a clear picture of how a case will be decided. All parties involved are certain how judges will rule on issues. It is simple—judges will strictly follow the law. This simple fact, that the law will not change from one situation to another, allows for court systems in Western Europe to process cases efficiently and cuts down on the amount of frivolous lawsuits. It is useless for an individual to attempt a case if he knows in advance that the law is not in his favor.

For Question 4, select one answer choice.

4. In the passage, the author is primarily concerned with
    - Ⓐ arguing for a universal application of Western European legal practices
    - Ⓑ decrying the rigidity and constancy of Western European legal practices
    - Ⓒ describing the potential benefits of Western European legal systems
    - Ⓓ defining the pros and cons of various legal systems
    - Ⓔ denouncing European law for its anti-consumer bias

For Questions 5 to 7, select one entry from the corresponding column of choices for each blank. Fill all blanks in the way that best completes the text.

5. Onlookers considered Justin a (i) _____ after watching him eat; however, little did they know that he was (ii) _____ following a weeklong hunger strike.

Blank (i)	Blank (ii)
Ⓐ miser	Ⓓ parched
Ⓑ glutton	Ⓔ famished
Ⓒ hoarder	Ⓕ sated

6. Because it is (i) _____ to (ii) _____ all of the costs associated with starting a new business, a certain level of flexibility should be built into any initial business plan.

Blank (i)	Blank (ii)
Ⓐ necessary	Ⓓ incur
Ⓑ challenging	Ⓔ anticipate
Ⓒ pragmatic	Ⓕ assess

GO ON TO NEXT PAGE

7. In 1948, the Universal Declaration of Human Rights was adopted by the United Nations. Its 30 articles ensured people's rights to freedom from torture and (i) _____, equal (ii) _____ under the law and a guarantee of a (iii) _____ based on the will of the people.

Blank (i)	Blank (ii)	Blank (iii)
Ⓐ slavery	Ⓓ compensation	Ⓖ country
Ⓑ asylum	Ⓔ protection	Ⓗ nationality
Ⓒ punishment	Ⓕ attention	Ⓘ government

Questions 8 to 11 are based on the following passage.

Unlike some classic European novels, American literature encompasses many different, even unique, styles and genres. One of the most interesting of these is the Southern Gothic subgenre. As its name implies, Southern Gothic literature is reflective of life in the American South. Southern Gothic maintains some of the characteristics of Gothic writing, such as plot development of the supernatural or the ironic. However, Southern Gothic does not focus on creating tension and suspense like other Gothic genres. Instead, Southern Gothic story lines examine Southern society and its underlying, often implicit, social structure.

Southern Gothic writers generally spurn the stereotype of the gentleman on the plantation and the glamorous Southern belle. Instead, the authors develop characters that are sinister or reclusive and not particularly pleasant on the surface. However, these characters usually have redeeming qualities that allow and encourage the reader to empathize with their situations or dilemmas. It is through these immoral and unhappy personalities that the Southern Gothic writer is able to present and explore moral issues of the American South, such as slavery and bigotry, without blatant accusations.

For Question 8, select one answer choice.

8. The main purpose of the passage is to
   Ⓐ explain how Southern Gothic writers use immoral personalities to explore moral issues in the American South
   Ⓑ explore the primary stylistic differences between classical Gothic and Southern Gothic
   Ⓒ argue that Southern Gothic is sufficiently unique to merit its classification as a distinct subgenre
   Ⓓ deny the necessity of tension and suspense as defining features of Gothic literature
   Ⓔ describe the identifying features of the Southern Gothic subgenre

For Question 9, consider each of the choices separately and select all that apply.

9. Which of the following can be inferred from the passage?
   - [A] Southern Gothic writers use their writings to subtly condemn immoral traditions like slavery and bigotry.
   - [B] Southern Gothic maintains certain elements of the classical Gothic tradition while breaking with other elements.
   - [C] The main characters of Southern Gothic literature frequently alienate readers with their unpleasant, even sinister, personalities.

10. Select the sentence that weakens the author's assertion that readers are encouraged to sympathize with Southern Gothic characters.

For Question 11, consider each of the choices separately and select all that apply.

11. Based on the attitudes displayed in the passage, with which of the following statements would the author most likely agree?
    - [A] Southern Gothic writers enjoy employing the character stereotypes of Southern plantation life.
    - [B] American literature sometimes diverges sharply from its European antecedents.
    - [C] Southern society is organized on clear moral guidelines of right and wrong.

GO ON TO NEXT PAGE

Question 12 is based on the following passage.

Researchers at the Shimizu Institute in Japan believe it is possible to terraform Mars by making use of the planet's own resources and by introducing genetically altered life from Earth. They hope these actions will speed up the terraforming process, not just by adapting Mars to support Earth-life, but also by adapting Earth-life to exist on Mars. These experts think they can use the Martian geology itself to jump-start the planet. The theory is that detonation of thermonuclear devices deep in the Martian mountains will trigger eruptions of hot magma that would melt the frozen atmosphere, thereby releasing the components necessary for life.

For Question 12, select one answer choice.

12. Which of the following, if true, would most weaken the experts' theory as explained in the last two sentences?
    - (A) Martian mountains are well-situated and easily accessible by remote mobility devices.
    - (B) Similar eruptions of magma on Earth have demonstrated the ability to enable life in hostile underwater environments.
    - (C) Mars' frozen atmosphere lacks the critical components necessary for life.
    - (D) Even if scientists could terraform Mars, the planet would eventually have all the same problems as Earth.
    - (E) Thermonuclear devices would be very dangerous to send to Mars.

For Question 13, select one entry from the corresponding column of choices for each blank. Fill all blanks in the way that best completes the text.

13. During the Elizabethan era of the mid and late 1500s, (i) _____ were common, including Christopher Marlowe and William Shakespeare, and tragedies were by far the most popular type of performance, despite their (ii) _____ endings.

Blank (i)	Blank (ii)
(A) journalists	(D) unanticipated
(B) playwrights	(E) exultant
(C) biographers	(F) heartrending

Questions 14 and 15 are based on the following passage.

For generations, Native Americans used myths and legends to explain the mysterious world around them. One such etiological myth originated with the Cherokee. According to the tale, at one time, far in the past, animals, birds, fishes, and even insects were able to communicate with one another. When humans arrived, however, life became more difficult because the creatures' habitats began to shrink. In order to protect themselves, the creatures decided to introduce disease to humans. The plant world, however, took sympathy upon the Cherokee and so provided a remedy for each of the diseases created by the creatures. It was because of this, says the legend, that the Cherokee turned to plants for antidotes and medicines for illness.

For Question 14, select one answer choice.

14. Which of the following describes the organization of the passage?
    - Ⓐ The author defines a theory then illustrates its workings.
    - Ⓑ The author argues for one side then presents a counterargument.
    - Ⓒ The author defends an early explanation of aboriginal medical practices.
    - Ⓓ The author introduces a subject then gives an example of it.
    - Ⓔ The author compares two versions of a creation myth to determine which is the original.

For Question 15, consider each of the choices separately and select all that apply.

15. The author mentions etiological myth probably in order to
    - A cast aspersion on Cherokee legends
    - B give the academic designation for legends that explain practices or events
    - C show how animals were thought by the Cherokee to be able to communicate with each other

For Questions 16 through 20, select the two answer choices that, when used to complete the sentence, fit the meaning of the sentence as a whole and produce completed sentences that are alike in meaning.

16. Eager to sell her home and move to another city, Kendra accepted the proffered purchase agreement with _____.
    - A reluctance
    - B humility
    - C enthusiasm
    - D probity
    - E alacrity
    - F aversion

17. Until Andrew learned to _____ a strict schedule, he seldom managed to complete his homework in a timely manner.
    - [A] infer from
    - [B] commingle with
    - [C] adhere to
    - [D] vacillate from
    - [E] inure to
    - [F] stick with

18. Although sometimes extremely _____ of automobile repair shops as a whole, people are unwilling to treat their own mechanics with equal criticism.
    - [A] reverential
    - [B] deferential
    - [C] contemptuous
    - [D] redemptive
    - [E] disdainful
    - [F] trusting

19. Consider the continuing pessimism of the political candidate, whose proposals are increasingly _____.
    - [A] dreary
    - [B] astute
    - [C] euphoric
    - [D] popular
    - [E] bleak
    - [F] versatile

20. He entered his supervisor's office with an _____ sense of doom; his misdeeds at the office party would certainly cause him to be fired.
    - [A] elemental
    - [B] impractical
    - [C] inadvertent
    - [D] inexorable
    - [E] assiduous
    - [F] unerring

STOP.
This is the end of Section 2. Use any remaining time to check your work.

SECTION 3

Verbal Reasoning

30 Minutes
20 Questions

This section consists of three different types of questions: Reading Comprehension, Text Completion, and Sentence Equivalence. To answer the questions, select the best answer from the answer choices given. Reading Comprehension questions appear in sets; Text Completion and Sentence Equivalence questions are independent. The questions will be presented in random order. Read the following directions before you begin the test.

Reading Comprehension Questions

Directions:
Multiple-choice Questions—Select One Answer Choice: These are the traditional multiple-choice questions with five answer choices from which you must select one.

Multiple-choice Questions—Select One or More Answer Choices: These questions provide three answer choices; select all that are correct.

Select-in-Passage: Choose the sentence in the passage that meets a certain description.

Text Completion Questions

Directions: Select one entry from the corresponding column of choices for each blank. Fill all blanks in the way that best completes the text.

Sentence Equivalence Questions

Directions: Select the two answer choices that, when used to complete the sentence, fit the meaning of the sentence as a whole and produce completed sentences that are alike in meaning.

GO ON TO NEXT PAGE

For Questions 1 through 3, select the two answer choices that, when used to complete the sentence, fit the meaning of the sentence as a whole and produce completed sentences that are alike in meaning.

1. The music store attracts an _____ group of customers; people with varied interests and lifestyles congregate there.
    A irate
    B assorted
    C apprehensive
    D aberrant
    E eclectic
    F optimum

2. Linda exposed the illegal actions of her company and was, unfortunately, _____ by her peers for her ethical actions.
    A adored
    B shunned
    C ostracized
    D relieved
    E celebrated
    F admired

3. Because the media corporation owned such a large portion of the news channels, it enjoyed remarkable _____ in the news market.
    A hegemony
    B discretion
    C atonement
    D monotony
    E zeal
    F predominance

Questions 4 and 5 are based on the following passage.

When home is approximately 2,000 feet under the surface of the sea, it is challenging to have your photograph taken. In Japan, however, a species of shark that is almost never seen because of its deep natural habitat came close enough to the top to grab the attention of some fishermen. This five-foot long, eel-shaped shark was caught and soon identified as a female frill shark, a primitive species that has gone through little alteration since prehistoric times. Cameras captured it while it was still swimming so that scientists could learn as much as possible from this single specimen of a mysterious species.

For Question 4, consider each of the choices separately and select all that apply.

4. Which of the following is implied about scientific documentation of frill sharks?
   - [A] Frill sharks are rarely studied because their habitats are inaccessible to most scientific equipment.
   - [B] Female frill sharks are easier to study than males.
   - [C] Photographic evidence is the best form of documentation for marine biologists.

For Question 5, select one answer choice.

5. Which of the following best describes the central issue with which the passage is concerned?
   - (A) presenting evidence of a marine animal rarely witnessed in nature
   - (B) arguing that ancient creatures still exist in a modern world
   - (C) celebrating Japan's tradition of aquaculture
   - (D) proving that commercial fishing boats are trawling too deeply in open water
   - (E) documenting the extinction of prehistoric fish

Question 6 is based on the following passage.

The very first line of the lengthy saga *Anna Karenina* gives the reader an immediate sense of Leo Tolstoy's main theme: "Happy families are all alike; every unhappy family is unhappy in its own way." From this morose observation, it is clear that Tolstoy's characters are probably not going to be bland or blithe. Throughout his novel, Tolstoy depicts the ambiguities and ambivalences felt by seemingly real people in real-life situations. The main character, Anna Karenina, has a quietly desperate air throughout the story. The reader first meets her in an attempt to talk her sister-in-law out of leaving Anna's adulterous brother. Even in this scene, where Anna most extols the joys of married life, she seems to be missing a part of herself. Despite her protestations, she only pretends to be happy and content.

For Question 6, select one answer choice.

6. Which of the following, if true, most logically completes the passage?
   - (A) Anna's brother, however, is quite content with his choices, and continues to act in his own interests.
   - (B) Tolstoy continues to weave Anna's story of sadness and self-deception until its tragic conclusion.
   - (C) Anna's sister-in-law decides that she must leave her husband for her own wellbeing.
   - (D) Tolstoy's other novels follow the same motif.
   - (E) Tolstoy's insistence on depressive characterization renders his novels almost unreadable.

GO ON TO NEXT PAGE

Questions 7 and 8 are based on the following passage.

Fear is a normal, legitimate response to genuine danger. However, when fear spirals out of control, becoming persistent and irrational, it constitutes a phobia. Phobias affect a significant portion of the American population. Some experts believe that nearly twenty-five percent of Americans live with irrational fears that prevent them from performing everyday activities. Phobias, like other anxiety disorders, can greatly affect quality of life. Generally defined as an unrelenting, anomalous, and unfounded fear of an object or situation, a phobia is normally developed from a past negative experience or encounter. Children might adopt phobias by observing a family member's reaction to specific stimuli. There is also data to suggest genetic factors linked to phobias.

For Question 7, consider each of the choices separately and select all that apply.

7. It can be inferred from the passage that theories about phobias contain which of the following elements?
    - [A] There is a qualitative difference between ordinary fear and phobia.
    - [B] Nearly three quarters of Americans live their lives unaffected by phobias.
    - [C] Tendencies to develop phobias may be inherited.

8. Select the sentence that explains the difference between normal fear and phobia.

For Questions 9 and 10, select one entry from the corresponding column of choices for each blank. Fill all blanks in the way that best completes the text.

9. In its first few hours out of the nest, a fledgling bird can find itself alone on the lawn, looking lost and (i) _____, where its main danger is local (ii) _____, especially in a residential neighborhood where there are many outdoor cats.

Blank (i)	Blank (ii)
Ⓐ abandoned	Ⓓ wildlife
Ⓑ appalled	Ⓔ predators
Ⓒ duped	Ⓕ predicates

10. Carolyn suffers from myopia, often known as nearsightedness, which necessitates the use of contacts or eyeglasses, and recent genetic studies indicate that it appears to be a(n) _____ condition.

Ⓐ inherited
Ⓑ contagious
Ⓒ predominantly
Ⓓ untreatable
Ⓔ discriminating

Questions 11 to 13 are based on the following passage.

Nine times as many Americans died in the farmlands near Antietam Creek in the fall of 1862 than died on the beaches of Normandy on D-Day, the so-called longest day of World War II. The bloodiest single day of war in the nation's history came when General Robert E. Lee's Confederate Army undertook its first engagement on northern soil. According to the Antietam National Battlefield park service, when the fighting had subsided, more than 23,000 soldiers lay dead or wounded, more than all of the dead or wounded Americans in the Revolutionary War, War of 1812, Mexican War, and Spanish-American War combined.

Just a week after his army's victory in the Second Battle of Bull Run, Lee resolved to advance the front into Northern territory. The vast farm fields of western Maryland were ready for harvest, and Lee saw in them an opportunity to nourish his soldiers, replenish his supplies, and turn the residents of the undecided border state to his cause.

For Questions 11 to 13, select one answer choice.

11. Which of the following most logically completes the first paragraph?
    - (A) How then did this terrible battle come about?
    - (B) The Confederacy was famous for the tactical genius of its generals.
    - (C) Clearly the battle strategy on both sides was ineffective.
    - (D) Despite these casualties, the war dragged on for another three years.
    - (E) It was an inexcusable waste of human life.

12. Which of the following statements about Maryland can be inferred from the passage?
    - (A) Numerous farmers in Maryland had freed their slaves before the commencement of the Civil War.
    - (B) While Maryland was not a Confederate state, some residents were sympathetic to the Southern cause.
    - (C) General Lee intended to pillage the farms of Maryland in order to feed his troops.
    - (D) Many Southern fighters were originally from Maryland.
    - (E) The battle at Normandy is more important than the battle at Antietam.

13. In the last sentence of the first paragraph, the author is most likely suggesting that
    - (A) the other American wars of the 18th and 19th centuries did not have heavy casualties
    - (B) the Antietam National Battlefield park service is an unreliable source of information
    - (C) the Battle at Antietam was the most significant battle of the American Civil War
    - (D) General Lee was overly encouraged by his success in the Second Battle of Bull Run
    - (E) the troops at Antietam suffered catastrophic losses compared to other battles in that century

For Questions 14 to 16, select one entry from the corresponding column of choices for each blank. Fill all blanks in the way that best completes the text.

14. The depiction of the (i) _____ koala bear is largely a misconception: koalas can be very (ii) _____ creatures that should never be approached in the wild.

Blank (i)	Blank (ii)
(A) ferocious	(D) fierce
(B) volatile	(E) hysterical
(C) affable	(F) assertive

15. It is surprising to observe that Susan's paintings have recently been criticized as (ii) _____, because her advocates have been touting her great (ii) _____.

Blank (i)	Blank (ii)
(A) ambiguous	(D) uncertainty
(B) feckless	(E) imagination
(C) banal	(F) incompetence

16. The supply of fresh water continues to be a _____ for most environmentalists since, surprisingly, over 97 percent of the world's water is un-potable because it comes from salty oceans.

    - (A) digression
    - (B) concern
    - (C) catalyst
    - (D) precept
    - (E) compromise

Question 17 is based on the following passage.

"Joy is the holy fire that keeps our purpose warm and our intelligence aglow. Work without joy shall be as nothing. Resolve to keep happy, and your joy and you shall form an invincible host against difficulties." This quote becomes yet more inspirational upon learning it comes from Helen Keller, a remarkable woman who overcame both blindness and deafness. Her decision to be joyful despite adversity no doubt contributed to her many impressive accomplishments. She succeeded in learning to communicate, and reached out to others with her meaningful speeches and writings.

For Question 17, select one answer choice.

17. Which of the following statements is most analogous to the quotation presented in the passage?
    - (A) Fire is an essential tool when respected and attended, but a massive destructive force if allowed to spread out of control.
    - (B) A child's mind is absorptive like the driest sponge, so great care must be taken to keep poisonous notions from infiltrating it.
    - (C) Sorrowful resignation remains the genius' malady, for truth and knowledge weigh heavy on the heart.
    - (D) Find your true purpose in life and your days will be filled with peace and harmony, your troubles will be few.
    - (E) Enthusiasm raises the sunken spirit and fosters creativity in even the most hardened heart.

Question 18 is based on the following passage.

On October 3, 1965, President Lyndon B. Johnson signed a law that sought to overturn four decades of discrimination. The National Origins Quota System, which had been in effect since 1924, determined which immigrants should be allowed to come to the United States based solely on their national origin. The 1965 Immigration Act changed all this by making individual work skills and relationships with current U.S. citizens the criteria for immigration. President Johnson captured the essence of this exciting change by declaring that "those who can contribute most to this country—to its growth, to its strength, to its spirit—will be the first that are admitted to this land."

For Question 18, select one answer choice.

18. The author's attitude toward the Immigration Act is best characterized as one of
    - (A) resentment
    - (B) derision
    - (C) appreciation
    - (D) wonder
    - (E) confusion

Questions 19 and 20 are based on the following passage.

English poet Elizabeth Barrett Browning, is probably best known for her collection of poems, *Sonnets from the Portuguese*. By title alone, one might assume that these poems were either translated from Portuguese or a product of Portuguese inspiration. Instead, the title refers to the author herself. Robert Browning, Elizabeth's husband, affectionately called her his "little Portuguese," on account of her dark complexion. Indeed, it was Robert, himself a successful poet, who secured his wife's literary fame through this volume of verse. While the poems in *Sonnets from the Portuguese* were intended as a private gift for him, he simply could not keep their beauty to himself. The book was subsequently published in 1850.

For Question 19, consider each of the choices separately and select all that apply.

19. According to the passage, which of the following may be inferred about Robert Browning?
    - [A] Despite his love, Robert Browning was unable to appreciate the true quality of Elizabeth Barrett Browning's verse.
    - [B] Robert Browning failed to take seriously his wife's literary ambitions.
    - [C] Robert Browning was well qualified to judge the quality of his wife's poetry.

20. Select the sentence within the paragraph that explains Barrett Browning's inspiration for the title of her book of verse.

STOP.
This is the end of Section 3. Use any remaining time to check your work.

SECTION 4

Quantitative Reasoning

35 Minutes
20 Questions

This section includes four types of questions: Multiple-choice Questions (Select One Answer Choice *and* Select One or More Answer Choices), Numeric Entry Questions, and Quantitative Comparison Questions. Read the following directions before you begin the test.

General Information:
Numbers: All of the numbers used in this section are real numbers.

Figures: Assume that the position of all points, angles, etc. are in the order shown and the measures of angles are positive.

Straight lines can be assumed to be straight.

All figures lie in a plane unless otherwise stated.

The figures given for each question provide information to solve the problem. The figures are not drawn to scale unless otherwise stated. To solve the problems, use your knowledge of mathematics; do not estimate lengths and sizes of the figures to answer questions.

Multiple-choice Questions

Select One Answer Choice

Directions: These questions are multiple-choice questions that ask you to select only one answer choice from a list of five choices.

Select One or More Answer Choices

Directions: Select one or more answer choices according to the specific question directions.

If the question does not specify how many answer choices to select, select all that apply.

The correct answer may be just one of the choices or as many as all of the choices, depending on the question.

No credit is given unless you select all of the correct choices and no others.

If the question specifies how many answer choices to select, select exactly that number of choices.

GO ON TO NEXT PAGE

Numeric Entry Questions

Directions: Enter your answer in the answer box(es) below the question.

Equivalent forms of the correct answer, such as 2.5 and 2.50, are all correct. Fractions do not need to be reduced to lowest terms.

Enter the exact answer unless the question asks you to round your answer.

Quantitative Comparison Questions

Directions: Some questions give you two quantities, Quantity A and Quantity B. Compare the two quantities and choose one of the following answer choices:

- **A** if Quantity A is greater;
- **B** if Quantity B is greater;
- **C** if the two quantities are equal;
- **D** if you cannot determine the relationship based on the given information.

Note: Information and/or figures pertaining to one or both of the quantities may appear above the two columns. Any information that appears in both columns has the same meaning for both Quantity A and Quantity B.

You will also be asked Data Interpretation questions, which are grouped together and refer to the same table, graph, or other data presentation. These questions ask the examinee to interpret or analyze the given data. The types of questions may be Multiple-choice (both types) or Numeric Entry.

Each of Questions 1 to 7 presents two quantities, Quantity A and Quantity B. Compare the two quantities. You may use additional information centered above the quantities if such information is given. Choose one of the following answer choices:

- Ⓐ if Quantity A is greater;
- Ⓑ if Quantity B is greater;
- Ⓒ if the two quantities are equal;
- Ⓓ if you cannot determine the relationship based on the given information.

	Quantity A	Quantity B	
1.	The increase in the area of a circle C when its radius is increased by 1 inch	The increase in the area of a circle R when its radius is increased by 1 inch	Ⓐ Ⓑ Ⓒ Ⓓ

	Quantity A	Quantity B	
2.	(30% of 50)+40	(50% of 40)+30	Ⓐ Ⓑ Ⓒ Ⓓ

	Quantity A	Quantity B	
3.	$\frac{1}{13}$ of 19	$\frac{1}{19}$ of 13	Ⓐ Ⓑ Ⓒ Ⓓ

$$x+y=4$$

	Quantity A	Quantity B	
4.	x	y	Ⓐ Ⓑ Ⓒ Ⓓ

$$2x+3y=18$$
$$x-4y=-13$$

	Quantity A	Quantity B	
5.	$x+y$	6	Ⓐ Ⓑ Ⓒ Ⓓ

	Quantity A	Quantity B	
6.	14(256)	15(255)	Ⓐ Ⓑ Ⓒ Ⓓ

	Quantity A	Quantity B	
7.	90,000	$(298.89)^2$	Ⓐ Ⓑ Ⓒ Ⓓ

8. While riding a bicycle, a person traveled 5 blocks in 2 minutes. At this rate, how many blocks will the person travel in 16 minutes?
   Ⓐ 8
   Ⓑ 10
   Ⓒ 16
   Ⓓ 32
   Ⓔ 40

GO ON TO NEXT PAGE

9. If $m-p=4$, and $n+p=18$, then $m+n=$
   - (A) 14
   - (B) 18
   - (C) 22
   - (D) 26
   - (E) 30

For Question 10, write your answer in the box.

10. What is the largest prime factor of 636?

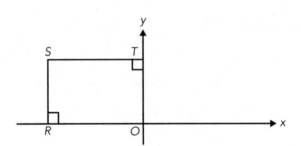

11. In the figure above, $RS=ST$ and the coordinates of S are $(k,4)$. What is the value of k?
    - (A) −4
    - (B) −2
    - (C) 0
    - (D) 2
    - (E) 4

For Question 12, select all the answer choices that apply.

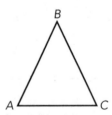

12. Triangle ABC shown above is an isosceles triangle.
    Which of the following statements individually provide(s) sufficient additional information to determine the measure of angle B?

    Select all such statements.
    - [A] The measure of angle A is 80°.
    - [B] The measure of angle C is 50°.
    - [C] The measure of angle A is 80° and the measure of angle C is 50°.

13. When the average of a list of course grades is multiplied by the number of courses, the result is n. What does n represent?
    (A) Half the number of courses
    (B) Half the sum of course grades
    (C) The number of courses
    (D) The average of the course grades
    (E) The sum of the course grades

Refer to the following graph for Questions 14 and 15.

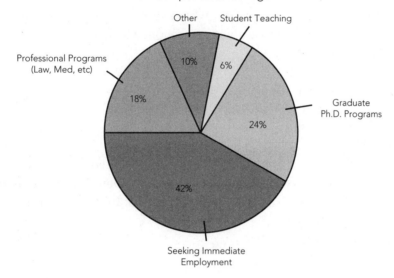

14. There were 1,650 graduates in the class of 2006 at Juniper State College. How many graduates entered Graduate programs?
    (A) 215
    (B) 248
    (C) 416
    (D) 396
    (E) 693

15. There were 1,650 graduates in the class of 2006 at Juniper State College. What is the ratio of graduates who are student teaching to graduates who are seeking immediate employment?
    (A) 1:4
    (B) 1:7
    (C) 4:7
    (D) 7:1
    (E) 42:1

GO ON TO NEXT PAGE

Refer to the following graphs for Questions 16 and 17.

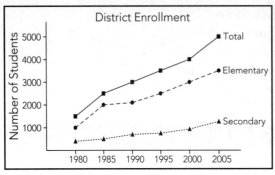
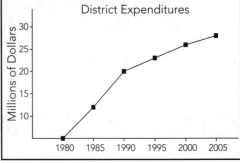

16. Of the following years, which showed the least difference between elementary enrollment and secondary enrollment?
    - Ⓐ 2000
    - Ⓑ 1995
    - Ⓒ 1990
    - Ⓓ 1985
    - Ⓔ 1980

17. The cost of books and materials accounted for approximately 30% of the school district's annual expenditures. In 1990, what was the approximate average cost per student for books and materials?
    - Ⓐ $1,500
    - Ⓑ $2,000
    - Ⓒ $3,000
    - Ⓓ $6,000
    - Ⓔ It cannot be determined from the given information.

Use the following information to answer Question 18.

Mr. Hernandez's students filled out a survey asking how many hours each student watched television over 7 days. The results from the survey are shown below in a stem-and-leaf plot.

Stem	Leaf
0	4 5 7
1	0 2 2 4 4 4 5 6 6 6 8 9
2	1 1 1 1 4 8

(Note: For example, 12 hours of television watched would have a stem value of 1 and a leaf value of 2)

18. Which of the following is the median number of hours of television watched during the week?
   - Ⓐ 6
   - Ⓑ 12
   - Ⓒ 15.5
   - Ⓓ 16
   - Ⓔ 21

19. If the volume of a cube is 64, what is the surface area of the cube?
   - Ⓐ 16
   - Ⓑ 24
   - Ⓒ 64
   - Ⓓ 72
   - Ⓔ 96

For question 20, write your answer in the box.

20. To get to Kaytie's house, Camilla must ride her bicycle 8 miles south and then 6 miles west. What is the shortest distance, in miles, between the two houses?

   ☐ miles

STOP.
This is the end of Section 4. Use any remaining time to check your work.

SECTION 5

Quantitative Reasoning

35 Minutes
20 Questions

This section includes four types of questions: Multiple-choice Questions (Select One Answer Choice *and* Select One or More Answer Choices), Numeric Entry Questions, and Quantitative Comparison Questions. Read the following directions before you begin the test.

General Information:
Numbers: All of the numbers used in this section are real numbers.

Figures: Assume that the position of all points, angles, etc. are in the order shown and the measures of angles are positive.

Straight lines can be assumed to be straight.

All figures lie in a plane unless otherwise stated.

The figures given for each question provide information to solve the problem. The figures are not drawn to scale unless otherwise stated. To solve the problems, use your knowledge of mathematics; do not estimate lengths and sizes of the figures to answer questions.

Multiple-choice Questions

Select One Answer Choice

Directions: These questions are multiple-choice questions that ask you to select only one answer choice from a list of five choices.

Select One or More Answer Choices

Directions: Select one or more answer choices according to the specific question directions.

If the question does not specify how many answer choices to select, select all that apply.

The correct answer may be just one of the choices or as many as all of the choices, depending on the question.

No credit is given unless you select all of the correct choices and no others.

If the question specifies how many answer choices to select, select exactly that number of choices.

Numeric Entry Questions

Directions: Enter your answer in the answer box(es) below the question.

Equivalent forms of the correct answer, such as 2.5 and 2.50, are all correct. Fractions do not need to be reduced to lowest terms.

Enter the exact answer unless the question asks you to round your answer.

Quantitative Comparison Questions

Directions: Some questions give you two quantities, Quantity A and Quantity B. Compare the two quantities and choose one of the following answer choices:

    A if Quantity A is greater;
    B if Quantity B is greater;
    C if the two quantities are equal;
    D if you cannot determine the relationship based on the given information.

Note: Information and/or figures pertaining to one or both of the quantities may appear above the two columns. Any information that appears in both columns has the same meaning for both Quantity A and Quantity B.

You will also be asked Data Interpretation questions, which are grouped together and refer to the same table, graph, or other data presentation. These questions ask the examinee to interpret or analyze the given data. The types of questions may be Multiple-choice (both types) or Numeric Entry.

Each of Questions 1 to 7 presents two quantities, Quantity A and Quantity B. Compare the two quantities. You may use additional information centered above the quantities if such information is given. Choose one of the following answer choices:

  Ⓐ if Quantity A is greater;
  Ⓑ if Quantity B is greater;
  Ⓒ if the two quantities are equal;
  Ⓓ if you cannot determine the relationship based on the given information.

	Quantity A	Quantity B	
1.	$\left(\sqrt{6}\right)^2$	$6\sqrt{6}$	Ⓐ Ⓑ Ⓒ Ⓓ

A $25 CD was bought on sale for $17.50.

	Quantity A	Quantity B	
2.	The difference between the original price and the price of the CD during the sale	75% of the original price	Ⓐ Ⓑ Ⓒ Ⓓ

GO ON TO NEXT PAGE ➤

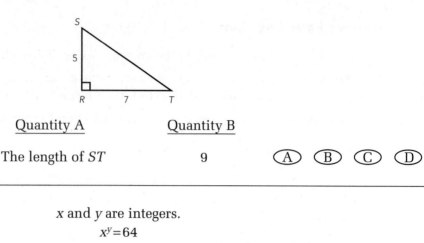

	Quantity A	Quantity B	
3.	The length of *ST*	9	Ⓐ Ⓑ Ⓒ Ⓓ

x and *y* are integers.
$$x^y = 64$$

	Quantity A	Quantity B	
4.	*x*	*y*	Ⓐ Ⓑ Ⓒ Ⓓ

A circle graph shows the various parts of a student's budget. The sector that represents housing costs is 20 percent of the total area.

	Quantity A	Quantity B	
5.	The degree measure of the central angle of the sector that represents housing costs	75°	Ⓐ Ⓑ Ⓒ Ⓓ

$$a > b > 1$$

	Quantity A	Quantity B	
6.	$\dfrac{b+1}{b}$	$\dfrac{a+1}{a}$	Ⓐ Ⓑ Ⓒ Ⓓ

x is a negative integer.
y is a positive integer.

	Quantity A	Quantity B	
7.	0	*x* − *y*	Ⓐ Ⓑ Ⓒ Ⓓ

8. The larger of two numbers exceeds three times the smaller number by 2. The sum of twice the larger and 4 times the smaller is 73. If a is the smaller number, which equation below determines the correct value of x?
   - (A) $4(3a+2)+2a=73$
   - (B) $4(3a+2)+2a=73$
   - (C) $(6a+2)+4a=73$
   - (D) $2(3a+2)+4a=73$
   - (E) $2(3a-2)+4a=73$

9. If x is positive and y is two greater than the square of x, which of the following expresses x in terms of y?
   - (A) $x=\sqrt{y+2}$
   - (B) $x=\sqrt{(y-2)}$
   - (C) $x=\sqrt{(y+2)}$
   - (D) $x=y^2+2$
   - (E) $x=y^2-2$

10. A shoe store charges $39 for a pair of a certain type of sneaker. This price is 30% more than the amount it costs the shoe store to buy one pair of these sneakers. A sales associate can purchase a pair of these sneakers at 20% off the store's cost. How much would an associate pay for a pair of these sneakers (excluding sales tax)?
    - (A) $31.20
    - (B) $25.00
    - (C) $24.00
    - (D) $21.84
    - (E) $19.50

11. If Jason traveled 30 miles in 6 hours and Becky traveled three times as far in half the time, what was Becky's average speed, in miles per hour?
    - (A) 5
    - (B) 15
    - (C) 30
    - (D) 45
    - (E) 90

GO ON TO NEXT PAGE

For Question 12, write your answer in the box.

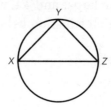

12. In the figure above, $XY = YZ$, and XZ is a diameter of the circle, having a length of 10 inches. What is the area of $\triangle XYZ$, in square inches?

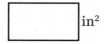 in²

13. The average of x and y is 16 and the average of x, y, and z is 22. What is the value of z?
   - (A) 16
   - (B) 22
   - (C) 34
   - (D) 45
   - (E) 66

Questions 14 and 15 are based on the following information.

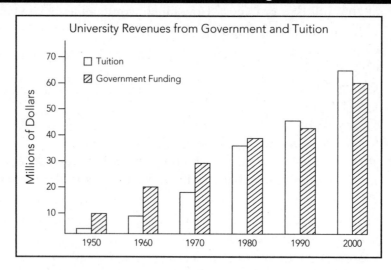

14. According to the graph, which of the following is the best estimate of the total revenue from government funding in 1990?
   - (A) $60 million
   - (B) $55 million
   - (C) $44 million
   - (D) $35 million
   - (E) $29 million

15. Each of the following is a valid conclusion that can be drawn from the information in the graph EXCEPT
    - (A) the total revenue from tuition and government funding in 2000 was $120 million
    - (B) between 1980 and 1990, the proportion of total revenue from government funding increased
    - (C) revenue from government funding increased every year from 1950 to 2000
    - (D) revenue from tuition increased every year from 1960 to 1990
    - (E) revenue from tuition increased at a greater rate than revenue from government funding

Questions 16 and 17 are based on the following information.

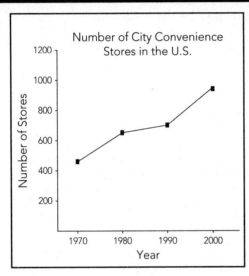
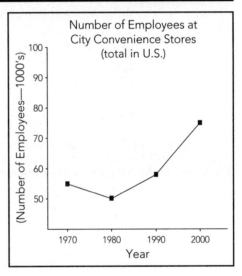

16. Each of the following is a valid conclusion that can be drawn from the information in the graphs EXCEPT
    - (A) from 1970 to 1980, the number of stores increased by approximately 200
    - (B) from 1970 to 2000, the number of stores approximately doubled
    - (C) from 1980 to 2000, the average number of employees increased by approximately 50%
    - (D) in 2000, there were about 75,000 employees
    - (E) from 1970 to 2000, the number of employees increased each decade

GO ON TO NEXT PAGE

17. Assume a 10% growth rate in the number of employees each year from 2000 to 2005. Based on this information, which of the following represents the approximate total number of expected employees in 2002?

    Ⓐ 82,500
    Ⓑ 85,000
    Ⓒ 90,000
    Ⓓ 90,750
    Ⓔ 135,000

For Question 18, select all the answer choices that apply.

18. A colored marble is to be chosen at random from a bag of marbles. The probability that the marble chosen will be green is $\frac{4}{9}$. Which of the following numbers could NOT be the total number of marbles in the bag?

    Select all such numbers.

    ☐ A 64
    ☐ B 72
    ☐ C 110

For Question 19, write your answer in the box.

19. When x is divided by 7, the remainder is 4. What is the remainder when $2x$ is divided by 7?

    ☐

20. The length of a rectangular kitchen floor is 3 feet more than its width. If the length of the floor is 12 feet, what is the area of the floor in square feet?

    Ⓐ 9
    Ⓑ 15
    Ⓒ 42
    Ⓓ 108
    Ⓔ 144

STOP.
This is the end of Section 5. Use any remaining time to check your work.

GRE Practice Test 3 Answers and Explanations

Answer Key

Section 2. Verbal Reasoning

1. A
2. "Researchers estimate...permutations and unique features."
3. D
4. C
5. B, E
6. B, E
7. A, E, I
8. E
9. A, B
10. "Instead, the authors...pleasant on the surface."
11. B
12. C
13. B, F
14. D
15. B
16. C, E
17. C, F
18. C, E
19. A, E
20. D, F

Section 3. Verbal Reasoning

1. B, E
2. B, C
3. A, F
4. A
5. A
6. B
7. A, B, C
8. "However, when fear spirals...it constitutes a phobia."
9. A, E
10. A
11. A
12. B
13. E
14. C, D
15. C, E
16. B
17. E
18. C
19. C
20. "Robert Browning...her dark complexion."

Section 4. Quantitative Reasoning

1. D
2. A
3. A
4. D
5. A
6. B
7. A
8. E
9. C
10. 53
11. A
12. C
13. E
14. D
15. B
16. E
17. B
18. D
19. E
20. 10

Section 5. Quantitative Reasoning

1. B
2. B
3. B
4. D
5. B
6. A
7. A
8. D
9. B
10. C
11. C
12. 25
13. C
14. C
15. B
16. C
17. E
18. A, C
19. 1
20. D

Answer Explanations

Section 1. Analytical Writing Parts 1 and 2

Because grading the essay is subjective, we've chosen not to include any "graded" essays here. Your best bet is to have someone you trust, such as your personal tutor, read your essays and give you an honest critique. Make the grading criteria mentioned in Chapter 6, "GRE Analytical Writing Assessment," available to whoever grades your essays. If you plan on grading your own essays, review the grading criteria and be as honest as possible regarding the structure, development, organization, technique, and appropriateness of your writing. Focus on your weak areas and continue to practice in order to improve your writing skills.

Section 2. Verbal Reasoning

1. **The best answer is A.** The passage is a factual description of a medical condition. Because perception is by definition idiosyncratic, synesthesia could be very difficult to diagnose, but relatively easy to describe.
2. **The best answer is:** *"Researchers estimate that there could be as many as 35 different broad pairings—sound/touch, taste/hearing, and so on—each characterized by many permutations and unique features."* This sentence gives an idea of how synesthesia might manifest itself (sound/touch, etc.) as well as the number of such pairings (35). It also suggests that these pairings may separate into subgroupings. Together, these give the reader an idea of the scope of the disorder.
3. **The best answer is D.** There is nothing in the passage to suggest that a single individual would experience shifting sensory pairings (i.e. sound/touch to taste/hearing), just that several individuals could have unique pairings. All the other choices are supported by the passage.
4. **The best answer is C.** The adjectives "efficiently" and "frivolous" indicate that the author approves of Western European legal systems. This supports choice C. The verbs in choices A, B, and E all connote the wrong tone.
5. **The best answer is B and E.** A weeklong hunger strike strongly suggests that Justin would be hungry ("famished"). The conjunction "however" calls for a contrasting idea in the first blank. A "glutton" is someone who eats to excess without legitimate hunger.
6. **The best answer is B and E.** The phrase "a certain level of flexibility" suggests a level of unknown risk. Because the actual risk is unknown, a predictive word like "anticipate" is the best choice for Blank (ii). Similarly, as the sentence suggests that it is impossible to plan for all the costs, the best choice for Blank (i) is "challenging."
7. **The best answer is A, E, and I.** Because the U.S. declaration was designed to protect human rights, Blank (i) should be filled by a word with a negative

connotation (i.e. "slavery"). "Punishment" is incorrect because it can be appropriate and deserved. Ideally, law exists to "protect" people from harm. "Government" fits Blank (iii) best because it describes how people are ruled within a country or nation.

8. **The best answer is E.** The first paragraph defines Southern Gothic in comparison to the broader category, Gothic. The second paragraph lists specific qualities and interests of Southern Gothic. Combined, the two paragraphs create a passage that describes the identifying features of Southern Gothic literature. The other choices are incorrect because they miss the tone or scope of the passage.

9. **The best answer is A and B.** Choice A is supported by the last sentence of the passage. Choice B is supported in the first paragraph. Choice C is contradicted in the second paragraph.

10. **The best answer is:** *Instead, the authors develop characters that are sinister or reclusive and not particularly pleasant on the surface.* This sentence is a counterargument to the author's main argument that readers are ultimately expected to empathize with the characters. It slightly weakens the author's argument for rhetorical effect.

11. **The best answer is B.** According to the passage, American literature encompasses unique styles and genres. This implies divergence from the earlier, mostly European, genres upon which the American forms are based.

12. **The best answer is C.** According to the passage, detonation of the thermonuclear devices would release specific components found in the atmosphere, and life on Mars would be possible. If those components were not in the atmosphere to begin with, they could not be released and life could not result.

13. **The best answer is B and F.** Christopher Marlowe and William Shakespeare are well-known "playwrights," and tragedies, by definition, have sad, or even "heartrending" endings.

14. **The best answer is D.** In this passage, the author introduces the subject of etiological myths (these legends are also called 'just-so stories') and then gives an example of one from Cherokee mythology. This best matches choice D.

15. **The best answer is B.** The author describes a type of legend that explains some aspect of the world then labels it with its academic name. Choice A is too negative in tone to be correct. Choice C is too narrow in scope.

16. **The best answer is C and E.** Since Kendra is eager to sell her home, she can be expected to accept an offer quickly. Choices C and E match this answer.

17. **The best answer is C and F.** The sentence suggests that Andrew must *follow* a strict schedule in order to complete his homework on time. Choice C and F both match this answer.

18. **The best answer is C and E.** Here, the negative conjunction "Although" is cancelled by the negative adjective "unwilling." Therefore, the blank should be filled by words meaning "critical." Choices C and E both fit nicely.

19. **The best answer is A and E.** The answer choices should be adjectives that match the negative sense of "pessimism." "Dreary" and "bleak" are the best choices.
20. **The best answer is D and F.** The clue here is the certainty of the firing. The answer choices both have the sense of something inescapable.

Section 3. Verbal Reasoning

1. **The best answer is B and E.** The customers are people with varied interests and lifestyles. "Assorted" and "eclectic" both reflect the meaning of "varied."
2. **The best answer is B and C.** Linda's behavior was "ethical," a positive term, but the results were described as "unfortunate." Therefore, you can anticipate that the action of her peers was negative. "Shunned" and "ostracized" are synonyms that capture this sense of negative action.
3. **The best answer is A and F.** The subordinating conjunction 'because' signals that the blank will be filled with a word that matches the idea of "large portion." "Hegemony" and "predominance" are synonyms that echo this meaning.
4. **The best answer is A.** According to the passage, the frill shark is almost never seen because of its deep natural habitat, where photographic documentation is difficult to achieve. These facts support choice A.
5. **The best answer is A.** Choice A matches the tone of the passage while covering the main topic, the relatively unknown frill shark.
6. **The best answer is B.** The passage introduces Tolstoy's main theme of personal uncertainty and unhappiness. Choice B describes how this theme continues to play out in the life of Tolstoy's main character. Therefore, choice B is the best answer.
7. **The best answer is A, B, and C.** Choice A is supported in the second sentence of the passage. Choice B is implied by the fourth sentence. Choice C is supported by the last sentence.
8. **The best answer is:** *However, when fear spirals out of control, becoming persistent and irrational, it constitutes a phobia.* This sentence defines phobia as fear that cannot be controlled or that results from unfounded causes. Thus, it makes a distinction between phobia and fear.
9. **The best answer is A and E.** The baby bird that is alone in a yard may appear to be "abandoned." Its main danger is from "predators," such as cats. The term "wildlife" is not sufficiently precise to be the correct choice.
10. **The best answer is A.** The word "genetic" is the clue that myopia may be an "inherited" condition.
11. **The best answer is A.** The passage needs a link between the first paragraph, which focuses on the catastrophic results of the Battle of Antietam, and the second paragraph, which focuses on Lee's reasons for advancing into Maryland. Only choice A leads the reader logically from one idea to the next.

12. **The best answer is B.** Maryland is identified as an undecided border state and Lee thought it could be swung to support the South. These points support choice B. Note that, while more than one answer choice is factually true, only choice B is implied within the passage.
13. **The best answer is E.** This last sentence serves to compare the losses at Antietam with those of other wars. It illustrates the scope of the casualties in a contemporary time frame.
14. **The best answer is C and D.** Because the first view of koalas is a "misconception," you can expect antonyms in the two blanks. For Blank (ii), "fierce" best fits an animal that should never be approached in the wild. For Blank (i), "affable" fits logically and contrasts nicely with "fierce."
15. **The best answer is C and E.** The two clauses in this sentence provide contrasting views of Susan's paintings, with the second clause providing the positive view offered by her advocates. "Imagination" is the most appropriate choice for blank ii, and therefore, "banal," or bland, is the best direct contrast to fill Blank (i).
16. **The best answer is B.** It makes sense according to the context that environmentalists would be "concerned" by the apparent lack of fresh water. Unlike fresh water, salt water is undrinkable by human beings.
17. **The best answer is E.** Joy is the theme of Helen Keller's exhortation. Happiness will inspire you and urge you to work harder. Therefore, choice E, which states that enthusiasm can accomplish the same things, is the most analogous statement.
18. **The best answer is C.** The tone of the passage is mostly neutral. However, the description of "exciting change" and the positive tone of Johnson's declaration indicate that the author feels positively about the 1965 Immigration Act. These two elements make choice C the best answer.
19. **The best answer is C only.** Robert Browning is described as a successful poet, so he was likely qualified to recognize talent in others, which supports choice C. Browning was also directly responsible for his wife's career as a poet, so choices A and B are contradicted by the passage.
20. **The best answer is:** *Robert Browning, Elizabeth's husband, affectionately called her his "little Portuguese," on account of her dark complexion.* Barrett Browning's book of poetry was called *Sonnets from the Portuguese*. The selected sentence explains that the Portuguese in question was Barrett Browning herself.

Section 4. Quantitative Reasoning

1. **The correct answer is D.** The formula for the area of a circle is πr^2, where r is the radius. Because the area is dependent on the square of the radius, it is not apparent what increasing the radius by 1 will do to the area. The original radius is not specified for either quantity, so the increases in areas cannot be calculated; the relationship cannot be determined from the given information.

2. **The correct answer is A.** To solve this problem, you must determine the value of each quantity. Quantity A is (30% of 50)+40. Because 30% of 50 can be represented as 0.30(50), or 15, the quantity (30% of 50)+40=15+40, or 55. Similarly, (50% of 40)+30=0.50(40)+30, or 20+30, which equals 50. Thus, Quantity A (55) is greater than Quantity B (50).

3. **The correct answer is A.** To compare the quantities, multiply the fractions by the whole numbers in each quantity. The quantity $\frac{1}{13}$ of 19 is $\left(\frac{1}{13}\right)(19)$, or $\frac{19}{13}$, which is greater than 1 because the numerator is larger than the denominator. The quantity $\frac{1}{19}$ of 13 is $\left(\frac{1}{19}\right)(13)$, or $\frac{13}{19}$, which is less than 1 because the denominator is greater than the numerator. Therefore, Quantity A (>1) is greater than Quantity B (<1).

4. **The correct answer is D.** Given that $x+y=4$, there are infinitely many pairs of (x, y) values that make the equation true. For example:
$$2+2=4$$
$$5+(-1)=4$$
$$(-3)+7=4$$
From the three examples above, it is clear that there are instances when $x=y$, $x>y$, and $x<y$. Thus the relationship cannot be determined from the information given.

5. **The correct answer is A.** To solve this system of equations, first multiply the bottom equation by -2 to get $-2x+8y=26$. Next, add the two equations together (note: their x-values will conveniently cancel out).
$$2x+3y=18$$
$$-2x+8y=26$$
$$11y=44$$
Dividing both sides of the equation $11y=44$ yields $y=4$. Using the original equation $x-4y=-13$, substitute 4 for y. Thus $x-4(4)=-13$, or $x-16=-13$. Adding 16 to both sides results in $x=3$. Therefore, Quantity A, $x+y$, equals $3+4$, or 7. Quantity B is 6, which is less than 7.

6. **The correct answer is B.** You could solve this by multiplying each quantity and comparing. However, you could also solve by thinking about the quantities in the following way:

14(256)	15(255)
=14(255+1)	=(14+1)(255)
=14(255)+14(1)	=14(255)+1(255)
=14(255)+14	=14(255)+255

Thus it is apparent that Quantity B is greater than Quantity A.

7. **The correct answer is A.** To solve this problem, you should recognize that 90,000 is equal to $(300)^2$. Because 300 is greater than 298.89, $(300)^2$ will be greater than $(298.89)^2$, so Quantity A is greater than Quantity B.

8. **The correct answer is E.** You are given that the person traveled 5 blocks in 2 minutes, which means that the distance traveled in 16 minutes can be found using a proportion. If x represents the number of blocks traveled in 16 minutes, then $\frac{5}{2} = \frac{x}{16}$. Cross-multiply and solve for x, as shown below:

$$\frac{5}{2} = \frac{x}{16}$$
$$2x = 80$$
$$x = 40$$

9. **The correct answer is C.** You are given the values of $m-p$ and $n+p$. If you note that $(m-p)+(n+p)=m-p+n+p$, which equals $m+n$, then this value must be $4+18$, which is 22.

10. **The correct answer is 53.** The best way to determine the prime factors of a large number is to use a factor tree. Start with 636, and divide by any available prime factor: for instance, two factors of 636 are 2 and 318. Next, 318 is divisible by the prime number 3, leaving 106. Finally, 106 is divisible by 2, which leaves you with 53.

11. **The correct answer is A.** To solve this problem, you need to know how to graph xy-coordinates. Because point k is in the upper left quadrant, it must be negative. Eliminate answer choices C, D, and E. You are given that RS=ST. Because the coordinates of S are $(k, 4)$, RS must equal 4 units. Therefore, ST must equal 4 units, and point S must be 4 units to the left along the x-axis. The x-coordinate, k, must be –4.

12. **The correct answer is C.** An isosceles triangle has two congruent sides, and the angles opposite those sides are also congruent. In any triangle, the total of all three interior angles is 180 degrees. Because you do not know which sides are congruent, neither (A) nor (B) alone is sufficient to answer the question; angle B could be either 80° or 50°. However, if you take both statements together, as in statement (C), you know that angle B must equal 50°, because $180°-80°-50°=50°$.

13. **The correct answer is E.** You are given that the product of the average of a list of course grades and the total number of courses is n. Recall that average, A, is equal to the sum of the course grades, G, divided by the number of courses, C; thus $A = \frac{G}{C}$. Because n is the product of the number of courses, C, and the average of the course grades, A, $n=AC$. Further, because $A = \frac{G}{C}$, multiplying both sides by C yields $G=AC$. Finally because $n=AC$ and $G=AC$, it follows that $n=G$. Thus n is the sum of the course grades.

14. **The correct answer is D.** To solve this problem, simply calculate 24% of 1,650; 1650(0.24)=396. You could also estimate to arrive at an answer: 1,650 is about 1,600 and 24% is approximately 25%. Therefore, 24% of 1,650 is close to 25% of 1,600, which is 400.

15. **The correct answer is B.** Because 6% of the graduating class is currently student teaching and 42% of the graduating class is currently seeking immediate

employment, the ratio of graduates who are student teaching to graduates who are seeking immediate employment is 6:42, which reduces to 1:7.

16. **The correct answer is E.** According to the graph, in 1980, the difference between elementary enrollment and secondary enrollment was approximately 1,000 − 500, or 500 students. In every other year, the difference in enrollment was at least twice that number.

17. **The correct answer is B.** According to the graph, district expenditures in 1990 were $20 million. Therefore, the school district spent about $6 million on books and materials. The graph shows that there were 3,000 students enrolled in 1990, so the district spent $2,000 per student on books and materials.

18. **The correct answer is D.** The median is the middle value in an ordered set of values. Based on the information given, the median of the set of values is 16.

19. **The correct answer is E.** Recall that the volume of a cube is equivalent to side×side×side, or s^3. If the volume is 64, then $s^3=64$, and $s=4$. Because there are 6 faces on a cube, the surface area will equal 6 times one of the surfaces, which are squares with side s; the area of one face is s^2. Therefore, the total surface area of the cube is $6s^2$, or $6(4^2)$, or $6(16)$, which equals 96.

20. **The correct answer is 10.** To quickly answer this question, draw a figure representing Camilla's travel:

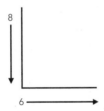

The shortest distance between the houses is a straight line, which corresponds to the hypotenuse:

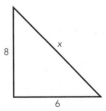

Because this is a 3-4-5 right triangle, the hypotenuse is 10.

Section 5. Quantitative Reasoning

1. **The correct answer is B.** To answer this question, you must recognize that $\left(\sqrt{6}\right)^2 = 6$; Quantity A is 6. Quantity B is $6\sqrt{6}$, which must be greater than 6.

2. **The correct answer is B.** To compare the quantities, first determine Quantity B. To find 75% of the original price, multiply the original price ($25) by 0.75: $(25)(0.75)=18.75$. Thus, Quantity B (18.75) is greater than Quantity A (7.50).

3. **The correct answer is B.** To solve this problem, calculate the length of ST using the Pythagorean theorem. Because RST is a right triangle, $5^2+7^2=ST^2$; $25+49=74$, which is equal to ST^2. Because $9 > \sqrt{74}$, Quantity B is greater than Quantity A.

4. **The correct answer is D.** Given that $x^y=64$, there are a variety of values for x and y. For example, if $x=2$, then $y=5$, such that $2^5=64$. However, if $x=8$, then $y=2$ such that $8^2=64$. Both examples are valid, yet in the first, $x>y$ and in the second, $x<y$. Therefore, a relationship cannot be determined from the information given.

5. **The correct answer is B.** To solve this problem, find the angle measure of a sector of a circle that encompasses 20% of the circle. Because there are $360°$ in a whole circle, a sector that is 20% of the circle would have an angle measure of 20% of $360°$, or $(0.20)(360°)$, which is $72°$. Thus Quantity B ($75°$) is greater than Quantity A ($72°$).

6. **The correct answer is A.** The best way to solve this problem is to pick numbers to substitute for a and b, keeping in mind that a must be greater than b, and b must be greater than 1. If you let $a=3$ and $b=2$, the quantity $\frac{a+1}{a}$ equals $\frac{4}{3}$ while the quantity $\frac{b+1}{b}$ equals $\frac{3}{2}$. In this case Quantity A is greater than Quantity B. Further, if you let $a=10$ and $b=9$, the quantity $\frac{a+1}{a}$ equals $\frac{11}{10}$, or 1.1, while the quantity $\frac{b+1}{b}$ equals $\frac{10}{9}$, or approximately 1.111. Again in this case Quantity A is greater than Quantity B. Even though the difference between the quantities $\frac{a+1}{a}$ and $\frac{b+1}{b}$ gets smaller as a and b get larger, Quantity A is always greater than Quantity B.

7. **The correct answer is A.** To solve this problem, determine how the quantity $x-y$ compares to 0, given that x is a negative integer and y is a positive integer. Because x is a negative integer, subtracting a positive integer from it would yield another negative integer with a greater value; therefore, the quantity $x-y<0$, and Quantity A (0) is greater than Quantity B ($x-y$).

8. **The correct answer is D.** To answer this question, carefully convert the given information into its mathematical equivalent. The larger number is $3a+2$; you are given that the smaller number is a. Therefore, the equation is $2(3a+2)+4a=73$.

9. **The correct answer is B.** When x is positive and y is two greater than the square of x, $y=x^2+2$. To find x in terms of y, solve the equation $y=x^2+2$ for x. First, subtract 2 from both sides to get $x^2=y-2$. Then take the square root of both sides such that $y-2$ is thought of as a single quantity: $x=\sqrt{(y-2)}$.

10. **The correct answer is C.** First recognize that $39 is 30% more than the cost of the sneakers for the store. This can be represented as 130%, or 1.3. Therefore, the store pays $39/1.3, or $30 for a pair of sneakers. A sales associate pays 80% of this price: $30(0.8)=$24.

11. **The correct answer is C.** You are given that Jason traveled 30 miles in 6 hours and that Becky traveled three times as far in half the time; Becky traveled 30×3 or 90 miles in $6 \times \frac{1}{2}$, or 3 hours. Therefore, Becky traveled $\frac{90}{3}$, or 30 miles per hour.

12. **The correct answer is 25.** The formula for the area of a triangle is ½(b)(h). The base of the triangle is 10 (the diameter of the circle) and the height of the triangle is 5 (the radius of the circle). Therefore, the area is ½(10)(5)=25.

13. **The correct answer is C.** You are given that the average of x and y is 16. Therefore, $(x+y) \div 2 = 16$, which means that $x+y=32$. It is not important to know what x and y equal individually, only to know that their sum is 32. Given that the average of x, y, and z is 22, then $(x+y+z) \div 3 = 22$, and $x+y+z=66$. Since $x+y=32$, then $32+z=66$, and $z=34$.

14. **The correct answer is C.** According to the graph, the bar that represents the revenue from government funding in 1990 is slightly below the line representing $45 million. Thus, $44 million is the logical answer choice.

15. **The correct answer is B.** According to the graph, it is apparent that revenue from government funding increased between 1980 and 1990. However, in 1980, revenue from government funding was greater than revenue from tuition, but in 1990 revenue from government funding was less than revenue from tuition. Thus, between 1980 and 1990, the proportion of total revenue that came from government funding *decreased*.

16. **The correct answer is E.** According to the graph, the slope of the line segment between the number of employees in 1970 and the number of employees in 1980 is negative (slopes down). Thus, the number of employees decreased between 1970 and 1980; the statement "From 1970 to 2000, the number of employees increased each decade" is therefore false.

17. **The correct answer is D.** You are given that the rate of increase is 10%. According to the graph, there were approximately 75,000 employees in 2000. Therefore, you should expect 75,000 + 7,500 = 82,500 employees in 2001. You should expect 82,500 + 8,250 = 90,750 employees in 2002.

18. **The correct answer is A and C.** You are given that the probability of drawing a green marble is $\frac{4}{9}$ or 4 out of 9. This means that the total number of marbles in the bag must be a multiple of 9. The question asks for the answer choice that cannot be the number of marbles in the bag. Therefore, the answer choice that is not a multiple of 9 will be the correct answer. Neither 64 nor 110 are multiples of 9.

19. **The correct answer is 1.** You are given that x divided by 7 leaves a remainder of 4. Assume that 7 goes into x one time with a remainder of 4: $x=11$. Because $x=11$, $2x=22$. 7 goes into 22 3 times, with a remainder of 1.

20. **The correct answer is D.** You are given that the length of the floor is 12 feet, and that the length is 3 more than the width. Set the width equal to w, and set up an equation to find the width.

$$3+w=12$$
$$w=9$$

To calculate the area, multiply the length by the width.

$$12\times 9=108$$

The area of the kitchen floor is 108 square feet.

APPENDIXES

APPENDIX **A** **GRE VOCABULARY LIST**
APPENDIX **B** **GLOSSARY OF GRE MATH TERMS**
APPENDIX **C** **ADDITIONAL RESOURCES**

APPENDIX A
GRE Vocabulary List

Although the following is by no means a comprehensive list, it does contain words that have appeared on actual GRE tests, each followed by a sentence or sentences appropriately using the word or a derivation of the word. The words are included here because they have been selected by experienced GRE instructors as representative of the vocabulary level that is expected to appear on the GRE.

A

Abate   to reduce or lessen
After blowing fiercely for hours, the hurricane winds at last began to abate.

Aberration   a deviation or departure from the norm
Harry's low grades in chemistry are an aberration; he is typically an A student.

Abeyance   temporary inactivity or suspension
For some time now, the dissenters have been held in abeyance; they have suspended all protests.

Abjure   to forswear or abstain from; to give up
Once King Edward VIII abdicated the throne to marry a commoner, he abjured all of his former titles.

Abrade   to wear down or rub away the surface of something
Years of exposure to the sea spray had abraded the face of the cliffs.

Abridge   to reduce the length of or diminish in scope (for example, written text)
The author recently published an abridged version of his original 600-page novel.

Abrogate   to end or do away with something
It is unlikely that the senator's push to abrogate any rights regarding free speech will be supported.

Abscond   to withdraw and hide, typically to avoid arrest
The fugitive absconded to Canada in an attempt to avoid arrest in the United States.

Absurd   extremely ridiculous or completely lacking reason
   The idea that Samantha would fail her test was completely absurd; she had studied for hours and was completely prepared.

Abysmal   very profound or deep; very bad
   Despite all of the advertisements promoting the new product, its first-quarter sales were abysmal.

Accretion   a gradual increase in the amount or size of something
   Increased organic matter accumulation has led to an increase in the accretion rate in the Mississippi Delta.

Acquisitive   characterized by a strong desire to gain or retain information or objects
   The acquisitive nature of the chimpanzee makes it appear almost human.

Acrid   harsh or bitter taste or smell
   Sean immediately turned the engine off when he smelled acrid smoke billowing from beneath the hood of his car.

Acute   quick and precise, intense; sharp, keen
   The acute pain in Sarah's wrist kept her from performing even the simplest activity.

   Henry was an acute observer; he quickly learned the rules of the game.

Adhere   to stick fast; to remain in support of
   In order to maintain order in his classroom, Mr. Blume required strict adherence to the code of conduct.

Adjacent   in the nearest position; next to
   Chase took a new job in downtown Chicago, but purchased a house in an adjacent suburb.

Adroit   showing skill and experience
   Steve was considered an adroit negotiator; he was often able to settle disputes when others had failed.

Aesthetic   appealing to the senses because it is beautiful
   The aesthetic quality of the painting was more appealing than its historical significance.

Affinity   natural attraction; inherent similarity
   Michelle's affinity for getting straight to the point made her a popular editor at the publishing house.

Alienate   to isolate oneself from others or another person from oneself
   Gregg often felt alienated from his classmates because of his illness.

Ambiguous unclear or capable of having more than one meaning
The student's ambiguous answer left the professor wondering whether the student had studied the assigned material.

Ambivalent characterized by uncertainty; unable to decide between opposites
His inability to show emotion left her feeling ambivalent about their relationship.

Amenable responsive to suggestion; willing
Josh was amenable to eating dinner early; he was ravenous.

Amiable friendly and pleasant
Joe was very amiable; as a result, he made friends easily at his new school.

Anachronism something existing or happening out of its time in historical order
Her yearning to be nothing more than a housewife seemed an anachronism in today's society.

Annotate to provide with extra notes or comments
In order to ensure the credibility of his students' sources, the professor asked the students to annotate their bibliographies.

Anomaly something that is different from the norm
The botanists were excited when they discovered the unique flower; it was a complete anomaly.

Apathy a lack of any emotion or concern
Mary appeared quite apathetic at her trial; she seemed unconcerned by the jury's guilty verdict.

Ardor intense feelings; passion
Scott's ardor for Julianne increased as he spent more and more time with her.

Articulate *v.* to clearly explain. *adj.* the quality of being able to speak clearly
Young children often find it difficult to articulate exactly what they are thinking.

Ascribe to attribute to a specific source; to assign a characteristic
It is not unusual to ascribe jealousy and pettiness to one's critics.

Asperity roughness or severity
The asperity of the desert climate in Death Valley prevents many people from visiting for extended periods of time.

Assay *n.* an analysis or examination. *v.* to subject to analysis; to examine
The diplomat carefully assayed the situation prior to making a decision.

Assert   to demonstrate power; to defend a statement as true
> It is often necessary for a parent to *assert* his or her authority over an unruly child.

Assiduous   characteristic of careful and persistent effort
> The journey to earning good grades is an *assiduous* one; consistent effort must be put forth.

Assimilate   to incorporate into; to make similar
> Many immigrants desire to *assimilate* quickly into their new community.

Assuage   to lessen or ease
> Mandy often used food to *assuage* her loneliness, a habit that led to her problem with obesity.

Assumption   something believed to be true without proof; unstated evidence
> Because Jennifer wore glasses every day, we *assumed* that she had poor eyesight.

Aver   to declare as true; to maintain
> The politician continued to *aver* that he was more experienced than his opponent, despite evidence to the contrary.

Aversion   strong dislike
> Kelly has such an *aversion* to strenuous exercise that she never goes to the gym.

B

Banish   to force to leave
> The deposed dictator was *banished* from his native country.

Benevolence   an inclination to be kind or charitable
> Mr. Horn's *benevolence* made him a beloved school principal; his generosity and understanding far exceeded that of his predecessor.

Benign   kind, mild, harmless
> Katherine was relieved to discover that her tumor was *benign*; she would not require surgery after all.

Bequest   the act of passing on; something that is passed on
> This collection of rare manuscripts was donated to the library as a *bequest* from Professor Austin.

Bereft   deprived or despondent
> Jill was *bereft* when she discovered that the coveted role had been offered to another actress.

Blithe   carefree or joyous; casual
> Ellen's *blithe* and outgoing attitude made her one of the most popular students on campus.

Bolster *n.* a narrow cushion. *v.* to support or strengthen
> The small business owner secured a low-interest loan to bolster his financial situation during a period of expansion.

Brazen bold or shameless; insolent
> His often brazen behavior at work led to his being reprimanded on a regular basis.

Burgeoning thriving or growing rapidly
> Although it was completely undeveloped a year ago, the vacant land is now home to a burgeoning commercial area, complete with a new shopping mall.

C

Cadge to beg
> The destitute man was relegated to cadging meals from local restaurants.

Capricious impulsive; prone to sudden change
> Jill's sudden move to Hollywood was considered capricious by the rest of her family.

Castigate to punish or criticize severely
> Jason was castigated by his teacher for turning in his assignment late.

Catalyst something that causes something else to happen, usually without being directly involved in or changed by the process; a trigger for an event
> Our classmate's recent job offer served as a catalyst for the rest of us to update and submit our resumes.

Censure *n.* a formal criticism or intense disproval. *v.* to express a formal criticism
> The prosecuting attorney was censured for a conflict of interest arising from his personal relationship with the plaintiff.

Chronicle *n.* a detailed narrative. *v.* to document or record
> Several biographers have chronicled the life of Albert Einstein, one of the world's greatest physicists.

Circumspect mindful of potential consequences; prudent
> A wise investor is circumspect about fluctuations in the market.

Cite to quote as an example or proof
> The company cited a 10 percent increase in sales as evidence that their new advertising campaign was achieving the predicted results.

Coalesce to unite or come together
> The different factions coalesced to form a strong group opposed to the current regime.

Coerce to force or threaten someone into acting a certain way; to compel
The jury did not hear the man's taped confession during the trial because police had coerced him into admitting that he had committed the crime.

Cogent convincing and reasonable
The teenager's cogent argument for a later curfew persuaded his parents to push it back to midnight.

Cognitive relating to conscious intellectual activity such as thinking, reasoning, and learning
Entering college at the age of 14, the teen had cognitive abilities far beyond most of her peers.

Coherence the quality of being logical and clear
The essay lacked coherence; it did not flow logically from one concept to the next.

Coincidental occurring by chance
The coincidental meeting of two old friends was a pleasant surprise for them both.

Commensurate corresponding in size, degree, or duration
He refused the job offer; the salary did not seem commensurate with his related skills and experience.

Complaisant showing a willingness to please; obliging
Eager to earn a large tip, our waiter was unusually complaisant.

Comprise to consist of; to include
Students enrolled in the music program comprised the university marching band.

Concede to admit or reluctantly yield; to surrender
The presidential candidate decided to concede defeat based on the latest poll results; he was too far behind to win.

Conducive contributive; favorable
The noisy restaurant was not conducive to holding intimate conversations.

Consternation alarm or fear
To her consternation, she found that she'd forgotten to bring her assignment to class.

Converge to meet or come together at a common point
Ambulances, police cars, and fire trucks quickly converged on the scene of the accident.

Convivial festive and sociable
There was always a convivial atmosphere at the annual holiday party.

Cordial friendly; gracious
The doorman at the luxury hotel cordially greeted all arriving guests.

Correlate to have corresponding characteristics
According to researchers, the length of time a student studies is roughly correlated to the grades that the student receives.

Corroborate to confirm, to substantiate with evidence
Further laboratory tests corroborated the scientist's theory that taking vitamins could help to maintain a person's good health.

Countenance n. facial features or expression.
The teacher had a stern countenance that intimidated many of her students.

Credulous easily deceived; believing too readily
Even the most credulous person would not believe the story that Mike had concocted.

Cryptic mystifying; hidden or concealed meaning
The cryptic hieroglyphics on the Rosetta Stone were finally deciphered using the Greek writings also found on the stone.

Culmination completion or climax
Finishing the marathon in less than four hours was the culmination of months and months of training for Elaine.

Culpable deserving of blame; guilty
Despite his claims to the contrary, the senator is likely culpable of misappropriating funds.

D

Debilitate to weaken or impair
Bob's broken leg left him debilitated and unable to attend school.

Decimate to destroy large numbers of; to inflict great damage upon
The rain forest is being decimated at an alarmingly fast pace; it is estimated that it could be completely gone within 40 years.

Decry to denounce or criticize
A loyal fan of classical music, Megan decried all popular rap and hip-hop artists.

Defamation a malicious or abusive attack on one's character
The celebrity sued the tabloid for defamation of character when the magazine published a story filled with lies.

Delve to deeply search through
　Many philosophers and scientists delve into the secrets of the universe.

Demise the end of existence; death
　The demise of the dinosaurs is a topic of much debate among paleontologists.

Denigrate to speak ill of; to belittle
　You should not denigrate a person whose opinion differs from yours.

Depict to represent or describe
　Many people disapprove of how Native Americans are depicted in old Westerns.

Deplore to condemn; disapprove of or regret
　Environmental advocacy groups deplore deforestation and industrial pollution.

Derision use of ridicule to show contempt
　Joe's harsh derision of his pesky younger brother set everyone on edge at the dinner table.

Derivative *adj.* copied or adapted. *n.* something derived
　There are zero-calorie sweeteners available that are derivatives of real sugar.

Desultory inconsistent and irregular, aimless
　The project leader's rather desultory speech left the team members uncertain of how to proceed.

Dexterity skill and ease of movement, especially of the hands; cleverness
　It took great dexterity, but the politician managed to evade answering every difficult question that the reporters threw at him.

Diatribe an abusive, insulting verbal attack
　The environmental activist launched into a lengthy diatribe against the developers who wanted to build a new mall in place of the city park.

Didactic intended for the purposes of moral teaching or instructing, even when such instruction is not necessary or welcome
　Professor McFarland's didactic presentations in the classroom tended to bore some students and outrage others.

Dilate to make larger; expand
　Jesse's pupils began to dilate as the sun set and the room darkened.

Diligent continuously putting in great effort
　Ben diligently trained for the marathon, running at least 40 miles per week.

Disabuse to free someone of believing something that is untrue
I hope that this most recent scandal will finally disabuse the public of its notion that the senator is infallible.

Discern to differentiate or distinguish; to perceive
The moon's distance from Earth makes it difficult to discern most of the features on the surface of the moon with the naked eye.

Disconcerting unsettling
Linda had the disconcerting habit of staring at the ground whenever she spoke.

Dislodge to remove from a former position
The small earthquake dislodged several tons of rock from the mountain.

Disparity the state of being different or unequal
There was much disparity between my perception of the judicial process and the actual manner in which the process worked.

Disperse to scatter or spread out
The crowd began to disperse as the concert came to an end.

Dissemble to disguise or conceal
The platoon's efforts to dissemble their preparations resulted in a swift ambush of the enemy the following day.

Dissident *adj.* disagreeable. *n.* one who disagrees
It took hours of careful diplomacy for the staunch political dissidents to reach an accord.

Dissipate to drive away; scatter
The wind helped to dissipate the smoke from our campfire.

Dissonance lack of harmony; discord
Band leaders know immediately by the piercing dissonance that a wrong note has been played.

Diverge to move apart, or extend in different directions; to differ in opinion
Though they agreed on most things, their opinions diverged on the topic of abortion rights.

Divest to get rid of
Howard was extremely lucky; he divested himself of $10 million worth of electronics stock days before its value plummeted.

Docile easy to train or teach
The normally docile students became very rowdy as the day's pep rally drew near.

Dubious unsure, skeptical
Mike was very dubious when his older brother, infamous for playing pranks, told Mike that he had a surprise for him.

E

Eccentric *adj.* departing from convention. *n.* one who deviates from the norm
Mary's style, considered to be very eccentric when she was young, led her to become one of the most popular fashion designers of all time.

Eclectic combining elements from many different sources or styles
Jenny's eclectic taste in movies ranged from musicals to comedies, dramas to action films.

Effrontery rude and presumptuous behavior
The general was unaware that his imperialist effrontery was only breeding contempt among the colonists.

Egregious noticeably bad or offensive
William committed an egregious error when he failed to mention his wife during his acceptance speech.

Eloquent very clear and precise; quality of being skilled in clear and precise speech
Julie's valedictorian speech was quite eloquent; she clearly articulated her hopes and dreams for a prosperous future.

Elucidate to clarify
Recent efforts to elucidate the text on certain ancient scrolls have yielded curious new perspectives on the political history of Babylon.

Emancipation the act of freeing or liberating
Minor children may petition a court for emancipation from their parents if they provide evidence of alternate housing and income.

Emollient *adj.* softening or soothing. *n.* a softening agent
Sarah rubbed an emollient over her dry, peeling, sunburned skin.

Empirical based on or provable by observation and experiment
The hypothesis had to be backed up by empirical evidence in order to be considered credible.

Emulate to follow an admirable example; imitate
As she entered law school, she hoped to emulate the success of her sister, who was already a prominent partner in a law firm.

Endorse to support or sign
The sports superstar was paid more than $10 million to endorse the new athletic shoe.

Engender to give rise to; originate
Professor Evan's good nature engendered a positive attitude among his students.

Enigmatic unexplainable, puzzling
  The Mona Lisa's enigmatic smile is legendary.

Entity a discrete unit or being
  Though the corporations worked in conjunction with each other, they remained separate legal entities.

Enumerate to state things in a list
  At his performance review, the employee listened to his boss enumerate several ways he could improve his performance in the workplace.

Ephemeral temporary, fleeting
  Considered a "one-hit wonder," the pop star enjoyed only ephemeral fame.

Equivocal uncertain or ambiguous
  Many lengthy court battles could be avoided if the legislature took more care to avoid equivocal language in the criminal statutes.

Erudite learned; having great knowledge
  After earning three doctoral degrees, Dr. Kidman was considered one of the most erudite professors on campus.

Esoteric understood by few people; mysterious
  Most of the subject matter in the novel is quite esoteric; the author is forced to overwhelm the reader with too much background information.

Espouse to choose to follow or support something
  Abraham Lincoln was famous for his refusal to espouse slavery in the North.

Estimable admirable; deserving of esteem
  His first attempt at writing a novel was estimable; nearly 1 million copies of the book were sold.

Ethical in line with the principles of right and wrong
  Only the most ethical people would return money from a wallet they find in the street.

Euphemism an inoffensive expression substituted for one that is deemed offensive
  The word borrowing is sometimes used as a euphemism for stealing.

Exacerbate to intensify bitterness or violence
  The terrorist attacks exacerbated the already strained relations between the two countries.

Exceptional having uncommonly great qualities
  Kevin was an exceptional basketball player, and received many offers to play at the collegiate level.

Excoriate   to denounce; to chafe
> *The film critics excoriated the film that was supposed to be that year's biggest blockbuster, emphasizing how overrated it was.*

Exculpate   to remove blame; acquit
> *The defendant was exculpated of the homicide charges when new evidence was found at the crime scene.*

Exhort   to urge or try to persuade
> *After graduating from college, Diana exhorted her parents to lend her the money to start her own business.*

Exigent   demanding immediate attention; urgent
> *In the exigent circumstances of the coup d'état, thousands of troops were dispatched to the capital city.*

Explicate   to explain or make comprehensible
> *The graduate student was unable to successfully explicate his thesis; therefore, he did not earn his degree.*

Expunge   to get rid of or erase
> *The speeding infraction would be expunged from John's driving record after he paid a $600 fine and kept a clean record for one year.*

Extant   currently existing
> *There are few extant copies of the Gutenberg Bible, four of which are in New York City.*

Extenuating   partially justifiable
> *Extenuating circumstances surrounding the motive for the assault meant Sean would serve less jail time.*

Extol   to praise or glorify
> *Ever the proud mother, Anna extols her child's accomplishments to no end.*

Extrovert   a person characterized by concern with things outside of himself or herself; an outgoing or gregarious person
> *In order to be successful as a salesperson, you must be somewhat of an extrovert.*

Extricate   to free or disentangle
> *It took rescue crews several hours to safely extricate all of the passengers from the plane that had crashed earlier in the day.*

Exultant   gleeful because of success
> *The exultant crowd cheered the soccer team on to victory in the World Cup.*

F

Fallacy   an error in reasoning
   It is a common fallacy that first-year law students spend every waking moment studying.

Familial   relating to the family
   Her familial ties kept her from moving too far away from the town in which she grew up.

Fathom   v. to come to understand the meaning of something. n. a measure of distance equal to six feet
   The complexity of the situation made it difficult to fathom a simple outcome.

Fatuous   foolish or delusive; smug
   We ignored Brendan's fatuous remarks about politics; he spoke strictly from opinion with no regard for the facts.

Feckless   lacking in purpose; careless
   Because more than half of the legislators are not running for reelection this fall, pundits predict another feckless session of the State House.

Feign   to fabricate or deceive
   She feigned astonishment when she walked into her surprise party; her best friend had previously told her about the event.

Feint   n. a deceptive, diversionary action. v. to make a deceptive show of
   The robbers used some smoke bombs in the parking lot as a feint while they discreetly took money from the cash drawers.

Fidelity   faithfulness or allegiance; often used to denote faithfulness in a romantic relationship, or faithfulness to a particular religion
   I admire dogs for their unshakeable fidelity to their owners.

Florid   flushed with color; ornate
   The stark realism of neoclassicism in painting replaced the florid idealism of the Rococo period.

Foil   to keep from being successful
   Her plans were often foiled by her failure to plan ahead.

Foment   to incite or agitate
   Ryan tried to hold his tongue; he knew that one of his sarcastic remarks would foment a fight that he didn't want to start.

Forage   to search for food or provisions
   During the cold winter months, many wild animals are forced to forage for scarce food.

Formidable capable of arousing fear or awe
The current championship team was a formidable opponent for the yet unranked team.

Fortuitous happening by accident or chance
The defenseman scored easily with a quick shot after the puck's fortuitous bounce toward him.

Forum a public meeting place; a medium for open discussion
The mayor held an open forum for discussion to learn what the people thought of his new proposal.

Fracas a noisy fight; a brawl
James was arrested for disorderly conduct after getting into a fracas outside the restaurant this weekend.

G

Gainsay to deny or contradict
There can be no resolution if all you do is gainsay each of my suggestions.

Garrison a military post; the troops stationed at a military post
The garrison was currently home to nearly 400 troops.

Garrulous very talkative
The normally garrulous teenager was very subdued at the party; she barely spoke to anyone.

Genre a type, class, or category
His favorite genre of music was classic rock, but he also enjoyed jazz quite a bit.

Gist main idea
I'm in a hurry, so please tell me the gist of the story.

Glib seemingly slick and clever, but lacking sincerity
The president's glib speech about the financial state of the company resulted in a general sense of unease among the members of the staff.

Gratuitous for no reason or at no cost
Her gratuitous acts of kindness earned her fondness and respect within the community.

Gregarious sociable; enjoying the company of others
It's a wonder Lynn can get a word in edgewise when speaking with her extremely gregarious sister.

Grievous causing grief or pain; serious
The spokesperson knew he had made a grievous error when he prematurely announced that all of the victims had survived the accident.

Guile cunning; shrewdness
> *I employed all of my guile to convince my housemates that I truly deserved the largest bedroom in the house along with the house's single parking spot.*

H

Hackneyed unoriginal, overused
> *The hackneyed plot of the television show led to its cancellation after only three episodes.*

Harrow to torment or cause suffering and agony
> *The prospect of a beach landing in broad daylight harrowed the troops for days before the battle.*

Hierarchy a way to rank or place things in order
> *The business's hierarchy allowed room for all employees to advance within the company if they worked hard enough.*

Heterogeneous made up of dissimilar elements; not homogeneous
> *Switzerland has a heterogeneous culture, in which German, French, and Italian influences are intermixed.*

Hypothesis a tentative explanation that can be tested by further investigation and experimentation
> *The graduate students working on the project presented a viable hypothesis regarding the outcome of their experiments.*

I

Idiosyncrasy a peculiar characteristic
> *One of the most annoying idiosyncrasies of the computer is that it must be completely restarted every two hours.*

Immutable not subject to change
> *People should know that their freedom is not immutable and must be protected whenever necessary.*

Impending threatening to occur
> *We changed our tee time to later that afternoon because of the impending rain.*

Imperturbable hard to excite or upset, very calm
> *Kevin's imperturbable demeanor during the storm helped keep his wife and children calm.*

Impetus a stimulus encouraging a particular activity
> *The upcoming race provided the impetus she needed to expand her training regimen.*

Implosion   a violent, inward collapse
   A careful implosion of the old stadium would prevent damage to adjacent structures and onlookers.

Inadvertent   unintentional, often related to carelessness
   His inadvertent pull of the lever started a chain reaction of leaks throughout the building's plumbing.

Inchoate   poorly formed or formless
   His inchoate political opinions were based largely on ignorance.

Incinerate   to set fire to and burn until reduced to ashes
   The leaves were incinerated quickly in the raging campfire.

Incongruous   inconsistent; lacking in harmony
   Carrie's colorful joke was incongruous with the deep conversation going on around her.

Incorrigible   impossible to change or reform
   The child was incorrigible; he refused to listen when his parents repeatedly told him to stop teasing the dog.

Indigenous   native; innate
   The Maori are the indigenous people of New Zealand.

Inevitable   impossible to avoid; predictable
   After spending the weekend doing everything but studying, it was inevitable that she would fail her exam.

Infer   to conclude from evidence
   Mr. Mauro was able to infer from his employee's attitude that she was not satisfied with her job.

Ingenuity   cleverness or imagination
   The world relies on the ingenuity of people such as Bell and Edison to conceive of tomorrow's technology.

Inherent   naturally occurring, permanent element or attribute
   The risks inherent in driving a car are surprisingly greater than those associated with riding in an airplane.

Inimical   harmful or unfriendly
   Doctors agree smoking is inimical to good health and longevity.

Innate   possessed at birth; a natural characteristic
   Linguists still don't know why humans have an innate capacity for language while other animals do not.

Inscrutable   difficult to understand; having an obscure nature
   Science still has little explanation for the inscrutable origins of matter and energy in the universe.

Insinuate   to subtly imply or insert
Andrew attempted to insinuate himself into the conversation by replying to a question that was not directed at him.

Insipid   dull; lacking in flavor or zest
Waiting in line for the movie, I was forced to listen to an insipid conversation between two young girls who could not decide which actor they found most attractive.

Insular   isolated; narrow-minded
The villagers displayed the typical insularity of small communities.

Integral   essential or necessary
The quarterback was an integral part of the football team's seven-game winning streak.

Intercede   to mediate, or plead on another's behalf
When Kelly learned that she had become the prime suspect in a police investigation, she called upon her lawyer to intercede.

Interpolate   to insert or introduce between, often to falsify
No one can be sure what fanciful stories were interpolated into the old chronicle by medieval scribes.

Intractable   difficult to manage; stubborn
Paul's intractable temper landed him in jail after a brief altercation with a police officer.

Inundate   to quickly overwhelm or exceed capacity
The government was inundated with requests for help after the hurricane destroyed or damaged over 10,000 homes and businesses.

Inure   to cause to accept something that is undesirable; habituate
Every winter it snows heavily in this area, but by now I am inured to the harsh climate.

Invariable   not subject to question or change; constant
Judge Owens is famous for his invariable demeanor, which is lauded by prosecution and defense counsel alike.

Irascible   easily angered
Grizzly bears are irascible beasts, which one would do well to avoid.

J

Jovial   full of joy and happiness
Noelle was in a jovial mood for weeks after getting engaged to her high school sweetheart.

Judicious   sensible, having good judgment
> Kate's decision not to take the job was quite judicious because she had no previous marketing experience.

Juxtapose   to place things next to each other in order to compare or contrast
> The artist juxtaposed some of his early sketches with some of his later works to show how much his style had changed over time.

K

Keen   quick-witted, sharp
> His keen sense of smell allowed him to figure out what was for dinner long before he reached the kitchen.

Kudos   praise for achievements
> The volunteers all received kudos for their work at the homeless shelter.

L

Lambaste   to scold or criticize sharply; to beat
> The critics lambasted the author's newest novel, saying he had become lazy in the wake of his last book's success.

Languish   to exist in a dreadful or gloomy situation; to become weak
> The convict had been languishing in prison for nearly 20 years.

Latter   the second of two things mentioned; nearer the end
> My parents offered either to buy me a new computer or to pay for a trip to Europe for my graduation, and I chose the latter, having never been abroad.

Laudable   deserving praise; favorable
> Jenny's efforts to raise money for breast cancer research were laudable.

Lavish   *adj.* elaborate and luxurious. *v.* to freely and boundlessly bestow
> He showered her with lavish gifts of jewelry and clothes in an attempt to win her over.

Lenient   easy-going, tolerant
> Sarah's parents were not lenient at all when it came to grades; she was expected to earn straight A's.

Lethargic   deficient in alertness; lacking energy
> Linda was lethargic all day; she had not slept at all the night before.

Listless   characterized by a lack of energy
> During his long illness, Michael became very listless and spent most of his time in bed.

Loathsome   offensive, disgusting
> His *loathsome* behavior ultimately resulted in his being fired; his employers had received numerous complaints from his coworkers.

Loquacious   very talkative or rambling
> My plans for a quiet dinner were disrupted by a *loquacious* patron seated at the next table.

Lucid   easily understood; clear
> The speaker presented a series of *lucid* arguments in favor of the antismoking law.

Ludicrous   laughable or foolish
> Mark's *ludicrous* budget estimations resulted in large financial losses for his company.

M

Magnanimous   courageous, generous, or noble
> Coach Davis was *magnanimous* in defeat and congratulated the winning team on a game well played.

Malevolent   purposefully wishing harm on others
> The villain in the movie was a *malevolent* old man who would stop at nothing to gain power over the citizens in his community.

Manifest   *adj.* clearly recognizable. *v.* to make clear. *n.* a list of transported goods or passengers used for record keeping
> The airline workers' dissatisfaction with their wages *manifested* itself as a two-week-long strike.

Mar   to inflict damage or blemishes on
> The surface of the antique table was *marred* during the move from the storage facility.

Melancholy   *adj.* glum. *n.* deep contemplative thought
> Reid attributed his *melancholy* mood to the weather; it had been raining for nearly a week.

Melodramatic   overly emotional or sentimental
> "I'm never talking to you AGAIN!" she exclaimed *melodramatically* to her sister.

Mercurial   prone to sudden unpredictable change; volatile
> Michael had a very *mercurial* temperament; he could go from cheerful to irate in a matter of moments.

Metamorphosis   a transformation or change
> The new CEO vowed that the struggling business would undergo a complete *metamorphosis*, and that it would soon be thriving and successful.

Meticulous   devoting a high amount of attention to detail
Janine was meticulous about her appearance, refusing to be seen in public without makeup.

Mettle   courage
The troops showed their mettle in the face of armed combat.

Minuscule   extremely small; unimportant
The acceptable error for this test is minuscule, so the research team takes the utmost care in executing it.

Miscreant   villain; evildoer
In typical fairy tale style, the heroine of the story overcomes the local miscreant, teaching him a lesson and earning the esteem of the townspeople.

Mitigate   causing something to be less intense, forceful, or harmful
The County Road Commission authorized the use of extra snowplows to help mitigate the hazardous road conditions.

Mollify   to calm down or alleviate; to soften
The experienced referees attempted to mollify the angry players before a fight broke out.

Munificence   the act of liberally giving
The soup kitchen was able to feed more than one thousand homeless people every day, thanks to the munificence of the community.

N

Nascent   just beginning to exist
Brett's nascent career in politics ended before it began when the public learned that he had been arrested for the purchase of narcotics.

Negligent   characterized by carelessness and neglectfulness
His often negligent behavior led to his being replaced by a more diligent manager.

Negligible   meaningless and insignificant
The difference between the two brands of baby food was negligible; both offered the same nutritional value.

Nostalgia   a bittersweet longing for the past
Every time I hear that song, I feel a wave of nostalgia for my college days.

Noxious   unwholesome or harmful
Environmentalists protested the construction of a new factory that would emit large quantities of noxious gases into the atmosphere each day.

O

Obdurate firm, stubborn
The governor was obdurate in her beliefs that schools needed additional funding for their art and music programs.

Obscurity the condition of being unknown
The 1962 hit single propelled him from relative obscurity in the Canadian north to fame and fortune in Los Angeles.

Obsolete no longer in use; outmoded or old-fashioned
Telegrams became obsolete with the development of the Internet.

Obtuse lacking intellectual clarity; blunt, or slow-witted
My law professor insinuates that his students are incredibly obtuse if they don't know the answer to one of his questions.

Obviate to render unnecessary
The brand-new underpass obviates the railroad crossing gates at the intersection.

Odious arousing or deserving strong hatred
The odious crimes committed by the gang members put them at the top of the city's most-wanted list.

Onerous very troublesome or oppressively difficult
The police had the onerous task of somehow convincing the assailant to set his hostages free.

Ostracize to eliminate from a group
Coworkers have ostracized the young welder since he first spoke out against the union.

P

Paradox a self-contradiction; something that appears to be self-contradictory, but is nonetheless true
It was a strange paradox that adding more capacity to the network actually reduced its overall performance.

Paragon an example of excellence
Mother Theresa was a paragon of piety and generosity.

Parse to break down into components
Mrs. Antoinette assigned our French class 100 sentences to parse into subject, verb, and tense.

Pedantic characterized by a narrow concern for detail, particularly in academics
My history teacher's hopelessly pedantic lectures left the class in a state of utter boredom.

Penchant   a tendency or fondness
   Her penchant for designer clothes was something that her meager salary could simply not support.

Perceive   to become aware of something, usually through the senses
   Perceiving the sadness in his voice, I asked him if anything was wrong.

Percolate   to slowly pass through
   Mountain spring water is generally safe to drink because it has spent decades slowly percolating through porous layers of rock.

Peripatetic   adj. moving or traveling from place to place. n. one who travels frequently from place to place
   My grandmother loves to hear stories from the peripatetic salespeople who occasionally come to her door.

Periphery   the outermost boundary of an area
   Paul jogged daily along the periphery of the lake, enjoying the view of the water as he worked out.

Perjury   knowingly lying under oath
   Witnesses whose intent is to deceive the court with their testimony may later be found guilty of perjury.

Perpetuate   to prolong the existence or idea of; to make everlasting
   That a high grade point average leads to a high standardized test score is a myth perpetuated among some educators.

Pertinent   relevant or appropriate
   Our professor warned us to read chapter eight very carefully; the information was pertinent to what would be found on our exam.

Peruse   to examine or review something
   Each day Liz perused the want ads in the newspaper, desperately trying to find a job.

Pervasive   capable of spreading or flowing throughout
   Because we lived on a farm, it was impossible to avoid the pervasive smell of cow manure at certain times during the year.

Phenomenon   observable fact or event; an unusual, significant, or outstanding occurrence. Plural is *phenomena*.
   Many cosmological phenomena have yet to be fully explained.

Pith   significance, importance
   Politicians seem to have a knack for obscuring the pith of an issue.

Placate   to calm
   The waitress tried to placate her angry patron by offering him a free meal.

Placid   calm or quiet
The placid lakeside resort in the mountains of Colorado was my favorite place to get away from it all.

Plagiarize   to copy another's work and pretend that it is original
The journalist was sued for plagiarizing an article from another writer and selling it to a national magazine.

Plausible   reasonable, likely
Her reasons seemed highly plausible; nonetheless, her friends found it hard to accept her unusual tardiness.

Plethora   excess or overabundance
The library has a plethora of books on the Civil War.

Poignant   profoundly moving; incisive
The audience sat stunned, moved to silence by the speaker's poignant remarks.

Polarity   the possession of two opposing attributes or ideas
The novel was based on the ironic polarity of the identical twins.

Postulate   to put forth or assert
Karl Marx postulated that Communism was the only successful way to organize the economy; he was wrong.

Pragmatic   practical
She was pragmatic in her approach to applying for the job; she thoroughly researched the company prior to her interview.

Precarious   in a dangerous state, lacking security or stability
Many start-up companies find themselves in a very precarious position when seeking additional funding.

Precedent   an example or event that is used to justify similar occurrences at a later time; custom arising from long-term practice
The student broke her family's long-running precedent and attended the University of Colorado instead of Colorado State.

Precept   a guiding rule or principle
The fraternity's founding precepts were love and equality among all of its brothers.

Precipitate   to cause something to happen very suddenly or prematurely
The bombings precipitated a massive wave of antiterrorism among the people of the target country.

Preclude   to prevent or make impossible
John's embezzlement conviction precluded him from getting another high-powered accounting job.

Precursor   one that precedes or suggests the approach of another
   The peasant uprisings of earlier decades are now considered to be precursors of the French Revolution.

Presage   an omen or other warning sign
   Some sailors believe that a red sky in the morning is a presage of storms coming that day.

Prescience   foresight; the power to see the future
   The captain's prescience for trouble at sea prompted him to replace the old life jackets he had on board.

Presume   to take something for granted as being fact
   Many college graduates with high grade point averages presume that finding employment will be easy.

Prevaricate   to lie
   It was obvious that Emily was prevaricating when her story changed slightly every time she told it.

Probity   integrity and uprightness
   It is important that those working at the clothing store display probity, for it would be far too easy for greedy employees to take whatever they wanted from inventory.

Prodigal   wasteful; extravagant
   Gone are the days of prodigal expenditures on social services by the government.

Profuse   plentiful or abundant
   After her foolish mistake, Maria offered profuse apologies.

Progeny   offspring or product
   My great-grandfather is proud of his extensive progeny.

Prognosis   forecast or prediction
   The economic prognosis was bleak; it looked like the recession had only just begun.

Proliferate   to grow or increase rapidly
   Computers, like any other technology, proliferate rapidly as production costs decrease and materials availability increases.

Promulgate   to proclaim; usually in reference to rules or laws
   At the Board meeting, the town trustees promulgated some new zoning regulations.

Propagate   to cause to multiply or spread
   The newly introduced plant species began to propagate quickly in the humid environment.

Prototype   an original form of something
The prototypes of countless sports cars will be debuted at the auto show next week.

Protract   to lengthen or prolong
Our train trip was annoyingly protracted by a series of unexplained delays.

Prowess   great skill or ability in something
Chandler's athletic prowess was overshadowed by that of his legendary older brother, who was named MVP all four years of his high school football career.

Prudish   exaggeratedly proper; righteous
My prudish mother wouldn't allow me to wear miniskirts, no matter how hot it got in the summer.

Q

Quaff   to drink heartily
After a long day at work, Chad quaffed multiple beers while waiting for his dinner.

Querulous   characterized by constant complaining or whining
The losing candidate's querulous remarks regarding his opponent were not included in the newspaper article.

Quixotic   unpredictable and impractical
The quixotic nature of the weather in April requires that you carry an umbrella with you wherever you go.

Quotidian   ordinary, occurring daily
Cell phone use has become a quotidian part of our existence; it's hard to imagine that only 20 years ago cell phones were used primarily in emergencies.

R

Rancor   bitter resentment
The prisoner's rancor was increasingly evident in his malicious glance at the warden.

Recalcitrant   stubbornly resistant; defiant
Joanna seemed to morph overnight from a polite child to a recalcitrant teen.

Recluse   someone who is withdrawn from society
Although the movie star has been in countless blockbusters, she lives as a recluse and refuses to give interviews or appear at publicity events.

Recompense   *n.* payment in return for something. *v.* to award compensation to
> You are certainly entitled to some <u>recompense</u> after all of your hours of hard work.

Reconciliation   the reestablishing of cordial relations
> It took hours of negotiations to bring about <u>reconciliation</u> between the two parties.

Recondite   difficult to understand
> Many students feel it is more helpful to read the textbook than attend the professor's <u>recondite</u> lectures.

Refute   to prove to be false; to deny the truth of
> The testimony provided by the prosecution's star witness <u>refuted</u> the statements previously made by the defendant.

Relegate   to refer or assign to a particular place or category
> The journalist was <u>relegated</u> from investigative reporting to writing obituaries after submitting too many substandard articles.

Renounce   break; reject
> Because of the scandal, the senator <u>renounced</u> all ties to the disgraced lobbyist.

Reparation   compensation given to make amends
> Some countries were unable to pay the <u>reparations</u> demanded after the war.

Reproach   to express disapproval
> Zach's wife <u>reproached</u> him for spending all of his time watching sports on TV.

Repudiate   to reject or refuse as valid
> Ellen <u>repudiated</u> the accusation that she had cheated in order to pass her exam last week.

Resolute   definite, determined
> Kelly is <u>resolute</u> in her decision to run a marathon this year, despite her current inability to run more than one mile without a break.

Resonant   strong and deep; lasting
> The <u>resonant</u> voices of the choir rang out through the concert hall.

Resplendent   dazzling or brilliant in appearance
> The bride looked absolutely <u>resplendent</u> walking down the aisle in her white gown.

Resurrect   to bring back to life
> Each summer, Renaissance festivals try to <u>resurrect</u> the spirit of the Middle Ages across the country.

Rhetoric effective use of language; a style of speaking or writing
The politician used his rhetoric to be voted into office, but whether he will actually use his power constructively remains to be seen.

Rigor strictness or severity
The nature of the study demanded extreme rigor in setting up the experiments.

S

Sage one revered for experience and wisdom
It is not wise to disobey the teachings of the tribal sages.

Sanctimonious feigning piety or righteousness
After a few years, the sanctimonious preacher was finally exposed and run out of town.

Sanction n. authoritative permission. v. to give official approval to
Our research proposal received official sanction from the university last week.

Satirize to insult using witty language
Television shows such as Saturday Night Live satirize many people and current events.

Sedulous persevering, industrious
In spite of the declining poll numbers, the senator's campaign manager remained sedulous to the end.

Skepticism an attitude of doubt or disbelief
Miranda's claims to be a psychic were met with skepticism by her friends and family.

Solace comfort, safety
Paul sought solace from the cold near the roaring fireplace in his living room.

Solicitous concerned; thoughtful
For a week after my surgery, my solicitous neighbors brought me meals so I wouldn't have to cook.

Specious appearing to be true or genuine but actually deceptive
Despite sounding credible, all of Jordan's arguments were specious.

Speculate to theorize on the basis of inconclusive evidence
The tabloids have been speculating for months that the celebrity couple is getting a divorce.

Spontaneous arising without apparent external cause; unrestrained
Charlotte's spontaneous laughter caused an uncomfortable pause in the conversation; nothing that had been said was meant to be funny.

Squelch to crush or silence
> The dictator *squelched* any sign of rebellion by making it public that those who spoke out against him would be jailed indefinitely.

Stanch to stop or check the flow of
> Carrie pressed a towel firmly onto the wound to *stanch* the flow of blood.

Static fixed or stationary
> The typically *static* price of corn rose dramatically when a major drought hit the Midwest and millions of acres of crops were lost.

Stint a length of time spent in a particular way
> Samantha's two-year *stint* as a court reporter was one of the most fascinating jobs she ever held.

Stoic indifferent or unaffected
> Kevin's *stoic* expression gave no clue about what he was thinking.

Subjective depending or based on someone's personal attitudes or opinions
> I think that my best friend is the greatest actress in the world, but my opinion of her is rather *subjective*.

Substantiate to validate or support
> I had to provide a list of all sources used in my research paper to *substantiate* the fact that I didn't plagiarize.

Subsume to contain or include
> The new Corporate Policy Manual now *subsumes* both the Customer Contact Manual and the Internal Procedure Manual.

Subvert to undermine, ruin, or overthrow
> My desire to go to class was *subverted* by my body's need for more sleep.

Surfeit an overabundance or excess
> The farmer donated his crop *surfeit* to a charity dedicated to feeding the poor.

Susceptible easily influenced or likely to be affected
> People who don't wash their hands frequently are much more *susceptible* to illnesses than are those people who regularly wash their hands.

Synchronized occurring at the same time and at the same rate
> The lights in the show were *synchronized* with the pulsing rhythm of the music.

T

Tacit using no words
> With a smile, Rob's girlfriend implied *tacit* approval of his gift of a dozen roses.

Tangential slightly connected; superficially relevant
Chandra's tangential remark added nothing relevant to the conversation.

Temperance moderation and self-restraint
When the constitutional prohibition of alcohol was lifted, citizens were left to manage their own temperance.

Tenuous very thin or consisting of little substance
My sister has a tenuous grasp of physics; she does not completely understand how the physical world works.

Torpor state of physical or mental sluggishness
No amount of incentives or creature comforts could lift the cloud of torpor that had overcome the office.

Tout to promote or solicit
Salespeople tend to tout the obvious benefits of a product, while distracting from any negative aspects of ownership.

Tractable easy to control or work with
Teachers are charged with the powerful task of molding tractable young minds.

Transcend to go above and beyond; to rise above
Through luck and hard work, he was able to transcend his humble origins.

Transgress to exceed or violate
Joel has repeatedly transgressed the laws against using a cell phone while driving.

Transpose to reverse the order of; interchange
When I copied down her telephone number, I foolishly transposed two digits.

U

Unalloyed pure; complete
The detectives needed more than four hours to extract the unalloyed version of events from the witness.

Unilaterally performed in a one-sided manner
When the high school principal failed to respond to numerous requests for more information, the school board unilaterally terminated his contract.

Unprecedented having no previous example
The coffee shop franchise launched new locations at an unprecedented rate, opening an average of eight new stores per day across the country.

Unstinting very generous; bestowed liberally
Sometimes the boss's unstinting praise of our work can be construed as disingenuous.

Urbanity refinement and elegance
Cindy's urbanity was apparent in the way she dressed herself—classic clothes with a touch of style.

Utilitarian useful or practical
The workers' coveralls were very utilitarian, but had no regard at all for style or looks.

V

Vacillate to swing or waver
In an emergency situation there is no time to vacillate, so first responders are taught appropriate courses of actions for a myriad of crises.

Variegated having a variety of colors or marks
Calico cats have variegated coats of many shades of brown, tan, black, and white.

Vehement forceful; displaying extreme emotion
In spite of vehement protests from his parents, Joey left Harvard and moved to Los Angeles to become an actor.

Venal corruptible, open to bribery
The success of mafia crimes relies on a steady supply of venal police officers and judges.

Venerable highly esteemed or respected; commanding respect
Dr. Sanford, a most venerable professor, received a standing ovation at his retirement party.

Veracity truthfulness
The veracity of his alibi was questioned when several witnesses saw him fleeing the scene of the crime.

Verbose wordy; long-winded
Most students were yawning and half-asleep by the end of the dean's verbose commencement speech.

Verisimilitude the quality of appearing to be true or real
Carol added several specific details to her story to lend it verisimilitude.

Veritable genuine or authentic
After months of privation in the wilderness, the Andersons enjoyed a veritable feast of turkey, mashed potatoes, stuffing, and carrot cake.

Versatile having many uses or a variety of abilities
She is a very versatile singer and is equally comfortable singing operatic arias or country-western ballads.

Vilify to make negative statements about; to malign
She was vilified in the press as "the other woman" in the divorce case of a married actor.

Vindicate to clear someone or something from blame
The suspect was vindicated when the person who actually committed the robbery turned himself in.

Virtually in almost all instances; simulated as by a computer
Surviving a plunge over Niagara Falls in a barrel was virtually impossible prior to the invention of reliable foam padding and rigid plastics.

Vituperate to criticize in an abusive way
The senator condemned and vituperated his political opponents in a series of angry speeches.

Voluminous large in volume or bulk
He produced a voluminous amount of published works during his 50 years as an author.

Voracious excessively greedy; ravenous
After his two-week wilderness camping trip, Pat had a voracious appetite.

W

Wane to gradually decrease
Randy's interest in his baseball card collection began to wane as he got older.

Wary cautious and untrusting
Emily threw a wary glance at the man who had been following her for nearly five blocks.

Whet to sharpen or stimulate
Before a large meal, I like to whet my appetite with a little wine and cheese.

Wily very sly, deceptive
The wily salesperson convinced my friend to purchase a car that was well beyond my friend's financial means.

X

Xenophobic distrustful of strangers or foreign people
Before traveling abroad, I had a xenophobic mistrust of all people who weren't American.

Z

Zealous very passionate or enthusiastic
As a dedicated and honest attorney, Kara remained committed to the zealous pursuit of the truth.

Zenith the peak point
Winning the Academy Award for Best Actor was the zenith of the actor's career.

APPENDIX B

Glossary of GRE Math Terms

This glossary includes many of the concepts tested on the GRE Quantitative section. We recommend that you thoroughly review difficult mathematical concepts, and refer to this glossary as necessary during your preparation.

A

Absolute Value   A number's distance on the number line from 0, without considering which direction from 0 the number lies. Therefore, absolute value will always be positive.

Acute Angle   An angle less than 90 degrees.

Adjacent Angle   Either of two angles having a common side and common vertex. For example, in the following figure, angles a and b are adjacent angles:

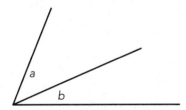

Arc   A portion of the circumference of a circle, as shown in the following figure:

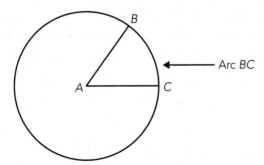

The complete arc of a circle has 360°.

457

Area The number of square units that covers the shape or figure. Following are the formulas for the area of some common figures:

- Square: side (*s*) squared (s^2)
- Rectangle: length (*l*) times width (*w*) ($l \times w$)
- Circle: pi (π) times the radius (*r*) squared (πr^2)
- Triangle: one half the base (*b*) times the height (*h*) ($\frac{1}{2} b \times h$)

Arithmetic Mean (*see* Average) The average of a group of values. Calculate the arithmetic mean by dividing the sum of all of the values in the group by the total count of values in the group. For example, the average of the 3 test scores 82%, 83%, and 87% is equivalent to (82 + 83 + 87) divided by 3; 252 ÷ 3 = 84.

Associative Property A mathematical property whereby the grouping of numbers being added or multiplied can be changed without changing the sum or the product. The associative property of multiplication can be expressed as $(a \times b) \times c = a \times (b \times c)$. Likewise, the associative property of addition can be expressed as $(a + b) + c = a + (b + c)$.

Average (*see* Arithmetic Mean) The arithmetic mean of a group of values. Calculate the average by dividing the sum of all of the values in the group by the total count of values in the group. For example, the average of the 3 test scores 82%, 83%, and 87% is equivalent to (82 + 83 + 87) divided by 3; 252 ÷ 3 = 84.

B–C

Base In geometry, the bottom of a plane figure. For example, in the right triangle that follows, *AC* is the base:

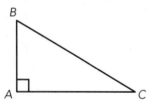

In algebra, the base is the number that is raised to various powers. For example, 2^3 indicates a base of 2 raised to the power of 3.

Circumference The distance around a circle. The circumference of a circle is equal to pi times the diameter (πd). The formula for the circumference of a circle can also be expressed as $2\pi r$, because the diameter, *d*, is twice the radius, *r*.

Collinear A term referring to points that pass through or lie on the same straight line.

Commutative Property A mathematical property whereby the order of numbers being added or multiplied can be changed without changing the sum or the product. The commutative property of addition is expressed as $a + b = b + a$. Likewise, the commutative property of multiplication is expressed as $a \times b = b \times a$, or $ab = ba$.

Complementary Angles Two angles for which the sum is 90 degrees.

Congruent A term describing any shapes or figures, including line segments and angles, that have the same size or measure. For example, in the triangle below, sides AB and BC are congruent, and angles A and C are congruent:

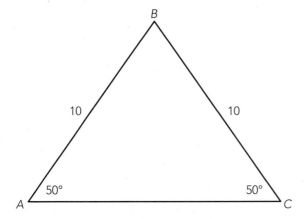

Coordinate Plane A plane, typically defined with the coordinates x and y, where the two axes are at right angles to each other. The horizontal axis is the x-axis, and the vertical axis is the y-axis, as shown in the following figure:

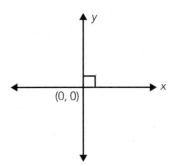

You can locate any point (x,y) on the coordinate plane by an ordered pair of numbers. The ordered pair $(0,0)$, where the x and y axes meet, is the origin.

The coordinate plane is divided into four quadrants, as shown in the following figure:

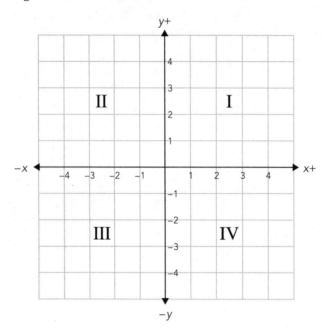

D

Decimal   The point that separates values less than 1 from those greater than 1. In our number system, digits can be placed to the left and right of a decimal point. *Place value* refers to the value of a digit in a number relative to its position. Starting from the left of the decimal point, the values of the digits are ones, tens, hundreds, and so on. Starting to the right of the decimal point, the values of the digits are tenths, hundredths, thousandths, and so on.

Denominator   The bottom part of a fraction. For example, in the fraction $\frac{3}{4}$, 4 is the denominator.

Diagonal   A line segment that connects two nonadjacent vertices in any polygon. In the following rectangle, *AC* and *BD* are diagonals:

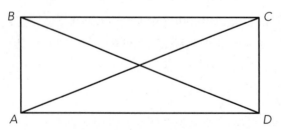

Diameter   A line segment that joins two points on a circle and passes through the center of the circle, as shown in the following figure, where AB is the diameter:

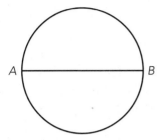

Distributive Property   A mathematical property observed when an expression involves both addition and multiplication. The distributive property is expressed as $a(b + c) = ab + ac$, where the variable a is distributed to the variables b and c.

Divisible   Capable of being divided, usually with no remainder. For example, 6 is divisible by 2, because when 6 is divided by 2, the result is 3 with no remainder.

E–F

Equilateral Triangle   A triangle in which all of the sides are congruent and each of the angles equals 60 degrees.

Exponent   A number that indicates the operation of repeated multiplication. A number with an exponent is said to be "raised to the power" of that exponent. For example, 2^3 indicates 2 raised to the power of 3, which translates into $2 \times 2 \times 2$. In this instance, 3 is the exponent.

Factor   One of two or more expressions that are multiplied together to get a product. For example, in the equation $2 \times 3 = 6$, 2 and 3 are factors of 6. Likewise, in the equation $x^2 + 5x + 6$, $(x + 2)$ and $(x + 3)$ are factors.

FOIL Method   A method of multiplying two binomials, such as $(x + 2)$ and $(x + 3)$, according to the following steps:

>Multiply the **FIRST** terms together: $(x)(x) = x^2$
>
>Multiply the **OUTSIDE** terms together: $(x)(3) = 3x$
>
>Multiply the **INSIDE** terms together: $(2)(x) = 2x$
>
>Multiply the **LAST** terms together: $(2)(3) = 6$
>
>Now, combine like terms to get $x^2 + 5x + 6$

Fraction   An expression that indicates the quotient of two quantities. For example, $\frac{2}{3}$ is a fraction, where 2 is the numerator and 3 is the denominator.

Frequency Distribution   The frequency with which a data value occurs in any given set of data.

Function A set of ordered pairs where no two of the ordered pairs has the same *x*-value. In a function, each input (*x*-value) has exactly one output (*y*-value). For example, $f(x) = 2x + 3$. If $x = 3$, then $f(x) = 9$. For every *x*, only one $f(x)$, or *y*, exists.

G–H–I

Greatest Common Factor (GCF) The largest number that will divide evenly into any two or more numbers. For example, 1, 2, 4, and 8 are all factors of 8; likewise, 1, 2, 3, and 6 are all factors of 6. Therefore, the greatest common factor of 8 and 6 is 2.

Hexagon A six-sided figure, shown below:

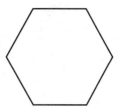

Hypotenuse The leg of a right triangle that is opposite the right angle. For example, in the right triangle in the following figure, *BC* is the hypotenuse:

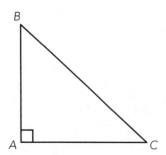

The hypotenuse is always the longest leg of a right triangle.

Improper Fraction An integer combined with a fraction. For example, $2\frac{1}{2}$ is an improper fraction (**see also Mixed Number**).

Inequality A mathematical expression that shows that two quantities are not equal. For example, $2x < 8$ is an inequality that means that $2x$ is less than 8. Likewise, $3a > 17$ is an inequality that means that $3a$ is greater than 17.

Integer Integers include both positive and negative whole numbers. Zero is also considered an integer.

Interior Angle The angle inside two adjacent sides of a polygon. The sum of the interior angles in a triangle is always 180 degrees.

Irrational Number A number that cannot be exactly expressed as the ratio of two integers. For example, π (≈ 3.14) is an irrational number.

Isosceles Triangle A triangle in which two sides have the same length.

J–L

Least Common Denominator (LCD) The smallest multiple of the denominators of two or more fractions. For example, the least common denominator of $\frac{3}{4}$ and $\frac{2}{5}$ is 20.

Least Common Multiple (LCM) The smallest number that any two or more numbers will divide evenly into. For example, the common multiples of 3 and 4 are 12, 24, and 36; 12 is the smallest multiple, and is, therefore, the least common multiple of 3 and 4.

Like Terms Terms that contain the same variable raised to the same power. For example, $3x^2$ and $10x^2$ are like terms that can be combined to get $13x^2$. Also, $-x$ and $4x$ are like terms that can be combined to get $3x$.

Line A straight set of points that extends into infinity in both directions, as shown in the following figure:

Line Segment A figure representing two points on a line and all of the points in between, as shown in the following figure:

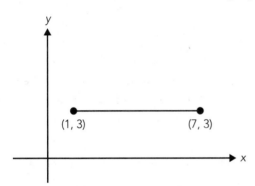

M–N

Median The middle value of a series of numbers when those numbers are in either ascending or descending order. In the series (2, 4, 6, 8, 10) the median is 6. To find the median in an even set of data, find the average of the middle two numbers. In the series (3, 4, 5, 6) the median is 4.5.

Midpoint The center point of a line segment. To find the midpoint of a line given two points on the line, use the formula $\left(\frac{[x_1 + x_2]}{2}, \frac{[y_1 + y_2]}{2}\right)$.

Mixed Number A number that combines an integer with a fraction. Mixed numbers are also called **Improper Fractions**; $1\frac{1}{2}$ is a mixed number.

Mode The number that appears most frequently in a series of numbers. In the series (2, 3, 4, 5, 6, 3, 7) the mode is 3, because 3 appears twice in the series and the other numbers each appear only once in the series.

Number Line The line on which every point represents a real number. On a number line, numbers that correspond to points to the right of zero are positive, and numbers that correspond to points to the left of zero are negative. For any two numbers on the number line, the number to the left is less than the number to the right.

Numerator The top part of a fraction. For example, in the fraction $\frac{3}{4}$, 3 is the numerator.

O–P

Obtuse Angle An angle that measures greater than 90 degrees and less than 180 degrees.

Octagon An eight-sided figure, shown as follows:

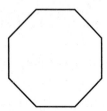

Parallel A term that describes two distinct lines that lie in the same plane and do not intersect. Two lines are parallel if and only if they have the same slope. For example, the two lines with equations $2y = 6x + 7$ and $y = 3x - 14$ have the same slope (3) **(see Point-slope Form)**.

Parallelogram A quadrilateral in which the opposite sides are of equal length and the opposite angles are equal, as shown below:

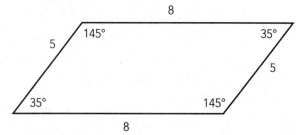

The sum of the angles in a parallelogram is always 360 degrees.

PEMDAS An acronym that describes the correct order in which to perform mathematical operations. The acronym PEMDAS stands for Parentheses, Exponents, Multiplication, Division, Addition, and Subtraction. It should help you to remember to do the operations in the correct order, as follows:

P First, do the operations within the *parentheses*, if any.

E Next, do the *exponents*, if any.

M, D Next, do the *multiplication* or *division*, if any.

A, S Next, do the *addition* or *subtraction*, in order from left to right, if any.

Pentagon A five-sided figure, shown as follows:

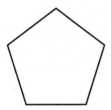

Percent A fraction whose denominator is 100. The fraction 25/100 is equal to 25% and can also be expressed as 0.25.

Perimeter The distance around any shape or object. Following are the formulas for the perimeter of some common figures:

- The perimeter (P) of a rectangle is equivalent to $2l + 2w$, where l is the length and w is the width.
- The perimeter (P) of a square is $4s$, where s is the length of a side.
- The perimeter (P) of other polygons is the sum of the lengths of the sides.
- The perimeter (P) of a triangle is the sum of the lengths of the sides.

Perpendicular A term describing two distinct lines whose intersection creates a right angle. Two lines are perpendicular if and only if the slope of one of the lines is the negative reciprocal of the slope of the other line. In other words, if line a has a slope of 2, and line b has a slope of $-\frac{1}{2}$, then the two lines are perpendicular.

Point A location in a plane or in space that has no dimensions.

Point-Slope Form The equation of a line in the form $y = mx + b$, where m is the slope and b is the y-intercept.

Polygon A closed plane figure made up of at least three line segments that are joined. For example, a triangle, a rectangle, and an octagon are polygons.

Polynomial A mathematic expression consisting of more than two terms. $2x^2 + 4x + 4$ is a simple quadratic equation, and also a polynomial.

Prime Number Any number that can only be divided by itself and 1. That is, 1 and number itself are the only factors of a prime number. For example, 2, 3, 5, 7, and 11 are prime numbers.

Probability The likelihood that an event will occur. For example, Jeff has three striped and four solid ties in his closet; therefore, he has a total of seven ties in his closet. He has three chances to grab a striped tie out of the seven total ties, because he has three striped ties. So, the probability of Jeff grabbing a striped tie is 3 out of 7, which can also be expressed as 3:7, or $\frac{3}{7}$.

Proportion A mathematical statement indicating that one ratio is equal to another ratio. For example, $\frac{1}{5} = \frac{x}{20}$ is a proportion.

Pythagorean Theorem This theorem applies only to finding the length of the sides in right triangles, and states that $c^2 = a^2 + b^2$, where c is the hypotenuse (the side opposite the right angle) of a right triangle and a and b are the two other sides of the triangle.

Q–R

Quadrilateral Any four-sided polygon with four angles. A parallelogram, a rectangle, a square, and a trapezoid are all examples of quadrilaterals.

Quotient The result of division.

Radius The distance from the center of a circle to any point on the circle, as shown below in the following circle with center C:

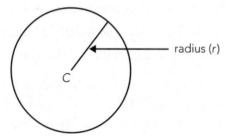

Ratio A mathematical comparison between two quantities. A ratio of 1 to 5, for example, is written as either $\frac{1}{5}$ or 1:5.

Rational Number A fraction whose numerator and denominator are both integers and the denominator does not equal 0.

Real Number Any rational or irrational number, used to express quantities, lengths, amounts, and the like. All real numbers correspond to points on the number line. All real numbers except zero are either positive or negative.

Reciprocal Given a number, n, the reciprocal is expressed as 1 over n, or $\frac{1}{n}$. The product of a number and its reciprocal is always 1. In other words, $\frac{1}{3} \times \frac{3}{1} = \frac{3}{3}$, which is equivalent to 1.

Rectangle   A polygon with four sides (two sets of congruent, or equal sides) and four right angles. All rectangles are parallelograms.

Right Angle   An angle that measures 90 degrees.

S–T

Sequence   An *arithmetic* sequence is one in which the difference between one term and the next is the same. For example, the following sequence is an arithmetic sequence because the difference between the terms is 2: 1, 3, 5, 7, 9. A *geometric* sequence is one in which the ratio between two terms is constant. For example, the following sequence is a geometric sequence because the ratio between the terms is $\frac{1}{2}$: 16, 8, 4, 2, 1, $\frac{1}{2}$.

Set   A well-defined group of numbers or objects. For example, {2, 4, 6, 8} is the set of positive even whole numbers less than 10.

Similar Triangles   Triangles in which the measures of corresponding angles are equal and the corresponding sides are in proportion, as shown in the following figure:

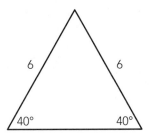

Slope   The change in y-coordinates divided by the change in x-coordinates from two given points on a line. The formula for slope is $m = \frac{(y_2 - y_1)}{(x_2 - x_1)}$, where (x_1, y_1) and (x_2, y_2) are the two given points. For example, the slope of a line that contains the points (3,6) and (2,5) is equivalent to $\frac{(6-5)}{(3-2)}$, or $\frac{1}{1}$, which equals 1.

Slope-Intercept Equation $y = mx + b$, where m is the slope of the line and b is the y-intercept (that is, the point at which the graph of the line crosses the y-axis).

Special Triangles   Triangles whose sides have special ratios. The following are angle measures and side lengths for special right triangles:

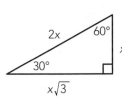
30-60-90 Triangle

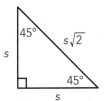
45-45-90 Triangle

Square A number multiplied by itself. Squaring a negative number yields a positive result. For example, $-2^2 = 4$.

Square Root Given a number, n, the square root is written as $\sqrt{n}$, or the non-negative value a that fulfills the expression $a^2 = n$. For example, the square root of 5 is expressed as $\sqrt{5}$, and $(\sqrt{5})^2 = 5$.

System of Equations A group of two or more equations with the same set of unknowns. In solving a system of equations, try to find values for each of the unknowns that will satisfy every equation in the system.

Triangle A closed plane figure having three sides and three angles.

V–Z

Volume A measure of space or capacity of a three-dimensional object. The formula for the volume of a rectangular solid is V = lwh, where l = length, w = width, and h = height.

y-intercept The point at which a line crosses the y-axis in the (x,y)–coordinate plane.

APPENDIX C
Additional Resources

The purpose of this book is to help you prepare for the GRE. While this book provides you with helpful information about the test and realistic practice materials to get you ready for the real thing, the following additional resources might be useful in your preparation:

ETS

Educational Testing Service (ETS) is the entity that creates and administers the GRE tests. The official GRE website at **www.gre.org** offers a wealth of up-to-date information about the GRE. Once you get to the Test Takers section of the website, you can download the POWERPREP® software, find out about test locations and fees, register for the test, learn about your score report, order additional score reports, and more.

Practicing to Take the General Test published by ETS, is a great source of practice material for the GRE. This book is usually available at all the major bookstores. Pick one up as a great complement to *McGraw-Hill's GRE*.

Advantage Education

Advantage Education offers many programs for students planning to go to graduate school, including programs that prepare students for the GRE, as well as admissions counseling. To learn about individual tutoring, workshops, courses, and other programs, visit **www.AdvantageEd.com**, or call Toll Free 1-888-737-6010.

Textbooks and Human Resources

High school and college textbooks are extremely valuable resources. The content areas tested on the GRE Quantitative section are the same content areas that you've been studying in school. Hence, textbooks cover many of the relevant skills and subjects you will need for success on the GRE. If you do not have your textbooks, your school library should have copies that you can use.

Don't forget to talk to professors and students who have some experience with the GRE. They might be able to shed some additional light on getting ready for the test. It is in your best interest to be as well prepared as possible on test day.